FLIGHT
OF THE
RONDONE

High School Dropout VS Big Pharma:
The Fight to Save My Son's Life

Patrick Girondi

Skyhorse Publishing

Skyhorse Publishing books may be purchased in bulk at special discounts for sales promotion, corporate gifts, fund-raising, or educational purposes. Special editions can also be created to specifications. For details, contact the Special Sales Department, Sports Publishing, 307 West 36th Street, 11th Floor, New York, NY 10018 or info@ skyhorsepublishing.com.

Skyhorse® and Skyhorse Publishing® are registered trademarks of Skyhorse Publishing, Inc.®, a Delaware corporation.

Visit our website at www.skyhorsepublishing.com.

10 9 8 7 6 5 4 3 2 1

Library of Congress Cataloging-in-Publication Data is available on file.

Front cover photo by Megan Euker

ISBN: 978-1-5107-7219-9
Ebook ISBN: 978-1-5107-7220-5

Printed in the United States of America

I have tried to recreate events, locales, and conversations from my memories of them. In order to maintain their anonymity, in some instances I have changed the names of individuals and places, I may have changed some identifying characteristics and details such as physical properties, occupations, and places of residence.

Dedications

I dedicate this book to my family members, the patients—many who should have already been cured. Had I been shrewder, the project would have never been interrupted in 2010. I apologize and ask for their forgiveness. I will continue to push and ask for your prayers.

To my three sons.

To the courageous doctors and researchers:

Ballas	Lucarelli	Rivella
Cappellini	Luzzatto	Rivière
Cohen	Maggio	Sadelain
Colavito	Moi	Sorrentino*
Crivelli	Montemurno	Tisdale
Galanello*	Park	Vullo*
Gesualdo	Perrine	Yannaki
Govender	Persons*	Wiech
Locatelli	Raino	Wilber

To the families who have picked me, the rondone, up from the ground and thrown me in the air:

Feldman	Ballantyne	Buccellato
Aliquò	Barr	Buckley
Antypas	Beecroft	Burger
Arbor	Bertucci	Capano
Arcieri	Borsellino	Caputo
Bailey	Botica	Catalanotto
Bacall	Bryant	Chambers

Ciaravino
Cirrottola
Clark
Colonna
Coluzzi
Creanza
Crognale
Daly
DeFrancesco
Dever
Di Leo
Distasio
Euker
Ernsting
Ferro
Finley
Fiore
Fratto
Fritzlen
Fulfer
Gavril
Girondi
Gornick
Hanley
Hanson

Hayhurst
Hillock
Holmes
Houlihan
Iacono
Johnson
Kazan
Kurgan
Lackowitz
Ladhani
Lapointe
Leonard
Liberti
Linconetti
Lockwood
Macchitelli
Marutzky
McCluskey
Meehan
Molaro
Napoli
O'Hara
O'Keefe
Palenic
Parillo

Pascello
Pepe
Petrosky
Pugliese
Remenick
Rubino
Salman
Segert
Segvich
Serritella
Sheehan
Shetty
Sion
Smith
Step
Sussmane
Swan
Tartaglia
Timm
Tito
VanHoutan
Vickrey
Walton
Wiech
Wilson

Thank you to these incredible journalists for sharing my company's story:

John Aquino, *Bloomberg*
Andrew Martin, *Bloomberg*
Dan O'Connor, *TrialSite News*
Charles Ornstein, *ProPublica*
Andrew Pollack, *New York Times*
Katie Thomas, *New York Times*

Thanks to these museums/galleries that supported and displayed Megan Euker's work about my company's story:

International Museum of Surgical Science, Chicago
Linda Warren Projects, Chicago
University Club of Chicago

Thank you to the office of the New York Attorney General:

Letitia James; Amy Mcfarlane; Saami Zain

Thank you to my music collaborators, past and present:

Marco Abbattista	Ronny G. and the Ultimate Concept
Massimo Allegretti	Band
Renzo Arbore	Sergio Langella
Peppino Barberio	Mino Lionetti
Ken Barnard/Street Factory Music	Enzo Matera
Mimmo Basetta	Giordano Mazzi
Antonio Benedetto	Enzo Melasi
Salvatore Centoducati	Eustachio Montemurro
Roberto Chietera	I Pooh
Giuseppe Chiefa	Antonio Sansone
Michele Ciccimarra	Alessio Santoro
Luca Debonis	Arturo Sanzo
Antonio Francia	Giuliano Scavetta
Farelive	Nanni Teot

Thanks to John and Patricia Moll for the cover shooting location at Moll Park,
Tampa, Florida.

Thank you to Skyhorse Publishing and Tony Lyons for believing in and publishing this
book and to Ted Kalem for making the connection with Skyhorse. Thanks to Julie Ganz
for helping to pull it all together. Thanks to Kevin Anderson/Kevin Anderson editors,
especially Erin McKnight and Rob Foreman. Thanks to Carl Segvich for assisting with
edits. Thank you to my agent Megan Euker for her undying dedication and persistence.

. . . and many more . . .

*Rest in peace

Contents

Prologue

"Put your hands in mine . . . close your eyes."

I took Santino's tiny hands into my own hands and observed him. "Tired of play-ing?" I asked.

He shook his head. I took stock of his condition as best I could through sight alone.

His forehead and cheekbones protruded—pushed outward by an overactive bone marrow that struggled to raise his blood levels. He was out of breath from running around with Nico and Enzo. Their hemoglobins were fourteen; his was nine.

"Put your hands in mine," I said.

He did. We never questioned each other.

"Close your eyes," I said as I squeezed Santino's hands, tighter and tighter, pausing for fifteen seconds. *Figlio mio* (my son), when I let go, you'll be charged with energy from Papà. You'll be able to fly like the rondone."

I released his hands, easing the pressure slowly. We breathed. The aroma of Panificio Santa Chiara's wood-fired focaccia filled the piazza, where I sat, and Santino leaned against me with his eyes closed.

My solution wouldn't cure his Thalassemia. But it would let him go back to his friends.

He gazed at his freed hands. "Pà, they're tingling."

I nodded. "Now go. Fly like a rondone!"

Santino shot away. "Papà! I can fly! I can fly!"

There are no words for the happiness I felt as I watched him dart back into his world—Piazza Duomo, Altamura. He dodged in and out of the crowded square to rejoin his friends, his paisans, his compatriots.

Piazza Duomo is its own universe. Built in 1200, the stone cathedral has witnessed centuries of comings and goings across the white stone streets. Altamura, and all of Eastern Italy, was at one time a crossroad for African, Arab, Asian, and European cultures, and as a result, many Italians are a darker shade than their African relatives, and many Italians have bluer eyes than people on their northern borders. I find it tragically funny when seemingly intelligent folks identify cultures with Crayola colors—as if it were that simple.

Minutes later, the kids dashed toward me.

"Papà!" Santino screamed.

"Signor Girondi!" Enzo yelled.

They got within a few yards. Santino was holding a *rondone*—a bird, also known as a swift.

Concerned and wide-eyed, the kids gushed ancient Altamuran words that could easily be mistaken for Arabic.

Rondoni (plural for *rondone*) arrive in late March from Southern Africa. They travel thousands of miles at speeds up to 140 miles per hour. The female rondoni lay eggs in the tiled roofs and crevices of the ancient town center. Catching insects for offspring, they swoosh round and round in precise patterns. When the rondoni depart in August, mosquitoes move in and retake the piazza.

Rondini are as strange as they are fast. Their long wings prohibit them from taking off from the ground. If they don't want to get stuck, they must take off from high elevations so they can throw themselves into the air and take flight again.

Occasionally, rondoni collide with something solid and fall to the earth. That must have been what happened to this one, I thought.

I didn't hesitate. I took the young bird in my hands, and threw him into the air with all my force. The higher I could propel him, the better chance the creature would have of spreading his wings again, of saving himself, of soaring, of living.

It was a good throw. The power of the launch took the winged marvel almost to Doctor Alberto's third-floor windows.

But the rondone began falling, faster and faster. The eyes of everyone in the piazza were on the bird. Each of us secretly, solemnly prayed for his wings to carry him to salvation. A moment of hesitation would smash the swift onto the white stone.

I had done my part. Now the rondone was on his own, alone in descent, within inches of the end of his life. I turned away, like most of the others did, not wanting to witness the almost certain loss of life.

I barely saw, and almost missed what became of the mystical creature. But as I turned my head, from the corner of my eye, I saw him swoosh upward.

The boys had not turned away. Their eyes were wide. They shouted and marveled at what they saw.

The rondone took flight.

A few of the spectators cheered and clapped. Relieved, I nodded gently to myself. I understood.

I was there to save the bird because, in much the same way, others had intervened to save me. The fact that I was there in the piazza, at that moment, was a living tribute to the many people who had launched me back into life's wind and returned me to the world.

I took Santino's hand in mine again. He looked up at me and smiled.

Chapter 1

Bliss

Every so often, when I was growing up, I'd find Grandpa Santino sleeping on our couch.

I wasn't sure where he lived. His face was gentle and kind. Sleeping there quietly, he reminded me of a little homeless boy. And I knew that when I woke to find him there, he would soon rise and disappear to his favorite part of the house—the kitchen.

If I woke up later than he did, I would be enraptured and dragged out of bed by the scent of Grandpa Santino's *sugo*. About once a month, he'd serve his treasured tomato sauce for our sacred dinner. I helped him make it, when he let me.

One Sunday, when I was maybe seven, I walked into the kitchen with its ancient wooden table and wobbly chairs. The cabinets were metal, painted brown, and the floor was clothed in a worn, stained linoleum. The original pattern was white with gold swirls. The white had turned off-white and then gray. The only thing resembling gold about the swirls were mustard stains that couldn't be scrubbed out of the cracks and crevices.

The kitchen was ten by twelve feet. The table with the six wobblies situated around it looked like they had come directly out of a scene from a film made about a second-hand store.

Grandpa stood with a wooden spoon in his hand. He was slender and all of five feet, two inches tall. His full head of hair was turning from black to silver. As he chopped the garlic, he seemed to look right through it and into another world.

He had seen so many things in his life. He had made the voyage to a new land. He had survived. There was a unique sense of satisfaction on his face. It seemed that simple accomplishments such as chopping garlic gave him a profound sense of purpose.

Grandpa's mother, Angela, always made the Sunday *ragu* or *sugo* with neck bones. Grandpa Santino was certain that they were an important part of the magic.

From time to time, Grandpa told stories about growing up in Puglia, his family, the olive trees, and the feast days dedicated to saints. I'd seen some photos with the various members of our extended southern Italian family. I envisioned myself with my hooked nose, wearing a cap, on a ladder leaning against an olive tree, gently raking the leaves, causing the green and black treasures to fall into the net placed on the ground.

Somehow, back then, in the strangest way, I was already a part of those trees, those olives, those saints. I had never really lived in America. The most formative years of my existence had been passed in an Italian ghetto, thousands of miles from home.

My mother's parents arrived in Chicago from Modugno, a town near Bari, in southern Italy, in the state of Puglia. Santino, my grandfather, dreamed of singing opera. Soon, Angela was born, then Maria, Vittoria, Vincenzo, and finally my mother, Sara. Antonia, my grandmother, disappeared shortly after my mother's birth, and was not seen again for more than thirty years.

Grandpa's steadiest income came from singing in bars. Ma grew up in foster homes. The bliss continued when she married my father, a proud Irish Renaissance man, dockworker, thief, and all-around gangster.

I was named Patrick, after the patron saint of Ireland. Ma decided I would be a physician. Soon I was joined by my brother and sisters, Greg, Marie, and Katy, all of us born twelve to fourteen months apart.

Our neighborhood was Little Italy on the South Side. 67th and 71st Streets, Ashland and Damen were the boundaries. The Saint Rocco Feast at Our Lady of Mount Carmel Church on Marquette (67th Street) was the highlight of our year. Each family saved for stylish clothing, and Grandpa practiced "O Sole Mio," "U Sorrento," and a half dozen other Italian tunes for his chance to exhibit his pipes.

Grandpa's gaze moved from the garlic to the window. I looked but all I saw was our neighbor's dirty windows. I was sure he saw much more than that. He was transported; he was somewhere else.

I purposely made a sound with my shoe. Grandpa looked to the side, and then at me, standing in the doorway, rubbing my eyes.

"*Prova*," he said gently, as he handed me the wooden spoon filled with the red elixir. The smile on his face emulated the warmth of the Mediterranean he came from, and in one action, one grin, he beamed more tenderness than my father had transmitted in his entire lifetime.

Grandpa's stay in Chicago was marred by a stark reality. It appeared that the stories told in the piazzas of Italy about streets paved with gold were mostly cruel jokes. Still, the US became an alibi for every Italian who did not arrive where he wanted to go in life, saying, "Had I only gone to America, I would have been a famous artist, chef, soccer player . . ."

Does anyone really arrive where they want to go?

The day before, Grandpa had sent me with a quarter to Sarli's Butcher on 69th Street to buy neck bones. Rosario Sarli was a sweetheart, and it was hard for me to imagine that he spent a great part of his life butchering animals. Mr. Sarli turned and smiled as I walked in. Mrs. Clemente was being served. Mrs. Scalise and Mrs. Fiore were waiting impatiently. It was almost five o'clock, and Rosario was happy about that. Saturday was the busiest day of the week.

Rosario Sarli was a kind man. He extended credit, and had a list of debts that he erased at Christmas for widows and single mothers. We were often recipients of his kindness. Today, he felt more generous than usual. Cassio's grocery store, across 69th Street, had opened a meat counter eight months prior, and officially closed it the previous week.

I returned home, gave Grandpa his quarter, the neck bones, and a warm salutation from our paisan, Rosario Sarli.

Looking up lovingly at Grandpa, I heard a noise at the front door. My body froze. Disaster would replace my Italian paradise if my father walked in and found Grandpa cooking. Matty, my father, despised the smell of garlic and hated anything Italian.

I also wasn't sure where my father lived. He showed up when he liked and we hadn't seen him in a couple of weeks. The house had been peaceful in his absence.

When he did show up, he helped himself to whatever he wanted, conducted his personal reign of terror, and then, after a few hours or days, disappeared again, back to wherever he came from.

He reminded me of the Loch Ness Monster—he reemerged into our lives as mysteriously, ominously, and unpredictably as that creature rose from its lake—but the beatings and torment were much more real than the fabled lake leviathan.

The noise subsided and no one arrived. My body relaxed and I scooted myself on the countertop next to my tiny Grandfather.

Grandpa looked at me sternly. "*Scendi di la,*" he said.

I smiled and we both pretended that he had not told me to get down. I watched his face. He knew he was being observed but he concentrated on his artwork. Grandpa's skin was olive-colored and smooth with no wrinkles. His eyes were soft and brown. His nose was that of a movie star, pronounced yet dignified.

After a few moments, he turned to me. "*Sei un brave uaggnòne.*"

I loved when Grandpa spoke to me in the Barese dialect. He was telling me that I was a good guy, and the sincerity with which he delivered his message almost convinced me that he was right.

I learned so much more than Italian from him. We once sat in my and my brother Greg's bedroom when my parents argued. "*Silenzio*," he hushed, as he raised his finger to his lips.

My mother was in the kitchen, screaming at my father about his unwanted visits, how he terrorized the village and went riding off on his horse, shooting his pistol in the air. My mother was standing up for herself—finally.

But it was short-lived. My father gave her a backhand. Her little body flew against the wall and slouched to the floor.

The Old Man grabbed her purse and walked out of the house.

Grandpa gently shook his head. We sat and waited, not wanting to walk in and further humiliate his daughter, our mother.

Grandpa told me stories of Italy, and the extended family, made up of "*compari.*" Pronounced "gombody," it is the title used for extended family members who baptize, confirm, or serve as testimony for wedding ceremonies. Persons also become compari through great acts of kindness.

Grandpa's favorite compari were Compare (singular for compari) Ciccio from Bitritto and one-eyed Compare Uncle Mike from Carbonara; both towns were walking distance from Modugno, Grandpa's town.

Grandpa's favorite moments were spent with his family, *compari*, Father Angelo from Our Lady of Mount Carmel, the local hoods (hoodlums), and the congregation, who often sat on my Aunt Vittoria's porch, reminiscing about their past in Italy and their brave plans for an American future.

Ma arrived like a lightning bolt out of nowhere, and I jumped off the counter. I didn't know it, but she must have had work that morning. I wasn't sure where she'd go. In the past, she was employed at IBM, Bays English Muffins, and as a helper to different families who needed someone for housework and or babysitting duties.

Wherever she went, she'd get mass in. Ma knew where all the churches were and what time the masses were, not only on Sunday but every day. Inside her purse there were never less than ten saints' holy cards and novenas. On the bus, and on her breaks at work, she prayed.

Ma always had a determined look on her face. Today was no different. I believed that much of Ma's determination came from her belief in "good." The saints were historical pillars of our church and our faith. They may have not been perfect, but their stories were inspiring. Ma made sure that there were always books about the saints in the house. Many of them were kids' books, and she insisted we read them. My knowledge of and therefore the presence of the saints were critical at all the important times in my life.

Ma was four-foot-eleven, but had the presence of someone over six feet tall. Her black hair was more of a mane, and it shook as she walked.

Ma had beautiful teeth and a divine smile. Her body was lean and proportioned as a beautiful Italian woman's should be.

She smiled to see me next to my grandfather, happy that I had jumped off the counter before she scolded me.

She looked at Grandpa sternly, correcting him for allowing me to sit there. She knew that Grandpa and I had a relationship that was different from any that he had with his other grandchildren. She approved, and hoped that his gentle ways might someday become my own.

Grandpa offered her a taste of the sauce.

Ma sipped from the wooden spoon. "Mmm, Pa, this is delicious. I got to run, save me some."

Grandpa smiled and Ma kissed my cheek. It just didn't get any better than this.

Raising four kids by herself, Ma accepted acts of kindness and borrowed money from friends, the church, and even neighbors. She was a stark contrast to my father, Matthew, who most called Matty. Matty would never accept charity but took what he wanted, whenever he wanted it.

Matty was a hard and good-looking Irish man with a scar from his right ear to the right side of his mouth. He was almost six feet tall and had curly brown hair that was always gelled. He had a smile that could melt a glacier or befriend a cougar, before he killed and gutted it.

My father was a South Sider from Canaryville, a neighborhood on the eastern front of the Stock Yards. He was a gangster and he liked being a gangster. He walked the walk and talked the talk. I witnessed him getting into fistfights with complete strangers. He always won.

I'm not sure if he did it purposely, but he spoke like the actor James Cagney. In fact, I often pictured my father squashing grapefruit in someone's face or getting blown up on the top of a gasoline holding tank, screaming, "Ma, I'm on top of the world!"

The Old Man and his colleagues from Teamsters Local 714 primarily worked at the McCormick Place, the Amphitheater, and the Hilton Hotel. They helped themselves to everything that wasn't nailed down and some things that were. His Ford van was always filled with everything from electric toothbrushes to ashtrays and rugs. His house was literally full of stolen duct tape—his solution for cracked walls, cups, windows, and shoes. The teamsters from 714 only worked when there were shows. How else were they supposed to make ends meet?

I don't recall ever making a conscious judgment about my mother or my father. There were attractive things about both of them.

Like so many South Siders, I also did not pronounce my H's, so like my fadder, the number three became "tree." It wasn't a conscious choice on my part to emulate him. It just happened.

We were often between homes. When we vacated one place, in search of another, we loaded up Ma's beige Rambler station wagon and headed out. Sometimes we'd have to sleep in the car.

Sadly, the Old Man never showed up when we desperately needed someone.

I deduced, early on in life, that stealing was something the Old Man and I had in common. For as long as I can remember, I felt the obligation to help my mother out. I shoveled snow, raked leaves, washed cars, and robbed garages and the occasional house. I even delivered newspapers, until I found that I could make almost the same amount of money by stealing them and selling them for scrap.

I think I preferred honesty, actually—but there just wasn't a lot of opportunity for that. I decided to shine shoes, but got caught stealing polish from a drugstore. The owner called the police, and when they arrived I squirmed and feigned the grief of a mother whale whose calf had just been devoured by sharks.

My mother never found out. I should have won an Academy Award.

Ma disappeared from the kitchen, headed for work, and Grandpa turned to me and smiled. Few people ever smiled my way. Ma insisted that I was misunderstood, but the nuns and most of the neighbors had a low regard for me, a classic juvenile delinquent.

The neighbors weren't all wrong to see me that way. Some of them had been my victims, and I had shoplifted more times than I could remember.

I looked at my grandfather, not knowing if I had any right to smile back at him. If I smiled back, was I confirming that I was a good boy when I knew that I wasn't?

Grandpa read my mind and looked sternly at me. "*Per tua madre, devi fare bravo.*"

It wasn't so easy for me to be good for my mother, or anyone else, for that matter. I'd seen her grovel and get beaten to the ground many times. I would not live her type of existence and I resented having to watch her live it.

Grandpa smiled tightly, as if my silence were the confirmation of our mostly telepathic conversation. He offered me another taste from the chipped wooden spoon.

I hesitated in another speechless gesture. Then I took the spoon, and the pact was finalized, as I let the tomato sauce roll on my tongue, past my tonsils, and down to my stomach. It made no sense for me to elaborate. At that moment, I was Grandpa's quiet, good grandson, that *brave uaggnòne.*

I guess it was okay for him to believe that.

Grandpa Santino looked at me softly and said nothing. He rolled the neck bones into a frying pan and cut up more garlic. He took a pinch of salt from the box and squeezed his fingers to distribute it evenly. The neck bones and garlic cloves began sizzling in the heated oil. I loved watching '*u maestro'* create his succulent potion.

Somehow, word spread whenever Grandpa cooked. Cousins and guests we hadn't seen for months miraculously showed up at dinnertime, and in good Pugliese tradition, everyone ate their fill.

Grandpa turned his attention back to the deep pot of tomato sauce. He stirred it lightly. It seemed that everything he did was done tenderly. He began singing, "*Al di lá; del bene più prezioso, ci sei tu. Al di lá; del sogno più ambizioso ci sei tu!*"

"Al Di La" is a song dedicated to a love so strong that after all, after life itself, survived. Although Grandpa never made it to perform in the lyric houses of the world, the performance that he gave me those mornings are documented forever in my heart.

In neighborhood bars, Grandpa sang for change they'd leave in his cap or throw at his feet. Any pay was meager, compared to the satisfaction he received from performing for others.

"Volare" and "O Sole Mio" were two of my favorites from his *repertorio.* It wasn't just that his voice was so lovely and fine; it was that his life was so tragic and coarse, and he was still able to sing. As I stated prior, his wife, my grandmother Antonia, disappeared not long after my mother was born, and for decades, no one knew where she was. The family wasn't sure if she had gone back home, was living a life of amnesia, or was dead—yet Grandpa sang. All of his children struggled day to day trying to make ends meet. Violence, alcohol, and drugs damaged each of their lives, and yet Grandpa sang.

I was putting the jigsaw puzzle together in my mind when out of nowhere my father's voice broke the heavenly flow of Italian music. I desperately hoped that my brain was toying with me.

It wasn't. The Old Man, a whiskey guy, who usually rolled to the runway on beers, was recovering from a night out with his friends in Canaryville that probably included a fight, a stickup, and/or someone being seriously injured.

He resented Italians in the worst way. I often thought it might be because there were some of them he could not bully or berate, and maybe this was why he was so adamant about slugging my mother and belittling my grandfather.

He often told me that I was Italian, not white. I wasn't sure what he meant. I had never seen a white person and I, myself, was tan. Most Italians I know don't know what you mean if you tell them they're white. A young Italian girl once told me, "Paint and paper can be white, but not people."

He referred to my clan as either degos or spics, and the way he slithered those words actually made me proud to belong to the group.

As soon as he entered the kitchen, the Old Man said firmly, "I told you, I didn't want you cooking that smelly shit in my house."

Grandpa grew silent, and I felt him step closer to me. Maybe it was I who stepped closer to him. At any rate, at that moment, we were inseparable.

"Why'd you stop singing, greaseball?" the Old Man taunted ("Greaseball," another of his favorite words, should have been included with "dego" and "spic," above).

There was an ugly stillness. The only sound was the sizzling of neck bones and garlic cloves in the frying pan. It was time to pick a side.

I didn't move and did the most ill-advised thing that I could have done. I stood my ground and looked into my father's eyes.

He stared back at me. "C'mere."

I didn't have the courage to say no, nor would my heart allow me to leave Grandpa's side. We were in Hadleyville and it was *High Noon*. Hours passed in those next moments, as all three of us realized that something would follow the end of the music.

Out of nowhere, a piece of gristle cracked and shot out of one of the neck bones. The first shot, although completely irrelevant, was fired—and it was all Matty needed to lurch into action.

He jumped at us. Grandpa gave no resistance as my father grabbed him by the neck, lifted him, and pushed him against the wall.

Grandpa couldn't breathe. His feet performed an arrhythmic ballet below his legs.

"No!" I screamed as tears flooded my eyes.

Grandpa's eyes softly communicated *cheet*, the word that told me to remain still and quiet.

My father then grabbed Grandpa with the other hand and dragged him to the back porch door. My father tugged him down the back stairs, Grandpa's body dangling as if he were a rag doll. I watched grandpa's feet as he panicked to stabilize his body weight.

For a moment my gaze locked in on Grandpa's grief-filled eyes. At the last stair, my father took my grandfather under the arms and threw him into the yard.

I watched from the back porch window, relieved that it was over.

It wasn't over.

Still in a rage, my father arrived at the top of the porch steps with the deep pot of sauce. Matty's eyes were filled with contempt. He wasn't only striking out at the tiny man, he was battling something much larger, his determination awe-inspiring, like he was in the twelfth round of a championship fight.

I looked at Grandpa and at my father's back. I wondered what I'd do if I had a gun.

With a Herculean grunt, my father jerked the pot, sending the sauce flying into the air. It sailed as if it were a flock of geese, and I watched the red splash and recalled that blood and sugo are the same color. I watched as hot red streaked Grandpa's face. He didn't move a centimeter.

My father threw the empty pot at him. Grandpa didn't flinch as it landed on the grass next to him.

The Old Man attempted to spit at my grandfather, but nothing came out. He zoomed past me as if I were no one. And in fact, I felt like less than no one.

Back in the house, Matty wanted to have some fun with my mother. When he couldn't find her, he left, like a hurricane, leaving damage in his path, yet nowhere to be found.

I ran into the yard to help Grandpa up. He shook his head and pushed me to the side. "*Ti sporcherai.*"

He didn't want me to get dirty, or so I understood. He took the garden hose and washed himself without even removing his shoes. It wasn't cold out, but it wasn't warm. Grandpa seemed unconcerned.

When I got into the house, the neck bones, garlic, and oil were burning. I turned them off and went back to the yard, to give Grandpa towels. He dried himself off as best he could, and then, hand in hand, we walked solemnly through the gangway and out to the street. I figured he didn't want to dirty the house with water and sauce. Maybe his pride kept him from wanting to enter the scene of his humiliation.

There were so many things I wanted to tell him. I could not help but believe that there were many things that he wanted to tell me.

Grandpa stopped. We gazed into each other's eyes. "*Vattene a casa.*"

I would listen and go into the house, but for now I paused and watched his back until he turned the corner.

My mother's unbending faith already had its grips on me. I didn't hate Matty. I was already prepared to forgive him, to look to the saints for strength in the face of what he'd done.

But I wasn't a pushover. Seeing the things my father did, and seeing so much more, in the neighborhood where I grew up, I learned to detest the strong who feasted on the weak. I had plenty of rage for them stirring in me, and stored up vengeance that I would gladly deliver in return for such cruelty.

Grandpa didn't come around much after what happened with my Old Man. I barely knew my father's people, and the world around me continued to be an Italian world.

Looking back on those years, I can truly say that, despite its drawbacks, life was full. And a full life to me is a blissful life.

Chapter 2

The Bliss Continues

M y mother continued to struggle. We often lived in the homes of friends and relatives, sometimes separately, sometimes together. Partings were tearfully agonizing, not knowing when or if we'd ever be reunited.

Ma juggled novenas and jobs. Whether together or separate, she dragged us to mass and put us through Catholic schools.

A few weekends, we lived in Ma's station wagon. During the day, we visited friends, relatives, and churches. After dark, we parked and slept.

We wobbled into a gas station at 51st and Ashland with a flat. Ma had six bucks. We slept there until the morning, when Uncle Vincenzo (Vince), Ma's brother, scrounged up a tire.

At five foot five, Uncle Vince was muscle and bone. He had a sixth-grade education, and like Ma, he would literally give you his last cent or morsel if you needed it. I call it the "Girondi Disease."

Uncle Vince and his wife, Alice, had five kids. There wasn't always food or electricity in their home, but he was forever an optimist. He taught my brother Greg and me to fish and play chess.

Growing up in the 1970s, the nation was in the throes of the great "busing" experiment. Politicians, from their protected pedestals, decided that kids would be transported across their cities, to forcefully integrate their schools and mix them together. While it sounded like a great idea to many people to make schools and children's lives less homogeneous, the results of the policy were mixed.

Busing left behind thousands of dismantled communities and dozens of destroyed cities. Public schools weren't places to learn anymore. They became battlegrounds, where you could get shot, stabbed, maimed, or killed. Communities went from being middle-class neighborhoods to crime-ridden zones of the economically challenged.

Uncle Vince's kids went to public schools, and his son Santino got stabbed at eight years old. As a result of busing and other shrewd social trials and economic situations, some of my cousins never made it out of eighth grade. Curing homogeneity also meant mixing people from very different backgrounds. The result of this experiment sparked violent conflict and bloodshed. What looks good on paper doesn't necessarily work in practice.

Catholic schools were, for the most part, spared the great social remedy of busing. The schools I attended remained as they had been. Religious folks taught us what they thought we should know, and provided guardrails to the youths they educated. Some, such as myself at very young ages, already showed signs of going off the road.

By my tenth birthday, I had lived at ten different addresses, mostly in the South Side's "Little Italy," where I was surrounded by dozens of cousins.

Eventually, the Old Man remarried. One year, when winter set in, my brother, sisters, and I lived with him and his new bride. Her name was also Sara. He called her "Butch" (eventually, the "u" was substituted with an "i"). She arrived with six kids from her first marriage: Coleen, Bobby, Casey, Clara, Jimmy, and Mark, who were all between the ages of two and seven. Matty had changed wives, but not much else.

Some Sunday mornings were spent kneeling in front of the TV, screaming, jiggling, and singing to dark-skinned gospel singers on *Jubilee Showcase*. Matty kicked and slapped us until we hit a frantic pitch.

In Little Italy of the South Side, Italian was the second language on the streets. In Italian communities in the US, as in Italy, clan members are relied upon to do what people in other places rely on strangers to do. *Compari* are on the front line of every family crisis, doing things that in other families are done by strangers in uniforms. Compari assist in recovering stolen property and doling out justice. In times of need, compari often loan money, taking the place of a bank. They're the household safety net.

Compare Ciccio was from Bitritto, three miles from my grandfather's town of Modugno. He baptized five of my cousins, and often loaded as many of us as he could into his '62 Ford to take us for Rainbow Ice Cream on 63rd and Damen.

The neighborhood was full of people the US government considered undesirables. Many men used aliases and were not strangers to the law. Compare Ciccio was an incredibly kind man, and we all missed him when he was deported.

Ma always had legal custody of us, but back then, legal custody didn't mean a whole lot. The government's nose wasn't nearly as involved in families' lives as it is today.

Imagine this. When we were kids, it was dishonorable to snitch on someone, anyone, even your enemy. If you did snitch on a sibling, you lined up for punishment after the disciplinarian was done with them. Today, things have dramatically changed. Each group whines, whimpers, and points fingers, often at individuals more victimized than themselves, using the media and attorneys to garner favors and cash from the imperfect system.

Ma didn't always have the funds necessary to keep us together. For a while, she got us back and we moved to 49th Street in the Saint Augustine Parish. Danny Stanic, a Polish kid from a family of twelve, became my shoeshine partner and best friend.

"I disappear in the morning, show up at night, and no one even knows I was gone," he'd say.

The neighborhood was full of struggling families and ruthless gangs that we aspired to enter; but for now, Danny; his brother Ricky; another friend, Stevey; and I made for the railroad tracks. Danny was thirteen, Stevey and Ricky eleven, and I was ten.

Bravery was everything; a few weeks prior, Stevey solemnly stood still against the garage as I whipped a dart that landed less than an inch from his armpit. Up next, I took my turn, as the hurtling projectile headed for my face. I turned slightly, not wanting to demonstrate cowardice, and it entered the side of my head. We paraded through the neighborhood, the badge of courage still in place. People gawked. I glared back. After a few hours and before my mother could see, I pulled the dart from my head. No pain; no big deal.

On other days, we flipped switchblades at each other's feet—but the railroad tracks were the true test of bravery. In just a few months, one kid lost his life and another his legs.

The freights traveled up to sixty mph between Ashland and the Dan Ryan. We timed it perfectly as an eastbound train came into view.

The train was within a few blocks of where we were standing.

"Me and Pat first," Stevey said. "Danny, you better be honest."

"I'm always honest, man. You know that, man," Danny snapped.

The train was a block away. Ricky and Danny lined us up evenly and stooped down to judge as Stevey and I rested our heads on opposite sides of the tracks.

The engineer clocked fifty-four miles an hour. He needed to slow down to avoid crashing at the Englewood Yard. It was too late to call anyone when he spotted us.

He hit the horn. We didn't budge.

Stopping 173 cars took time.

The train thundered. The horn bellowed. Braking hard meant jumping the track. The uniformed man on the front of the locomotive frantically waved his arms, whelping silenced screams. The steel grate was within inches of us. I threw myself away and grabbed an iron pole that was stuck in the dirt.

The irate ogre swooshed, moving to and fro as I brushed myself off.

"I couldn't see when Stevey flinched!" Danny yelled.

"I ain't doing that! Call me chicken or whatever! I ain't puttin' my head on those tracks!" Ricky shouted.

"The caboose!" Danny yelled.

We soberly walked to where Stevey had rested his head. There was no sign of him. Danny wore funeral eyes, and tears welled up in mine, when Stevey jumped out from behind a pile of garbage, laughing. We all hugged, and Danny and I pretended we would not have cried if he'd really been dead.

Occasionally, the brute machine that could have killed us so many times was our victim. We broke its locks and stole hidden treasure, unburdening it of fruit or even pool sticks. We dodged the railroad dicks, who supposedly aimed their guns at our asses.

Two neighborhood kids pulled their families out of poverty, each losing an eye to the pepper-spraying rifles of the railroad men. I'd gladly have done that myself, but I was afraid I might lose both eyes.

By the end of summer, we moved a few blocks away to live with Ma's friends, Uncle Rory and Aunt Kay Brown. They had two small children, Emmy and Kevin. Uncle Rory supported his family and us by doing small burglaries and selling drugs. I already knew that *illegal* did not necessarily mean *immoral*.

I was always an "ends justify the means" kind of guy. Going in and out of bars, shoe shining with Danny, I had developed a real liking for Slim Jims, the stringy pieces of sausage that were sold for a dime in most neighborhood saloons. Times were skinny, and I was dying for the taste of one. I raked the house for pop bottles to refund and was still short.

I saw Aunt Kay's purse hanging off the chair in the kitchen. The coast was clear. The house was quiet.

As my sticky fingers graveled the bottom of Aunt Kay's purse, Uncle Rory appeared. I'm not sure where he came from, but I was consumed with guilt. What would Ma do now? Where would we go?

I barely closed my eyes when I went to bed. I prayed all night. Surely the Lord would intercede and help me out. The hours I waited until light sneaked through the blinds were the longest years of my life.

The following day, Uncle Rory introduced me, as his nephew, to the owner of the little grocery store across the street. He got me a job sweeping and stocking shelves. I should have known better not to worry so. Uncle Rory might have been a drug dealer and a thief, but he was an A-class, good guy.

A few days later, Ma visited and we walked alone on 51st Street. I loved music, and had sung "The First Noel" for the whole school the previous Christmas. For weeks, I had been banging out a new song, "Drumbeat," on coffee cans, plastic buckets, and pieces of tin in the alley. I had practiced it four hundred times, and wanted to sing "Drumbeat" for Ma.

As I was about to begin, she turned to me. "Patrick, I have something to tell you," she said in a low tone.

I was slightly taller than she was. I looked into her eyes.

I was never sure what she might say. Her life was one tribulation after another.

"What is it, Ma?" I asked.

"Son, I'm going to have a baby."

My mind raced. *How could that happen?* I saw the pain in her face, grasped the situation, and hugged her.

"Good, Mom, I'll have a new brother or sister." I was sure that I had spoken the words, but was not certain where they came from.

Ma cried quietly and squeezed me. "I knew that I could count on you. I knew it," she said, and embraced me even tighter.

The Old Man's wife was knocked up as well. So now we would be twelve, four from my mother and father, my mother had a new arrival on the way, six in the brood with the Old Man from his second wife, and Paulie, their newest arrival. My, how wonderful life was. I hear my first song "Drumbeat" in my head every time I begin penning a new tune.

This year, we'd spend Christmas with Uncle Vince, his wife, and five kids. Ma wanted a holiday to remember, and got her wish. As we rushed around Christmas Eve, it began snowing. Ma made purchases with Irwin's signed business card. Each week, Irwin arrived and collected whatever Ma had to give him toward the balance. He was never cross or impatient, and though he was Jewish, he was more Christian than most any Catholic I've ever known.

On the back of the card was the amount Irwin guaranteed for his client. He knew each of the families he dealt with. He knew the work they did and the estimated amount of monthly bills they had to pay. Irwin had to be a good judge of character and a good risk manager. After all, he had four kids of his own to feed.

I often look back with fond memories of "our Jew," Irwin Rothstein. Families like ours were often in grave financial straits. Evictions, and electricity and gas being cut off, were common. Yet Irwin cared enough to gamble, and it was his courage that made life more bearable for our family and many like us.

Irwin's card was the first credit card I'd ever seen, good at all the shops at Jefthro Plaza on Roosevelt Road. As we went from store to store, each merchant scratched the old balance, wrote the new one, and signed the card.

With only one purchase left, we entered the toy store. Ma quickly targeted a gift for my sister, Katy.

"I would like that doll, please," pointing as she spoke.

The tired, elderly shop owner reached up and grabbed the doll, knocking two other toys down.

"How much is it?" Ma asked with dignity.

"Seven dollars, madam," the merchant responded.

"Why so expensive?" Ma inquired.

"Its face, hands, and feet are porcelain, madam."

"What about that one?" Ma pointed to another doll.

The Old Man's back ached, reaching up. His face twisted with pain as he handed it to Ma. "Madam."

Ma examined the doll. "No, no, this won't last a week," she said as she handed it back.

"Madam, we're about to close," the merchant said.

"Yes, I know, but I just can't buy any old thing. It's Christmas."

"Yes, for you it is. For me it's just another long day. Now, how much money can you spend?"

"$1.75" was written on the back of Irwin's card. She rummaged through the holy cards in her purse to capture loose change. Her fingers finally made it to her secret hiding spot. There was a crack on the inner floor inside of Ma's purse. That sacred crevice was the home of Ma's "never broke dollar." She promised to never, ever use it—but it was Christmas.

"I can spend three dollars," she said, with a little less dignity.

"I have those stockings filled with hard candy. They have little, plastic dolls inside," he said.

Ma stared.

"I'm sorry, I'm closing," he said.

My stomach turned. I could have easily stolen any doll I wanted. Who could stop me? Certainly not him—but Ma would never go for that.

Some months prior, Ma had sent me to Neisner's Dime Store to buy some plastic drapes. I stole them instead. She caught me putting the money back in her purse and marched me back to Neisner's to pay. It was the first time the manager remembered someone returning to pay for stolen merchandise.

"How much is that one?" Ma pointed. The doll was wearing a pink outfit and had a pacifier in its mouth. I thought the cheeks were a bit too rosy. But what did I know about dolls?

"$4.75," the store owner answered.

"I'll take it," Ma said.

The store owner thought that he must have mistakenly heard, "Three dollars."

"Gift wrapped?" he grunted more than asked.

"Yes, please." Ma's voice turned sheepish.

She gave him the card and $1.25. "I'll get the other $1.75 to Irwin."

The owner pulled the package back. "You'll not leave this store with that doll unless I'm paid in full. These are the rules and Irwin knows it, too."

Desperation and tears flooded Ma's face. "It's Christmas," she offered.

"This is what you teach your children on Christmas, to run around spending money that you don't have? This is your religion, Santa Claus?"

Ma stumbled and sobbed. "I'm one of Irwin's best customers."

The man stood firm. I held Ma's arm as we walked out. The car wouldn't start, and I convinced a man to give us a jump start. The window wipers cleared the snow, but I don't know how Ma drove through the tears.

Later, at Uncle Vince's house, Uncle Vince consoled her. "Sis," he said, "I have a job lined up after Christmas. I'll buy her the most beautiful doll in the city."

Ray, the Mexican woman who lived downstairs, overheard the story while sipping coffee with Aunt Alice. Ray left and returned fifteen minutes later. The neighbors never knocked on each other's doors. Ray was carrying a package with her.

She winked at Ma and Aunt Alice. "Come into the bathroom," she said.

Uncle Vince tried to see what was going on.

"Women's stuff, Vince," Aunt Alice chided as she closed the door.

Once in the bathroom, Ray opened the package, revealing a beautiful porcelain doll. "My grandmother gave her to me, but she was too pretty to play with. I want Katy to have it," Ray said.

Ma wept with joy, opened the door a crack, and called me in to join them.

They rewrapped the gift and with the precious cargo hidden in my sweatshirt, I went down and played with the lock on the icy car door. Once it was opened, I lay the porcelain doll in the sack with the other gifts. I covered the sack with a sheet, to wait until it was time to lay them out for Christmas morning.

Hours later, in the apartment, I heard Ma whispering my name. I rose cautiously, tiptoeing to avoid the children who blanketed the floor. I headed down the stairs, to get the gifts from the car, so they'd be under the tree when my brothers and sisters awoke.

I glanced ahead, at the car.

The window on the passenger side was broken.

I knew what that meant. I knew it was futile, that everything was gone. I glimpsed inside anyway.

Walking up the stairs, I thought about the words of the cranky, old merchant. "This is what you teach your children on Christmas, to run around spending money that you don't have? This is your religion, Santa Claus?"

I hesitated before opening the door leading to Uncle Vince's. There were just no words for the anguish that would fill my mother, an anguish that I suspected would be more than most anyone could bear.

Still, it had to be done. My hands were freezing. I welcomed the pain as I reached for the doorknob. I stopped and hesitated once more, knowing Ma was on the other side of the door, enjoying that unique ecstasy that only giving can bring.

I thought about a person falling from the splendor of a sunny mountain into the depths of a dark valley. I opened the door.

As I surmised, Ma was anxiously waiting to unload my hands and spread the gifts under the tree. At first, she appeared confused as she looked into my empty arms. Then she looked into my eyes. I gently shook my head. She looked to the floor, walked into the kitchen, sat at the table, put her head in her hands, and softly cried.

We went to mass, shared our cousins' toys, and feasted on pasta and neck bones.

I wondered and then hoped that some other kids were enjoying the toys that were stolen from us. At least my mother's sacrifice would have not gone in vain.

Chapter 3

A Typical Adolescence

For the most part, the whole stepfather/mother thing involves a whole lot of wishful thinking. Over the next period of my life, I needed to cope with the things one copes with when one of his parents marries a certified lunatic.

I mean, he had *papers*.

My brother Francis was born, and then my sister, Anne. Their father, Robert Meyer, was a heavyset German. Ma was happy that he agreed to have us all live together. Things got confusing when people asked how many siblings I had. I decided back then that my half brothers and sisters and stepbrothers and -sisters were all my brothers and sisters. By 1970, there were thirteen of us.

My other seven brothers and sisters lived with the Old Man in Bridgeport.

Marie, Katy, Anne, Greg, Francis, and I lived with Meyer and Ma in a third-floor apartment on 78th and Winchester. I made friends with some neighborhood musicians, and we formed a garage band.

Greg was ten, and I was almost twelve. Meyer convinced Ma to let us spend time alone together. We easily fit into the bucket seat of his '66 Dodge Charger. The car leapt as the motor sucked air into the carburetor. The speedometer needle jumped to over 100 miles an hour as we headed south on the Dan Ryan Expressway. I studied every detail: the street signs, the odometer, the expression on Meyer's face.

Ma's Girondi Disease attracted her to people that she could help, that she could save. Robert Meyer, who worked in his family's gas station with his older brother, had an abundant share of trouble. He did a stretch in jail, and spent time in a few of the state's sanitariums. He erupted into violent fits, drank heavily, and was schizophrenic. A dozen Mother Teresas couldn't have saved the guy.

Just after passing the Indiana border, we pulled into an oasis. I glanced at the surroundings. Meyer turned the car off and smiled.

"You are my sons, now. We're a family. Do you fellas want something to eat, ice cream or chips or something?" He smiled warmly at us.

Greg glowed. I stared. Meyer's smile turned treacherous as he glared back at me.

His eyes were frosty, his teeth crooked, and his breath reeked of decay. "You're a punk, aren't ya?"

I cringed deliberately as his breath hit my face.

"I know how to deal with punks," he said. He grabbed my shirt, his mechanic hands covering most of my chest. He raised my face to his.

"Greg, run," I said.

"Run where?" Greg asked.

"Just run," I said a bit louder.

As Meyer raised his hand to slap me, he spotted two Indiana state troopers walking toward the car. He released me, grinned, and lowered the window. "My sons," he nodded, "these are my boys."

In my mind, I saw a vision of my mother crying as her dream family fell to the roadside. I smiled. One of the officers winked.

Meyer watched the state cruiser disappear in the rearview mirror.

He beamed; any sign of anger had vanished. "Greg, you are good boys, aren't you!"

"Sure," Greg replied.

"Then you should have what you want!" Meyer said enthusiastically.

"I want a Pepsi," Greg said confidently.

Meyer dropped his brown leather wallet between the seat and the door. "Oops! What a shame, I forgot my wallet," he said as he gazed at Greg.

I saw him drop the wallet. That meant there were two possibilities. Either he was a lunatic, or he was trying to give me acting lessons.

"I'm sorry, Gregory." Meyer looked away, and turned back, grinning. "I know! I have a friend that works here. He's off today. You guys stick a few things into your shirts. I'll figure out how much we owe, and I'll pay him when I have my wallet."

"You want us to steal?" Greg asked.

"Absolutely not," Meyer replied.

Meyer placed his hand on my head, rubbing harder and harder. "You're my sons. Daddy wants you to have what you want, but don't let anyone see, or my friend could get in trouble." He winked.

Greg and I walked into the oasis store.

"Greg, don't take anything," I said.

The shop was doing a brisk business. Grabbing a few things would have been a piece of cake, but I didn't want to give Meyer the satisfaction. It wasn't about refusing to steal. It was about defiance. I walked past Greg, trying to offer cover as he slipped the bottle of Pepsi into his shirt.

We returned to the car.

"What did my boys get?" Meyer asked.

Greg pulled the Pepsi out from under his shirt. Meyer opened the bottle with his teeth. He then looked at me.

"And what did you get, Patrick?" Meyer asked.

"I didn't want anything," I said.

His eyeballs darted as far left as they could go while still remaining in his head. They slowly rolled back and set on me. He stared intensely. His lips moved slowly, as if maneuvering tons of weight making strange forms for over 10 seconds but no words came out. He then grinned and started the car.

Heading toward Chicago, Meyer pulled onto the shoulder.

"Your turn to drive, Patrick," Meyer said.

"I don't know how to drive," I replied.

Meyer grabbed the door handle, hesitated, and then looked at me. He removed the ignition key. "That's right, Daddy's going to teach you."

Cars zoomed by as he carelessly flung his door open. A horn screamed as a car skidded, just missing him.

"Screw you!" Meyer yelled, throwing up his middle finger to the passing cars. He stood erect and proud, daring any of them to stop.

He entered the passenger door, lifted Greg, and moved him next to the window. "Don't drop your Pepsi, son. It's a sin to waste."

Greg sipped his pop. Meyer pushed me. My legs bumped against the stick shift divide.

"What are you doing?" Greg asked.

"Daddy's got to teach you things, doesn't he?" Meyer asked kindly.

Greg continued drinking without saying a word.

"I'm going to teach Patrick how to drive. When you're older, I'm going to teach you how to drive," he said devotedly.

Meyer pushed his body against mine. "If you don't move into the seat, I'm gonna hurt you." The volume of his voice was perfectly flat. The intent, however, was as rigid as the command of a marine general.

I moved into the driver's seat. Meyer started the car. "Pull the seat up so you can see, son," he said kindheartedly.

I reached for the door handle. Meyer stared at me, "You'll be sorry if you do that." He grinned and looked at my brother. "If you really don't want to, Gregory can drive."

I glanced at Greg. "I'll drive," I said.

Horns blew as I eased the car into traffic.

"Faster! Faster! You're going to get us killed!" Meyer urged.

With my eyes frozen on the white lines, I gripped the steering wheel tightly and pressed the gas pedal; we gained speed, but cars continued flying past us. He sat on the divide and put his foot on top of mine, pushing the gas pedal to the floor. The carburetor screamed. The car jumped. My hands were fixed tightly to the steering wheel. If Greg wasn't in the passenger seat, I'd have already crashed it into the guardrail.

Twenty minutes later, we were home. Meyer smiled as he greeted Ma, hugging Greg and me to his side. "Dinner ready? Me and the boys are starving."

Ma beamed at her three men. I smiled thinly, doing all I could to not break her heart. "Looks like you boys had a good time," she said.

"And we're going to have plenty more," Meyer said, "We're going to have plenty more."

Meyer would steal money from my mother's purse and blame us. I once watched him eat an entire package of raw hot dogs. He later swore that he hadn't eaten even one. A few times, I walked in as he asked my mother for beer money.

Ma was now the single breadwinner for six kids and a lunatic. Anything could turn him into a beast. Things worsened when he argued with his brother at the gas station. Now he was unemployed, and always home.

As the climate deteriorated, he convinced Ma that I was the real problem. Ma, somewhat of a tragic optimist, remembered that I, in fact, had always been a bit of a challenge. She sent me to stay with various relatives and friends for a "settling-in period."

During the settling-in period, I traveled back and forth. One morning, during Christmas break when I was home, Meyer called my sisters Marie and Katy into the kitchen. The house reeked of urine. One of them had wet the bed. Ma fearfully watched the drama unfold. Meyer condemned Katy, who according to him was intentionally trying to make him look foolish by not admitting guilt. He took off his belt. Katy shrieked. Ma grabbed Meyer from behind and took the belt from his hand. In one movement, Meyer flung Ma onto the ground and broke off an eighteen-inch long couch leg. The couch toppled. Meyer hit Katy on the legs with the couch leg. None of my siblings were cowards. Greg, Marie, and I ran in front of Katy. Ma joined us.

Meyer threw the leg down and glared. "These kids will never amount to anything," he said, hesitating for a moment, as if searching for the right words. "You're always picking them over me. If this is how it's going to be, I'm not going to stay here." He walked out, my mother in hot pursuit.

That night, as Meyer slept, I lay in the bottom bunk next to Francis. I reached under the bed, almost hoping I wouldn't find the baseball bat that I had borrowed from Doug Winters.

My fingernails touched the wooden bat. I never had forgiven myself for cowering when the Old Man beat Grandpa. I had a chance to amend things.

I rolled the bat out. The light from the stove clock shone off the barrel. I gazed at the floor, sliding the weapon until my fingers were at the bottlecap.

I took a deep breath. I stood. I knew I had to move quickly. If someone stirred, and Meyer woke, I'd be at the business end of the Louisville Slugger.

Francis's leg moved. I was conscious that the ruffling didn't faze me.

I stood and walked to Ma's bedroom. Meyer, the unwanted guest, was sleeping soundly, his nostrils making gentle rustling sounds.

I took the bat in both of my hands. I didn't want to kill, but I also didn't want to leave him alive.

I measured the swing and whacked him in the stomach.

He erupted, gasping for breath.

I didn't stick around for the next bats. I fled and slept in my friend Doug Winters's basement, not knowing exactly what might happen next. After a week, Ma communicated to Doug that things were calm and I could return home.

I wasn't convinced, but I was out of options.

When I came home, Meyer was outside, carrying groceries to the apartment.

I moved closer, convinced that I could outrun him if I had to.

He saw me. He dropped the bags.

I slipped. He tackled me, rubbing ice and slush into my face. He didn't stop there. Neighbors watched as Ma's tiny structure flip-flopped like a rag doll on Meyer's back. His panting was the last sound I heard. He rose proudly, king of the jungle. I lay unconscious, surrounded by bloodstained slush.

When the union of Ma and Meyer ended, our movement from 78th Street was restricted. We couldn't afford much in rent. Sometimes we left an apartment because a neighborhood changed from bad to worse; other times we were tossed out because

Ma couldn't pay the rent or because I, and to a lesser extent, my brother Greg, were punks, delinquents, or—as Ma and some others kindly contended—misunderstood.

Many of the guys in Little Italy wore Big Apple or Berretto newsboy caps. I took to wearing one of them too. Grandpa wasn't around much anymore, but I visited him from time to time. When I'd go see him, I wanted to bring some of the neighborhood with me and wore the newsboy cap religiously. It was my uniform, the uniform of an Italo-American—not Italian, not American, not really white and not really Arab.

Grandpa lived in the basement of an elderly Polish woman's house on 72nd and Artesian. When I visited, I rapped on the window in the gangway. He'd peer out and then walked to meet me at the back door. He wasn't singing much anymore, and his gentleness had given in to reality. He was going to die a pauper with his family in shreds, five thousand miles from home.

He opened the door and made a path through the labyrinth of hanging, wet clothes. It wasn't much, but it was enough: a bed, hot plate, television, bathroom sink, and toilet. I wondered how he washed himself, but never asked. All that was really left of his life was Wrigley's spearmint gum, of which he always offered me a piece, along with the latest on the Chicago White Sox, whether it was baseball season or just news about spring training. The break between the end of the baseball season and spring training games must have been a real challenge for him.

I was twelve and a half when Grandpa Santino died. The funeral was on 69th Street in Old Little Italy. The parlor was full of family members, priests, and criminals, speaking Italian. It was no secret that Santino's family was broken and broke; almost everyone brought an envelope. I remembered thinking that Italy must be a horrid place, for my family to have moved here to live like this.

It may not have been the life that Santino had dreamt about when he left Modugno, but it was beautiful. I loved every part of it.

On one of my first nights busing tables at Club el Bianco, on 63rd Street, a few drunkards made threatening advances on Terry, the hostess. I was twelve, maybe thirteen. I moved next to her. Hidden behind my back, I had a screwdriver in my hand. Enrico, the owner, arrived, and threw the rowdies out.

"Kid, where'd you get that screwdriver?" he asked.

"Off the ledge, in the ice room," I responded.

"What were you going to do with it?" he asked.

"I was going to stab them if they went after Terry," I said.

Enrico loved me. His twenty-five-year-old son, Butchy, didn't.

Club el Bianco was famous for its thirteen-course dinner, "Festa alla Bianco." Actually, in Italian, the "el" in Club el Bianco should have been "'il," but like so many misspelled Italian names, it eventually became cost-prohibitive, or just plain inconvenient, to fix the errors. I liked how it rang.

A busboy like me had to memorize the courses, remembering that minestrone came after the relish trays, with spoons and bowls already in place for the waitress who arrived with piping-hot soup. No one hustled like I did. Better service meant better tips, and the waitresses argued over who I'd work with. But busing didn't bring in a lot of cake, so I took up other activities, and thankfully, rarely got caught.

The few times I got pinched was for theft. Each time was different, and mostly I was able to make a deal with the police officers, whom we affectionately called "coppers." If it did get in front of a judge, they were usually all too happy to believe the bologna I gave them. The prisons were full, and I was just a kid.

I was also a great talker and fast on my feet. Most of my beefs were cookie crumb stuff, and most coppers passed on the paperwork, especially since my stories were so interesting.

My family moved into a home, a "hole" owned by Johnny Rossi, my Aunt Angela's boyfriend. The place was infested with millions of cockroaches. At night, whole pieces of the ceiling were covered with them.

At one point, "Uncle Johnny" arrived, promising to evict us and make Ma pay for the damage we had caused to the house.

"The roaches were here and the house was in shambles when we arrived," Ma pleaded.

I moved to my mother's side. Uncle Johnny called us scum. Ma's tears flowed, and I socked him in the gut. He doubled over, pushing Ma away as she tried to comfort him.

"That kid's a hoodlum," he groaned, "he's gonna be just like his father."

Ma was angrier at me than he was.

F

On one of Ma's many visits to Saint Augustine Church, she met Father Pasquale Faro, a teacher at Saint Joseph's Franciscan Seminary. Ma hoped that the seminary could break the grip of the streets on me. She pleaded like the old woman pleaded with the king, in the Bible parable. Her persistence was rewarded.

In freshman year, I packed up and moved away from home to live with the Franciscans. A total of eighty-three students in the whole school were taught by sixty-two Franciscan brothers and priests.

Being in the seminary was one of the happiest times of my youth. There was no stress. I just had to pray, take a few tests, and behave. If I didn't behave, I had to not get caught. Sure, I thought of home, or my homes, but I was convinced that I wasn't missing much. Over the years I learned that things didn't change a whole lot.

When I returned for Christmas break, things were normal—the TV didn't work, the gas and electricity were going to be turned off, the phone had already been disconnected, and rent hadn't been paid in three months. I intended to pay for the television repair by shoveling snow and busing at Club el Bianco.

My brother Greg and I loaded the broken television onto a borrowed wagon. The sidewalks were icy, and the wind gusted a hurtful cold. We navigated the precious freight carefully into the electronic repair shop on 69th Street and Wolcott.

"What do you fellows need?" the repairman asked.

"The set's busted," I replied.

"Well, let's open her up, maybe it's just a tube."

While staring at my good-looking self in the gray-black TV screen, I heard a yell and watched a man run toward us from the back of the shop. All of our eyes were fixed as a dark, brown residue fell from the inside of the set. It spread across the counter in every direction. It was mayhem.

The owner and his assistant worked furiously to contain the live roaches. They screwed the cover onto the set and scraped the roaches and their dead relatives into a cardboard box.

We knew to always check our clothes for roaches before leaving home. I didn't think to check the television.

"Get out of here, you filth, get out of here!" the repairman screamed. "Get out of here before I smash you like one of your roaches!"

I stared at him, looking into his eyes; I actually wanted him to try.

On summer break, I carelessly pursued Marilyn, an attractive twenty-four-year-old Club el Bianco waitress. The story began. I was fourteen. It may not have been politically correct, or legal, but I learned more from her than I learned from any ten women in my life (against modern hysteria, I kind of think every boy should be able to have the experience).

26

Marilyn was just a hobby. I did serious prowling all summer. Next to our house, or should I say Uncle Johnny's house, lived the Olive family.

We didn't always get along with the Olives, and that's a shame, considering that in the Catholic church an olive branch is used as a gesture of peace. I was more or less in tune with my church. But when I thought of the Olive sisters, I mostly considered the homophone for peace.

Dale Olive, the eldest, was a bullying muscle head. Tom, his younger brother, was a few years older than me, and at times he seemed to despise Dale as much as I did.

One evening, the Olive brothers called me to their basement. They had been told that I took indecent liberties with their sisters, Terry and Rochelle. Though I denied the accusations, they had already decided to teach me a lesson for Terry, Rochelle, Marianne, Kim, and Joanie, other girls on the block.

At eighteen, Dale still hadn't had the pleasure. I, a fourteen-year-old punk from the worst family, living in the dirtiest house, was breaking records. He wasn't even slightly amused.

Thinking of me being with Terry confused Tom, Dale's younger brother. She was fifteen and homely. He was more interested in allegations involving Rochelle; she was only twelve. Pointing out that Rochelle's breasts were bigger than Terry's probably wouldn't have helped; at any rate, Dale wrapped a chain around my neck. I punched and kicked until I heard Grandpa Santino's voice calling me from heaven. I walked toward him, but woke up on a fallen bicycle and broken glass.

The experience bound me even tighter to Ma's religious conviction, Grandpa, and his culture. Going forward, I had absolutely no fear of death. I knew that no matter what happened, Grandpa was actually waiting for me in what us Franciscans call a better place.

All these wonderful experiences . . . seriously, I guess, I'm just lucky.

Before Easter of my sophomore year, Father Edward, the Saint Joseph Seminary Dean, went through a list of my infractions, which wouldn't exactly be used to canonize me. I stole bacon from the kitchen and cooked it in the forest when I should have been at Sunday mass. I had fistfights with Jimmy Passer and Gayton Burke. More recently, I had been caught on the lawn of a nearby hotel, making out with the daughter of a local businessman. The girl's father personally visited the seminary, and reported the incident to Father Edward. The words that the disgruntled parent employed struck the good father like Chicago winter winds.

As a result of all of these altercations, I was forbidden to return after Easter.

In almost two years of living among the Franciscans, I have nothing but kind things to say about brothers and priests, even Jesuits. I would dearly miss Father Ambrose, the soft-spoken Italian priest who tended the livestock. His simplicity just struck me as the closest thing to truth that I knew in a man.

My disappointed mother didn't want a bad apple to spoil the bushel. She forbade my return. As a consequence, I went to live with the Old Man in Bridgeport, a blue-collar neighborhood next to Chinatown, on the South Side of Chicago.

While going back and forth between my parents, friends, and the seminary, the old Little Italy disappeared. The community went from predominantly Italian to predominantly African American in the blink of an eye. It confused me. I spent years of nights yearning for days gone by. I forever wore the newsboy cap that a lot of the "guys" wore in Little Italy. An important part of my past, in time, it became a part of me.

Chapter 4

Bridgeport

People of almost any nationality lived in Bridgeport, but the Irish predominated the South Side (37th Street), ruled over by the 11th Ward/Daley political family, and the Italians lived on the North Side (26th Street), run by Dominick and the Italian organization.

By coincidence, the Old Man lived at 26th and Halsted, almost the farthest north you could go and still be in the neighborhood. Home was a tiny shack with three bedrooms, each of them six by nine feet. The abode leaned to the right, and was held together by thousands of strips of duct tape stolen from "The McCormick Place," or one of the other places where the Old Man worked.

Coleen and Clara slept in one room, the five boys in another, the bride and groom in the last bedroom, and I slept on the couch. I enrolled myself at De La Salle, an Irish Christian Brothers boys' high school, close to Bridgeport. Carmine Ferri quickly became my best friend. His family was from Sorbo San Basile, a tiny town in Calabria, Italy. The Ferris lived on 31st and Wells in Bridgeport. Soon I was a regular at their home.

I had to pay my own tuition. After school, I took the L and a bus to the Southwest Side, where I worked at the Silver Transmission Shop from 3:00 to 5:30 p.m. on weekdays and all day on Saturdays. Three evenings a week, I bused at Club el Bianco. When I wasn't at school, working or hanging with my new Bridgeport buddies, I was with Marilyn.

Morris Greenberger, Silver Transmission Shop's owner, went by Morry Green. He robbed everyone that walked in the front door. He'd do the same if they walked in the back door, but insurance dictated that clients weren't allowed in the garage.

Morry could sell a rosary to the pope. I watched, and I learned.

Johnny dropped the transmissions, and after Dave, the bench mechanic, finished his handiwork, the transmissions were spray-painted silver and reinstalled. Morry did five or six of these some days, and got his clients for $500 to $1,500. Most customers didn't know what a transmission was, and most mechanics didn't touch them.

The customers' autos were usually immobile. It was expensive, towing a car around the city to check prices, and the tow truck drivers were usually in on it, getting an extra ten bucks from Morry for every client they hauled in. Things worked like clockwork, unless you were the customer, who must have felt like he had been given an enema with the wide part of a ball bat.

If you let Morry hold your car title, he'd put you on a payment plan. He accepted almost any form of currency: paintings, statues, baseball cards, coupons, or even store rebates.

Morry read customers like billboards, and sensed immediately if one had a drug problem, or if one was aching from divorce. He divested those who didn't know the value of money, and coaxed the sensible into making nonsensical decisions. Women who were older than him blushed when he told them that he was treating them like he would his own daughter—which was likely true.

Morry attempted to cheat everyone by adjusting their hours, scribbled on the calendar. Employees, no fools, would readjust in order to live better. Merchandise was stacked everywhere, and we had absolutely no guilty feelings about walking out the back door with Morry's booty.

I robbed car parts and sold them to Morry, who bartered them off, mostly to auto body shops. Sometimes, I stole parts from Morry himself and sold them back to him, obviously at a discount. Shoe shining had been my university. Under Morry, I got my master's, and met more con artists in a week than most people meet in a lifetime.

Our house reeked from unwashed clothes, particularly socks. On one of the Old Man's sober stints, he noticed the odor and ordered socks to be changed daily. Each evening, we marched into the front room, showed him our socks, and told him the color of yesterday's socks.

Half the time the washer was broken and the laundry wasn't always done regularly, so Bobby swapped his dirty socks with Casey, Mark switched with Jimmy's dirty socks, and then the next day Bobby would change with Jimmy, and Casey with Mark.

The odor persisted. Out of fear, Butch defended her daughters. The girls always did the housework.

We were purposely making him look foolish, the Old Man said.

He barked and we paraded in front of him. My brother Mark was eight, and had a lisp. His words were plagued by the "sh" sound. It drove the Old Man nuts.

The Old Man stared at us one by one. It was kind of like standing against the wall, facing a firing squad.

"Mark!" the Old Man screamed.

"Yesh shir?" Mark meeked out.

"What color were your socks yesterday?"

"Red, shir."

"No dey weren't! Dey were blue!"

Tears began tumbling down Mark's face.

"I'm going to ask you again. What color were your socks yesterday?"

The house was perfectly silent. Even the cars on busy Halsted Street made not a sound.

"What color were your socks yesterday?!"

Mark looked to his mother, but there was no safety there. They both knew that. We all knew that. There was no safety anywhere.

Without moving his head a hair, Mark glanced around, looking for some type of solution.

"They were red, shir."

"Are you calling me a liar?"

"No, shir."

"Den dey weren't red, were dey, you dirty liar?"

"Yes shir, I mean, no shir."

The Old Man looked at the rest of us. "Your brother's an idiot."

The Old Man looked at Jimmy, who also had a slight lisp.

"Do you know what idiots do, Jimmy?"

"No sir."

"Do you want to know?"

"No sir, I mean yes sir."

"Dey eat deir socks."

The Old Man glanced at each of us again. "Mark, eat your socks!"

Mark choked and cried silently as he got about half of his reeking sock into his mouth before the Old Man stopped him.

Few outsiders ever entered this haven, where the Old Man helped himself to whatever and whomever he wanted. He loved a show, and one of his favorite entertainments was using the family's German shepherd "Sarge" as a disciplinary tool.

He pointed, said "Get him," and Sarge attacked. Sarge always broke skin, but eventually, we learned to block most of the damage with our closed fists. It was traumatic, watching him pounce on my younger brothers.

Toast and tea were breakfast and dinner. Two tea bags were allotted per meal.

I arrived in the neighborhood at fourteen, but immediately it was my home. My friends, the Arcieris, Baileys, Bertuccis, Billses, Boticas, Ferros, Ciarvinos, Frattos, Fitzpatricks, and Ramoses, became my family. We routinely bailed each other out of colorful circumstances, including jail. Most bail deposits were no more than a few hundred dollars. Of course, this represented only 10 percent of the actual sum forfeited, if one didn't show up for court. Lots of time was spent rounding up bail money, for charges ranging from disorderly conduct to grand larceny or assault and battery.

Folks in Bridgeport, Chicago, and the major US cities, including FBI agents from all over the country, knew very well who the members of the 26th Street crew and the Old Neighborhood Italian-American Club were. When one of my closest friend's uncle and cousin were found frozen and dead in their bullet-ridden trunk, no one asked, and everyone knew.

I eventually did some things with an outfit guy named Squeaky, and ran parlay cards at school. A customer picked six teams. If he won all six, we paid thirteen to one.

I liked and respected the boss (he and some of his crew were depicted in the story of Las Vegas in the movie *Casino*). The Bridgeport boss was accused by the FBI of putting his victims on meat hooks before killing them.

It was easy money, pedaling parlay cards or doling out phony hundreds. The Italian Organization didn't scare me or most of the neighborhood people. Many poked fun at them and the wannabe mobsters in their waxed Fords and Cadillacs.

Slim Torre was an enforcer. One summer day, my friends and I waited in an alley for him, his soldiers, and his three-foot-long cigar to pass by on the street that crossed the alley. When they did, we pulled our pants down and wagged our personal gear at them. 400-pound Slim never caught us, but he did eventually catch a sixty-year sentence for murder.

Rooks was the public relations, soft side of the organization, and Penny Candy ran the biggest book for the outfit at the Board of Trade. They were among the boss's top men, and both were kind "uncles" to me. The boss was a sucker for the underdog.

Usually, thieves paid some fee to his organization. My father, who had seven kids to feed, was given a pass.

ⵕ

One day the Old Man walked in with a toaster he stole off an exhibition counter. Butch loved her gift, but was duly warned to keep it clean or have it thrown out the window.

The Old Man locked the front door at nine p.m. (or whenever he felt like it). Whoever was outside remained outside. The first time I slept on the concrete porch, I felt him look out the window at me from time to time. I purposely didn't look back. Maybe Spartan love is true love.

Some nights, I slept at my mother's or in Carmine's basement. Grandpa Santino had spoken Barese, a Puglia dialect. I learned a Calabria dialect from the Ferris, and soon affectionately became *shrompolatto*. In the dialect of Sorbo San Basile, in the province of Catanzaro, where the Ferris were from, *shrompolatto* was used to designate people who didn't know how to behave and didn't care to learn.

It was a bitter cold, windy evening. Anywhere in the house more than fifteen feet from the space heater, was in the forties. The Old Man walked into the kitchen, turned the toaster upside down, and shook it. Crumbs fell onto the counter. He pitched it through the window.

That night, everyone shivered under clothes and blankets. The Old Man likely had antifreeze in his system. The next day, he instructed my brothers and me to duct tape the broken hole closed. It was too cold for the duct tape to stick to the glass. We put cardboard on the inside and the duct tape held on to that and the wooden part of the window. The broken windowpane wasn't changed for years.

The only visitor at our home was the Old Man's best friend, George Murphy. George was a jovial guy who killed people for a living. Every time he visited, he offered us a hundred-dollar bill. The Old Man would not accept and not allow us to accept charity, so George ripped the paper note into four or five pieces and let it fall to the ground. As soon as the Old Man and George left, Butch taped the bill together. At Christmas, George ripped five one-hundred-dollar bills. George may have exterminated some, but he was a savior to us.

I was in and out of police stations. At fifteen, I had lived in fifteen residences and been in front of judges at least fifteen times. The police often got aggravated with me, because as many of my friends said, I stepped in shit and came out smelling like a rose.

Some said that I could talk a squirrel out of a nut. I wasn't sure how it was that I was so lucky. Looking back, I think I was just good at analyzing situations and figuring out the best exit strategy.

ᚠ

Enrico's son took over at Club el Bianco. He caught me shooting craps with some delivery truck drivers in the alley behind the restaurant. I was fired on the spot.

A waitress's daughter got me a job at Northwestern Hospital, washing dishes. The pay was over four bucks an hour. I continued supplying stolen auto parts to Morry, and was making a few hundred take-home a week. I was living big.

The forty employees in the hospital kitchen were all dark-skinned. On my first day, I walked in while six of them were punching the time clock. I received the welcome of a debt collector.

Ryan Banks, a lanky guy three or four years my senior, smirked. "You lost, cracker?" he asked.

I grinned. "I'm looking for the supervisor, Abe Birch," I replied.

I wasn't white enough for the Old Man, and for most of the hospital workers I was *too* white. . . Crayola colors, kinda silly. Honky, Whitey, White Trash, Cracker—they were all names I answered to while working at the hospital (were those people committing hate crimes)?

It meant nothing at all to me. I was brought up on, "Sticks and stones will break my bones, but names will never hurt me."

After a week on the job, I was in the locker room, buttoning my uniform, when Ryan Banks entered. "Honky," he said, "You gotta stop working so hard. You're making us look bad."

"I need this job," I replied.

"How old are you, white boy?"

"Fifteen." I moved to exit. Banks blocked me.

A heavy, dark-skinned woman with a net over her hair and in hospital whites passed as I pulled the door open. "Ryan Banks, you leave that skinny, little white boy alone. You're older and twice his size," she said.

"Come on, Big Mamma, he's gonna make us all lose our jobs."

"No, he won't, if you do your job, you loafer."

Things were escalating quickly, and Banks grabbed my arm. Big Mamma grabbed the other. "Boy, you let him go or I'll give you what for, and a whole lot of it," she threatened.

Banks looked at her and released my arm. "I'll get you when she's not around to save you, white boy," he growled.

Big Mamma returned to the food line. As the trays passed, the women read the order and scooped on vegetables, meat, fish, Jell-O, broth, etc. All the line women wore white smocks and white mesh nets that covered their hair and much of their faces, making it difficult to tell them apart.

A few weeks later, my supervisor, Abe Birch, who was studying for a promotion, asked me if I was any good with algebra. I told him I was okay with it, and he asked me to help him prepare for a promotion exam. The next day, "kiss ass" was written in white spray paint on my locker door.

I was at my most vulnerable when I changed. As I scurried into the hall, I ran head-on into Banks. He said a few phrases about my algebra lessons that wouldn't be published in the *American Catholic Weekly* and grabbed me by the neck. A coworker passed, as if we were invisible.

"I told you I'd get you when Big Mamma wasn't around to save your skinny ass," he slithered.

Ryan Banks took me into a headlock and ran me into the wall. My heart beat fast as I felt his fist hit my forehead. I grabbed his arm as he pulled back for another shot. His arm slipped down around my neck.

As I squirmed, a woman in white ran toward us. I felt it as she caught Ryan Banks on the back with a soup ladle.

"Ouch! Big mamma! Ouch, woman! Leave me alone!" he screamed.

Ryan released me, and I gasped, slipping to the floor. Big Mamma took three more good swings.

"I told you to leave that skinny white boy alone and I meant it!" she screamed.

Big Mamma didn't say another word or hang around for thanks. Later, I walked to the women dressed in white. I recognized Big Mamma by her glasses. I thanked her. She just nodded, and continued with her work.

My career as a street mechanic, stealing cars and car parts ("Midnight Auto") helped me pay my tuition and assist Ma. My brothers and I helped the Old Man sell stolen loot mostly on the weekends out of our garage.

According to the police, my brothers and I eventually became just another of the many Bridgeport hoodlum clans.

Eventually, I stood in front of Judge Darren Stokes, at 61st and Racine, for stealing a battery out of an unmarked police car parked on 35th and Wallace—in the *police* lot. Officer Dumbrowski was the arresting officer.

Cops routinely "confiscated" our alcohol, fireworks, and stolen loot. I guess Dumbrowski was incensed when the tables were turned. How could anyone actually have the gall to rob from them?

Dumbrowski tugged hard on the cuffs, as we made our way through the parking lot to the police station.

"You're a big, tough guy, arresting a fifteen-year-old," I said.

He tugged harder.

"Hey, big boy, how you gonna run a mile and a half in twelve minutes this year?" I asked, when we were almost to the station.

Here I hit a sore spot. He had nightmares about the exam. He shoved me to the ground.

When the case finally got to court, Dumbrowski showed up early. He wouldn't miss this for a Ricobene's breaded steak sandwich.

I walked to the rail that separated the court from the lawyers, defendants, and spectators, and approached the court clerk. "Excuse me, ma'am. My name is Patrick Carmichael. I have a case today," I said in an angelic voice.

The woman pushed her glasses closer to her face and found my name. "You'll be called, sit down," she said.

After five cases, I heard, "Patrick Carmichael! Arresting Officer, Dumbrowski!"

I gazed down at my shoes as the judge watched me walk up slowly. I made my eyes water, thinking about when Grandpa died.

Dumbrowski approached the bench, his pants jammed into his buttocks crack, like they were forced in there with the handle of a hockey stick. He stood inches away from me, on my right.

"The defendant is charged with theft," the clerk said.

"A car battery, from a police car, in a police parking lot," Dumbrowski blurted.

The judge raised his hand as he examined my file.

"Patrick, aren't you tired of coming here?" the judge asked.

Dumbrowski stared at me. A tear ran down my cheek. I wiped my nose and sniffled.

"Where are your parents, son? You're a minor," the judge said.

"My parents are divorced. I'm living with my father, but he was hurt at work and couldn't come," I blubbered.

"Son, this is a serious charge," the judge said.

"Yes sir, I know, sir. I'm sorry. I'm so sorry," I said.

Dumbrowski was furious. He had to stop the performance and help the state recognize that I had all the makings of a career criminal. I felt Dumbrowski's shoe pushing on my right foot. Jerking would interrupt the show. I remained still, the pain helping the tears flow.

Dumbrowski was exasperated. "Your Honor, this kid is a punk."

Using the chance to move unnoticed, he put more pressure on my foot. The judge raised his hand. Dumbrowski stilled.

"Son, do you promise to not steal again?" the judge asked.

I wiped my nose with my shirtsleeve and used the chance to jerk my foot out from under Dumbrowski's shoe.

"Yes, Your Honor," I said meekly.

I left, truly thankful that I rarely got caught. It was a close call, but in a worst-case scenario I'd eventually end up behind bars. Ten percent of the neighborhood was there. I'd have company.

I was with the Old Man once, when a tow truck cut us off at a traffic light. We caught up with it at the following red light.

We could see the driver had a passenger with him. The Old Man growled, as he opened his door, "If you don't sock the passenger, you'll get what I'm going to give to the driver."

I walked up to the truck, grabbed the frightened guy from the cab, and while the Old Man went to work on the driver, I winked and pretended to punch his friend. He played along.

Surviving was sometimes challenging. At four a.m., I walked three miles in the snow to pick the Old Man up at the Star Bar on 48th and Halsted. I banged on the door and heard two pops. Light broke through two small holes just inches from my face. I dodged behind the brick wall next to the door and yelled, "It's Matty's son!"

Jimmy McCarthey, the owner, opened and examined the bullet holes. "Kid, you yell before you knock, not after."

I was the closest thing George Murphy had to a son, and the day I turned sixteen, he and the Old Man decided it was time to ordain me. They were about seven years late.

The festivities began in the early afternoon on Lake Street. The Old Man climbed into the van with a dark-skinned hooker. While waiting, George schooled me on women. "It's like eating. If you get accustomed to a certain flavor, that's what you want. I used to love chinks. That's all I wanted, but lately I like dark meat."

The Old Man crawled out and fastened his pants. "Your turn," he said, pointing to George.

"It's the kid's birthday," George said, smiling paternally. "Go ahead, kid."

I thought George's coat buttons were going to pop off with pride as I stepped up. The Old Man closed the door and George lit a cigarette.

The woman and I exchanged warm glances. "Come here, sugar," she said.

She gently put my hair behind my ear. I tenderly made love to her, and she gasped at all the right moments. As I finished, she smiled and waited until my eyes fell to hers. "All women are hookers, baby," she said.

I pushed firmly, to celebrate our oneness. At that moment, I was hers only, and she was mine. Her beam was amorous. "If a man shows up on Christmas without a gift, he ain't getting any Christmas pie," she smiled.

I sneaked a ten-dollar bill into her hand.

The Old Man opened the door and offered me a cigarette. I declined. George climbed in. An L train moved overhead, but I could still hear loud noises after it had passed.

I looked into the van and my father stopped me as I went for the door. Years ago, a knife had sliced a line from his left ear to his mouth. He grinned. The scar seemed deeper and uglier than I had ever noticed before.

"Let him have his fun, he'll be in a better mood," he said.

George's massive back moved as he seemed to work the woman over. Her mascara rolled like droplets of rain mixed with dirt. I again grabbed for the door, ready to take on George and my father to protect the woman I had loved. Her eyes fixed on mine, she winked and shook her head.

As we headed west, I watched her turn north off Lake Street. The van screeched to a stop. "The whore stole my wallet!" the Old Man screamed.

The tires screeched as he pulled a U-turn. I pointed my finger south. "She went down that street!" I yelled.

We were in hot pursuit, going in the wrong direction. I smiled. George fixed his glance on me. He smiled, too.

That evening, the Star Bar was full of truck drivers, hookers, drug addicts, and professionals (most would say professional criminals, but I know accountants, doctors, and lawyers who are far more criminal than they were).

"What song should I play on the jukebox?" George asked.

"Danny Boy," Matty said quickly.

"I played 'Danny Boy' twenty times," George said.

"Play 'The Star-Spangled Banner,'" the Old Man said.

George returned and said sadly, "They don't have 'The Star-Spangled Banner.'"

"Then tip the jukebox over," the Old Man said calmly.

A patron smashed a beer bottle on another's face. "Take it outside!" yelled the owner, Jimmy McCarthy.

Moments later, a crash froze everyone in the bar. George stood over the flipped jukebox, looking at the Old Man. Broken pieces and rolling quarters went everywhere. The patrons eyed each other before diving for the spoils.

Brothers Raymond and Oscar owned the Novak Brothers Gas Station on 65th and Kedzie. I'm not sure why they called it a gas station; the pumps didn't work.

Raymond, the elder, was always in bad sorts. He constantly eyed me, suspecting that I was a thief. I wasn't minimally offended; he thought that of most people. Friends and I were constantly there for repairs, borrowing tools or getting advice. I spent much of my free time at the Novak Brothers shop. When I wasn't there for a spell, Murph, the old guy who ran for parts, filled me in on the news.

Raymond didn't like when I and what he called my band of misfits were around, but he had been anxiously waiting for me to show up for more than a week. When I arrived, he smiled widely, something he did only in special tender moments, such as smashing flies or running over cats. He had to get the truth about "Red's starter."

Red was the flamboyant owner of the Go, a jumping nightclub on 63rd Street. Red was a fanatic about his hair and clothes, but his most precious fixation was for his '66 Pontiac Bonneville. The car was "cherry."

Red was the shop's most important client. Raymond, as head mechanic, was Red's official mechanic, and being anything to Red was stressful. Red showed up whenever the motor made any sound that wasn't a kitten purr. If the car took more than two seconds to start, Red headed for Novak's Station to complain.

Sure, Raymond thought, *he doesn't open until eight p.m., so he has lots of time to bust balls.*

Raymond was tempted to throw him out, but Red paid in cash on the spot, and the place was beginning to look like a used car lot, from all the customers who couldn't pay their mechanic bill.

A week or so prior, Raymond woke with a headache from arguing with his wife about loaning money to his worthless son. In the shop, he closed his eyes, trying to relieve the pain, opening them only to see Bobby towing Red's Bonneville onto the lot.

Christ, the car left here with a new starter a few days ago, he thought.

Bobby walked over to Raymond's brother Oscar, preferring not to be yelled at. "Oscar, Red's pissed. We got to get this in," Bobby said.

"Screw Red," Raymond said, looking at Bobby and his younger brother, Oscar. "And Bobby, wipe that frickin' grease off your face!"

Bobby squinted into the filth-caked mirror, moving his head to and fro, smearing grease into his skin.

"What's wrong with it?" Oscar asked.

Bobby's face became a question mark. "Don't know. It's completely dead. The battery's got plenty of juice. It must be the starter."

"We just put a starter in there! I told J and M, no rebuilt starters! I don't give a damn what they cost new! Who wants to listen to that arrogant pimp today?!" Raymond hesitated, "or any day, for that matter?!!!!" Raymond screamed even louder.

They put Red's Bonneville up on the fourth bay. Raymond, Oscar, and Carl ("The Guru") were busy on the other three bays. Carl was nicknamed "Guru" for his uncanny skill at misdiagnosis. If Carl thought the problem was the alternator, it meant that the alternator was not the problem.

"Oscar!" Bobby called. "Come look at this!"

Oscar, puffing his ever-present cigar, put his pliers down and walked over to Red's car. He looked up at the bottom of the motor and began laughing.

Raymond watched, not able to think of one possible thing that could be funny. He walked over. Oscar pointed, and Raymond looked up and rubbed his mechanic's hat. "Well, I'll be damned," Raymond said.

"I don't believe it," Oscar said as he shook his head.

"Should I call J and M?" Bobby asked.

"No. Don't touch a thing. Call that pimp." With a rep to protect, Raymond turned away so no one could see him smile.

Red arrived fifteen minutes later. His hair was slicked back and his clothes pressed. He never, ever entered the garage, not wanting to soil the soles of his shoes.

"Have you imbeciles fixed my car yet?" He looked at them one by one, assuming they'd be too embarrassed to answer. "If this keeps up, I'll have to rent an apartment across the street," Red said, quite impressed with his cleverness.

Raymond lovingly smiled, and waved Red in.

"I just had my shoes polished." Red threw the toothpick out of his mouth as he spoke. "It's the starter, right, kids?"

Raymond nodded. "Yeah, now get in here or we won't touch it."

That hit a nerve. "What the hell are you talking about? Last week you changed the starter. Now fix it! And I ain't paying for the tow!" Red screamed.

"Yes, you are," Raymond said gently, "now come in here, I got to show you something."

Red couldn't stand seeing Raymond happy. "I got my business and you got yours. Fix the car," Red said.

Raymond's face turned as red as a fire truck. "Get in here! Goddamnit, you arrogant son of a bitch!" he shrieked.

The eyes of the mechanics, customers, and even Murph, the old guy who mostly slept while watching the front, were all pasted on the unfolding saga.

Red cleared his throat and spit. "It's the starter, right?"

"Yes," Raymond replied smiling, calmly noting that his headache was gone.

"Well, Ace, it's on warranty, fix it," Red said, turning toward the street, "and I ain't paying for the tow!"

"We ain't touching nothing! It's not our responsibility, and the tow's eighty bucks!" Raymond yelped.

Red twisted angrily. Oscar winked at him and said, "Bobby, sweep a path for Red."

Bobby swept a trail to the Bonneville, and Red walked judiciously to his car. Raymond pointed up into the motor.

Red's face went blank. The goddamn starter was gone. The electric tape that was wrapped around the hot wire was wearing a string, tied like a miniature bow tie.

Red put his hand on his head. "What the . . . Well, I never."

Red's hood was always chain locked. Taking a juiced starter down on the street was dangerous (a spark, fire, or move that could cause the car to fall were all possibilities) and the temperature hadn't been above zero in a week. Raymond was convinced that I did it. Who else could have? Who else would have? And what was the meaning of the string bow tie?! He thought to himself loudly.

I walked in. Raymond and I were soon nose to nose. "You're a lunatic, and it does no good to ask a lunatic to rationalize his actions." Raymond walked away, shaking his head.

All eyes were on me. Raymond rushed back. "Did you steal the pimp's starter?"

I winked. "Come on, Raymond, do you think I'm crazy?"

Honor prevented anyone from snitching, and I suspected that Raymond hoped I'd steal the entire engine next time. He'd give anything to see the look on the pimp's face for that.

F

Sergeant Steele ran the 63rd Street police station lockup. His pride in abusing prisoners was the only thing bigger than his stomach. I found myself in his workplace more often than I would have liked. He resented my insolence, and always pulled me out of the lockup to stand in lineups. I assumed that he believed that the more questions he asked meant the higher the possibility that someone would finger me for a crime. He asked me banal questions, to which I responded with even more banal answers. He took special pleasure in commanding me to turn, step forward, look side to side. He yearned for someone behind the one-way glass to finger me, more than he yearned for a Whopper with cheese.

"Number four, what do you do for a living?" he asked.

"I seduce daughters of fat police sergeants," I responded calmly.

Steele had two daughters.

Later that night in my cell, he slapped, punched, and kicked me. I stood, fell, and laid quietly until he finished. There was no upside in shrinking, the way I did for judges, and I wouldn't give him the satisfaction.

Most law officials were convinced that I was more than a few eggs short of a dozen. The crazy things that some of them saw me do reminded them more of a film than real life. That's why the flatfoots (I get tired of saying "coppers") who arrested me knew exactly where to find me when I disappeared from the station after being arrested for assault.

An hour prior, I entered Pepe's Tacos for dinner with Laura, an Irish girl. I had been trying for months with her and was full of hope.

The Mexican waiter, who thought he was Spanish—Don Juan himself—began openly flirting with my date. I had eaten in the place plenty of times, but this was the first time that I laid eyes on him. I listened in almost disbelief. He stood there grinning at me in a white shirt with a large red waist belt, all the while making comments about my lass. His hair was dyed orange blond. I stared and thought, *how could anyone who looked so funny smirk at me?*

I looked back at him.

"Don Juan, get me an enchilada suiza dinner." I turned to Laura. "Laura, what would you like?"

Before she could answer, the banderillero smiled and gazed at her. "I could suggest something for the pretty lady," he said in a thick Hispanic accent.

Laura smiled. I couldn't figure out if she smiled at him or at the attention. I wasn't really entertained.

"Listen blondy, don't be talking to my date."

"I was just trying to suggest something of taste." He looked at me and frowned almost disappointedly. "I'm not sure that you could do that."

"Stop it, lover-boy."

"Why don't you let her decide for herself?" He gawked at her the way a wolf might gaze at a fallen doe. "Would you like to hear suggestions that I have for you? I mean, for now with the food?"

I didn't look at Laura. "You want my suggestion for you? Stop. Because if you don't, you're gonna get slapped."

"Oh, you're a tough . . .?"

Before he could get "guy" out of his mouth, I stood up and slapped him on the side of his head. He grabbed his face in disbelief. The owner called the cops.

"Now get me my enchilada suiza dinner and get her . . . what do you want, Laura?"

"I want to leave," she said calmly.

"Why, because this goof caught a slap?"

"I want to leave."

Lover-boy moved back to the kitchen and I tried to save my project. I mean, I had put the chances of bedding this Irish vixen at 30 to 40 percent.

"Please stick around, honey."

She just looked at me and shook her head. Moments later, she was heading for the door and almost right after, two policemen arrived. I thought they'd have been quicker. The station was only two blocks west of the restaurant.

They looked at the owner, who nodded at me. I looked at them. "Guys, I already lost my date for the night and I've been working on her for months. Could we consider that like justice served?"

They weren't impressed and had recognized me from being arrested other times.

"Get up, wiseguy."

They took me to the station, but did not handcuff me. When they returned with coffee, I was nowhere to be found.

Infuriated, they jumped in their cruiser and found me calmly eating in Pepe's, without my Irish date. "Get up," one of the officers growled.

"Can I finish my dinner?" I asked.

"Get up or I'll stick your dinner up your ass," the other cop said.

I gingerly dabbed my mouth with a napkin and got up. "You should see someone about that temper, you're in a high-stress occupation," I said.

The owner and Don Juan watched as the police pushed me toward the door.

"Temper, temper," I said.

"Just cuff him, there are cameras in here," one whispered to the other.

I turned and winked at the owner and Don Juan. "I still say you got the best enchiladas suizas in the city!"

"Està muy loco," the owner said.

Don Juan nodded. "Mucho."

Chapter 5

The Street Saves

Carmine Ferri's older brother, Mercurio, seemed not to trust anyone. He certainly didn't want a half-breed anywhere near his sisters Rachele and Giovanna, but one afternoon he came upstairs and looked at Carmine and me.

"*Vene ca!*" he yelled.

There was an issue at the Giglio family home. The Giglio's were DPs—displaced persons; a term used to designate new arrivals of any nationality. The Ferris and the Giglios arrived ten years earlier from Calabria. The newly arrived were DPs. Their children were kids of DPs.

The Giglio family rented an apartment to people that Signor Giglio, who went by Totò, described as hillbillies. Mercurio wanted my help. He, Carmine, three other guys, and I piled out of the car and into the Giglio family's yard. Mr. Giglio was waiting anxiously. "*Sono ubriachi e ricchioni. Danno le botte alle mighiere!*" Totò screamed.

I understood this to mean that the problem tenants were drunken, cowardly, wife-beaters. I assumed that they were also behind paying their rent.

"*Va e pigh acidd e dange tante mazzeit!*" Totò yelled to the troops.

We filed up the stairs with the intention of doing just as Totò told us, to "beat the shit out of them." We kicked the door down and dragged five long-haired guys out onto the lawn. The police arrived before anyone was killed. They cuffed everyone. Mercurio gave orders for no one to speak in English.

There were too many of us to fit into a single paddy wagon. One of the coppers made a comment that it was too nice out to spend the rest of the day booking DPs who didn't speak English. The hillbillies told Totò and the police that they would be moving out. We were freed—and I officially entered the family.

I loved the idea of "all for one and one for all" that Bridgeporters seemed to have. I was a part of that.

45

Our house was just down the street from the office of the outfit guys, the big boss Dominick, the underboss Slim, and their gang. My horizon expanded, and my past scrapes with the law helped me fit in. Folks knew I could be trusted.

Squeaky was a middle-aged inventor-handyman. He lived on 24th Street but was employed by 26th Street. Chinatown was rapidly expanding, and there were already twenty restaurants along Wentworth Avenue between 22nd and 25th Streets.

The North Side of Chinatown was home to the State Way Gardens. These were government-sponsored housing projects filled with poor people. Their presence made Chinatown a tough area. Many customers left without paying, and some patrons physically abused the restaurant owners who tried to make them pay for their food.

Problem and solution: the 26th Street guys sold insurance to the Chinese restaurants. Each client got a card with Sweetboy's phone number on it (one of Dominick's captains). That was their insurance card. When someone called the number on the card, within minutes, five guys with bats arrived. That was long before the Chicago Police would have shown up.

Not all of the Chinese restaurant owners wanted to pay. That's where Squeaky came in. His laboratory (garage) was full of homemade gadgets, long-armed fingers, clippers for hard-to-reach alarms, cameras, and different-sized torches and tanks for safes.

Squeaky told me I could earn twenty bucks. I was all ears. "What do I godda do?" I asked.

"You godda go take a dump in Chinatown." Squeaky laughed uncontrollably, like some mad scientist, and pointed to five hanging balls.

"Your dump's gunna be one of dese." I reached my hand toward the balls.

"Don't! Don't touch 'em! You moron!" Squeaky yelled, thoroughly irritated. He grabbed a pair of scissors, cut an eight-by-eight-inch piece of newspaper, and enveloped a ball into it.

"Come here and learn something, jackass," Squeaky said.

I followed him through the clutter to a desk. He turned on an antique lamp, reached into the top desk drawer, and took out tweezers and cuticle scissors.

He cleaned his glasses with a handkerchief. "This is a dried sponge soaked in paste. That's the paste."

Squeaky gently dipped the tip of his finger in a tin can filled with a white concoction and licked it. "You know, kid, I'm the brains of 26th Street. Homemade silencers, magnet sticks for safes, wire cutters to splice but not short . . . What do you know? They'd still be sticking up liquor stores without me."

"I know, Squeaky. Why do I godda take a dump in Chinatown?"

Me and Squeaky talked d' same way, not pronouncing our Hs and had a certain lazy fall to our voice pattern. We were "guys."

I went over to Chinatown. The owner of Three Happiness eyed me as I walked into the place.

"Boy, where you go?" he asked in a Chinese accent.

"Sir, I think that my parents are eating in the back," I said politely.

He nodded.

I walked to the bathroom and dropped the ball into the toilet. When it got to the size of a handball, I flushed.

Insurance from 26th Street was cheaper than a plumber.

Not long after my sixteenth birthday, in 1974, George Murphy was found in the South Loop Hotel with two bullets in his head. I didn't negatively judge George for his alleged career. Growing up in the neighborhood, we had been reminded dozens of times that since the Korean War, the US had been responsible for the murder of millions. The armed forces rarely discipline the murderers, and often award medals to those responsible for killing the most people. George was a decent guy. The news saddened me.

The Old Man was proudly solemn. George's death reminded him of his favorite film, *White Heat*, with Jimmy Cagney. The way he saw it, George died the way he lived. And now the Old Man carried a pistol, always. After George's death, when at a bar, the Old Man would shovel five thousand quarters into the jukebox playing Eric Carmen singing "All By Myself" over and over again.

After a string of murders, the Star Bar license was revoked. The Old Man now drank across the street from our house at Bruno's on 26th and Halsted.

One night walking home, he broke his leg in three places. He was only insured while on the job. He laid on the couch, watching television, waiting for the union to call him back to work. He did this until he was angered by a documentary about giving clemency to draft dodgers. He threw a glass through the picture tube. Now he just laid on the couch.

I walked in as he ordered Butch and her two whores (pet names for her daughters) to get him milk and a bologna sandwich. Butch still walked with a limp from a mini-stroke, but was happy to hobble into the kitchen for the king. She lightly salted and put mustard on the Oscar Mayer bologna sandwich. Butch cut it carefully into triangles, the only way His Highness would eat it.

He drank the milk, tossed the plastic cup into the kitchen (Butch gave him plastic cups after the episode with the television). He then sat up and fed the sandwich to Sarge. Butch constantly reminded him that she felt he favored the dog over her. He constantly reminded her that she was correct.

Finally, after almost a month, the union called. Colleagues arrived and moved the Old Man into a car. He told me to wipe the smirk off my face, as he invented a few new phrases to describe the pain.

The Old Man supported me and my brothers and sisters. I was appreciative and wasn't smirking. Maybe he thought that I should have been.

The makeshift ambulance drove to McCormick Place. They took the Old Man out of the car, laid him on the dock, and called a bona fide ambulance.

People from Bridgeport didn't count on the police to protect them. They took care of their own families and neighborhood. Visitors would tread lightly, and rightfully so. Baseball bats were the preferred instruments of peace.

One night, a dark-skinned kid, hopped up on PCP, wandered into Armor Park. He got baseball batted. The kid didn't come out of the coma until three months later, when he died. The news made a racial thing out of it, but the kid would have been ball-batted even if his skin was orange.

Life was fascinating, full of girls, adventure, and arrests; finally, it seemed that paradise might come to an end. I was again in the courtroom above the police station at 61st and Racine, in front of Judge Darren Stokes.

"Mr. Carmichael, I've seen you far too many times. Always showing up with no mother or father."

"Sir, we can't find my father and . . ."

The judge pushed his glasses up on his nose and spoke. "Now, on—" he said, then paused and looked at the court clerk.

"November 4th, Your Honor," the clerk responded.

"Now, on November 4th, young man, bring enlistment papers to the US Armed Services of your choice, or you'll be incarcerated until your eighteenth birthday, at which time your case will be reevaluated." He gently nodded and winked.

A week earlier, he gave the same ultimatum to Tony Burke, another neighborhood guy, for stabbing someone. Tony went into the Marines. I was still sixteen, and the Air Force was the only branch of the military that offered delayed enlistment. I didn't much consider the ramifications of going to jail, which appeared to be a less attractive alternative.

I rang the doorbell of the house on 73rd and Artesian. I noticed the drapes move. The motion stopped. It wasn't a heating vent; maybe a cat or someone was watching me. No one answered. I rang again, looking ahead but focusing on the window from the corner of my eye. The drapes again moved slightly. I was beginning to not like the dynamics. The door opened to a two-inch gap.

"What do you want?" a man asked.

"I'm leaving for the military and I wanted . . ."

"What do you want?!" the man screamed.

The door swung open, I was dragged in, and it slammed shut. I was surrounded by an odd stench. The room was colored between dim and dark.

My eyes began to refocus. A lighter, held by a man sitting on the floor, lit up the room; there was a Tupperware bowl with baggies and a scale on the table in front of him. The room dimmed as he sucked flame into the pipe.

He looked into my eyes, grunting as he exhaled. He was the man I had come to see. "Crack the blinds, it's OK, he's my nephew," Uncle Rory said.

Murky light shone in and he smiled. His face was drawn, his eyes beady and split to a slither. "Your mother told Aunt Kay you're going to the military," he said.

There was a rustle coming from behind Uncle Rory. I looked. There was a child sleeping on the couch. I focused and recognized the boy. It was Kevin, Rory and Kay's son; he was twelve, maybe thirteen.

I never bought into condemning men and women for one or even a few bad acts in their lives. If we were all prosecuted for law infringement, there wouldn't be enough jails. There wouldn't be a person to emulate or a statue, or portrait left in the world. The government, often manipulated by special interest groups, decides who to pursue.

Who ends up behind bars has little to do with the law and less to do with justice.

I smiled tightly and bid goodbye to a great man to whom I owed a substantial debt.

At Lackland Air Force Base, in San Antonio, Texas, I had lots of time to think. I owed so much to so many: Ma, the Ferris, Big Mamma, Judge Stokes, a whole bunch of neighborhood families, and the priests, brothers, and teachers at Saint Joseph's and De La Salle. It was a long list, and though I didn't graduate from high school, I had made it to another juncture.

Basic training was meant to be tough. The drill sergeants attempted to intimidate the new recruits. A few times, I smirked while Sergeant Markum barked orders at me. Markum screamed in my face, shoved and pushed me down (I was, in fact, smirking at this yoyo).

By the fourth week, he'd had enough.

Feeling that there was nothing that could make me enthusiastic about *hup, two, three, four* and risking life and limb for the next commercial enterprise, Markum moved to have me undesirably discharged. He was absolutely right to do that; with the disappearance of "Little Italy," Bridgeport was my home, and the neighborhood Santa Lucia Fest was my Fourth of July.

Master Sergeant Davis couldn't completely ignore Markum's wishes. In my fifth week of training I was moved to the motivation platoon for hard-to-discipline recruits. In reality, my fellow cohorts were a mixed batch, mostly kids from big cities and a few hicks. I wasn't really interested in making friends. I just wanted to do my time and get out.

We spent our days and evenings weeding on our hands and knees or digging and then refilling holes that the guy next to us had just dug. The red ants, which everyone called "piss ants," were especially fun when they tracked up our legs and arms, stinging and leaving welts all over. My six weeks of basic training became eleven, but it wasn't a big deal to me. I made it.

After I was finished with basic, I was transferred to Lowry Air Force Base in Denver, to become an electronic countermeasure technician.

When I was younger, living with Uncle Rory, I had done some intramural boxing at Sherman Park. When I arrived at Lowry, I joined the base boxing team. I felt it might keep me on the straight and narrow. Six months later, I was shipped to the Mountain Home Base, about sixty miles outside of Boise, Idaho. Two weeks after I arrived, Ma wrote to me that Uncle Rory had died of an overdose.

Within a month, at Breakers West in Boise, I fought and lost my first and only pro fight. I weighed in at 156 pounds. I was eighteen, and the other guy was twenty-nine. I had five, maybe six amateur fights behind me. He had fifty. The guy beat me fair and square. I put down the gloves. It just didn't provide the rush or the satisfaction that I hoped that it might have. Besides, back in Chicago, if I had real issues, boxing would not likely remedy them.

On base, Andreas Schmitz, a tall, husky son of a Pittsburgh cop, was my best friend. One evening, Andreas and I were in the recreation room, watching TV. A group of guys came in to use the pool table. It got loud. Andreas turned the TV up.

They got louder, so Andreas turned it up again. He returned to his seat (this was not a remote control set) and found it occupied.

I followed Andreas to the door, but before I made it out, he was back inside, swinging a twenty-pound cement-based ashtray like it was a lasso. The pool players ran, giving no resistance. We trashed the room, and the next morning we were arrested.

This was not my first scrape on base. Fortunately for the commander and me, my mother had written to the Red Cross, asking that I be granted a hardship discharge and be returned home to assist the family. Colonel Armstrong remembered me as being the guy who stole the metal Colonel flag off his car. He had also read the file about me being arrested for fistfighting with some redneck from Kentucky in front of the mess hall. He didn't think twice when he saw the report about the destruction of the television room.

"Grant the hardship discharge and get him off base," Armstrong told his assistant.

I left for Chicago. Andreas got an undesirable discharge and was shipped back to Pittsburgh.

Again, I stepped in feces and came out smelling like a rose.

Back home, in the spring of 1977, I applied for a job at Cameron Miller, a company that made electric gadgets for veterinarians. Vets used these electric coagulators to heal wounds, mostly on pooches. My credentials were flawless: Air Force, Electronic Countermeasures School, Academy of the Air Force School of Soldering, etc. Electronic Countermeasure School was supposed to have prepared me for fixing radar and other sophisticated defense and weapons equipment.

Truthfully, though, like many of my service buddies, I couldn't tell a transistor from a raisin. The civilians fixed all the planes. After a few vets got electric shocks, and a few pooches checked out, I got fired.

Things with my mother were normal. She had my five brothers and sisters living with her. A few of them worked, but as usual, my mother's life was framed in economic shambles. I applied for what seemed to be hundreds of jobs and finally interviewed for a job as a dockhand with Nathaniel Poppel, a boss at Great Lakes Supply on 50th and Morgan. Poppel liked to give you the impression that he was tough. I didn't care much; maybe he was.

"Well, kid, can you drive a truck? We got two drivers, a Jew and a dego. When they're both sick, you get an extra buck an hour to drive. Can't have the job if you don't drive a truck," Poppel said.

"That was my job in the Air Force," I told him.

We were on the dock and Poppel told me to get into the truck for a test drive. A short gentleman working on the dock heard Poppel and yelled, "the brakes are out on that truck!"

Fortuitous indeed; I had never driven a truck in my life. I was hired on the spot. The guy that had yelled was my new boss, a five-foot, sixty-year-old Croatian named Joe Horvat.

Great Lakes specialized in supplies for the steel mills, South Works, Bethlehem, US Steel, and a handful of smaller companies. I mostly filled orders in the warehouse.

My coworkers were Ron, the Polish order checker; Shillelagh, the Irish packer, who was widowed with a ten-year-old son; Mike, the tool room manager; Johnny Griff, a half–Irish, half–American Indian forklift driver; and Joe Horvat, the Croatian boss. Poppel was the interface between the administrative offices and the warehouse. I rarely saw him, and strangely enough, he forgot about my test drive.

Joe Horvat could not stand to be idle. This suited me, and we hit it off. After seeing me pissing next to him he began calling me "Moondick." Soon everyone called me Moondick. I never remembered being happier.

Joe subsidized his income with the Candy Store, an old steel locker painted green and filled with cigarettes, aspirin, nylons, chewing gum, and candy. He kept it immaculately clean and in meticulous order.

"That locker put my daughter through college," he'd say two or three times a week.

Numbered bins ran along the dock walls for smaller items. The tallest bin was about fifteen feet high. We began loading the trucks at six a.m. Joe yelled out numbers, and I used the lower bins for steps, running, jumping, and swinging to retrieve the item in the corresponding bin. We must have been entertaining; by seven a.m., the white collars from upstairs arrived to sip coffee and watch the show.

Joe shouted, "N17, you Moondicked Monkey!"

I darted, snatched the item, and dropped it into the small pack box on the truck.

In the lulls, I sang.

I turned twenty at Great Lakes. In the evenings, I still ran Midnight Auto Parts, but my absolute favorite pastime was fishing. Friends made comments about me, the short, ugly, big-nosed, Italian-looking guy who always caught women. It's a numbers game. The more you fish, the more you catch. I fished at train stations, bus stops, hospitals, churches, funerals—just about anywhere.

My first time driving the Great Lakes truck, it was fully loaded with six feet of pipe hanging off the back. I left broken windshields and dented cars up and down my route.

I was sharing an apartment with Jim Bob Hailey on 38th Street when I got a call from Buck Willis and Dennis O'Rourke. There was no one nicer than Dennis O'Rourke, a good-looking Irish guy who had been with the same Italian girl, Jackie, since before time. He may have been good-looking but we called him Neer, for his protruding ears.

Bucky Willis and Neer were gamblers. Bucky and his father, Dicky, were famous neighborhood "Black Cats." If Dicky bet a horse, a football game, a baseball game, or a number, it was a guaranteed loser. Many asked him who he liked so they could bet the other way.

Bucky was a good athlete without an athlete's body. He and his father struggled as many struggled. I sometimes slept on their couch. When there was no money, Bucky went to a local restaurant and bought tea. While waiting, he helped himself to ketchup, salt, and pepper, went home and used it to make what he called "real home-made tomato soup."

My car was busted. Bucky, Dennis, and I took a bus to Sportsman Park to bet the "steam"—the winner of a fixed race. The steam's name was Miss Moon. She ran in the seventh. Normally, we'd pay absolutely no attention to Bucky, who couldn't pick the winner in a one-horse-race. But Dicky, Bucky's dad, knew a guy named Branack. Branack was a legend for fixing races, and he owed Bucky's dad a favor.

We came up with twenty-seven bucks. Miss Moon was still thirty-to-one, so I also pitched in our return bus fare. She led early, and by the Clubhouse turn was six furlongs ahead. I could taste the sausage and peppers Ma would cook when I brought over the groceries. Bucky was going to pay back rent, and Neer was going to square with his bookie and buy a gift for his girlfriend.

We jumped, screamed, and joyously yelled until Miss Moon fell in the bushes five yards from the finish line.

Dennis and Bucky stayed and flipped tickets. Flipping tickets meant kicking tickets with your shoe to overturn a winner. *Right, good luck with that.*

It was freezing out. The valets warmed up clients' cars to get extra tips. I climbed into one of the idling cars and drove home, ditching it on 39th Street by the railroad tracks.

Dennis O'Rourke (can't call a floor manager "Neer") was the floor manager for a small firm on the Chicago Board Options Exchange. As a gambler, he'd have been super-rich, if he'd only bet against the teams he picked to win.

Burton Hartz, the Floor Manager for Chicago Corp, bailed Dennis out of major jams more than a few times. Markets were crazy busy, and Burton desperately needed runners, the people that ran orders out to the trading pits.

Dennis came through, and Chicago Corp hired Bucky Willis. Bucky told Neer he didn't want the job. Of course, Bucky was another successful gambler, and he was into the "guys" for ten, maybe even twenty, thousand. He lost count, but needed some—any—kind of income to keep his kneecaps in good shape.

Bucky, like most neighborhood guys, did not take orders well. Phone clerks yelled at him, "Get this order out! It's a market!" (Market meaning that a customer wanted an immediate transaction, buying or selling at the best offer or best bid. This was different from an order to buy or sell at a particular price).

Half the time, Bucky had no idea where the stocks even traded. He waltzed around looking for them like it was Easter Sunday. He was eventually labeled "What the Fuck Buck."

With minutes left in the trading day, a phone clerk received an order to buy two thousand IBM calls at the market. Bucky was the only runner at the desk. "Take this!" the mustached phone clerk screamed, jamming the order into Bucky's chest.

Bucky looked at the phone clerk's hand, back at his face, and then grabbed the order.

The guy was panic-stricken. The order was already time-stamped. There were more than five minutes remaining before the exchange closed. This meant that the client's order was guaranteed to be filled. If Bucky didn't get the order out, the market would close and the clerk would be liable for any loss incurred—well, at least whatever he was due in bonus. If the stock opened substantially higher the next trading day, missing the close could literally cost millions.

Bucky stared and kept staring.

The phone clerk's mustache silently moved up and down.

Bucky was one of the tougher guys from 37th Street. I remember driving in the pouring rain to Donavan Park and watching his and Dennis O'Rourke's shadows teeing off on one another until I sloshed through the mud, pleading with them to stop.

Bucky read the mustache quivers like a stock broker reads the ticker tape. The phone clerk realized that his shield of authority, as far as Bucky was concerned, was about as useful as a character witness for a child molester.

The phone clerk bit his lip and got the quivering under control. Bucky noticed and wanted to laugh. Instead, he nodded gently and handed the order back to the phone clerk. "Stick this up your ass," he said firmly.

Bucky being fired left Dennis in a bad spot. He needed a quick replacement, and offered me the job. I mentioned the idea to Ma, who was ecstatic that I wasn't in jail. She asked, "Why would you leave the docks to go to uncertainty? There were worse jobs. What would you do in the stock market without a high school diploma?"

One of the first things Joe Horvat told me when I got to Great Lakes was to not hang with Johnny Griff. Joe got his way; over that weekend Johnny was found sitting outside a Cicero bar with an ax that split his cranium to the bridge of his nose.

I told Joe Horvat, who was still shaken from what happened to Johnny Griff, about the offer to go work at the exchange.

"Don't worry, Joe," I said, "I ain't goin' nowhere. It's us, Joe," I said in a happy-go-lucky manner to my Croatian father.

Joe grabbed me by the neck, "Kid, this place will close with the mills. Get out of here. Make more of your life than I did of mine."

Joe held on to me. I didn't understand. What was going on? My mind raced; there'd be no more shows on the docks while I was loading. The hundreds of laughs Joe and I shared would cease forever.

His hand was hard and firm against my neck. My breathing was somewhat obstructed.

Emotions were easy for me to express, but not for Joe. His hand was still around my neck. I doubt he ever communicated anything more profoundly than he did then. "You take that job. You hear me. Damn it! You take that job or I'll kill you with my own bare hands," he said.

Chapter 6

The Street Leads to the Pits

I popped out of bed at six a.m. There was no way I was going to be late for my first day at the Chicago Board Options Exchange. I threw on my pants and shirt and rummaged through the drawer, grabbing for my gray striped tie—my only tie.

Without looking, I put it over my head and tightened it.

The tie was covered by a black stain. I mentally raced back to the day that I had untightened my car's oil cap with it. It would have been nice, had I remembered that the day before.

I walked into the gangway at 3736 South Lowe, went down the stairs to the basement, and ran my hand over the top of the entry ledge. I grabbed the key, opened the door, and flicked the light on.

The washer and dryer were silent but ready for service. I walked ahead and stepped into Dennis's room. His bed was disheveled, but he wasn't in it.

Opening the closet door, I grabbed a tie, which happened to be ostentatious yellow. Yellow was good. I dropped my grease-stained cloth onto the floor and headed out of Dennis's room. As I got back to the washer and dryer, a man in his underwear bounced down the steps. I paused, expecting Dennis; instead, it was Dennis's father, Mr. Ray Ray O'Rourke. He was in a pair of briefs, without a shirt.

He looked directly at me as soon as his foot hit the last step. I had no idea what he was thinking or what I could do to make him stop thinking it. If I darted, it would be worse.

"Good morning, Mr. O'Rourke."

He continued staring but didn't answer.

I raised the tie. "It's my first day. Dennis got me the job. I needed a tie."

Mr. O'Rourke's face didn't change, not even slightly. He just stared. I tried to smile. After another five uncomfortable seconds, I tightly grinned, turned, and walked out the door.

I headed to the jacket and badge room. I expected Dennis to be there. He wasn't. I waited my turn and gave the woman my name.

"Who will you be working for?" she asked.

"I think it's called Chicago something," I let out.

"Oh, you *think?* Don't you know who hired you?"

"I got hired by Dennis O'Rourke but not to work for him."

I felt that I was being observed, and I turned slightly to my left. A tall, handsome man with not a hair out of place was staring at me. Burton Hartz.

"You the guy Dennis O'Rourke sent?"

"I nodded."

"Nice tie." He didn't give me a moment to thank him for the compliment. Instead, he looked at the woman behind the desk. "He's one of mine," Burton said.

I had never seen this guy before, but the way he said, "He's one of mine," made me want to get to know him better. He spoke the phrase with a smidgen of pride and familiarity.

Everyone that worked on the floor had to get fingerprinted. I got fingerprinted. I wasn't too concerned about what might pop up. I was getting a job as a runner, for Christ's sake. That was the bottom of the heap. Armed bank robbers could get jobs as runners.

I had my picture taken and received a temporary badge and a beige-orange jacket with the words "Chicago Corp" stitched thickly in black, over the right chest pocket.

It was 1978, I was twenty years old, and I was officially a Chicago Corp runner. I put the jacket on and followed the parade toward what I assumed would lead me to the exchange.

I'd never seen anything like the trading floor. Thousands of people in brightly colored jackets were packed together like 42nd and Broadway at 11:59 p.m. on December 31st. It could have been a costume ball. From a distance, it resembled a Jackson Pollock painting. It must have been here where the saying, "It was so loud that you couldn't hear yourself think," was invented. Wherever you looked, there was action. It was unbelievable that I was even here.

The pace on the floor was infinitely faster than on the docks. I began learning a new vocabulary: options, strikes, puts, calls, and stops. I sprinted orders out, but I didn't do it for the phone clerk or Chicago Corp. I hustled for Joe, and for everyone who ever loved and believed in me, knowing that if I ever made it, I could help many; and that is what guys like Joe are all about.

Everyone on the floor wore identification cards. The "guys," the real guys, were the traders and brokers. They were exchange members and had their names and initials on big, blue badges. It was like Bridgeport, except that in the neighborhood, the South Bridgeport guys were members of the Daley political machine, and the North Bridgeport guys were part of Dominick's crew.

The floor was a wild circus, where rules were followed when convenient. Shining shoes, busing tables, washing dishes, being in the sanctity of the seminary, handing out parlay cards, working with Morry Green, and stealing and selling stolen cars and parts had all prepared me for this chapter of my life. It was a world made just for me.

I recalled, from when I was shining shoes, my trips to the next bar, and the bar after that, as I headed up the street with my shoeshine box. I remembered the time of day that I entered, the bartender, and the crowd. I remembered if I was welcomed, tolerated, ignored, humiliated, or booted.

I recalled the customers' faces, how much they paid, and what their dispositions were. Were they sooty and black from the rolling press, or clean and neat supervisors? Did they tip more when they were drunk or sober? Were they prone to violence? Did they try to impress the guy next to them by humiliating me, or did they try to be kind, as recompense for past deeds?

I could often read people like I read a street sign.

At Club el Bianco's, I studied the most efficient way to get tables cleared. Would the glasses need emptying? Would the food need to be gathered onto one plate? Would I be able to stack them one on top of the other without them falling off my tray?

Shoe shining taught me to think of every moving piece. No two taverns, clients, or days were ever even remotely similar.

The seminary taught me inner peace. I had no choice but to reflect and realize what an unimportant thing I truly am. Humility makes every task easier to accomplish.

Handing out the parlay cards was an art. You remembered the players, the guys who needed coaxing and the guys who wouldn't play unless it was Friday.

Stealing auto parts and cars took patience. Timing was everything, and if you pushed it, your risk was far greater. The greater the risk, the more trouble you ran into.

Morry introduced me to the reality of business. The nuggets I found in those four walls have helped support some of my most critical projects.

These experiences and the characters I met prepared me for the exchange floor. When I got there, it felt as if I had already been there for centuries, a place where it's hard to bluff grit and impossible to hide a lack of talent. The exchange floor is a place where gladiators go face-to-face, toe to toe, using cunning and wit as weapons, risking sums of money that others would easily jeopardize their lives for.

I'm not speaking of the spineless lot of Goldman Sachs and J. P. Morgan, who employ traders who sling around billions of others' money. I'm talking about the entrepreneur who risks his own skin.

There were over two hundred stocks in about thirty-five pits. The first day was a real challenge. The phone clerk gave me a map and handed me an order. I couldn't make heads or tails of the map and had no idea where I was going.

"IBM, hop!" the phone clerk yelled.

I looked at my map and saw the general direction. By the time I got closer, I was bumping into people. Not being the tallest guy in the room, I spent seconds bobbing to and fro, reading the stock signs on the book (the book was a kiosk in the center of the pit, staffed by exchange employees).

I returned and a phone clerk handed me another order, "Kennecott Copper, get it out there and wait for it!"

I was greeted by comments such as, "Where the hell have you been?" "Why'd it take so long for the fill?" and "Are you crawling the order out there?"

By the end of the day, I was mentally exhausted. I had to come up with a strategy. I was too short to easily spot the target when I arrived close to its location. I was struggling to recall where the different stocks were.

The following day, I got onto the floor at six a.m. I was alone, except for the sounds of the timestamp clocks ticking. I walked around, and using known stocks like General Motors, General Electric, International Business Machines, and Holiday Inn as pillars, I created my own map.

By the end of the second day, I knew where every stock on the floor was.

Chicago Corp had a dozen phone clerks, positioned six on each side of the floor. Theoretically, a runner's job was to keep the phone clerks content.

Just as I kept the waitresses happy by busting my ass busing their tables at Club el Bianco, I made the phone clerks happy. By the end of the first week, every phone clerk looked for me when they had large orders that needed to get to the pits and back in a hurry.

My favorite phone clerks were Earl Black and Packy Schultz. My least favorite guy was "Fat" Ethan Hansel. Ethan Hansel was officially a trade checker, but often, by the middle of the day, he was moonlighting as a phone clerk.

Ethan Hansel loved giving orders to people. For whatever reason, he seemed to especially love giving orders to me, and no matter how fast I got the order out, or how fast I returned with a filled order, it was never fast enough. He *always* had a smartass comment to make.

He seemed to be nice to the other runners, but for whatever reason he seemed to despise me. I started to believe that he was jealous because unlike me who was fit, he was a fat ass. That wasn't my fault. He just needed to stop eating so much.

Still, I wanted to expand my learning and get in his face. After a week or so of abuse, I devised a plan. On Monday morning, I got to the floor at 6:30 a.m. That's when the trade checkers' day began. Their job was to unravel the errors (out trades) involved in the millions of transactions that had taken place between traders and brokers the prior trading day. Traders made transactions for their own accounts or their company accounts. Brokers transacted for third parties. Both had to be exchange members to conduct business on the trading floor.

Some out trades were resolved simply, such as listing Goldman Sachs as the buyer instead of J. P. Morgan.

Other errors were not so easy to resolve, such as when both sides thought they were buying, or selling. These errors often cost millions, and the two sides usually split the pain or the gain.

Ethan Hansel spotted me and gave me a weird look. I followed him and his clipboard around the floor. After twenty minutes or so, he turned to me.

"What the hell are you doing?" he asked.

"I want to learn how to be a trade checker," I replied.

"Did Hartz tell you to become a trade checker?"

"Nope."

"Then get off the floor until eight."

"Nope."

"Nope? Nope?" He asked in an astonished tone.

Ethan continued to check trades, and I continued to follow him. Later that day, Burton Hartz, the Chicago Corp floor manager, tapped me on the shoulder.

"Hey kid, what are you doing coming down on the floor with the trade checkers?"

"I want to learn."

Burton stared at me and nodded.

After three more days of following Ethan Hansel, he began asking me to run to the desk to look for orders or for the time stamps on the green copies of the filled orders. If I hadn't done it, Chubs himself would have had to wobble back to the desk. It was convenient for him, and for the inside legs of his corduroy trousers. It was also a sign of acceptance to me.

I continued to arrive on the floor every day at 6:30. When a trade checker was swamped, or when one didn't show up, I filled in. At the close of every day, I stuck around until every order was back at the desk. Some days I was there until 4:30 p.m., and the last guy to leave the place. At that hour, the isolation was as pronounced as the reigning chaos had been just a few hours before.

I was learning the whole game, inside and out. I didn't ask for a raise or a position. I knew that the education I was giving myself was priceless.

Some guys thought I was after their job. I wasn't. I was after something infinitely more important. I was after their knowledge. One morning, while trade checking, I responded to Ethan Hansel in a way he resented. He shoved me. I didn't react.

It wasn't strategically the time to react. I waited outside the exchange the next morning at six a.m.

For whatever reason, Burton Hartz arrived early that day. He walked up to me. "What are you doing kid?"

"I'm waiting for Ethan Hansel."

"Why don't you wait for him on the floor?"

I squirmed a bit and hesitated. Burton had been around the block a few more times than myself.

"Why don't you wait for him on the floor?" he asked again.

"I'd rather wait for him here."

Burton scrutinized my face. "What can you do here that you can't do on the floor?"

"I can fight him."

"Oh, you're going to fight him?" Burton asked with the calm of a psychiatrist at his first appointment with a client.

I nodded.

"What for?"

"He pushed me yesterday while I was helping him check trades."

"Oh, so now you're going to fight him?" Burton asked, moving his head gently.

"Yeah," I said, nodding slightly and looking side to side. "There's no one out here. It'll be a fair fight."

"Oh," Burton said affirmatively, again nodding his head.

A few moments passed, and people were beginning to arrive and enter the revolving doors.

Burton smiled and put his hand on my shoulder, "Give him a break this time. I'll speak to him, and I promise that he'll never push you again."

We walked into the building. Burton kept his hand on my shoulder all the way up the two long escalators that led to the floor.

Observing the saints and the sinners, the pure and the puritans, I grew day by day. Direction may have ruled the market, but psychology ruled the warriors, and the warriors won and lost the wars.

The floor was a place where rules were bent into nonexistence. Behind it all was a code of honor; your word was your bond. I noticed trader superstars who defined their behavior in decency, "eating, but never being a hog, leaving enough food around for the smaller traders."

Borrowing from my shoeshine friend Danny, Uncle Rory, and the Franciscans, I invented my own official creed: "Man's law is optional, God's law is mandatory." And guess what? I fit right in. If I saw a confused or hesitant runner and knew that he had an important order, I'd grab it out of his hand and get it out. This was against the rules. Runners were mostly designated to specific phone clerks and had to follow a next-in-line order. I had learned long ago that the same rules which protect order often represent the greatest impediment to progress.

Many of the rules that governed the behavior of runners, phone clerks, floor managers, traders, and brokers were for the most part illogical on the chaotic trading floor. Throwing rules into the dumpster, where in my opinion most belong, made good common sense. Eventually, other runners, phone clerks, and the whole line of command at Chicago Corp learned to appreciate my bending of the rules and regulations for the benefit of the team. In time, I observed that rules were often used to aid mediocrity and empower the bullies. As a consequence of all of the above, I believe that common decency and common sense should reign supreme.

I wasn't sure what was going to happen to me on the floor, but it sure felt like whatever it might be, it would be good.

At night, I passed the guys in front of Shinnick's, the bar around the corner where I lived with my friend Jim Bob Hailey on 38th Street.

"Hey, kiss-ass!" they yelled, "Are they paying you for overtime?"

In the early morning, trade checkers sought me out to help them understand complex situations that arose when trades did not match up.

When the bell rang, all the phone clerks sought me out to run their orders. Still, I was only a runner and at the bottom of the food chain. I loved it.

The floor was turbulent and thunderous. Stress rained down like a tropical storm.

If a broker or a trader had a particularly bad day, there was no risk in snapping at the runner. A bad or late fill was because the runner was slow. A lost order must have been misplaced by the runner. In short, at the bottom of the totem pole, the runner was constantly being yelled at, spit at, cursed at, humiliated, and often, some were reduced to tears.

The brokers and traders routinely put on shows, teasing, ribbing, and demeaning the runners. It was like basic training, except here, if you made it through, there just might be somewhere to go.

Slowly, I became a kind of celebrity runner. Even the traders and brokers noticed something special about me. I only realized this because they never gave me shit.

"Optionette" was the name given to a beautiful girl runner—who, most claimed, was only on the floor to snag a broker or trader husband. The women wore $500 outfits to a job that paid $1,200 a month. Maybe something was amiss.

The boss of the firm Berken Drick, Stuart Wilmott, and his second-in-command, Billy Fisch, famously had the most beautiful Optionettes on the floor. They recruited them and if you didn't have drop-dead gorgeous looks, you need not apply.

Billy Fisch eventually got his talent off the floor and married a porn star. Years of marriage later, he confided to me that it was still a challenge for him to get laid by her.

Todd Mann was the Merrill Lynch broker in the Teledyne pit, and he was uglier than the Merrill Lynch bull. This did not prevent him from being immensely impressed with himself.

I usually just ignored him; however, one day when there was a trading lull, I arrived at his pit with an order. I looked up at the option board. The order was far away from the trading price and wouldn't be filled anytime soon. Instead of returning to the desk I spied Todd Mann, who was berating a young, tall, skinny runner. While doing so, Todd looked over at the beautiful Optionette leaning against the pit book (the exchange kiosk called a "book," where brokers deposited away from the market orders to be handled by the exchange employees).

"You're a fucking moron, kid! I told you to wait for the order. Why didn't you?" Todd screamed.

"I didn't hear you," the kid said feebly.

"You didn't hear me! Have you got shit in your ears, boy?"

"No, sir."

The kid turned.

"Hey, get back here!" Mann screamed. "I'm not done with you."

The kid turned back. His face was beet red, and I thought that he was about to break down.

I looked at the kid's badge. His name was John.

I walked in between John and Todd.

"Hey John," I said, "they're looking for you at the desk."

John was confused. Mann was pissed and dumbfounded. No one, let alone a runner, ever dared to interfere with his act of humiliating a serf. "I'm not through with that kid," Mann said, trying and failing terribly to look intimidating.

I nodded slightly. "Yes, you are."

Todd had seen me before. He knew I was a runner for Chicago Corp. He flew up the stairs, toward me, never leaving the Optionette out of his sight.

John was walking back toward his desk.

"Hey! Hey! Where do you think you're going?"

John continued to walk. Mann would not be humiliated, and now concentrated his efforts on me. "Who the hell do you think you are?" he screamed.

I just stared at him. He grabbed me by the collar and brought my face close to his. "Don't do that," I whispered softly.

He pushed me slightly away from him. "What?"

I smiled. "Get your hands off me and don't ever touch me again," I said softly.

By now, the rest of the Teledyne pit was watching us. Morgan Church, one of the other brokers, came over and intervened.

"Todd, leave the kid alone. I don't think he's kidding."

Todd lowered his hands and I walked away.

Following my own creed, I never burned bridges, and I tried to help anyone and everyone I could.

I still found time to hang out. One Saturday evening, a gang of workers from White Sox Park wandered into Shinnick's. A fight broke out and, as was customary, combatants were ordered to take the battle to the street.

Bucky turned to me calmly. "Wanna go outside and watch?"

I nodded. Bucky waved to Eddy Shinnick, who was bartending, and said, "Give me two. I'm going outside to watch the fight."

We walked through the crowd and sat on the hood of a car with our legs dangling. Within a few seconds, the brawl had swayed near us. A long, skinny combatant bumped Bucky.

"Hey," Bucky said, "watch my legs."

After thirty seconds or so, the same guy was back.

"Hey, I said, watch my frickin' legs," Bucky said patiently.

"Hey, screw your legs, man," the fighter replied.

Bucky sipped his beer and shook his head. After less than a minute, the guy again bumped Bucky's legs, consequently sending Bucky's second beer into a free fall.

In one movement, Bucky caught the bottle and smashed it on the guy's forehead. Blinded by his own blood, Junior stumbled toward us. "Man, did you see that guy who hit me in the head with the bottle? I'm gonna kick his ass!"

Bucky finished what was left of his first beer before answering, "No, but move away from me, you're gonna get blood on my shirt."

The great majority of brokers and traders gained access to the floor through connections, family, and other. Miranda Rose was one of those. She was attractive, about thirty-five, and one of the few female traders on the floor. Most of the day, she watched stock and options prices on the terminals. On a good day, she was quiet and miserable. On a bad day, she was rude and spiteful. The brunt of her wrath was dished out on—you guessed it—defenseless runners.

She squinted to read the tiny print on the screens with her hands clasped behind her back, waiting for a runner to get close.

Miranda must have been having a losing day.

A runner came within her orbit and she grabbed the unsuspecting victim by the collar.

"You almost stepped on my toes!"

I glanced down. She was wearing sandals, and her toes were long. My guess was that he would have tripped before he stepped on them.

The runner was one of those twenty-year-olds who looked like he was fifteen. He was terrified and at a loss for words. Miranda let his collar go and grabbed his badge. He looked down at her hand.

She ripped the badge off. "I know your floor manager!"

She probably did, I thought, and would likely perform fellatio on him if he'd show her big orders before they were sent out to the pit.

This kind of thing was common and worked like this.

Big orders to buy moved prices up, and big orders to sell pushed prices down. If a trader knew there was a big order to buy, he or she would go to that stock and buy in front of the order. When the order arrived, they'd then sell what they had bought back to the order. Doing so, they were guaranteed riskless profit. It was called front-running and was a rudimentary example of insider trading. It was a layup, a no-brainer . . .

Back to Miranda.

The kid just stood there (some are men at six, and others not even at eighty-six years old).

There wasn't anything I could do to help him. If this was his demeanor, he was in the wrong place anyway.

The fact is that Miranda terrified most, which in itself was hilarious. What was she going to do—sock you? If you got fired, she was doing you a favor. Where was a runner going, anyway? The turnover rate was astronomical, and few were able to make anything resembling meaningful careers there. In the history of the exchanges, and out of the thousands of traders, only a handful had made it up through the ranks starting as runners.

Morgan Church, the largest broker in Teledyne stock and options, was demanding and unbearable to work for. Most called him eccentric. If he'd been poor, he'd likely have been put in an institution. He wore a new bow tie each day, and when the trading day ended he cut it in two. He went through clerks like bow ties and was always looking for new talent. A good clerk could save hundreds of thousands in errors; a bad clerk could have the opposite effect.

I brought an order to Teledyne. Church grabbed me.

"Hey kid, I want to talk to you," he said in his chronically cocky voice.

"Oh, yeah? What'd I do?" I asked.

"I don't have time now. Meet me in Brokers Restaurant after the close."

I didn't think of much else the rest of the day.

Brokers was jammed with traders, brokers, clerks, and, of course, beautiful Optionettes.

Morgan rated his own table in the second room. Accompanying him was head of operations, Eric Sarr.

"Sit down, kid," Morgan said.

Church's team never broke for lunch. The floor closed at 3:10. It was now almost 4:00. Eric looked annoyed; maybe it was hunger pains.

"What do you want to eat, kid?" Morgan asked.

I put my hand in my pocket to feel for money. Morgan noticed.

"Don't worry, kid, it's on me," he said.

"Give me a cheap steak," I quipped.

Church laughed. "Cheap Steak" became my new nickname.

Eric looked even more annoyed. After I left, he told Morgan that he'd like to slap the cocky look off my face. "He's trouble," Eric said.

Church, who valued Eric's instincts, hired me the next day.

Traders made transactions for their own or their company's account. Brokers executed for clients—fill 'em and bill 'em. Brokers could make orders discretionary, "squeezing" in an attempt to get traders to pay higher or sell lower. In wild markets, squeezing could work against the broker. If even one option traded above his offer, or below his bid, he would be obligated to personally fill the customer. It could, and often did, cost millions.

The group in the Teledyne pit was an interesting tribe, with a historic rivalry between the pit's largest traders: Ernest Givings, an east coast WASP; and Corey Vann, a New York Jew.

Givings borrowed his strength from rules, regulations, and, of course, money; Vann found his power in his lack of adherence to the rules, his personality, and, of course, the money he was accumulating.

Saying they despised one another would be a gross underestimation of their true feelings. Tense relationships often touch the foundation of everything important to us—in this instance, power and money.

A typical greeting from Corey to Ernest was, "I'm sad to see that your train didn't crash on the way in from your gay suburb." Corey's passion and spirit showed true conviction.

There were a few other stocks traded in the pit, but Teledyne was the star. In the few weeks I had been there, it traded down to 100, and then up to almost 500. Traders on the floor called it "The Widow-Maker." It became illiquid in an instant, often leaving no path of escape.

Church rounded off the pit personalities well, flying into berserk rages over insignificant discrepancies. Once, he ranted for fifteen minutes because someone stole his lucky pen (a chewed-up Bic). It was likely thrown out by the cleanup crew; all the same, traders (therefore everyone) paid attention to him because he had the biggest deck in the pit.

"Deck" refers to the group of orders that a broker held. The larger the stack of orders, the more power one possessed. If you got on a broker's bad side, he'd stop hearing your bids and offers, sometimes for weeks. Morgan Church wasn't shy about using this leverage.

Because Teledyne moved so quickly, Morgan usually banged orders out. Traders also needed to be quick. The stock price that was needed to hedge and make the trade profitable could disappear in a flash.

Lonnie Katz was Jewish, from New York, and addicted to Quaaludes. He was a regular in the pit. It could take him up to a minute of drug-induced mumbling to make the simplest phrase understood.

It was a normal morning. Givings and Vann were exchanging their typical greetings, which today were a bit more colorful than usual. This was likely due to the fact that they each had accumulated massive contrary positions; if one earned, the other lost and vice versa; your death is my life sort of situation.

Vann pranced in, "You're a gay WASP fairy parasite," he gleefully spouted.

"Offensive language is against the exchange rules," Givings responded.

"Screw you and the exchange, a bunch of WASPy fruits, always with each other's flutes up each other's asses," Corey slithered. "Besides, since when is telling the truth illegal?"

Ernest cleared his throat and stared at the stock screen.

"How many more Dec (December) 420s (420 strike) do you wanna sell? Are they cloggin' up your dark crevice along with your boyfriend's rod? This stock is gonna blow. You'll feel 'em up around your throat," Vann said kindly.

Ernest shifted his weight from one leg to the other.

"Don't worry," Vann continued, "my uncle sells pianos in Brooklyn. I'll get a cord that you can fix yourself with. Would you like a nice C sharp?"

Ernest contemptuously looked at the exchange employees who worked in the pit's book (exchange kiosk).

"I hope you're all listening," Ernest said. "You'll be called as witnesses."

"Then when you're dead I'm gonna stick a broom in your ass and sweep the floor with you . . . Just how much money did daddy leave you, you racist WASP homo?"

Ernest lost a hundred grand every point the stock climbed. The rats in his skull were running rampant through the thoughts he knew to be facts. It was hard for him to keep his head from bobbing. He and his North Shore elites had discussed the problems of riffraff many times. According to Ernest, Vann was typical of his money-grubbing race, no morals or ethics unless there was a dime involved. The specialist (managing all Teledyne stock orders in New York on the New York Stock Exchange) was also Jewish. Givings was sure that the brethren were in cahoots, and futilely complained to the Securities Exchange Commission about the incestuous scumbags.

He would have never sold all of those December 420 call options to Church if he knew it was Vann buying them. Morgan Church would fill orders for the devil. He was a WASP, but was rumored to have a Jewish great-grandfather, which some said explained a lot about his despicable behavior.

It was rumored that Vann paid double brokerage in cash to induce Morgan Church to break rules. Had Church told the truth about the house (the company that clears trades) on the orders, Ernest would have known instantly. Vann was the only trader clearing 007 in the pit.

Church gave up the wrong firm so Ernest would not be suspicious and continue selling. If Ernest reported Morgan to the floor officials, Morgan would say Ernest misunderstood and then go deaf to Ernest (certain economic suicide).

Ernest heard a strange sound and felt something wet on his neck.

"Floor officials! Call floor officials!" Givings screamed (floor officials were the exchange police).

Randall Farms, a tall Texan floor official and Merrill Lynch broker in the Houston Oil pit, headed to Teledyne. Farms had little use for Givings, who thought his word was holier than God's. Texans were confused about these types of claims, unless the people who made them were other Texans like George Bush or Rick Perry. Farms also had absolutely no use for Vann, or any Jew, unless they were killing, as he called them, "sand niggers."

He noticed me and remembered I had been a runner for Chicago Corp. *The Jews help each other*, he must have thought, looking at my nose. Church's grandfather was a Jew, and Sarr, his right-hand man, was also a Jew. Randall liked when things made sense, like the invasion of Saudi Arabia he supported to resolve high gas prices.

Ernest held the collar of his shirt with his head to the side. A hocker, one of those nice thick green ones, was lying motionless on his neck.

Randall tried to verbally trap Vann, whom he knew to be the culprit. That, of course, did not work.

Randall turned to me. "Who spit on Givings's neck?" Randall Farms screamed as he leered into my eyes.

"Not sure. Why don't you put it in a tube and do a saliva test?"

"Hey, smart guy, if you saw who spit on Givings's neck, the rules of the exchange are clear. You must tell me or lose your job," Randall Farms said.

"I didn't see anything," I said.

"But you're right here," Randall slithered; there was no risk in trying to intimidate the new guy.

"I was putting the deck in order."

Frustrated, Randall stepped toward Givings.

"Clean your damn neck, Givings! It's disgusting!" he yelled.

Farms stared at the smirk on Vann's face. "I'm going to catch you, Vann," Farms warned.

Vann offered Givings a handkerchief. Givings growled.

Farms turned to me again, "You're getting off to a bad start, sport." He glanced at my nametag. I'm sure he was thinking, *What the hell kind of name is Patrick for a Jew?* He jerk-turned and steamed off quietly.

I studied traders and brokers, observing everything about them. This included but was not limited to their shoes, clothes, whether they changed ties, whether they sweat, twitched, blinked when nervous, and or made tiny lip movements which sometimes indicated that they were communicating with themselves. I must admit that Vann's style had a natural appeal.

One morning, Crete Hogg, a Teledyne trader, grabbed me by my green and white checkered trading jacket collar.

"Get Church at the Tangiers hotel!" he yelled at me.

I didn't have the vaguest idea what he was talking about.

"Call him now! Call him at the Tangiers hotel! He's got an order somewhere and I want to fill it!"

I looked at Crete's hands, then at him. He let go of my collar and I walked to the desk. There was no Tangiers hotel in Chicago, but there was an Algiers on Archer Avenue. I called and walked back into the pit.

"He ain't there," I said.

"Call back and tell them to look at the pool!" Crete bellowed.

I called again and returned. "They said that they don't have a pool."

"The hell they don't. I've been there a hundred times," Crete growled. "Give me the number! I'll call them!"

Crete examined the number. "What's the area code for Las Vegas?" he yelled.

Eric Sarr walked into the pit. "What's the problem, Crete?" Eric asked in his usual tone of superiority.

"I told this kid to get Church. He's playing games," Crete said.

Eric looked at me with his usual contempt. "Don't worry, Crete, tell me the problem. I'll help you. The kid's slow."

I had no idea that Church was in Las Vegas. I figured that Morgan was off, hanging around Chicago. I felt like the idiot I was.

I decided to study harder. On and off the floor, I became a full-time student. I studied license plates, adding their digits; the panels and floors on the insides of elevators; faces; cracks in sidewalks . . .

After the Hogg episode, things with Church went downhill. Whenever Sarr could fault me, he did.

Fortunately, it wasn't all gloom. I cleaned up shooting craps at the company Christmas party, and things seemed a little better. I bought gifts for my whole family and was ready to begin the year fresh.

It was Friday in mid-January. Church was still on break. The week's payroll checks were on Sarr's desk. I grabbed mine. I made less on the floor than I did on the docks. Still, I saw through the blur a possibility of helping a lot of my folks through eventual opportunity on the exchange floor. This, however, didn't change the fact that I was two months behind in rent for my new apartment.

Monday morning, Eric stormed up and interrupted me while I was checking an out trade (when two trades did not match up) with the Berken Drick broker.

"Where's your check?" he demanded.

"I cashed it," I replied.

"Impossible, it wasn't signed!" Eric yelled, a crowd forming.

"Mine was," I calmly replied.

"Morgan Church is in Hawaii. Who signed your check?" Eric snarled.

"I did," I replied calmly.

"Oh, you did?"

Eric pimp-slapped me.

I socked him and with this one action, Cheap Steak became dead meat.

Buried in debt, I remembered my mother's advice to "stay put." I wanted to be back on the loading dock, but if I went back, what would I tell Joe Horvat?

I hadn't broken God's law. I hadn't robbed anything. The money was rightfully mine anyway. Church was back after a week and saw things Eric's way. If I forged one check, I'd forge another.

I trudged up in the middle of a trading day to get my final pay. A little Chinese-looking (Taiwanese) guy wearing a trading badge, named Harvey Wan, sat in the office. While waiting, we spoke shop. Finally, he asked me why I was fired.

"I socked a guy," I said.

He hired me on the spot.

Chapter 7

A Man from Taiwan

Harvey Wan was a trader. That's where the real money was.

My first day, I understood why he hired me. Socking Eric had won me a reputation.

"Chinaman" jokes didn't bother Harvey. He explained that he liked the United States because everyone here hates everyone else. This made business easier. He did, however, have a problem with brokers and traders wasting time, making squinted eyes, and saying "Rots of ruck," instead of trading with him. He was an options seller with massive positions; lost seconds often meant lost revenue.

Most of these inconvenient distractions ended when I began following him into the pit.

Harvey Wan's strategy was to teach his method to clerks and then financially back them to trade for him on a split-profit deal, usually meaning fifty-fifty. He hired and fired many before my arrival.

Steve Tyler, a trader for Harvey, was nine years my senior, Chicago, west side Irish, married, and father of three. He constantly kidded himself about being overweight. I, instead, was in shape, working out, flexing even while walking. I wanted to be ready if something came my way, and I sensed that something would.

Harvey constantly rode Steve for being fat and stupid. After clerking a few weeks, Steve told me, "Harvey's impressed with you."

"Oh yeah, how do you know?" I asked.

"He never criticizes you," he replied.

Harvey's family lived in San Francisco. He rented a studio at the stylish McClurg Court Towers. His only furniture was a couch and a TV set.

"Little Chinaman" was our name for the feisty little guy. Tyler checked both ways, whispered the phrase, and then laughed hysterically.

The trading strategy Harvey taught put a trader at a disadvantage when stocks moved violently. Movement meant adjusting the position and losses.

Tyler's earnings were erratic. Harvey's belittling escalated.

Watching a guy getting kicked when he was down was torturous. I wanted to quit a half dozen times, but Steve Tyler always talked me into staying.

Eventually, Steve's wife put it to him: "Get a steady income or a new address."

IBM had bad earnings. Stocks moved wildly all over the floor. Steve had big losses, meaning there would be no weekly draw. He knew what he had to do. I knew, too, and in front of me and with tears in his eyes and mine, Steve Tyler resigned.

Harvey waited for Steve's speech to end, then calmly looked at me. "You wanna trade?" he asked.

"No," I quickly responded.

Steve stared, weighing each word. "Pat, do it. I got three kids. You got nothing to lose and talent to make it. Do it for me."

Seconds passed in frozen silence. Steve leaned toward me to whisper, stared at Harvey, pulled back, and spoke clearly. "Show the Chinaman," he said proudly.

I lied about having a high school diploma on the membership application, and within a few weeks was trading Harvey's account as a delegate. I took "BPT," for Bridgeport, as my trading initials. Within a year, I had gone from dockhand to trader.

The lying part didn't bother me in the least. Many times we have to break man's law to follow God's, and after all, I'm not true to my words. I'm true to my friends; just like almost every kid in my neighborhood proved, one time or another, by lying under oath to a judge for a friend.

Harvey didn't allow traders to take a penny from their account until their profits covered the position margin (position margin is the calculated amount required to cover risk). My margin was rarely under 20,000. This meant that I couldn't take a dime out of my account until I had over $20,000 in profit to cover the margin. If I had $21,000 profit with a margin of $20,000, I would be able to draw $500, or 50 percent of the profit. Trading like Harvey Wan, my account balance swung violently. I wasn't getting many draws. The money I made in Midnight Auto Parts helped make ends meet.

ABC Junk Yard on 139th was about twelve miles from Bridgeport and my favorite place to pick up car parts. If you found one Ford, you found them all. If you found one Toyota, you found them all.

I got the Nova door and loaded it into the car. On my way back, the tie rods broke. I adjusted the tires by kicking them, riding a short distance, and then kicking them again. There weren't a whole lot of turns in the twelve or so miles, but it still took me four hours to get home.

I moved my trading to the Mobil Oil pit and plopped $1,500 down on a used Lincoln Town Car. The following day, I dropped sixty . . . thousand. My $1,500 was forfeited, but the lesson was worth millions (literally).

I immediately went away from Harvey's style of trading. I started carefully calculating risk, hedged all my trades, and began chipping away. Harvey seemed to pay little attention, and may not have even noticed that I began making a steady income. Instead, Harvey would make a half a million in a month and then lose $200,000 in a day.

I managed to get Harvey to Shinnick's Pub. Sean McCrory formed his eyes into slits, asking forgiveness for the bar not having rice wine (today, Sean is Vice President of the Fraternal Order of Chicago Police Officers).

I was driving Harvey home and traveling east on Jackson.

"Slow down, you go too fast," Harvey said in his strong accent.

"Yeah, I know." As I spoke, I gently pumped the brakes. Pumping the brakes usually worked. It was not working.

"I say slow down! You go too fast!" Harvey yelled.

"Yeah, you're right, hold on," I said calmly.

The emergency brake went straight to the floor and we smashed into the car in front of us. Three dark-skinned guys jumped out. I slowly opened my door, stepped out, smiled modestly, and confronted them.

"Sorry, my brakes went out. Are you OK?" I asked firmly, yet with kindness and respect—a lot of respect.

"If there's any damage, I'll pay for . . . I—I'm really sorry."

I noticed a dent on the bumper and scratches on the trunk door.

"That's OK, man," the leader said. "Car's all messed up anyway."

"Sorry again," I said. They jumped into their car and sped off. I cruised mine to the curb.

Drinking and fighting is a Bridgeport ritual. Many Mondays, I showed up with black eyes, bruises, and/or scratches. Harvey occasionally grimaced at me, but my fellow traders loved being entertained by recaps: how a girl slipped on ice and I ended up socking her boyfriend; how a guy from the neighborhood was getting beat up by five cops, so I got arrested for assault on a police officer; or how a bus driver, reading the newspaper, leaving an old lady waiting in the rain, got me arrested for destroying property and battery.

Josh Balkus was a Lugan (someone of Lithuanian descent) attorney from the neighborhood. He once lived above me in one of the flats I rented. I had been using him to get the wrinkles out of shirts for almost two years. Some weeks, he made more on my legal issues than I made trading.

Wanting to concentrate on trading and life, I decided to modify my entertainment; women are by far more pleasurable than a hangover, a sock in the face, or spending a day or two in Cook County Jail.

My apartment on 38th Street was the neighborhood flophouse. I never turned anyone away. It was my turn, God was good to me, and I would be good to others. The way I figured, almost any of them could have done what I was doing, better than I did. Like the hedge fund gurus and the so-called super CEO's, I was just a son of fortune, "The Hoochie Coochie Man."

Conscious of my good luck, I was respectful and soft-spoken with friends and fish, though a decent neighborhood fish (girl) would have nothing to do with me, at least not in public.

Lots happened on 38th Street. There were women, brawls, and barbecues. While I was home in bed, some of the guys were around the corner eating at Dock's Grill. A businessman and two of his rent-a-girls were eating at the opposite end of the bar.

One of the neighborhood guys dared Sean McCrory to take the businessman's hat off his head, and of course he did. A brawl began and the two girls punched, kicked, bit, scratched, and were far more operative than their CEO. None of the Bridgeport guys would sock them.

Afterward, outside my apartment, my friends noticed a purse on the car hood. McCrory remembered the businessman grabbing for it during the ruckus. It was Rob Kelly's car, so it was Rob Kelly's property.

Inside the apartment, Kelly opened the purse and pointed the .22 it contained at a chair in my front room. The bullet went through the panel wall, mushrooming on the mattress rail six inches below my head.

I woke up and found my friends laughing. It was the lesson of the bicycle chain and Star Bar all over again. I was invincible.

The following weekend, we brawled in a suburban lounge (change takes time). The Hometown (name of the suburb) police showed up and we scattered. Six days later, Bucky, McCrory and I were heading through Hometown at 4:00 a.m. I ran a light, and a police car was on me in an instant. The officer was alone in the squad, and we were only a few blocks from the Chicago city limits. There was no way he'd step on Chicago police toes and chase us into the city. Besides, fuck him.

He chased us for eight miles, deep into the South Side ghetto. I braked hard on Garfield Boulevard. He may have thought we were surrendering. He jumped out of the car, revolver in hand. I hit the gas; by the time we hit 47th Street, he was a block behind. A kind truck driver, seeing our plight, cut the copper off. We pulled into an alley behind Jim Bob's, and twenty seconds later, rejoiced when the flashing lights went flying by. I reported the car stolen. All's well that ends well.

If I'd have had more brains, I would have noticed this type of behavior to be very peculiar and extremely risky. I think I had an inner conflict. I assumed that I'd never be successful because I didn't deserve it. Why try to protect something you will never possess? Maybe I needed to hear Grandpa Santino tell me that I was a good guy, un *brave uaggnòne*. Maybe I'd believe him.

Four months later, driving Harvey Wan home, I blew a light on 11th and State. Chicago's Finest stopped me. I looked to my left and gazed into the blunted barrel of a .38 Special. I knew the model and the routine. I put my hands on my head and gently exited. They cuffed me and put me in back of the squad car.

My name was printed on their computer screen, with the words "outstanding warrants," "resisting arrest," and "endangering the life of a law enforcement agent." I told them about my car having been stolen—but two Chicago coppers had been gunned down a week prior, and they were still hurt and on the cusp of fear.

Cuffed, they allowed me to go back to the car and inform Harvey. I banged on the window with my forehead. Harvey jumped. I informed him that he needed to find alternative transportation home.

Members have the right to trade in any pit on the floor, but the regulars (traders who stood in a particular pit daily, monthly, sometimes for a whole career), fought desperately to keep newcomers out. They attempted to protect the castle, hoping to avoid splitting the pie. They used all weapons at their disposal including and not limited to physical, mental, and financial intimidation. Some guys got scared off by a look, others by threats, and still others by a shove. Sometimes new arrivals left because they got lonely, tired of the silent treatment and not being heard by the brokers and therefore left out of trades. It could get real comical.

I was probably too stupid to be intimidated and when people got a bit too hostile, I asked whoever, no matter how mean or how big they were, if they wanted to take the discussion off the floor. On the way down the escalator I calculated how I would fight them. If they were too big, I was going to jump on them before they got off the escalator. I walked off the floor with guys several times, but most guys started speaking to me while we were heading down on the escalator. I moved from Mobil Oil to the Monsanto pit.

The big traders in Monsanto were Steve Fossett and Nicky Tarson. Steve was a wealthy, square kind of a guy with a reputation for being ruthless. Nicky was studious and quiet. He came from and traded with a Minnesota financial group.

Steve welcomed new traders. His style was to pick a direction and go with it. He wasn't interested in the crumbs that spreaders, guys like me, went after. One day, after watching me scalp 500 bucks in a trade, Steve said, "Now you can go home."

His comment wasn't so outlandish. It took me a week to make that on the docks. The pond wasn't going anywhere; I left for the neighborhood.

On the floor, as I explained before, trading errors were usually split between brokers and traders. The rule existed to fight corruption but there were no rules against gifting cocaine, hookers, or cars.

If I had an error with another trader, I split the gain or loss with them but I took all the errors that I had with the brokers, winners and losers. They were fine with the arrangement. It took all of the risk out for them. This confused everyone; trading is about accumulating money. Most say that if you go bust, no one will help you. I was giving much of mine away. I came from a different place, and besides, the more I gave, the more people collaborated with me, and consequently, the more I earned.

Nicky Tarson's trading strategy was somewhere between that of Harvey Wan and Steve Fossett. He viewed my networking, particularly the fact that I always took the losses in an out trade, as a sort of bribery.

I thought of it differently. The brokers usually made a dollar in commission for every contract that they filled. Traders usually made more. Why shouldn't I eat the whole error? It was what was fair to me. Because of this, the brokers made sure that I was included in every trade.

At the end of each day, the closing prices are tallied up to give each exchange member an equity statement. If you had a thousand calls in your account, and you were able to push the closing price up one point, you would artificially inflate your account by $100,000. Unbeknownst to me, Nicky was in trouble. Each night, to keep his account in the black, he did acrobatics, pushing the prices of the options he owned up, and the ones that he had sold (was short) down.

His theatrics might have attracted unwanted attention from the SEC, or at least the exchange regulatory people, but he was going broke, and this risk was not a priority.

It's common practice for the big funds to do the exact same thing at the end of each quarter. It's called window-dressing, and helps to inflate bonuses, etc.

I usually walked off the floor when New York closed at 3:00 p.m. The options closed at 3:10 p.m. One day, I stayed. Nicky began selling calls that I wanted to buy. I wasn't sharp enough to understand what was going on. With thirty seconds left, he asked the floor brokers for their bids, sold them, and offered the Monsanto December 80 calls at eight, seven and a half, seven, six and a half, and six.

"I'll pay seven for a thousand of 'em, what are you doing?" I asked.

Closing the calls at seven meant Nicky was out of business. He charged me and I socked him. He fell like a brick. Seconds later, he rose. I imagined that he wanted to come after me, but instead he charged toward the huge window bordering the trading pit. It was four floors down. I raced to stop him. Luckily for us both, he ran head-on into a runner and they both fell to the floor.

Randall Farms, the Texan floor official who had first noticed me as the ugly Jewish kid in Teledyne, arrived and fined me $1,000 for cracking Tarson. Consequently, Nicky never returned to the floor. Had I known his situation, I'd have helped him push the options down.

A few weeks later, I had to pay the fine or be barred from the exchange. I asked Harvey permission to take money out of my account. Harvey disagreed with me; the fine for socking someone, in his opinion, was not a business expense.

I followed Harvey to the members' lounge. I needed the dough.

"Hi Harvey, mind if I sit?"

He watched the ticker and did not answer.

"Harvey," I started again, "I need some of my money."

Ten seconds later, he spoke. "You never come here. Since I make you trader, you big shot. You call me Harvey now, but I know what you call me when I not listen. You call me Chinaman, that like niggah."

"I'm sorry you see it that way, and I appreciate the chance you gave me, but I need some of my money. I gotta pay the fine or they won't let me on the floor."

"Your margin is too high."

"Harvey, have you ever calculated how much money I made for you in three months?" I politely asked.

"I don't care, I take risk," Harvey rebutted.

By then, I was calculating risk far better than most firms. "My position has little real risk," I pleaded.

Harvey blew up. "You embarrass me! You fight on the floor!"

"I was a victim of circumstance."

"I not pay that fine, you pay out of your pocket."

"I will," I said firmly, "if you give me some of the money you owe me."

"You fired," he said.

I left, not caring if I ever got my money. What concerned me was that I was again out of a job. Where would I work? What would I tell Ma, and Joe Horvat?

I felt blue about being fired. I shouldn't have. On the floor, a haven of rich kids, guys who were willing to physically defend themselves were rare. I was, therefore, a precious commodity. Word had somehow gotten around that I was out of work.

The next day, O'Connor and Associates offered me $40,000 plus a trading bonus. A trader, Jake Nolan, introduced me to the owners of Securities Options Corporation (SOC), a clearing firm for traders owned by Skippy Stein and Jarrett Rose. They offered to front a few seat leases ($1,300 a month) and put up some cash so I could trade my own account.

I was twenty-one. I knew options and the markets. Most important, shining shoes taught me how to read people. As I did on most Saturdays, I went to see Joe Horvat. "Go for it, kid," he said.

Father Frawley, the Irish priest who had baptized me, said, "Take the guaranteed money. Trading is risky, and your mother needs your help."

My mother, sure that I had misunderstood, said, "If it's true, take the $40,000. That's more than most make."

Being a true man of democracy, I accepted Skippy and Jarrett's offer.

Chapter 8

Groovin' on a Sunday Afternoon

S teve Fossett and other guests turned, hearing spinning tires and the noisy engine of
my newly acquired '73 Cutlass. I pulled a U-turn in front of Tufano's Restaurant,
jumped out of the car, and threw the keys to the valet.

Clay Canon (future president of the Board of Trade) remembers having only one
thought when he watched me: "It must be true what they say about that guy."

I wasn't impressed with money or power. That evening was a first and one of
my only appearances with traders or almost anyone outside of my neighborhood.
By the time dinner was over, none of them would ever forget that BPT stood for
Bridgeport.

I'd like to mention that Fossett eventually became a record-setting aviator, sailor,
and adventurer. He was the first person to fly solo nonstop around the world in a bal-
loon and in a fixed-wing aircraft. In September 2008, a hiker found Fossett's identification cards in the Sierra Nevada Mountains, California, leading shortly thereafter
to the discovery of Fossett's plane wreckage. Fossett's only known remains, two large
bones, were found half a mile [800 meters] from the crash site, probably scattered
by wild animals.

Seeing talent in me, floor brokers Bruno and the Turk invited me to the Houston
Oil Pit. Talented traders became big traders, and they paid floor brokers big commissions. Randall Farms was a tall Texan floor broker/official in the Houston Oil Pit. He
wasn't a fan of what he called "street scum."

Traders Craig Butler and Booby Suss were New York Jews. Lorry Irving was a sweet
guy from Chicago. There were other, less colorful regulars, and I settled in.

After three weeks, Jarrett Rose called me into his office. "Kid, I forgot to put money
in your account before leaving," he said kindly.

"That's OK, there's about $3,000 in there."

"Oh, you scrounged it up, hah?" Jarrett asked.

"No, Jarrett, I made it," I replied.

"And the fine?"

"Paid," I responded.

"And your haircut?" (meaning, margin).

"I'm fine," I replied.

"And your seat leases?" Jarrett inquired.

"All taken care of," I said.

I never looked back, and did all I could to repay Jarrett and Skippy for the break they gave me.

Some days, I realized just how unique my situation was. My mind would glide pitilessly over past experiences like a seagull looking for baby turtles. Now, I love turtles, and as a result am not fond of the viciousness and lack of scruples of the seagulls as they rip the tiny creatures apart, but this is how my mind worked, tearing each detail to shreds, often profiting from a tiny morsel years after the fact. An idle mind is the devil's play shop.

Recalling details of the past helped me keep perspective. Shoe shining, Midnight Auto Parts, Sarge's attacks, being shot at, strangled, and of course the Seminary, made for an interesting balance.

I was no better than the other billions of earth's inhabitants (surely I was luckier); had I not been born, where and when, had I not known Big Mamma, Judge Stokes, Harvey, Joe Horvat, Dennis O'Rourke, and Bucky Willis, I would have never gotten this break.

Success is 99 percent luck. Luck and clinging tightly to my roots made me special, to some.

Booby Suss's (Baby Booby, to me) clothes were loud and mismatched. He was overweight and had a bald head with frizzy side hairs that stood on end. His thick eyeglasses turned his eyes into beads. His mustache grew below his chin, and he constantly played with it and sucked on it. This drove Randall Farms nuts, which consequently made me love Baby Booby even more. During trading lulls, Baby Booby and I told each other our stories and exchanged our thoughts on life.

There was no apparatus that could measure Baby Booby's hatred for women whose toes hung over the front of their sandals, and Booby hated summers for that reason. They were everywhere. Unfortunately, for Booby, some women on the floor, like Miranda Rose, wore sandals as their floor shoes in the winter.

Miranda Rose's toes were way over.

"When she walks, it's as if they're holding on by themselves. They're like Doberman pinscher feet," Booby scowled.

To Booby's disgust, Miranda came to the pit several times a day. After he said "pinscher feet" a few times, he wrote "PINSCHER FEET" on an electronic Quotron (machine that reflected stock and option quotes). "PINSCHER FEET" would remain on the screen until someone else erased it to look up a stock.

Mike Nolan (Jake Nolan's brother), another Houston trader and friend, occasionally drove in with Booby. Weather permitting, Booby stopped on the way to visit Sinbad, Lincoln Park Zoo's famous gorilla.

Booby returned to the car frowning, smirking, or smiling. He'd say, "They don't look good today, Mikey," or, "He loves 'em today, Mikey."

Curiosity got the best of Nolan, and one day he decided to follow Booby into the zoo. They passed the zebras and camels, and then were face to face with Sinbad.

Booby looked at Mikey and raised his arm. "Stay back, he doesn't know you. I brought my wife here. He threw shit at her . . . He's a good judge of character." Booby nodded confidently.

Sinbad sat close to the cage bars, watching Booby.

"Hello, partner," Booby said in a brotherly tone.

Booby pulled a small paper bag out from under his baggy sweater. Sinbad looked at Mikey, whose eyes were glued to the unfolding events. Booby threw the bag. It landed inches from Sinbad. Sinbad glanced at the bag and back at Booby.

"What do you think about 'em today, old buddy?" Booby queried.

Sinbad pursed his lips and grabbed the bag with his right hand, raising it to his face.

"They didn't have the red gummy pennies. I got the fish. The fish are almost as good as the red gummy pennies."

Sinbad looked in the bag with one eye.

"Come on, old pal. You've been hot. Papà needs a new pair of shoes."

Booby glanced at Mikey.

"Papà needs a new pair of shoes?" Mikey asked.

Booby put a finger to his pursed lips.

"Shh." Booby whispered, "he doesn't appreciate sarcasm."

"Sorry," Mikey whispered.

Booby turned back to Sinbad. "He doesn't mean anything. He's just another stupid human."

Sinbad gazed at Mikey with a look of superiority.

"Well?" Booby asked.

Sinbad remained still.

"I promise, next time I'll bring fish," Booby said, almost pleading.

Sinbad frowned at Mikey and at Booby. Mikey startled as Sinbad roared and waved his hands.

Booby nodded. "Thanks, buddy, sorry about the fish. They said they'll have 'em in a few days. Can you believe they make them in Minnesota? I didn't think they made anything in Minnesota."

Sinbad screamed.

"I know, no excuses next time. Come on, Mikey," Booby said.

After a few steps, Booby stared at Mikey. "I thought so; they're oversold, Mikey. They're going to scream today, Mikey."

That day, the market rallied 3 percent, the largest daily move that whole year.

I concentrated on making good trades and having a good time. I was generous by nature, so I had very few arguments with other traders in the pit, though I could disagree vivaciously about principles. People's behavior fascinated me and I especially enjoyed it when I sensed that certain traders thought of me as an idiot, though for the most part I concurred. Consequently, with seemingly little effort on my part, money accumulated and I was soon one of the larger traders in the pit.

Craig Butler, a tall Russian Orthodox Jewish trader, was tired of how I was treated by everyone, including the brokers and the exchange employees who worked behind the book. Reputation's critical on the floor, and Craig was known as a tough guy.

One day Craig and I simultaneously bought an order from the book. The rule is, "First takes what he or she wants." Not sure who was first, the worker behind the book split the trade equally. Craig thought that he was first and demanded all the trade. In his mind, this was an opportune time to show everyone who the real king of the jungle was.

The altercation became physical, and we were pulled apart. Randall Farms called in another floor official. After speaking with the book employee, the floor officials decided that the trade would remain split fifty-fifty.

Craig hurled threats of reprisal, but things calmed and the floor quietly settled into a trading lull.

Out of the silence, I spoke.

"Hey Craig, lick this," I said as I motioned down with my eyes.

Booby watched in disbelief.

Craig screamed, "The pig showed me his pecker!"

Floor officials rushed in. Craig's testimony was useless without a witness.

Craig disliked Booby, who often spoke of eating pork ribs and bacon. Booby shrugged. "I didn't see anything."

Randall Farms believed Craig. "You just couldn't make something like that up." Farms was Head Floor Official of the entire exchange and felt humiliated that this could be happening in his own pit.

My display was like kerosene for the lamp in Booby's head. Several times a day on the Quotron, the words "The BPT Show" would appear and the snake came out. The event became renowned, and traders from different pits tried to catch the exhibition.

"That's why Joey Horvat called you Moondick," Booby would randomly say, several times a day.

In a year's time, I had gone from being a dockworker to a well-known trading personality. I was now twenty-two years old.

Randall Farms waited patiently for a chance to write me up on some major exchange infraction. He became further irritated when Lorry Irving, a trader, pit sage, and director for the Juvenile Diabetes Foundation, became my friend.

Lorry said I was a mensch. Life was one big adventure, and in the pit, we were one big, happy family, mostly.

One afternoon, I received a call from my old boss, Burton Hartz. I arrived at the General Electric pit. Burton wanted my advice on a trading error. Blake Ross, one of Chicago Corp's House Brokers (the term used for a broker that only worked for one firm), had completed a spread incorrectly. Brokers are paid on a per-contract fee. House brokers are on salary, and earn a discretionary bonus based on the volume of contracts traded annually. Blake was a 40k (before taxes) per year guy. This was the salary of most house brokers. The biggest part of their compensation came through commissions.

Instead of buying a spread, which involved more than one different option, he sold it. Usually, these errors were quickly resolved. The traders would cancel the trade, and the broker would execute the order correctly.

With little movement in the stock price, the price of the spread should also not have moved. Unfortunately for Blake, the GE traders refused to cancel the transaction. Blake now had to buy the spread twice, once for the client and another time for himself, because he had mistakenly sold it to the GE traders.

The pit's rooster, Benjamin Tisch, cleared his trades at SOC, the same clearing house as myself. I recalled seeing him rifling cans of pop from the refrigerator into his briefcase on Jewish holidays. When confronted by Jarrett Rose, Benjamin brazenly told him that if he didn't like him taking pop home, he would look for a new place to clear his trades.

Burton Hartz and Benjamin's discussion about Blake's mistake became heated. I, in a hurry to get back to my pit, interrupted.

"What's the problem, Burt?"

"Pat, where would you sell this spread?" Burton asked. As he spoke, he handed me a spread ticket to buy 400 General Electric time spreads.

"What's the market?" I asked in a tone that reflected my willingness to help.

"Mind your own business," Benjamin growled. "We don't come to your pit, stickin' our nose where it doesn't belong."

I didn't like the way he stole pop, the way he looked, or his whining. I ignored him and addressed Burton.

"What's the skinny?" I asked.

"They're trying to stick Blake up for 20,000. He mis-filled the spread, and the stock hasn't moved. It was 1½ to 1¾. Now, the scumbags say it's 1 ¾ to two." (A scumbag is the sack that holds testicles.) Some of the scumbags had heard of me.

"Hey guys, give him a break," I said. "He fills paper. He ain't no trader."

"We'll let him out at 1¾," Benjamin growled.

My presence had already saved Blake $10,000.

"Come on guys, the stock hasn't moved . . . What goes around comes around," I said, smiling.

"All right," said Benjamin. "We'll sell it at 1⅝." Benjamin looked at Blake, "We're doing you a big favor, next time be more careful."

The bullet was down to $5,000. Burton nodded to Blake who, with tears in his eyes, began writing.

I interrupted. "Blake, I sold you four hundred spreads at 1½. Girls, I bought the spread four hundred times at 1⅝."

I wrote the ticket and left. It cost me five Gs. By then, I had 20,000 in my account. I'd make more.

Each afternoon, trade by trade, after the close, I meticulously calculated my profit and loss. If I had a good day, I gave twenty bucks to Allen (Little Dick) and Robby, the two guards at the exchange entrance.

Allen became "Little Dick" on a bet. He, I, and as many guys as could fit in the exchange men's room, went in there and determined that I was longer. After the result was announced, I laughed and whispered "Little Dick" in his ear. He lost by less than an inch.

He'd yell back, "Man, you're short, ugly, and got a pecker like a beagle. My guy's been retired for a long time . . . Kids are too expensive." From that day on, he's affectionately "Little Dick" and I'm still "Beagle." We are still friends today.

I hired Peter Bellus, a kid I'd known since I was fourteen, to clerk for me and my growing positions. Peter's father objected. In their home, my brother Greg and I were known not affectionately as "Sneaky Eyes" and "Car Thief."

Peter has a nervous personality. He loved me but hated the BPT Show and the way I pushed buttons.

Miranda Rose rarely traded. She was still occupying her days terrorizing runners and disgusting Booby with her toes. One day she came and stood on the top step in our pit. Her facial expression was that of someone with an upset stomach. She held her right wrist in her left hand and squinted to read the numbers on the Quotron. Booby had just written "PINSCHER FEET" on the Quotron screen. Miranda noticed the curious phrase and was wondering what it meant when she felt something touch the inside of her hand. Gently squeezing, she slowly looked down, and screeched.

Randall Farms heard Miranda's screech, searched me out, and was disappointed to see me calmly talking to Booby.

"Oh my God!" Miranda gasped. "He put his thing in my hand!"

Randall stared at me and opened his floor official fine book. "You'll never make another trade on this floor! That's sexual harassment!"

One by one he looked at the traders in the pit. "Which one of you cowards saw BPT standing behind Miranda?!"

Everyone, including the workers behind the book, shook their heads or shrugged. Booby removed his moustache from his mouth. "Randy"—Booby knew he hated to be addressed as "Randy"—"Patti hasn't left my side for an hour."

Farms grimaced and looked at Craig Butler. This was Craig's chance to even things out. Craig looked deep into my eyes and took a breath. "I didn't see anything."

Randall slammed his pencil and fine book at the floor with all his might. They limply bounced. Everyone was waiting for his next move. He stared at the floor, the fine book, and then at Booby. After a few moments of silence, he yelled, "You can stick your moustache back in your mouth, Suss!"

Randall then looked at the rest of us and said, "You're all scumbag morons!" and stomped out of the pit.

"He seems very upset, Patti. I think that Randy should get some kind of help, see an anger counselor or something," Booby said considerately.

It is unbelievable, the stories some people invent to get what they're after.

Later in the day, Little Dick came to the pit. "The police are waiting by the bank of elevators," he whispered.

Little Dick and Robby risked their jobs, escorting me down the stairs that were only supposed to be used for fires or bomb threats. Miranda was infuriated that I had not been arrested. She argued with the police. I made a few phone calls. Without a witness, the police refused to pursue the situation further. Shortly after, Miranda moved to Paris.

Many innocent victims have found that even an untrue accusation can be fatal. A couple of bucks to buy a few fellows lunch likely saved my career and millions.

Within weeks of Peter's arrival, I had my first $5,000 day. After work, Bucky watched me jump on the hood of my '73 Cutlass. "You're really screwed up, ya know? You wanna buy a beer?"

On the way to the exchange the next day, Peter stopped the car at St. Anthony—All Saints on 28th and Wallace. I said a prayer and dropped five one-hundred-dollar bills into the poor box. Funny how things turned out; the church was right down the block from Uncle Vince's house, where thieves had made off with the Christmas gifts. Maybe my generosity was helping one of them now. *What a wonderful graceful restitution that would be*, I thought.

I began spending every day after work at Armour Square with the Titos, Boticas, Ruffalos, Frattos, Ferros, and of course Carmine Ferri. I felt embarrassed by my wealth and tried to do good while I had it, knowing that nothing lasts forever. There was no way for me not to spread it around. As a result, most assumed that I always had more of it.

I formed the neighborhood Pony League, sponsored the Valentine Boys Club Boxing Team, founded the Robin Hood Foundation, and hired more workers for my company, Bridgeport Securities Group.

Almost all of our employees were neighborhood guys, and if they weren't, they soon became neighborhood guys. I trained each and every one of our hopefully, future traders personally. Often ten or more of us would go walking through the neighborhood, sometimes at six a.m., other times in the evening after the close.

On our walks or even in the car on the way to work, I'd explain spreads and strategies; *why* trades worked or didn't work; *when* trades could work in their favor or become disastrous. Most important, I taught them how to calculate risk.

I preached about how important it was for them to give back and how hogs got slaughtered. I tried to demonstrate to them the meaning of friendship and loyalty.

Never wanting to waste time, when I was given the opportunity, I also taught different types of spreads to female acquaintances.

When I was not teaching and/or bonding, I was singing and writing. Singing and writing had a calming effect on me. Initially, I sang cover songs, but eventually began writing my own stuff. I didn't write music, so I'd record the tune from my head and find someone who played the piano or the guitar to help me get the chords down.

Soon Peter and a few other guys began trading for my (their) company. With our earnings, we began buying exchange memberships instead of renting them. I encouraged each trader to buy his very own.

If there were ever floor officials called to a pit where we had traders, I made it mandatory that we all show up in case one of the brothers needed a hand.

We looked like a pack walking down the streets of the neighborhood and in fact, on the floor, people called us the Bridgeport Securities Gang instead of Bridgeport Securities Group. I didn't mind. Either one sounded fine.

We opened an office on the second floor overlooking the L train on Van Buren Street. The window with toilet paper hanging down to the street below was our window. The office with speakers hanging out on the ledge, blasting my songs, was our office. If someone yelled at the fat copper standing against the wall to go and get himself another doughnut, the scream came from one of our guys, in our office.

The family grew. Rocco Arcieri and Nicky Carvotta joined the Bridgeport crew. Rocco stumbled onto "Sister Tom," a middle-aged man who was convinced he was a Catholic nun.

Trading could be stressful, and entertainment was crucial. We called Sister Tom ten times a day on speakerphone.

"Hello, good sister," Rocco would say.

"Hello," Sister Tom would answer.

"Sister, I heard that the Sunday mass schedule has changed. Can you give me the new times?"

"I didn't hear anything about that."

"Yes, you did," Rocco insisted.

"No, I didn't hear anything about the Sunday mass schedule being changed," Sister Tom responded impudently.

"Yes, you did," Rocco chided.

"I did not. You take it up with Father Carl," Sister Tom snapped.

"Let me talk to him."

"He's not here."

"Yes, he is," Rocco contended.

"No, he's not," Sister Tom insisted.

"Yes, he is. Why are you being such a lying little sister?" Rocco asked.

"I am not," Sister Tom responded.

"Yes, you are," Rocco said.

Churches were a big part of our community, and I encouraged our traders to be humble and to stay close to their churches. I did as well.

In October, Bridgeport bought thousands of pumpkins. A truck drove the Bridgeport Securities Group merry men from parish to parish, handing pumpkins out to any kid who showed up. Blutto, the driver, made up the schedule and allotted an hour for each church. Rocco, Russell Dicecca, the great Patty Bo, myself, and the rest of the gang lay in the back of the truck on top of the pumpkins on the way to Saint Mary's.

Rocco jumped onto the front of the truck next to Blutto's door. "Stop at 28th and Gratten," he said.

When we arrived, Rocco banged on the door of a white-framed house. A middle-aged man answered. "Are you Sister Tom?" Rocco asked.

"Why, yes, I am," Sister said with a kind smile.

"This is for you." Rocco handed the pumpkin to the good sister, and we all got off the truck and took a group picture. Sister Tom was elated, and was one of us.

On the way to another church, one of the guys lobbed a piece of pumpkin off the truck, shattering the windshield of a passing bus. The crisis team, led by Martin Robin, an ex-copper/political consultant and brother-in-arms, handled it.

Handling it usually meant getting to the right person to quash a storm. This may have included some sort of payoff. It may have included a lot of other things that I'd be an idiot to write in a book.

I met Martin through my contact with the Daley organization. Richard J. Daley had been mayor from before I was born until '76. His sons Richy, John, and Bill then took over. They got neighborhood people jobs and promotions, took care of the poor and downtrodden. They also accumulated money and power.

Through the Daleys, I also met Ronny Moreno, Martin Robin's friend and an Italian American attorney living west of Bridgeport in the heavily Polish 12th Ward. Mr. Fixit, Martin Robin, thought Ronny should run for 12th Ward committeeman. If he won, we could use the spot and clout to help our people.

For Ronny to even have a chance, we needed the backing of Donald Winski, the eighty-three-year-old committeeman who was living full-time in Florida.

"How would an Italian get elected in the 12th Ward, the most Polish Ward of the city?" Winski laughed.

Martin proposed, win or lose, that we lease Donald's offices, make his daughter our secretary, and throw him a going-away bash, guaranteeing him at least $100,000 in political donations. Committeeman Winski accepted.

Moreno's chief opponent was a very angry gentleman named Stan Kowalczyk. He told everyone about Winski's true residence in Florida and riled up the electorate nicely. "How could a committeeman living in Florida represent people living in the 12th Ward on the Southwest Side of Chicago?" I thought it was a fair question.

The ward's population was Polish. Polish people vote for other Polish people. Martin Robin, Moreno's campaign manager, knew exactly what to do.

The day before the deadline, seven completely unknown (to Chicago politics at least) contestants deposited the required signatures to get their names on the ballots. Now, instead of Moreno vs. Kowalczyk it was Moreno vs. Kowalsky, Kaminska, Kowalska, Kachanowski, Kachmarzinski, Kacimarcik, Kowalczyk, and Kachnycz. Not one of the K's got over 10 percent of the votes. Moreno was swept into office.

I quickly became a political insider. The present county clerk, Racic, was in a tough race against Heather Stucker, an Independent, backed by Mayor Harold Washington. The Chicago political machine wanted to siphon votes from Stucker to safeguard Racic and the 1,500 jobs in his office. After a few meetings, journalists were called and I became a candidate for county clerk.

The Bertuccis, La Monicas, Baileys, Billses, Frattos, Ramoses, and dozens of other neighborhood families became my army. As in any good Chicago race, there were fistfights, broken windows, name-calling, and treachery. Within days, I regretted my decision to run.

I was a topic on radio and television shows. Dozens of articles were written about me; some were even true. *Chicago Magazine* did an article called "Fonzie Gets Rich." The *Chicago Post* did an article, "Trading Faces, Looking at the Many Sides of Pat Carmichael." I was coined a Don Johnson lookalike (astonishing what money can do).

Chicago Post reporter Donald Brath wrote about the Miranda Rose incident in "County Clerk Candidate Generous As He Is Ornery." When it got to the part where I had to deny or admit, I responded and he printed, "no comment." Today, Donald is the editor of the *Chicago News*.

My main campaign topic was support needed for the Vietnam veterans. This had absolutely nothing to do with the office I was running for. I received 82,000 votes, and Racic sneaked back in by less than 15,000 ballots against Stucker.

It was a great first showing, and the press disseminated rumors of me running for mayor, governor, and eventually president. I don't think they got it. When I told people I'd never run for office again, I meant it.

They knew I'd change my mind. I mean, who didn't want power and glory and fame?

I didn't. I just wanted to help people.

Martin Robin and Bridgeport office manager Dirken Scott ran Robin Hood, the entity we used to organize charitable activities.

After Bob, a pizza deliveryman, was robbed and killed on the South Side, we delivered a pizza to his family. Written on the front of the napkin bag were the words "Remembering Bob." Inside was $2,000 cash.

A boy had terminal cancer and we sent him and his whole family to Disney World. A man was given six months to live, and we bought him a video camera to record his thoughts to be left to his child, who was then in the womb of his pregnant wife.

There was no limit to what the group of merry men would do to make someone happy. Eventually, we touched people all over the country.

After the election, I left for Italy and spent time with my grandfather's family. Many were entertained by the way I spoke Italian, a mixture of Calabrese and Sicilian dialects (from the neighborhood) with a Chicago accent. My cousin, Alfonso, gave me the nickname "U Carneveil," meaning I was as entertaining as a carnival.

Zio Cosimo, my grandfather's seventy-year-old nephew, watched over me as a son. He even insisted on holding my hand when we crossed the streets. Males in Italy often walk arm in arm and are quite physical. After the twentieth time of jerking my hand out of his, he understood. Somehow my grandfather's presence always felt strongest when I was together with Zio Cosimo . . . we were bonded forever.

In Italy, women do not change their surnames in marriage, and they run the households. Home is the nest of the family, and nothing is more important than family. This situation makes many Italian husbands "puppet kings."

Understanding Italy is not an easy thing. Some of the common sayings there are:

"With one pubic hair a woman can pull the cart that two donkeys can't budge."

"If a woman cannot charm her way into her husband's heart to attain what she wants then she is an incapable fool."

"The biggest thieves are the rich and the politicians, so even the little guy should be allowed to steal." Italy actually passed a law in 2016 that no one can be prosecuted for stealing food if they are hungry.

Italians see sex as a simple part of life, like the church, pasta, and work. Guys tease and grab at each other's crotches, women at each other's breasts. Folks openly kid about the size of one's ass or whatever.

"Is that whopper growing?" grandfathers ask grandsons as they poke at them with their canes. There would certainly not be enough jail cells in America for all the "sex offenders" in Italy.

Chapter 9

America's Most Eligible Bachelor

E veryone chased something on the floor.

Optionettes pursued lives of luxury through marriage; some sported three-inch fingernails and wore $1,000 outfits to a runner's job that paid spit. Traders often humiliated male or less attractive female runners in an effort to impress the gorgeous predators. Personally, I found less extravagant women far more appealing. I was always attracted to the simpler things, and believed women to be the most beautiful creatures on the planet.

Occasionally, the investment paid huge. Some Optionettes landed big fish, conceived a child, divorced a short time after, and were economically set for the remainder of their lives. Talk about nice trade.

The company paid our troops' legal fees for fights, damage to property, etc. Some months, attorney Josh Balkus billed Bridgeport tens of thousands.

The Hometown police chase, when the police chased (and lost) me from Hometown to Bridgeport was still dangling. Until now, my attorneys were able to get me seven continuances. To obtain the seventh continuance, my attorney Chester Chawak faked a heart attack right in the courtroom. It was the only choice he had, with the judge being so stubborn and all.

The court date finally arrived. We were ready. We had a stolen car report, and tickets placing me in Italy. The state had no eyewitnesses. Case closed.

Attorney Balkus figured it was a no-brainer, open-and-shut case. Instead of him showing up himself, he sent Trenton, a green assistant. Trenton approached the bench and heard the district attorney tell the clerk that the cop from the chase would identify me. Of course it was a lie. I mean the cop never got close enough to the car to see my face. Still, this could mean jail time.

The economy was tough, and Trenton was new. The courtroom was cold, but he was sweating.

The clerk called my name. Trenton rushed ahead of me.

"Your Honor, we need a continuance," he stammered.

"Denied," the judge said without looking up.

"Your Honor, you must give us a continuance. Ou-ou-our client is not happy with his counsel," Trenton said, regaining his nerve.

The beet-red judge stood. "He's not happy with his counsel, eh? We're not happy with your client! He's scum and making a mockery of this court. No continuance! Gather yourself and prepare for trial. Your client's going to jail, it's just a matter of how much time he'll serve!"

"Your Honor," Trenton mumbled.

"You'll be called. Prepare for trial," the judge said sternly.

Another case was called, and Trenton attempted to reason with the hard-nosed district attorney. She wasn't impressed with me in the least. She rejected Trenton's request for a jury trial, and if I admitted guilt, she was willing to offer six months for evading arrest and six months for endangering the life of a law enforcement agent. If I didn't accept the deal, I could go away for years, she told Trenton.

I never understood the system. It was the idiot copper who pursued me in a high-speed chase for a traffic infraction. He should have been on trial in my opinion. I mean, no common sense whatsoever. He should have been fired on the spot.

So here we were. If we accepted, I would spend at least three months behind bars. Peter was stunned. "Pat, if you're convicted of a felony, you can't trade anymore. It's an exchange rule."

"That's a good one. Who's more criminal than Goldman Sachs?"

"Please," Peter said, beginning to sweat. "What will we do with your positions? They're huge. Who could manage them?"

"You," I calmly replied.

"No way. The position is way bigger than I could handle."

Trenton was desperately trying to get Josh Balkus, his boss, on the phone. He turned to us. "It's no use, he doesn't answer," he said. "What am I going to do?"

"Offer them money," I said nonchalantly.

"What? You're nuts. I can't offer them money."

"Tell them we'll pay $2,000 on each charge for probation."

They countered with $3,000, and I paid $6,000, got probation, and no receipts. I was able to glide smoothly through turbulent skies. I mean, if I fell and ended up off the floor, I'd just go back to where I was, and that wasn't so bad.

Among the new Bridgeport recruits was my brother Casey. I loved him and all of my step- and half brothers and sisters. In the neighborhood, it didn't matter much what name you went by. Many changed their names and/or had nicknames or aliases. I had driver's licenses under three different names, because you never knew when you'd have to ditch one.

Bridgeport Securities Group grew in size and profit. Dirken Scott was the administrative captain of the ship, and he was loved by all. I said it a hundred times: "Dirken's a better man than I could ever be."

Dirken's widowed mother raised nine kids. She told Dirken to invite me to their home whenever he liked, and especially when she made smoked butt and cabbage, my favorite. I became a regular at the Scotts' home.

In 1980, I bought a house on 35th and Union. Larry Smith lived four doors down.

Larry's father, Al, was a Georgia hillbilly; his mother, Tam, was a devout Catholic, Sicilian, and the first woman to ever call me both a fuzzle nuts and cad. She loved me to death. I was soon part of the family and found them to be an ideal couple. Tam would sit on the couch saying the rosary and Al would be next to her watching porn on the television.

I had a key to their front door, and a few times a month, at six a.m. I let myself in, to jump on Tam's bed. She yelled and screamed while Al made coffee. Damn! It was a wonderful life.

Eventually, Larry came to work for Bridgeport Securities Group.

Our company continually sponsored dozens of programs—kids' sports, boxing, baseball teams, battered women's organizations, and families in distress. From time to time, I was asked to explain company philosophy.

I'd say, "We'd rather give a thousand to someone who needed it than spend a thousand on something that we didn't need." Bridgeport Securities Group—dedicated to doing the right thing.

My old boss, Eric Sarr, married the Jewish princess of his dreams. She was now suing him for divorce. Eric was trading in the Merc pit when Morgan Church called.

"Hey Cheap Steak," Morgan said, "Sarr is trading like an idiot. He lost a few hundred thousand last week. His position is huge, the other traders hate him and won't let him out. I think he might get suicidal."

If Eric kept losing, he would soon have to puke out of his huge position. This meant big profit to the regulars as he'd be at their mercy to close at the prices they dictated.

By now, I was an expert at analyzing even the most intricate trading situations. Sarr's position was large and hemorrhaging money, but all he really had to do, to de-risk, was buy the January, March "Fifty" time spread 500 times. The hemorrhaging would then stop and he could take his time to get out.

I walked into the pit. The pit traders knew I had socked Eric a few years prior. A few suspected that I had come to stick a knife in the wounded man. This would be good. It might push him off the cliff.

"Jan-March fifty, what's the market?" I asked.

"The market's five to six and three quarters," a trader replied.

"Eric, what will you pay for 500 of them? It's what you need," I said.

Eric studied me and then he studied his position card for over a minute. During the silence, several unhappy men stared at Eric and then back at me.

Finally, Eric nodded and looked at me. "I'll pay five and a half for 500."

"Sold," I said. I turned to my brother Casey, who was now my clerk. "Write it up," I said. The next day, I stuck a Bridgeport trader in the pit to get out of the position. Slowly, we were all over the floor.

Sid Feldman's father was a Russian Jew who immigrated to South America and then to the United States. Sid married an Irish Catholic. They raised their brood in the Irish neighborhood of Canaryville, which borders Bridgeport's south end. The Feldman children married Irish Catholics and by the time Sid was sixty he was a Jewish grandfather to a bunch of Irish Catholics.

One day I walked into the *Bridgeport News* office to get in a story about baseball registration. While talking to Sid's secretary, I inadvertently said a swear word and was assailed by the cigar-chomping owner, Sid Feldman. He lectured me about the rudeness of using cusswords in front of women (he had two female secretaries). I apologized.

Sid was on the board of the Valentine's Boys and Girls Club. He ended up liking me, and through him I became the club's youngest treasurer. Sid's son, Joe Feldman Sr., made a buck parking cars. At one of the Valentine fundraising dinners, Joe Sr. introduced himself to me and asked me if I'd hire his son, Joey Jr.

Joey Jr. worked for Bridgeport on the trading floor for four years as a clerk before becoming my partner and one of the greatest traders I've ever known. Life took many turns. Eventually, in the darkest hours, it was Sid's grandson, Joey Jr. who was the saving light.

As I've mentioned, Bridgeport gravitated to two points, the predominantly Italian mob on 26th Street and the predominantly Irish mob on 37th Street. As the years ticked by, the 26th Street mob was becoming the remnants of the failing mafia and the 37th Street mob was becoming the remnants of the failing Daley political dynasty.

Sometimes wounded bears are the most dangerous. I was aware of my surroundings.

To me, life was a function of what I could do for others. I bought tickets to Daley's fundraisers and was obviously a member of the Italian-American Club, founded by the neighborhood boss Dominick.

Sweetboy Leone, Penny Candy (Rino Fini), and Rooks whistled me in to meet with Dominick. The Leones kept the unions in line, Penny Candy ran the book at the Chicago exchanges, and Rooks was the soft side, interfacing for the outfit with churches and families in trouble. For years, Rooks and Penny Candy were like uncles to me.

I walked in to see Dominick, suspecting that he was going to shake me down. He began speaking about the neighborhood and the new Italian-American Club.

Unfortunately for Dominick and many others, the government wanted to give Las Vegas and loan-sharking to the corporations. The neighborhood was under siege, with the FBI digging up yards and parks, looking for bodies. I saw the writing on the wall and was wondering what Dominick and his men were doing to shelter themselves.

I paid close attention to Dominick's every movement and word.

"If you kill one guy," Dominick continued, "they want to put you in jail, but if you put a uniform on and kill twenty guys they give you a medal, go figure," Dominick said.

By the end of the meeting, it was clear what I had to do.

I didn't call the FBI; instead, I honored Dominick's request and bought the gifts for the Club's Christmas party. I was embarrassed that I hadn't thought to offer before I was asked.

I treasured my friendship with the "so-called" mobsters who were infinitely more honest than most politicians or businessmen I knew. On my trips to Vegas, I was a guest at Caesars Palace. Caesars was owned and operated by the Chicago Italian organization. My comped stays there more than made up for the price of the Christmas gifts.

The betting books, loan sharks, jewel thieves, hijackers, businesses, and casinos paid homage to 26th Street. The federal government called this "extortion, illegal and immoral." They were eventually replaced by car title loan shops, private police protection, the state lottery, off-track betting, gambling boats, and gambling firms.

The government spent billions to knock the wise guys out and pocketed billions to hand their turf over to the corporations. Practical people say that at least big business pays taxes, but if you analyze Apple, Goldman Sachs, and General Electric, you can't even say that.

My affiliation with 26th Street and frequent trips to southern Italy helped feed rumors about me, my money, and my influence. Some of the rumors greatly exaggerated my wealth and my power; some underestimated them. But all the rumors were a small price to pay. I loved to be with my grandfather's people, in Modugno, where I felt right at home.

In Italy, the church, government, and mafia wrestle for control. Without an absolute boss, the country breathes freedom not known in other mono-power-centered cultures, whether they're called democratic or not. If someone molested your child in Italy, it's taken care of quickly by the families who still run the nation.

Organized crime has its perks, but is far from perfect. Two guys from my close friend, Carmine's town, Sorbo, were found in the trunk of a car with multiple bullets in them. Dominick never allowed drug dealing in the neighborhood, and rumor was that the two paisans were doing just that.

I practiced Italian with Carmine's family and other neighborhood Italians. Over the years Carmine's mother, Zia Anna, had become a second mother. She organized all the cooking at Bridgeport Securities Group Christmas parties in the basement of Santa Lucia school. They were love bashes. Everyone ate and danced. Each kid got a gift. I sang (that's the price they paid).

Among our Bridgeport troops were recently unemployed roofers and parking attendants. A university degree was not only not necessary, in our eyes, but was actually an impediment to being hired by us. If someone had a degree, finding employment was easier, so they were less needy. Secondly, people with advanced education often have inflated ideas about what they know, including what they know about the markets.

We were mechanics. We didn't need any smart guys with big opinions taking a position and blowing us out of the water.

Our base of influence grew as we used knowhow and power to help others. On the floor they called us thugs, but in the neighborhood they called us saints.

I was on the Oprah show as a "rags to riches" story.

"Did you know that you would be a success?" Oprah asked me.

"I had a feeling that I'd do something big," I replied, "but wasn't sure if it would be legal."

The audience laughed. I couldn't figure out why.

"You're cute," she said.

Sam Freifeld was the real reason I went on the Oprah show. Sam was Saul Bellow's agent. Saul was a big guy who had won the Nobel Prize in Literature in 1976. I had written a book, *Diamond in the Rough*. Sam Freifeld was also my agent. He loved the idea of me going on Oprah and convinced Oprah to plug my book.

Oprah showcased *Diamond in the Rough*, and years later I entered the special club of being a repeat guest.

Being on her show was no big deal. I had been on dozens of shows, and she wasn't even from the neighborhood. She seemed likable, but if she had become such an essential part of so many lives, something has gone awry.

When being interviewed by an ABC reporter, I told her that I wanted to marry a virgin.

"Bingo, talk about hate mail."

I mean, what's wrong with that?

As the internet took over our lives, truth took a back seat to rumors that branded me a drug lord, mobster, devil, and saint. Some of the press coined me a chauvinist. The director of the Hull House baptized the phrase "Bridgeport's Guardian Angel" for my help with their battered women program.

One night on Grand Avenue at D'Amato's Italian restaurant with my gang, I threw a packet of butter across the table, missing my target but accidentally hitting a busboy. I gave him a hundred-dollar bill as I left. The next day, a story in the *Chicago Post*, written by award-winning journalist Ray Hanania, was titled "Chicago's Bad Boy Tosses Butter, 100 Dollars a Throw."

I went to De La Salle to watch a baseball game. I met Brother Richard Kelly, who was sure that I had just been released from prison. In fact, neither my notoriety nor my money changed the fact that I still had legal issues. Having money did make them easier to deal with. When I was a kid, I had to make up stories to tell the authorities all by myself. Now I could afford to pay attorneys to do it.

I walked into the police station at 35th Street. The desk cop waved me back to where they held prisoners. My friend, Rob Kelly, was one of four detainees handcuffed to the wall. Two plainclothes police typed at desks in the middle of the room. We'll call them Peter and Paul; police are sometimes also apostles.

One prisoner muttered and shook. His pants were stained, and there was a scent of urine in the air.

"Please give me a cigarette. I'm dying, here," he moaned.

"Shut up!" yelled Peter.

"Please," he whimpered, "just one cigarette."

Peter walked up to the bellyaching man.

"You just want one?" Peter asked gently.

"Yes, please just one. I need it. Please."

Peter lit a cigarette; the prisoner was full of anticipation; Paul arrived and also lit up; and just as the cigarette got to the man's pursed lips, Peter pulled away and both of the apostles blew smoke in the prisoner's face. Tears formed in the hostage's eyes.

In the past, Chicago police have been referred to as "Dicks" as well as "Pigs."

Peter turned to me unkindly, and said, "What do you want?"

I nodded toward Rob Kelly. "I got bail money."

"Oh, that jagoff? He likes drinking and driving. One day he'll kill a little kid. If you're bailing out a child killer, you're probably a jagoff too."

"You're quite the charmer." I smiled narrowly. "It's three in the morning. Could we just take care of this?"

Peter and Paul walked out without responding. Coffee break. I stared at the lighter and cigarettes on the locker.

"No," Kelly pleaded, "don't even think about it."

I put a cigarette in the consoled prisoner's mouth and lit it for him. He inhaled relief as I placed the cigarettes and lighter back on the locker. Moments later, the servants of justice arrived, carrying paper and coffee. The prisoner stared at his cigarette and then put it back in his mouth and puffed.

Peter glared into my eyes. "Who gave the gay boy a cigarette?"

My eyes locked with Peter's eyes. There really wasn't a lot to think about.

"I imagine you studied logic in the academy," I quipped.

Peter and Paul laid their coffee on the desk and slowly approached me. Peter removed his cuffs.

"As you can see, I'm the only person not handcuffed." They were now in my face. I looked from one to the other. "I'll gladly pay you for the cigarette," I said obligingly.

Peter shoved me. I socked him.

Within seconds, every available peace officer within the thirty-mile radius arrived. I instinctually clamped my mouth to protect my teeth.

Minutes later, with a swollen, bloodied face and clumps of hair missing from my head, I was dragged to a cell. I was bailed out from the jail at 26th and California four days later. I was charged with aggravated battery, resisting arrest, destruction of city property, and disorderly conduct. Stunningly, Peter and Paul ignored the fact that I had offered to pay for the cigarette. I was also charged with burglary.

ᚨ

My first day back to the trading floor was a hectic day in Kennecott Copper and Occidental Petroleum. There was news and both were bouncing around like super-balls. Peter Bellus was now a trader. My brother Casey had also moved up. My new clerk, Nicky Carvotta, was checking my position on the floor.

I was in the traders' lounge with cards spread out in front of me. Someone arrived. Without looking up, I smelled Sonny Handelsman, a six-foot-four giant, famous for two things: his girlfriend, who was a dead ringer for Morticia from *The Addams Family*, and his foul odor. Guys literally gifted him bars of soap.

Sonny was a cowboy. He bought or sold, then watched in pain or ecstasy. He was down tens of thousands this morning, and was not jovial.

"I'm counting, find another table," I said without looking up.

Lounge tables were squashed together; everyone within a tire toss could hear us. He sat, jarring the table toward me. I didn't look away. "Sonny, I can smell you. Please take a stroll?" I said calmly.

This was a perfect opportunity for Sonny to let off some steam.

"Screw you and the horse you rode in on," Sonny said.

I guess he wanted to also *speak* like a cowboy.

I lunged across the table and grabbed him by the neck. Sonny stood. I had made a great miscalculation. I went from looking down, to looking across, to looking up at him. What an idiot I truly am. If he got ahold of me, he'd kill me.

Running seemed the most intelligent choice. Still, a tarnished reputation would have horrendous ramifications. Others would find courage to challenge me and my traders all over the floor. I let him go and swung, purposely just missing his nose.

Sonny looked at my still bruised face. He looked at my eyes. I watched back with a serious gaze. He was deciding. I took another swing to force him into a choice.

Seconds passed. The whole room, full of traders, was captivated.

I waited and saw Charlie back up slightly. "Someone get ahold of that guy, he's crazy!" Sonny yelped.

Two of my sisters moved into a two-bedroom flat that I bought in the neighborhood. My mother got a new car. One of my brothers got a down payment on a house. I started the De La Salle scholarship contest. Neighborhood students won monetary prizes for writing essays on why neighborhood and family are important.

Father Frawley (the priest who baptized me) called me when he had a cause. And in response to one of Father Frawley's calls, Peter Bellus and I arrived at Visitation

Catholic Grammar School. Sister Bernadette pulled Derek, a skinny, dark skinned, thirteen-year-old eighth grader out of class.

Derek wanted to enter Quigley South Seminary High School, but his family lacked funding for it. I wrote a check. In the summer, at lunch, he told me he made the honor roll. I tingled inside. He also told me that he was going to a public school in the fall. His parents still couldn't afford tuition at Quigley.

"Keep the grades up and things will take care of themselves," I said.

We paid for all four years. Derek graduated with honors and went on to college, where he also excelled. Today he lives in Florida with Jessica and their three sons. We're best of friends. Every big move that he makes I'm in on, and vice versa. We are brothers.

It is a wonderful life, George Bailey.

Trading, like any other business, has its peaks and valleys. Fortunately, because of our instincts and lack of greediness, the valleys were rarely too deep. Having said this, the company hit a rough spot. Our positions were enormous and we had zero liquidity.

The De La Salle scholarship contest arrived at the same time. I made an appointment with a bank to borrow money. The following day, things turned, and I canceled the appointment with the bank.

Zia Anna Ferri asked me to hire Johnny Dicecca. I could never refuse her. In time, Johnny and I became inseparable friends. His mother, Katey, was a traditional, loving, Italian mother. I was invited to every family wedding and baptism. In their home I was a member of the clan, present for every holiday.

Mr. Dicecca (Mario) told his son, Johnny Boy, "You know, that kid doesn't have to do all those things that he does for everyone."

On a hot summer day, Johnny Dicecca and I walked past Loeber's Rolls-Royce. A dark-skinned salesman stopped us and confided that he needed to show hustle or lose his job. He asked us to take a test drive. In shorts and T-shirts, we followed him into the showroom. I got behind the wheel of the white Silver Shadow. The salesman got in the passenger seat and Johnny in the back.

The manager ran out and leaned on the driver side window. "Where do you think you're going with these two characters? They are not going to buy a Rolls-Royce."

"I, I, I . . ." the salesman stuttered.

"You, you, you, nothing!" screamed the manager.

"Hey dickhead, get your arm off the car." I shoved his arm, stepped on the gas, made rubbery screeches on the concrete showroom garage, and spun out into the street.

"Lost that job," the salesman said.

When we returned, the manager walked swiftly toward us, looking threateningly at the salesman. I got out of the car, walked to the office, and on the way pushed the manager again. "I said, get out of the way, dickhead."

He stared. I stopped, hoping he'd give me a reason to sock him. "I'm gonna buy this car," I told him.

Peter Bellus arrived with a check, and Johnny and I drove out in the Rolls. Family and friends used it and my new Porsche for communions, weddings, and proms. I rarely drove either cars.

They were shiny, but they just weren't me.

Chapter 10

Brothers Mikey and Paulie

Because of experiences similar to my own, my fourteen-year-old brother Paulie, Butch's and the Old Man's youngest son, lived in the Lawrence Home for Boys. I wanted him out. I hired the former head of the Department of Children and Family Services, who would now go against the Department of Children and Family Services . . . nothing like fighting the system with the system.

Paulie's social worker wanted Paulie to stay put. He was too violent to be on the streets.

The case hit the papers: "Chicago's bad boy had a little brother who was Chicago's little bad boy."

We won, and Paulie moved in with me at 3512 South Union.

Two weeks after his arrival, Paulie came home with a kid his age named Mikey Fontana. Mikey had family issues. He was sleeping at friends' houses, and occasionally in the park on 37th Street and Wallace.

I walked into the house a few weeks after Mikey moved in.

"Where's Mikey?" I asked.

Paulie started crying. "He's gone, we got into an argument. I said some things that I shouldn't have said."

I had been expecting the day to arrive when there was trouble between a brother and a friend.

"Get in the car," I said.

Paulie's tears fell like the pounding rain outside. We looked through the spaces that the wipers left, but Mikey was nowhere to be found. After forty minutes in the monsoon, my heart skipped. Mikey was sitting, head in lap, on a porch on 35th and Emerald.

"You get him," I said.

They walked a few minutes in the storm before getting into the car.

We sat drenched in the front room. Silence blanketed the room until I was able to organize my thoughts. "I don't want to know what happened. I'm going to say this once. I love both of you with all my heart, and in our home there are not two brothers and a friend. We're three brothers. Got it, Mikey?"

"Yep," Mikey said, crying.

"Got it, Paulie?"

"Yes, I'm sorry," Paulie said meekly.

Nothing further was ever said.

That Sunday, we attended mass at Santa Lucia, in the heart of the Italian part of Bridgeport. I was proud of my brothers, and taking them to mass, standing with them in front of the Lord and my fellow Italo-Americans was moving for me. It sent a strong message to the Lord and my compatriots about who I was and what I believed.

The house at 3512 was full of laughs, love, and characters. I insisted that Mikey and Paulie help others, respect their elders, and attend mass on Sunday.

I believe that sinners need mass more than anyone, and I'm a follower of the greatest commandment, "Love others as I have loved you."

Christ didn't need to die on the cross. He could have given in to the pressure and "admit" that He was wrong to condemn bullies and raise up the meek. But He didn't. He loved mankind more than His own life.

The Catholic church is a great thing. I love it like my mother, and when my mother gets diabetes or makes a mistake, I still love her. The same goes for my church. When I sit in any church, synagogue, or mosque, I feel that I can absorb the millions of prayers, tears, and elations that have been expressed in the abode. Sitting in these wonderful edifices is a gift on earth, which I treasure more than words can express.

I gave Mikey and Paulie a choice; they could either enter sports or work in the afternoon after school. Both boxed with the Valentine Boys and Girls Club.

Paulie's bouts were frustrating. He had raw talent, but was lazy at boxing, and at everything else. He only started hustling when he felt the rope on his back. The fights were three rounds, and he lost most of them. Mikey, on the other hand, went on to be the ranked number nine heavyweight in the world by *Ring* magazine, fighting Trevor Berbick, Iran Barkley, and Dwight Muhammad Qawi, three champions.

Rossi Calo was a childhood friend from the neighborhood, an aspiring author, painter, and musician, usually a step ahead of most. We played spades, and he was into me for almost twenty bucks. He walked into the kitchen (we never locked the door and all were welcome) to find Paulie eating a bologna sandwich.

"Where's your brudder?" Rossi asked.

"Which one?" Paulie asked with a smile.

"Oh yeah," Rossi said, "the older one, with the beak."

Paulie laughed. "You crack me up, Rossi."

"Yeah, you too," Rossi said, as he headed out the door into the backyard.

"Rossi!" Mikey yelled. "What's happening?"

"Not much, not much, how bout wit you? How's school?" Rossi asked.

Mikey shook his head.

"I understand," Rossi said.

The yard had a small, $500 swimming pool, surrounded by a $5,000 wooden deck.

I was lying next to Mikey. I sat up. "Spades?" I asked.

"Got no cake," Rossi said.

"Your credit's good with me." I smiled sinisterly.

"Don't want no more credit," Rossi said. "What are you reading out there?"

"Some guy gave me this book about chess. It's in Italian, and I can't make heads or tails out of it," I replied.

"You play chess?"

"Why, you wanna play for a few bucks?"

"Nah, I told you, I have no funding. But I have a chess set in my trunk. We can play for fun."

Rossi poured the pieces onto the table. I put the knight where the rook should have gone and the king where the queen should have gone, etc.

"What time is it?" Rossi asked.

"About two, why? You got to go somewhere?"

"No, I got some time." Rossi cleared his throat. "You said that my credit was good here, right?"

"Yeah, how much do you owe me?" I asked.

"Nineteen bucks. Do you want to play for nineteen bucks?" Rossi asked.

"The whole tuna? Nah, if you lose, it's thirty-eight bucks. Where you gonna get that kind of loot? I'll play you for a deuce."

"I got collateral," Rossi said seriously. "A guy at the University of Chicago was going to give me 200 bucks for one of my works."

"One of your works?"

"One of my art pieces, one of my paintings."

"Why didn't you tackle him?" I asked.

"I swear on my mother," Rossi said.

"Serious stuff. How is Fanny [Rossi's mother]?"

"Fine, fine. Do you want to play?"

I quietly stared and then spoke. "Go get the Rembrandt."

Ten minutes later, Rossi walked in with his painting. I looked at it and said, "Someone was willing to pay 200 for a dog walking a tightrope?"

"Your nose is in the way. That's no dog. It doesn't look anything like a dog." Rossi smirked, as an artist might.

"Rossi, it's made of sticks and it's got four legs and a tail. Is it a fox?"

"Beak, you may know something about the stock market, but you can't tell a dog from a donkey in the art world."

"Looking at it closer, I see your point. It's definitely a donkey," I said.

Paulie walked in. "Hey Rossi, why's the dog walking the tightrope?"

Rossi stared at me.

"You told him to say that," Rossi said.

"Rossi, I was here with you," I said.

"While I was gone, you told him to say the stupidest thing that popped into his mind when he saw my painting." He paused. "You're both imbeciles, so your analysis is the same."

"I never seen anything quite like it. It's unique—exquisite, even," I said.

Rossi stopped me cold. "If you can spell either of those words, I'll give you a fin."

"You'd lose," I said. "Even Paulie could spell dose."

Paulie glanced in our direction and finished his water, "I'm goin' back out by Mikey."

Rossi smirked. "Paulie struggles spelling 'Paulie.'"

"Don't be so tough on him, he tries hard," I said. "If you lose this game, the painting's mine."

"Absolutely," Rossi said. "Categorically."

Mikey and Paulie walked in, and now all four of us looked at Rossi's painting.

"Hey Rossi, why's dat dog walkin' on the clothesline over the fire?" Mikey asked. "If he falls, he'll be a hotdog." Mikey laughed.

"Einstein, it's a donkey and that's the circus crowd. *We're* the crowd. We're the crowd! You artistic illiterates."

"Us?" Mikey asked.

"We, *we* are the crowd," Rossi said firmly.

"I snuck into the circus once. I didn't like it," Mikey said.

"Don't get it, Rossi," Paulie said. "No crowd would watch no donkey walk on no string, 'cause it would break."

"Rope. If you two blockheads study for a few decades and put what you know together, you'll figure it out."

"That ain't nice," Mikey said.

"Yeah, that ain't nice," Paulie added.

"Yeah, that ain't nice," I said.

"All right, we all know that I ain't winning no contest for being amiable. Let's play," Rossi said in a commanding voice.

Mikey looked at Paulie as they walked out. "He does it on purpose, talking so we can't understand him. 'Amiable.'"

"OK, Beak, let's get going," Rossi said.

I reset the pieces correctly and beat him in a dozen moves. Rossi stared at the board. I opened a switchblade, sliced the painting, and threw it out the door into the swimming pool. Mikey and Paulie watched the painting float to the bottom.

"Hey Rossi, da dog can't swim," Mikey quipped.

"It's a donkey, you 'artistic illiterate,'" Paulie said.

Rossi grabbed a butcher knife and moved on me.

"Ahh!" he screamed as he raised the knife.

Paulie and Mikey joined me as I ran through the yard. We didn't return until Rossi's car was no longer parked in front of the house.

Weeks later, I read an ad in the *Chicago News*. "Heirloom silverware set missing from the area of Clark and North Avenue. No questions asked."

I picked up the phone and dialed the number written at the end of the ad. A woman answered.

"Ma'am, my grandmother had her silverware stolen years ago. She never got over it. I feel really sorry for your loss."

"Thank you," she replied. "That's kind of you. The missing silverware has been in my family for almost 150 years. It's not the economic value but the sentimental value."

"Ma'am, you sound like such a nice person, and I'm sorry for your loss. You said that there'd be no questions asked."

"Oh yes, no questions. And I'm willing to pay a small reward."

"Ma'am, I'm not interested in any reward. I think I know who has your merchandise, and I've tried without luck to convince him to return it to you."

At the end of the call, I gave her the address of the person who had taken her family heirlooms.

It was midnight. Rossi didn't notice the plainclothes detectives sitting in the unmarked car. He quietly opened the door so as not to wake up his mother.

The detectives arrived and dragged him into the house. They searched for twenty minutes. Rossi explained that he had nobody's stolen silverware, and had no idea what they were talking about. No silverware was found.

Rossi immediately began scheming revenge. He was sure that it was a Sammy or Alan Bino move, brothers famous for neighborhood pranks. He'd get them.

Life is full of fountains of knowledge and wisdom. Kevin Dever, also known as Calhoun, or Cal, is one of those fountains. He's Joe Feldman Sr.'s (my business partner's father's) best friend. Kevin drinks only when alone or in company. He's never been married, and says the best two words he never said are "I do."

He parks cars and pickets for whatever union calls. He's a sinner and a saint. As far as I'm concerned, the essential part of friendship is love and not what one does in his or her free time. He's my guardian angel, and when in Chicago we walk at six a.m., not 6:05 or 5:58. I swing five-pound weights and he tells stories, giving me an angle on life that no one else ever has.

Kev, in his sixties, has strong Irish characteristics. His bald head used to be covered by red hair. He has a beer belly and walks ten miles a day.

To Cal, the Vietnam War was about selling Coca-Cola and opening up McDonald's in Asia. He could give you the scoop on most politicians and tell you the latest on twenty different topics. He reads newspapers from end to end every morning. When he isn't sleeping, he's watching documentaries.

His apartment is in a building owned by the Feldmans in Canaryville, the mostly Irish enclave that borders Bridgeport on the south. The building was an old tavern.

His place is disorderly, you have no idea, but I'm more at home there than at any ritzy health club.

Initially, when my sons called him "Uncle Kevin," he turned away nervously, but he loves them just like he loves all of the little Feldman grandkids—"paycheck spenders" he calls them.

His dream is to win the lotto and stick a bomb under Father Flanagan's statue at Boys Town in Omaha. Father Flanagan said, "there's no such thing as a bad boy."

"That's 'cause he never lived in Canaryville," Kev quips.

One day, while walking, falling clumps of salt fell from a city truck and bounced around our feet. "Patti boy. Patti boy! Did you see that? I got hit in the head. This'll be worth big bucks. I was gonna write a book! It was gonna be a bestseller! Now I can't remember it. Get me an attorney!"

Kevin is just another guy with the Girondi Syndrome. He claims to dislike Muslims, Catholics, Mexicans, and Blacks, and would do anything for any of them.

He loved to hump, and Mr. Dever was an equal opportunity employer. He accepted all shapes, colors, and sizes. He never asked about religion or political preference. The ladies were mostly dark-skinned girls from the projects down on 43rd Street. Most humped for a few bucks in food stamps and/or whatever he had in the fridge. "Some came in from the cold just to get something warm in their stomachs," he claimed.

Once, he introduced me to a beautiful, milk-chocolate cokehead. A few weeks later, I asked him where I could find her.

"I ain't tellin' ya, and ain't introducing ya to any other girls!"

"Why, what did I do?" I asked innocently.

"First, you're a Catholic. What do you think those statues you talk to that never answer back *would* say if they ever did answer you?" he prodded. I smirked and he smirked.

He reentered. "Secondly, you got a lot of nerve! You gave that dame twenty bucks!" He looked to the side and turned back to me. "Now they all think that they're call girls!"

It didn't matter where Cal hid his money, he always forgot; and whether it was under the mattress or in a pair of pants hanging in the closet, once he went into the bathroom, his guests found it.

He had a lady friend with only a foot, having lost three limbs to frostbite. Kev was happy when she visited. "She can't roll me," he said.

Kevin is more divine than most any priest I have ever met. He loves and isn't looking for payback. In return, he's loved back.

"Every time someone told me they were going to pray for me I caught a cold or broke a bone," he says.

Growing up, Cal found the no meat Friday particularly humorous. "The bishop eats a ten-dollar lobster, and I go to hell for eating a twenty-five-cent hotdog."

"Dickhead, have you ever seen God? Can you tell me what he looks like? If he's so merciful, why doesn't he kill all the politicians?"

"I seen God clearer one night in a saloon on 41st Street than I ever saw in any church."

Once, he and friends stole a pony from the circus and drove it around in a convertible. They parked and let kids pet it.

One kid asked, "What kind of dog is that?"

The following morning, Cal covered the pony's eyes with a newspaper as a friend tugged the rope, coaxing the terrified creature down the three flights of stairs from Cal's apartment.

The apartment building owner, Ole Man Schroner, was cutting grass. He heard the clapping horse hooves and looked up. "Hey! Kevin, what are you doing?" he asked.

"I'm covering his eyes. He's afraid of heights."

Cal is one of my many doctors. Lord knows I need them all.

My house was a party house, whether I was present or not. I was away for the weekend. The house was full and Sylvia, a friend of Dirken, stopped by.

After a glass of wine she removed her thick eyeglasses—only fair that they all see her pretty eyes. Sylvia was in a very romantic mood and took turns getting romantic with everyone, including my visiting Italian cousin Alfonso. After his turn he said in his improving English, "She no drink."

It was raining heavily and Dirken had already left. There was no one left with a car to drive Sylvia home. She ended up walking out with Pasty, an unusual neighborhood guy.

Their stroll ended a block from the house at the police station. Sylvia was angry, maybe because she didn't get a ride home, or maybe because Alfonso complained. She made accusations of sexual assault. It was my house and both my brothers were present and looking at some serious charges.

Martin Robin discovered Pasty told the police that he would testify, so Pasty was soon handcuffed in a motel, close to the airport, in a bed that Fat Larry (Smith) laid in. Larry (5'11 and 250-plus) told him that if he opened his mouth without being asked, he'd kick his teeth in.

Pasty was quietly terrified. This was the first time he had been handcuffed by a man. His mind raced, filling in the squares. It was my house, I had lots of money, no high school diploma with relatives in Italy and many Italian friends. Larry's mother came from Sicily. It was obvious, he was a hostage of the mafia. There was no other possible explanation.

"Hey Pasty, wanna coke?" Larry asked.

Petrified, Pasty didn't answer.

"You want a coke or not, stunad [Italian dialect for idiot]?" Larry screamed.

"Yeah, that would be all right," Pasty whispered.

"The pop machine is by the bar in the motel lobby," Larry said.

Larry stared at Pasty before he uncuffed him.

"If you pull anything I'll baseball bat you," Larry said.

Pasty stared, petrified. "I won't pull anything, Larry. And I can't go nowhere, I'd get lost."

Larry handed Pasty two singles and quarters.

"Get a coke for yourself," Larry said.

"What about you, Larry?" Pasty asked sheepishly.

Larry looked at Pasty and smiled. "Yeah, you frickin' stunad, get me one, too."

"I'll be right back," Pasty replied. "You can count on me."

After five minutes, Larry grunted and rolled off the bed. He walked into the motel offices and spotted Pasty sitting with his back to the door, speaking to the motel security guard. Larry quietly approached.

"I'm a witness against a boss in the mafia. Who knows how many people he has murdered? Now they want to murder me because his men are being accused of raping a woman. I'll get some sort of award, I'm the only one with the courage . . ."

Larry put his arm around Pasty's shoulder, looked at the guard, and made circles around his own right ear. "Pasty, are you ready to come back now? It's time for you to take your medication," Larry said gingerly.

"Yeah, yeah, I'll come," Pasty peeped.

Larry winked at the security guard, who smiled at Larry and then at Pasty. "This nice man will protect you from the mafia," the security guard said patronizingly.

Pasty swallowed.

It was nerve-racking for everyone, except me. Things would work out.

In my cousin Alfonso's nightmare, he was in a US prison. His family, fearful of planes, took a boat to America. It disappeared at sea. He was desperate to leave, but his unquestionably insane cousin (U Carneveil) wouldn't give him his plane ticket. "U Carneveil" was directed at people who live life with a bit of insanity.

Ten of us were eating out. I argued with Alfonso about him refusing to eat onions. My phone rang. I quietly listened and hung up. "Hey, you frickin' ungrateful DP, you should eat everything on your plate, especially when someone else is paying for it," I said.

"You eat honions if you like dem. I don't eat honions," Alfonso replied insolently.

I screeched to a halt in front of the 35th Street police station, where Sylvia and Pasty had signed the complaint. Alfonso, seated behind me, watched as I got out of the car and grabbed his door handle.

"We'll see if you eat 'honions' in jail, you ungrateful DP!" I screamed.

Two policemen walked by, recognizing me as a friend of Station Commander Jackie Burke. I winked at them and everyone in the car (except Alfonso) realized that the coast was clear. Martin Robin had arranged a part-time job with the park district for Sylvia's cousin. As a result, Sylvia returned and told the police "the truth," that she made the story up to make her boyfriend jealous.

Everyone laughed, while my cousin and I had a tug-of-war to get the door open. Alfonso was sweating beads. Finally, I surrendered the handle and told him in Italian that we were in the clear.

He wanted to kill me. In time, he wouldn't be the only one.

Alfonso liked America, but missed home, and like all Italian males, at that time, had to serve a year in the military. Alfonso's mother, Zia Maria (my grandfather's niece who I called "Zia," or "aunt," out of respect for the bloodline and her age), was frantic about the situation.

Alfonso hated the military, went on a hunger strike, and ended up in the military hospital in Bari. While visiting, I took Alfonso's mother, Zia Maria, to see her son, my cousin, Alfonso.

We arrived at the huge sliding steel door in the early evening. Alfonso's mother knocked. A guard opened the trapdoor.

"I'd like to see my son," Zia Maria said (in Italian) with the authority of a five-star general.

"Who is your son, ma'am?" the guard asked nervously.

"My son is Alfonso Prato!" she yelled.

"Sorry, ma'am. I'll see," he meekly replied.

He returned. "May I see some identification?"

"I don't carry identification!" she snorted. "I never leave my house!"

"Ma'am, I need to see identification."

"Are you telling me that you'll stop a mother from seeing her sick son? One who needs his mother?" Zia Maria screamed.

Other mothers arrived and stared at the guard.

"Ma'am, I'm sorry, these are the rules," he said timidly.

"Stop all this nonsense, my son is ill!"

"Ma'am, don't you have anything to prove to me that you are your son's mother?" he asked, cowering.

She lifted her dress and pointed to her crotch. "He came from here! Damn it, he came from here! That's all the proof you need."

Other mothers joined in. "She's right, he came from there! Let her in!"

The soldier opened the gate and escorted us to my cousin; after all, this was Italy, and though Italians constantly complain about their plight, many of them have the greatest lifestyle on the planet.

As was tradition, Dirken Scott dressed as Santa on Christmas Eve. He walked up and down Halsted Street in the neighborhood and handed $100 bills of Bridgeport money to the homeless, drunks, and drug addicts. When he was finished, he dropped into Shinnick's for a nightcap, and sipped a beer close to the entrance in the packed bar. On the other end of the saloon, visitors (not neighborhood people) were drinking.

"Hey Santa, you got any toys for me?" yelled a visitor.

Dirken smiled and raised his beer in salute.

"Hey Santa, you don't need any padding!" the visitor laughed. "Santa's a fat ass!"

Dirken smiled and finished his beer.

"Goodnight and Merry Christmas, Dirken," Duke, the bartender said.

Dirken headed toward the bathroom and the group of visitors. He calmly socked the impolite patron in the forehead. Loudmouth went down like a ton of bricks.

Dirken put a hundred on the bar. "Duke, their drinks are on me."

Things with the Old Man were normal. He insisted that my friends buy his stolen merchandise, and that Paulie should not be within a block of him. "Keep the punk away from me," he told me. "I'll kill him." I never knew what Paulie did that riled up the Old Man, but the Old Man was mostly a mystery.

After George Murphy's hit, the Old Man rarely hung out with anyone, and continued to have scarce contact with the rest of his own family, who saw little reason to interact with him.

I started seeing Seana, a ballet dancer from the Joseph Holmes Dancing School. I'm not sure why, but on a cold December morning I drove to my father's mother's house with her. I had met my grandmother five or six times in my life. Maybe I subconsciously wanted to say that I had made it, even though their clan had never had anything to do with us.

While I was in the bathroom, Grandma Carmichael told Seana, "Stay away from him. He's a no-good hoodlum that will end up in jail."

I really didn't blame her. Where does a twenty-six-year-old high school dropout find all that cake? "Unlawful activity" was the only possible answer, to a normal person.

An evening with my father at a restaurant on 31st Street changed my life.

"Kid, I want to tell you somtin'. You're a good man, but I tink you should know," he said.

I watched inquisitively. It was hard for him to surprise me.

"I ain't your fadder, kid."

I paid the bill, and within a month I legally became Patrick Carmichael Girondi.

Chapter 11

Beginning Life as Girondi

L ouis Fellini, like myself, was an adopted son to "Penny Candy," Rino Fini.
Louis's uncle was the Acme Armored Truck Heist mastermind.

Louis liked trading, but also concentrated on a career robbing currency exchanges, small financial shops where people paid bills, made money orders, and wired funds. Things began well. He walked into a half dozen places with a gas can and walked out with bundles of cash.

The place on Archer was empty. He entered, gas can in hand. "I'm gonna pour gas in your window and light a match if you don't hand me all the cash in the drawers," Louis threatened.

Until the place on Archer, Louis had run into employees. The guy behind the counter at this one was the owner.

"Go ahead," he said, "I ain't giving you a dime."

The owner hit a button that locked the entrance door electronically, walked out, and pointed a pistol at Louis, who ran through the large glass window, still toting the empty gas can. A bullet passed through his hand and another lodged in his left thigh.

Emergency rooms call the police, when you arrive with gunshot wounds. Louis was nursed back to health on Penny Candy's couch, with supplies from Sipich's friendly neighborhood pharmacy.

The Robin Hood Association continued functioning as an anonymous organization, sending sick kids on vacations, helping people in financial need, etc. With Martin Robin and Dirken Scott as managers, the organization gained a reputation. Eventually, the Chicago newspapers wanted to know who was doing all the good deeds without taking a bow.

Reporters began snooping, and Dirken sneaked to get the request letters from the PO box. As always, he was a man who dedicated his time and energy to what he believed was right.

It was about 10 p.m. Some of the guys and I headed home from the Southwest Side. I drove down Central Avenue and spotted a small commercial passenger jet taking off from Midway Airport. I drove through the fence and watched the faces of the confused passengers as I hit the gas.

We lost the race, and the plane took off without event. The guys were in stitches as I pulled back onto Central.

"Pull over," Dirken said.

He walked home. For days he hardly said a word to me. I felt horribly. I didn't remember ever letting a friend down like that before.

I told Lorry Irving the story, adding, "I try to be a good, religious person."

Lorry took me by the arms and looked in my eyes. "You're not a religious person, you're a spiritual person," he said gently.

His warmth had me fighting back tears. "What's the difference?" I asked.

Lorry put on a smile that only he was capable of. "Religious people fear hell. Spiritual people have been there."

Having money has its advantages. Whenever I was charged with breaking the law, I just paid attorneys and I was never convicted of an infraction. It also gets attention from the ladies. In '86, three Italian girls from Melrose Park, a predominantly Italian suburb, came looking for me at the Valentine's Boys and Girls Club.

Back then, blue-collar Italians who tended to stay in what was left of the Italian enclaves in the major cities ran the Italian community in the US. That was until the nineties, when Dominick and his crew went to prison. The story was portrayed in the film *Casino*, and in fact, the girls hunting me down went to school with the daughters of the Spilotro brothers, who were killed at the end of the film.

From 1975 onward, more Americans moved to Italy than vice versa. Most of the Italians who did not move back home moved out of the Italian areas and/or died off. The communities withered, and those remaining are a painful shadow of a once-glorious people, a race all of their own, *the Italian American.*

Janet Davies, ABC reporter, arrived with her camera crew to my house. I was one of America's most eligible bachelors in *Playgirl* and a local star. It was my second interview with her. She set up in my backyard on the deck next to my pool. During the interview, she asked if I would ever get married. I told her that I'd like to marry a girl from my grandfather's town, Modugno.

Pamela, seventeen, and Lucrezia, sixteen, were sisters. Nicole, their friend, was also sixteen. They had read a Chicago newspaper article based on the Janet Davies interview. The sisters claimed that they were from Modugno.

The sisters had also read about Seana, the ballerina from Kalispell, Montana, in another newspaper article. This did not stop them from visiting Bridgeport often, where they met the Diceccas, Ferris, and other family members. We grew acquainted with one another.

Pamela and Lucrezia's mother was born and raised in Modugno. I showed up at her house on a Saturday morning. Her father worked at Zenith and came home every day for lunch. Today he'd find a surprise.

Pamela's mother looked at me and explained to her daughters in Italian, which I mostly understood, that their father would get angry and never allow Pamela to date anyone like me.

I was dressed normally, a tight T-shirt, tight jeans, and a body-molded leather jacket. The attire might not have said "mobster," but to most, it definitely reeked of something less than wholesome.

I draped my leg over the arm of the chair. Pamela pushed it off. I put it back up and stared at her. She put her finger in her mouth and nodded her head slightly, displaying her nervousness about the situation. Her mother began yelling about my leg when the door opened and the king of the castle walked in.

"Who is this man?" he said in perfectly cold English.

"My name is Patrick Girondi."

He looked at my leg. "Why are you here?"

I didn't believe that it could get colder than eighty below, but I was wrong.

I moved my leg off the arm of the chair and onto the floor. "Nice chair," I said.

He definitely knew I wasn't intimidated by his frosty tone, or his rigid behavior. His lips disappeared into his mustache. His wife and all three of his daughters' eyes were on him.

"I came to ask you sometin'." This time, I purposely left the H out.

"OK. Ask and leave."

I stood up and looked at him eye-to-eye. "I'd like to date your daughter, Pamela."

His dagger-sharp eyes were glacial. "No. That's impossible."

I grinned. "OK." I walked out. Pamela screeched and chased me to the car.

What the hell did I care what an arrogant little greaseball said? If I wanted to see someone, anyone, I'd do so.

Months later, I phoned and told Pamela's sister Lucrezia about Mr. Dicecca's lung cancer diagnosis. He didn't have a long time left. She began crying. To soothe her, I suggested we'd go to mass together on Sunday.

Lucrezia's father discovered our plans, beat her, and threw her out of the house.

At seventeen, Lucrezia could not wed without her parents' permission. Vince Berke, a political friend, organized a church wedding in Mexico City. Accompanied by Vince and his wife, we flew to Texas and drove across the border in a rent-a-car. Lucrezia, like me, seemed to be following a selected predestiny.

Lucrezia changed into her wedding dress in a gas station. We arrived at the church only to discover that the priest had fallen gravely ill and had been hospitalized.

The Berkes returned to Chicago, and Lucrezia and I went to Las Vegas, where Dominick and the 26th Street crew ran Caesar's Palace. I was on home turf and a nonpaying guest in the presidential suite.

Bridgeport Securities accounts were intermingled between traders. I required that any trader getting married must have a prenuptial agreement in place to protect the company. I was no exception to the rule. Lucrezia signed the prenuptial agreement, and using documents to make her twenty-three, we married at a wedding chapel.

I left phone messages and mailed letters, but her father refused to communicate with me or Lucrezia. So much for my dream of a warm Italian family.

Mr. Dicecca supported his peculiar sisters-in-law as if they were his own sisters, helped anyone who asked, and towered over life in his simplistic and loving ways. In September 1987, I was called to the hospital. The room was filled with the immediate Dicecca family and beeps and the sound of oxygen. Occasionally a nurse crept in with shots of morphine.

Mr. Dicecca borrowed grace and dignity from the exemplary life that he had lived, raised his hand to his face, blew a kiss, and was gone. It was the most beautiful thing I had ever seen.

Uncle Vince drove Lucrezia back and forth from Bridgeport to Mother Guerin Girls High School to finish her senior year. She didn't seem to be interested in school, but I wanted her to finish. Finishing what you start is a sign of character, and I wanted a woman of character.

In October 1987, the market crashed, leaving a trail of suicides and blood in its aftermath. Many attributed the crash to the same calls and puts that fed our lives and dreams.

I owed Harvey Wan a lot. I had learned how not to trade from him. Bridgeport made a fortune, and in two days Harvey was wiped out. He almost took the First National Bank of Chicago with him.

This is an excerpt from the *Chicago News*:

> "The trader responsible for more than $50 million of the recent losses of National Role Corp, options unit was identified in court papers as Harvey Wan, a nine-year veteran of the Chicago Board Options Exchange with a history of trading violations."

We, meanwhile, bought three New York Stock Exchange memberships, and Bridgeport became a respected force on the nation's trading floors.

These were some of the phrases I used in many interviews on trading:

> "A good trader needs to know the difference between greed and hunger."
>
> "Arrogance has no place in the trading place. It ensures certain death."
>
> "Socrates's phrase, 'The person who knows the most is he who admits that he knows nothing,' especially applies to traders."
>
> "It's psychology that causes one trader to make 2 transactions a day while another makes 20 in an hour. It's psychology that helps one see only opportunity while another sees only risk."
>
> "A successful trader is made of instinct, luck and controlled impulse."

Harvey retired to live with his family in San Francisco.

At seventeen, Lucrezia was still a minor in her hometown of Melrose Park (an Italian suburb outside of Chicago). Her father complained to the Melrose Park police about the situation. A Chicago Police car was dispatched to pick her up at our home at 3512 South Union. Lucrezia, according to her driver's license, was an official resident of Chicago. In Chicago, one was considered emancipated at sixteen.

Zio Saverio, Lucrezia's father's brother, arrived with his wife, Zia Caterina, from Altamura. Altamura is Lucrezia's father's town, roughly twenty miles from Modugno.

Lucrezia's mother was from Modugno. Lucrezia was raised in Altamura. If I had realized this before, there may not have been a wedding.

The four of us met in a small restaurant on North Avenue, near Lucrezia's parents' suburb. Her aunt made it clear that if Lucrezia wanted, she could return home with no questions asked.

She refused, turned eighteen, and again signed the marital agreement.

Lucrezia loved to shop. One day, she earned me sixty dollars by buying two pairs of shoes that were half-price.

"Why didn't you earn me $120 by buying four?" I asked.

Lucrezia found my friends to be a lucky bunch. They dropped off golf clubs that fell off trucks, and steaks that were given away because freezers had broken. Everyone in the neighborhood treated her like royalty.

Unfortunately, her father's vendetta endured.

We left for Italy in the spring of '88.

The plane touched down at the Palese Airport, just outside Modugno. The airport is in Bari, a city of 400,000, and the capital of the Apulia region. As Lucrezia and I stepped off the plane, I saw some of my relatives waving from the airport. We gathered our luggage, and two of my cousins took our bags and walked us to the car.

It was only April, but it was already in the eighties. We drove through the industrial area between the airport and Modugno. The harsh, unique smell of smashed olives (*sansa*) came from the olive oil mills, or *frantoi*.

A few months prior, I had wired money to my Zia Maria to buy a home for me in Cassano, a town of twenty thousand in the hills between Modugno and Altamura.

Lucrezia gazed out the window of the old car and seemed less than impressed.

Before going to Cassano, we ate at my Zio Cosimo's home. Everyone was warm, though there were a few dissatisfied relatives who hoped I might have married someone closer to the family: a commarra (commarra is the feminine version of compare) or even a second or third cousin.

We ate and were accompanied by many of my relatives to our home in Cassano. My people left before midnight. I was looking to get to bed and to business. Lucrezia was concerned with other things.

"I didn't come to Italy to wait on people," she said as she walked up the stairs to the night part of the home.

I pretended to ignore her. I wanted to take care of business, and knew that bickering would eliminate any possibility of that.

"I said that I didn't come to Italy to wait on your relatives and I know you heard me," she said as she walked into the bathroom.

"Don't worry. They won't be here every day," I said.

"You don't know these people like I do. As long as there is free food and a good time, they'll be here every day and night." She took her toothpaste out of her bag of toiletries.

"Come on, let's not fight," I said. "It's our first night together in Italy. Let's enjoy it."

"I have my period," she said.

We were planning to have our church wedding in June, and in fact things pretty much went how they started. Still, she was my wife, and someone like myself would marry once in a lifetime.

She was saddened that her family still refused to speak with her. Most evenings, she whimpered before falling asleep.

We went around, looking at different halls and churches. One day we went to Our Lady of Grace Church in Cassano. That evening, her mother called, and they spoke for the first time in months. We scheduled our wedding mass to be held at that church.

One day, Lucrezia's three uncles, Giovanni, Dionisio, and Saverio, invited me to go mushroom hunting in the Murgia. The Murgia is an empty, vast land that occupies hundreds of square miles in Puglia. Altamura is at the Murgia's northern crest. The area has rolling hills with millions of rocks growing out of them. In the grassy patches between the boulders grow the delicious Cardoncelli mushrooms.

The Murgia was delightful for mushroom hunting, and a great place for a murder. All they'd have to do was ditch my car. "The crazy American must have gone back to America." I put my chances of making it back at 50 percent.

We made it home with five kilos of mushrooms, and I was relieved when they did not ask me to park in the garage.

Our wedding reception was held at Hotel L'Olmo (The Elm), which was owned by Don Enrico Cramarosso. Enrico was also known as One Arm Rico. Some of Lucrezia's family attended, but most did not. Her father had made it clear what he thought of the union.

Don Enrico was built like Jabba the Hutt from *Star Wars*, and had only one arm indeed. Some said he lost it to disease; others said that it had been stabbed, burned, and or shot off. He was the local boss, who made a fortune and a reputation dealing in cigarettes, booze, art, and anything and everything else. He exerted incredible influence over all of Italy and the Italian community in the US. Hotel L'Olmo had its own zoo with live panthers, lions, an elephant, and a giraffe.

In time, Don Enrico consulted with me about investments and certain delicate situations involving US customs and US law. I gained his confidence and that of his brother Egidio, "Il Nero." I became their friend and American consultant.

Italy was heaven to me. It was like going back to Little Italy on the South Side of Chicago. Lucrezia was less impressed. She terribly missed the US, particularly the shopping malls.

We left for our honeymoon in July, visiting Rome, Paris, and London. We didn't return to Cassano until late fall.

I missed my friends and family in the US, and was happy to get back to Chicago. Lucrezia was ecstatic. Things with her immediate family were still tense, but on Saturdays and Sundays she was at the malls.

My dream of giving opportunities became a reality for less than 50 percent of those who passed through Bridgeport's doors, but everyone who entered got a shot. I spent hours with recruits and their families, teaching them, encouraging them, and reminding them about the importance of trading and money.

More times than not, it was the trader who saw the light. "Pat," they'd say, "I just can't do this anymore. I'm losing too much of your money." They carried with them memories of a group of guys who loved and helped one another.

Over the years, my brother Paulie was arrested repeatedly and booted out of three different high schools. Mikey Fontana graduated from De La Salle.

In 1989, Joe Feldman took the position in front of the Bridgeport Securities *Gang* (his grandfather, Sid, was the one who recruited me for Valentine's Boys Club). The nation was in the grip of a horrendous drought. We entered the commodity markets, soybeans in particular.

The Milton Group hired educated people from the wealthy North Shore to become their traders. William Milton was the founder, owner, and head trader. His grandfather had been a cornerstone of the exchange. Until recently, William Milton's group had run the soybean options pit, but the brutal price swings caused by the drought, which had attracted us, didn't suit the Milton Group style of trading.

The commodities opened at 9:30 a.m. and finished at 1:15 p.m. There were a few new regulations, but to me, trading was like riding a bike. In the middle of the soybean pit, I absorbed the looks of curiosity and animosity that all new traders get. I was a veteran. All of these antics were child's play for me.

During the noontime lull, a small, mustached Dent Financial Fund broker named O'Halloran entered. Leonard Dent was riding high. His fund was on every big commodity move. His brokers instilled awe and fear in traders who were afraid to be on the other side of a "Dent trade."

Everyone whispered as O'Halloran raised his hands. I smiled at the spectacle, which conjured the image of Moses dividing the Red Sea.

"August twelve-dollar calls!" O'Halloran screamed, as if he were a lion tamer with a whip.

A few traders weakly responded, "Two and a half bid and three and a half offer."

"I'll sell two thousand at three and a half! At three! I'll sell two thousand at two and a half!" O'Halloran's stare was intimidating, and most looked away.

"You idiots said that you were two and a half bid!" he screamed as an arrogant victor would.

A trader in the back quipped, "I'll buy five at two and a half."

"I'm not selling a five lot! I want to sell two thousand! I'll sell them at two! I'll sell them at one and a half!"

"Buy 'em," I said.

All eyes darted and fixed on me; it would be fun watching the new guy get bludgeoned. If that happened, they'd feel a bit better about their own situation. The weak often seek weakness to gain strength.

"That's a Leonard Dent order!" someone yelled.

"That's the end of the new guy," another added.

O'Halloran, somewhat entertained, sized me up. "How many do you want?" O'Halloran screamed more than asked.

"How many do you want to sell?" I asked calmly.

"You heard me! I want to sell two thousand!" he shouted, turning beet red.

It was idiotic, selling a cheap option with that much time left, with the present wild swings and lack of liquidity. He was pushing them down to buy them.

"I'll buy 'em," I said.

"I'll sell you, I'll sell, I'll sell you—you—two thousand," he stuttered.

We scribbled on our trading cards. He tripped as he ran out of the pit. The rest of the spectators gawked at the incredible spectacle; a Dent broker had been flustered by the new guy.

Moments later, O'Halloran was back. Surprise. "August twelves, I'll pay one and three-quarters!" he screamed.

The table was turned. A few laughed and teased him as a drop of sweat rolled off his funny, red mustache. "I'll pay two! I'll pay two for two thousand!" he screamed, not looking at the only guy who had them to sell—me.

All eyes were immobile and glued. "If I sold them back at three and a half, I made a $200,000 profit."

People were waved in from the other pits. Phone clerks came out of their cubby holes to watch the oppressor squirm.

"Hey, O'Halloran. I'll sell you two thousand at two and a half," I said. I knew I could easily have gotten him to pay three and a half or even four.

"Sold," O'Halloran said. "I'll buy two thousand at two and a half" (at the Board of Trade, you say "sold" whether you buy or sell—silly, but true).

He nodded gratefully. Each cent represented fifty dollars; two thousand cents was $100,000, a small loss for a firm that was making hundreds of millions.

I was instantly a celebrity, with a noticeable, obvious defect; I lacked "killer instinct." I could have gotten three and a half or even four or five. I walked away from the lion's share of the meat.

Bridgeport settled in, and our guys especially liked the hours, 9:30 a.m. to 1:15 p.m., giving us more time to make prank phone calls.

Roger Nimitz was a small trader who wrote books about options. *Those with talent trade, the others teach.* Fingernails against a blackboard were more pleasant than his voice. "I'll sell the August thirteen straddle at 130!" he shouted (selling the straddle meant selling both the call and put of the same strike price and month).

It was not William Milton's day. His clearing firm (bank) told him to put two million in his account or cut his position in half. In the middle of a divorce, he had less liquidity than patience. He needed to buy the thirteen straddle a thousand times, or the clearing firm would buy it for him. Clearing firms were not traders. When they liquidated positions, they did so quickly, without much consideration for price. It could wipe William Milton out.

I was about to ask Roger to stop spitting and yelling in my ear, when I caught the fury in Milton's eyes. William Milton rushed Nimitz. "I bought a thousand straddles at 130!" (130 cents is $6,500, times a thousand is $6.5 million, just to give you an idea).

Paralyzed, Roger turned white.

"Goddamnit, I bought a thousand at 130!" Milton screamed.

If a trader made an offer or bid and didn't put a number on it, as Nimitz had done, the person who said "sold" decided the quantity.

"I'll sell you ten," Roger murmured.

"Floor Officials! I bought one thousand!" Milton screamed as he began assailing Roger physically. "I bought a thousand! I bought a thousand! You didn't put a number on it!" Milton screamed and shoved him.

Roger felt his knees buckle. He had $48,000 in his account, and couldn't afford to sell more than twenty straddles.

I grabbed Milton as he grabbed Roger. "You don't want them. The straddle is going to collapse," I whispered.

Milton glared at me.

"I'll sell you a thousand at 129, but you don't want them."

The difference between a thousand at 129 or 130, was $50,000. I was offering Milton a $50,000 gift.

Floor officials arrived, and William Milton quietly walked out of the pit without making a transaction. Paramedics were called for Roger, who believed he was having a heart attack.

Two hours later, William Milton returned and bought the straddle for 110. My advice saved him a million dollars. Had I sold it to him, I would have made $950,000.

In those wild years, Bridgeport traders not only survived but prospered as modern-day gladiators. "Live and let live" was our modus operandi; one morning, I ate an error for $250,000, and told the broker to make a donation to the Valentine's Boys and Girls Club. The error would've cost him $125,000. Exchange rules said that we should have split. How could I, we, do that? The broker would have been wiped out, his family destroyed.

ꞅ

The commodity pits rarely attracted the attention of small investors or the federal government. The NYSE and NASDAQ were where the spotlight was hot. That would soon change.

On January 19, 1989, the *Chicago News* revealed that the government was investigating the Chicago Exchanges. Chicago Board of Trade Chairman Karsten Mahlmann refuted the report. His statement, when questioned, was that "He had and has no knowledge of surveillance activities of any nature being conducted on the trading floors or any other Board of Trade location."

The government would not comment on any investigation.

The floors were rumor mills. In fact, when there were trading lulls, in the midst of the thousands of people on the floor, the main topics were sex, sports, the latest rumors, and drugs—in that order. You could hear most anything. No one really paid much attention to the new rumbling about a government investigation.

Settling in, the Bridgeport group treated the pit as a brotherhood. Most everyone had a nickname: a guy who wore a toupee was Wiggy; Billy was the Bearded Lady; John was Hair Helmet; and Mark was Mr. Peabody.

Marianne, the only female trader in the pit, tapped out and was liquidating her position. She didn't make her situation public, but I got wind of it. Someone noticed ridiculous prices going up on the quote board.

"I'd sell them two cents lower!" screamed a trader.

"I'd buy them a nickel higher!" screamed another trader.

"Call floor officials!" screamed one of the larger traders outside our group.

I whispered in his ear. "I'm putting those prices up, helping a friend."

Everyone quieted as I sold Marianne contracts under the bid and bought contracts over the offer, making sure she'd have something left in her account to begin life outside the pits.

Man's laws are optional. God's are mandatory.

In September, I received a peculiar call from a person who, at that time, was more of an acquaintance than a friend. The federal investigation had not been a mere rumor. The soybean market was at the center of the government's attention, and the noose was closing quickly.

I was in our office. I hung the phone up and stared at the wall. The government needed big fish to keep the public angry and the politicians supportive. I saw prison bars and court scenes. I read the headlines: "Oprah Rags to Riches Guest is Really a Crook." "One of America's Past Most Eligible Bachelors is Also an American Thief."

I knew all too well about government damage, often to completely innocent people. Various studies estimate that in the United States, between 2.3 and 5 percent of *all* prisoners are innocent. This means that there are likely over 100,000 completely guiltless people in our prisons. A study looking at 1970s and 1980s convictions in Virginia, matching them to later DNA analyses, estimated wrongful conviction at 11.6 percent. A 2014 study published in *Proceedings of the National Academy of Sciences* made a conservative estimate that 4.1 percent of inmates awaiting execution on death row in the United States are innocent, and that at least 340 innocent people have been executed since 1973.

I thought hard. My initials, or one of my traders' initials, were on every large order in the soybean pit. Bridgeport was also a force in wheat and corn. With the government's power and money, the FBI could convict Mother Teresa for prostitution. I certainly wasn't Mother Teresa.

I told everyone to go home. I needed to make a call.

I grabbed the phone and called John, my Greek travel agent. I didn't even tell Lucrezia to pack until an hour before we needed to leave for the airport, the very next day.

Within twenty-four hours, the floor was in panic mode. The rumors had been true. Everyone was desperate to know if they would fall into the government gauntlet.

Within weeks, headlines all over the country were filled with the new hottest story.

A headline in the *NY Times*: "46 Commodities Traders Indicted after a 2-year FBI Sting;" *LA Times*: "Massive Fraud Uncovered at the Chicago Board of Trade;" *Chicago News*: "Indictments Name 46 Traders and How FBI Worked Trader Scheme."

Puglia is beautiful in the fall or any season, especially when the FBI has infiltrated your business. Dirken and the rest of the crew were extremely disappointed. My church wedding was just a year prior. Now it appeared that I might be in Italy indefinitely.

Chapter 12

Rules Can Be Broken in Chicago or Lausanne

The plane landed at what today is the Karol Wojtyla Aeroporto in Bari (named after Pope John Paul II).

Despite stinging letters from Lucrezia's father, demanding that we not be welcomed, Lucrezia's immediate family was replaced by her Altamuran aunts, uncles, and cousins. I fit in like a puzzle piece. Zia Chiara and Zio Mimmo, the aunt and uncle Lucrezia had grown up with, became her full-time Italian parents.

For now, Italy was home, and no longer a vacation rendezvous. My Italian family from Modugno, made up mostly of third to fifth-generation cousins, embraced me and I, them.

We drove through Modugno, my grandparents' town, toward Altamura. Both towns are in the province of Bari, and residents are considered Altamurani or Modugnesi. Both are also considered Baresi and finally Pugliesi because Bari is in the state of Puglia.

I wanted my wife to be comfortable. We set up house in Altamura.

Dirken filled me in daily. In the following weeks, the government revealed the depth of the federal commodities probe. Each day, Chicago traders woke to screaming newspaper headlines, threats of criminal charges, and promises of stricter rules to regulate trading abuses.

Nothing scared them more than the knowledge that our private enclave had been infiltrated by a bunch of government snitches who are themselves above the law.

Gary Mason, Bridgeport's broker in the bean future pit, was an honest, likable guy with a wife and two kids. We listed him as an employee, to get his family on the Bridgeport Group insurance plan for cheaper coverage.

In the middle of the night, the FBI visited his home.

"You'll do hard time. Your wife will divorce you. Your kids will grow up without a father. We know that you love them," the kind, public servants concluded as Gary's wife and their six- and eight-year-old sons wept.

Their message: give us the big fish or suffer the consequences. If you don't have any, make them up.

The FBI visited Bridgeport's office. Dirken politely answered none of their questions. He did tell them, per my instructions, that I would be in the following week.

Dirken, sucking on a stick, wearing a fishing cap, had a fishing pole in his hand. Two Bridgeport traders, Ronnie (Jim Bob Hailey's brother) and Chris (Dennis O'Rourke's brother), were hanging out the window.

"Now!" Chris yelled.

Dirken dropped the line. They laughed.

"You scared the shit out of her!" Ronnie said.

While Dirken reeled the fish up, FBI agents entered the office.

"Where's Girondi?"

Dirken began slowly removing the stick, attached to a large lollipop in his mouth.

"What are you doing?" The second agent asked.

"Taking the lollipop out of my mouth," Dirken answered.

"I'm talking about over there." He pointed to the window.

"We're fishing," Dirken said, answering an obvious question.

"Where's Girondi?" the first agent asked more firmly.

"He'll be here next week," Dirken said.

Chris turned. "Oh my God! Here comes chubby out of Boni Vino's."

"Tell me when," Dirken said.

"You said that last week." The 'G' man said seriously, while unsuccessfully trying to stare into Dirken's eyes who had already turned toward the window.

"This is serious," the second agent growled.

"Now!" Chris hooted.

Dirken dropped the line. "Fishing is a serious sport," Dirken responded.

"Hey. We're the FBI," the agent said.

On Van Buren, the overweight copper jumped and menacingly looked up at the rubber fish that waved over his head.

"I know, you told us it was serious last week," Dirken said serenely as he reeled the purple fish up.

"You won't be doing a lot of fishing in jail," the first agent said.

"Where is he?" the second agent asked.

"I think he's somewhere in Europe. They're seven or eight hours ahead or behind, but he did say that he was getting on a plane Thursday. It might be Wednesday or Friday here," Dirken said.

"Do you have a number where we can reach him?" the first agent asked.

Dirken tightened the line around the fish's tail. "I don't. I'll try to get a number if he doesn't make it in."

Dirken turned to fish, and the agents disappeared.

"Morons," Ronnie said.

"They're screwing Gary Mason. Some say he's going to cop a plea," Chris said.

"You live till you die," Dirken said.

The FBI considered extradition, but weren't even sure where I was. They visited my mother and others who knew me. Strangely enough, they couldn't find anyone who wanted to help snare Chicago's bad boy . . . most of my friends and family had some experience with government authorities. None were shaken, and many were proud to send the oppressors on wild-goose chases. *I'm true to my friends, not to my word.*

The FBI returned to our offices the following Friday. They flashed a paper that they said was a warrant—maybe it was. Dirken told them to take what they wanted and offered the name of Bridgeport's accountant.

At one time, the US floors were bastions of true capitalism, with many rags-to-riches stories, like my own. But Goldman Sachs, J. P. Morgan, and Bank of America brought this to an end. They took the exchanges away from penny capitalists and gave it to the people who own the FBI—the corporations (or as I call them, corruptorations).

In fact, the US attorney for the northern district of Illinois claims to have launched the investigation in 1986, following complaints to federal authorities by Archer-Daniels-Midland Co., about the way its orders were being handled in the Board of Trade's soybean pit.

Archer-Daniels-Midland, today a thirty-billion-dollar conglomerate, used government intervention to extend their influence over the commodities markets. The FBI was the exact same tool they used to give Las Vegas to the real criminals, the corruptorations.

In the neighborhoods of the US, the FBI was used mercilessly to stop those horrible thugs who were selling parlay cards, running illegal lottos, illegal gambling, and prostitution. The claim was that gambling ruins families, and prostitution—oh, prostitution!—is a horrible scourge that abuses women.

Today, lotteries are legal in every US state.

"If a man shows up on Christmas without a gift, he ain't getting any Christmas pie," my friend in the back of the Old Man's van told me years prior.

As soon as I arrived in Italy, I set up a relationship with Italian and Swiss banks. Not yet under an official investigation, I moved funds out of the US while I still could.

Not crazy about uncertainty or inactivity, I began trading from Fortissa Options and Futures in Lausanne, Switzerland. We hired linguists in Chicago to teach our soon-to-be European traders Italian and French (this took guts; most could hardly speak English).

Ludwig Bigi owned Fortissa. Fortissa was one of the founding members of the first electronic options exchange in the world, the Swiss Options and Futures Exchange. Ludwig was also the chairman of the Swiss Options and Futures Association. His wife and close friends called him Tod (you figure it out).

Bridgeport traders transacted business from Fortissa's offices in Lausanne, a city in the French-speaking Canton of Vaud. They slept at the Bigi villa in Vufflens Chateau, a fifteen-minute drive or half-hour train ride from the offices. The villa had a built-in swimming pool and spectacular view of Lake Geneva (the French called it Lac Leman). We had use of their large attic, and Bigi, his wife, and their three children, were warm hosts.

Bigi's father had been a Swiss diplomat, and Ludwig grew up in Africa, Europe, and South America. He spoke seven languages fluently, and expressed strong opinions in all of them.

The astronomical fees were a challenge. Bridgeport was often paying tens of thousands in fees and commissions each week. Despite the expense, Bridgeport's Swiss operation was profitable.

Computers were changing the world rapidly. I was sadly confident that the electronic markets would eventually eliminate floor trading. We made another deal with Jon Von Payton, a Swiss attorney from Zurich, to trade the Deutsche Termin Borse (German Exchange) from his RWG company offices in Frankfurt, Germany. We rented a townhouse in Frankfurt, hosting our Chicago traders and Paul and Neil, trading cousins from Birmingham, England. We were quickly profitable as well in Germany.

I was sick with grief, thinking of the torture that trader and broker families were going through during the witch hunt in Chicago.

The FBI's whole case seemed to be based on a minor trading infraction that they coined "Curb Trading." A floor broker was obligated to fulfill any order timestamped before 1:15 p.m. Particularly on busy days, many orders arrived after the closing bell. The broker had to trade the order into his or her "error account," along with the risks that accompanied carrying positions. The beans often swung wildly overnight. If a floor broker went home with twenty bought or sold contracts, his year could be wiped out the following morning.

To help out, guys like me would use the closing price and take the contracts into our own position. There was no fleecing anyone. Customers were satisfied, and the broker's risk became the trader's risk.

The FBI claimed that the customer did not get the benefit of the competitive "open outcry" market. Since many customers were out of state, it was a federal crime.

It was later understood that government rats had been on the floor for years. The trading pits were jam packed with thousands of traders, brokers, and clerks. It was easy for the FBI to infiltrate them, like a crud bringing a bomb to Times Square.

I comprehend that some may not be crazy about me calling these people "rats." They enticed others to commit crimes, and then snitched on them for committing the crimes they had enticed them into committing. Also, with the help of the G (government), these were the same people who violated federal law by lying about their names, education, employment, banking, and financial information to buy memberships at the exchanges and become members of said exchanges. Instead of going to prison for breaking the law, they got promotions. Let me know if you think of a better name for them.

FBI agents Reardon and Hopkins bought their own seats (taxpayers really bought them), each costing in excess of $300,000. Reardon entered the soybean futures pit. Hopkins went to the treasury bonds—the world's most heavily traded financial instrument.

Meanwhile, two bearded agents, calling themselves Stuart Martin and Jefferson Harding, had infiltrated the Standard & Poor's 500 stock index futures, claiming to work for a company called Marlin International Trading. These guys really spent your money. They had luxurious suites, hand-carved marlin statues, hand-painted marlin logos, and statues of two golden marlins at the office entrance.

The rats entertained, socialized, and secretly recorded conversations using hidden tape recorders and wireless microphones disguised as pens and rings.

The FBI worked hand in hand with the press to make villains out of some really nice people; that's not to say that there aren't any Benjamin Tisches out there. The problem is, the Benjamins follow the rules to the letter. Think of the wonderful doctor who charges $500 a visit; he's legit, too.

Gary Mason did not cooperate with the FBI. Mason claimed that not one cent came to him as a result of any rule infraction or wrongdoing, for which he was convicted. The government could not prove otherwise. In fact, the investigation discovered that curb trading was a common practice and condoned by CBOT officials.

Still, trading after the bell was an infraction. Gary lost his job, family, reputation, and did four and a half years in a federal penitentiary. His wife divorced him and remarried before he was released. Today he sells insurance. I won't dare put the name of the company in the book. The G would likely look him up.

In Altamura, Lucrezia was pregnant with our first child. As crazy, mischievous, and trying as I may have been, there was no way that the Lord would deny me a male for my firstborn.

Gathering it all in, sometimes my own thoughts numbed me.

It was all so incredible. My son would have my grandfather's name. There would be another Santino Girondi born in the Bari province of Puglia, where my grandfather was born. The fact that I made my name Girondi made the situation and my conviction that much more extreme.

I would be a good father, wouldn't I?

We moved in with Zia Caterina and Zio Saverio, my father-in-law's brother and sister-in-law. They were the couple who had previously flown to Chicago to make peace between my in-laws and us. Their home was larger than Zia Chiara and Zio Mimmo's, the aunt and uncle who had raised Lucrezia. Caterina and Saverio had five children. I loved them all.

On March 29th, the very pregnant Lucrezia went for a final checkup. She was eight months pregnant. Everything was fine, and the baby boy would be born at the end of April. I had the right to follow Italian tradition, naming the first male child after my father, or, in my situation, my grandfather.

Easter was in April. The doctor knew that Lucrezia loathed the name Santino. "You could also follow another tradition, naming your children after the saint's day on which they are born. Your son will be born during Easter. Name your son Pasquale," he said ("Pasqua" is Easter; "Pasquale" is the boy's form).

Lucrezia wished she had thought of the idea. I wished the doctor would have minded his own business.

My son was born two days later and almost a month ahead of schedule, on March 31, the date that Grandpa had died, twenty miles from Grandpa's town. My son welded the past to the present, never again to be severed. Santino.

Shortly after Santino's birth, Lucrezia's father spoke to her by phone. It was their first communication in almost three years. Lucrezia was twenty.

I wanted another five children in quick order. Lucrezia was having second thoughts about living and raising children in Altamura, a town of 50,000 (71,000 today), twenty-five miles from Bari, a city of under a half-million inhabitants. She felt that she had left the backward country as a child only to marry it as a young woman.

Traveling turned me into an avid reader, sometimes getting through three or four books a week. I was frequently interviewed as a financial expert/celebrity. In Paris, on a radio show, I said, "Napoleon Bonaparte is my favorite Italian." The interviewer seemed physically disturbed. I continued, "He was born to two Italian parents, one from Rome and the other from Tuscany. His first language was Italian, and Corsica was not yet in French hands." Despite his reputation, Napoleon was an incredible liberator and is still my favorite Italian (the victors write history).

More and more, the markets were becoming video games. On the European exchanges where we traded, huge transactions went up at the click of a button. Bridgeport began calling member banks for trades, and before long we were also phone trading. One, two, three, and voila. Bridgeport's profits skyrocketed. As a consequence, someone else's nosedived. Dresdner and Deutsche Banks were the first banks to prohibit dealing with us. Soon, we were blackballed in all of Germany.

Cut off from phone trading, we retaliated in other ways. "Hey Adolf. Give me a quote in the Volkswagen 360-380 November."

"My name is not Adolf; I think that you are trying to anger me."

I visited a spa in Baden-Baden, Germany, with heated swimming canals. It was ten below, and you swam outside in eighty-degree water. I went to the second floor, where garments were prohibited.

Walking with a towel around my waist, I spotted the prettiest redhead I had ever seen. I mean, I usually don't lean toward redheads, but I was in love. I followed her into the sauna.

When I rose to follow her out, a man dressed in white entered. He spoke in German and wasn't happy. After a bit of confusion, he ripped my towel off, exposing my briefs. He wanted me to remove my undergarment and though at attention, I refused to follow his order.

Imagine getting thrown out of a place for not exposing yourself.

It wasn't always easy for American traders to assimilate. Russell Dicecca, Johnny Dicecca's cousin, had boxed for our Valentine Boxing Club. He now traded in Switzerland. He left the Lausanne office starving, and walked into the only restaurant in Vufflens Chateau.

A cute, dark-haired, English-speaking girl greeted him. Russell ordered fondue with potatoes. Fondue is a hot bowl of melted cheese—the cheeses and liquors vary depending on where you are in Switzerland.

The waitress disappeared behind a small, wooden door. Other than an elderly man sipping kirsch (a cherry liquor) at the bar, the restaurant was empty. The waitress returned, her face unsettling. Russell prepared for the worse, suspecting that they had run out of fondue.

"Sir, I'm sorry, there is no fondue with potatoes," she said.

"You ain't got no potatoes?" Russell asked.

"Oh yes, we have potatoes."

"You ain't got no fondue?"

"Oh yes sir, we always have fondue."

"Well den, what's the problem?"

Russell didn't like to be played with. His hunger blunted his patience.

The girl moved her weight from one leg to the other. "Sir, the chef will not serve fondue with potatoes in it," she responded courteously.

Russell was baffled. "Well, what do you mean? He don't got no potatoes?"

"No, I mean yes, we got—have—potatoes."

"You said you got fondue. What's d' problem?"

"He will not make fondue with potatoes in it. He says that it is sacrilegious."

"I'm paying. Tell him I want potatoes in it."

The girl went to the kitchen and returned. "I'm sorry, sir, the chef refuses," she said, almost whispering.

"I'm the one that will eat it!"

The owner appeared, in a white chef hat and a black waxed moustache. The girl translated. "The chef would like to know what your problem is?" she asked.

Russell wasn't sure whom to speak to. He looked at the owner, then at the girl. "Tell him that I want fondue with potatoes."

The girl translated. The chef's patience was waning. There were too many foreigners in Switzerland, and now an American was going to tell him how to make fondue. He spoke quickly and forcefully.

"The chef," the girl said softly, "says that he did not ask you to come to his restaurant. And if you want to eat dinner here, you must eat the food the way he prepares it."

Tempted to sock the chef, Russell instead stared at the girl. "Ask him if he ever heard of customer satisfaction?"

The girl translated, and the chef replied.

"The chef wants to know if you ever heard of a free country?"

The owner waited until she finished her translation, and then disappeared through the kitchen door.

"Sir, is there something else that you might like?" the girl asked meekly.

Russell glanced out the window and then back at the waitress.

"I'd like a fondue and an order of pommes frites (fried potatoes)."

A quarter of an hour later, the girl brought a bowl of fondue. After a few minutes, she noticed that Russell still hadn't touched his food.

"Your fondue will get cold, sir," she said politely.

"I'm waiting for my pommes frites," Russell responded wryly.

"The chef told me that I couldn't give you your pommes frites until you finished your fondue," she softly replied.

Trading in Lausanne for over a year, Bucky called me in Altamura.

"Bucky, what's going on? How are the hookers treatin' you?"

"They want 200 francs for lookin' at your crotch. Forget about that. I gotta get home."

"What's wrong?"

"I have a toothache."

"They got dentists in Switzerland," I responded.

"Swiss dentists took out gold fillings for the Nazis. They ain't goin' in my mouth," he replied.

It was Christmas, and a trip home was three grand, so he went to a Swiss dentist. After a few weeks, we spoke again. "All fixed up with the dentist, Buck?" I asked.

"Yeah, all fixed up. Thieves," Bucky slithered. "I told you."

"What'd they do, steal one of your gold fillings?"

"Always kidding! I go the first time and he charges me 180 francs, says he's got to do a pipe or something. What are they, frickin' plumbers?"

"Canal, Buck, not a pipe, root canal," I interjected in a low tone.

"Whatever, I go back after ten days and he gets me for another 180. If I was in the neighborhood, Arnstein would've yanked it for twenty-five bucks . . . weasels."

Conversations with Bucky were always interesting and always urgent.

"Hey Buck, what's up?" another one started.

"I'll tell you what's up. You got to tell the Bigis I ain't a fucking rabbit!"

"Is there any particular reason I need to do that, Buck?"

"Yeah! They go into the yard, pick weeds, and feed them to me!"

"Do they eat the weeds as well?" I asked.

"Yeah! But they pick the shit out of the backyard."

"They call that a garden," I said calmly.

"Yeah, but these green and purple mixed weeds!"

"That's called a salad, Buck."

Chapter 13

Italy Fits and Destroys

Initially, I attempted to convince Lucrezia to attend mass with Santino and me. She reminded me that I didn't always make mass in the US. I didn't get her point, quite frankly. I was now a father, she was now a mother, and a spiritual foundation is essential for any child.

It wasn't so obvious to her. She considered mass to be old-fashioned, and thought I was out of touch. On Sundays, Lucrezia slept.

I took Santino to the children's mass at La Trinità on the border of the old city of Altamura. As I stood there with my son, it reminded me of mass at Santa Lucia with my two brothers, Mikey and Paulie. At mass, I was now telling the Lord and all my new paisans that this was my son.

During the children's mass, two women kept an eye on the young flock for pastor Don Ciccio. Whispering, fidgeting, or any sort of misbehavior was quickly addressed.

One Sunday, we sat behind a tiny, eighty-year-old woman. Each time the boy in front of her moved, she had to shift to see the altar. Finally, she stepped up onto the kneeler, grabbed him by the hair, and slapped his ears.

One of the guards, Vincenza, observed and nodded approvingly.

Concentrating on volatile stocks, Bridgeport's European profit rocketed. At the end of the year, I attempted to convert Swiss Francs into Italian lire. Credit Suisse, Fortissa's bank, informed me that all Fortissa accounts, including mine, were frozen.

On further investigation, I learned that Laro, a Fortissa trader, had lost a fortune and left for Australia. A half-million dollars of Bridgeport money was gone, Fortissa employees hadn't been paid in months, and the firm was 3,000,000 Swiss francs in debt.

Mr. Bigi had no personal wealth. His villa was rented. The only way to recover my losses was to take the firm over; doing so would also help protect Mr. Bigi from embarrassment and legal trouble.

Francois, Credit Suisse's attorney, claimed that the bank's position was to help its client, me, recover my funds. I believed him, and also knew that Credit Suisse didn't like newspaper articles, especially since International newspapers were writing about Nazi money held in Swiss banks that belonged to Jewish families. I began calling the shots, and Mr. Bigi wandered the offices as a beleaguered ship captain.

An attorney took fees for a name search, and Fortissa became Bridgeport SA. Lord Bridport of Geneva sued anyway. I laughed it off and faxed the lord a page of the Chicago White Pages showing dozens of Betty's Beauty Shops. I told him I was no fan of Switzerland and that I'd sell him the company for 3,000,000 Swiss francs. He could then name it whatever he liked. He was apparently angered by my offer. I told him I'd accept 2.8 million.

In Switzerland, both defendant and plaintiff are required to send funds covering court costs and the other party's attorney fees ahead of the court date, in case one loses. Our attorney asked for a 50,000-Swiss-franc court check. I decided that BPT Trading was a perfect name.

Sebastiano Morici, a Swiss trader, became my friend and right-hand man. Tough nights were followed by focused days. In the first year, we breathed life into the insolvent company. Credit Suisse watched as the hole filled; still, I needed to control all of the Fortissa shares, and 25 percent were held in lieu of a personal Bigi loan by the Swiss Volksbank.

While in Switzerland, I met many Swiss bankers. Until then, I had known dozens of businesspeople, European and not. I'm not pretending to be a mind-reader, or to be able to see through walls—but this is my summation of how things likely went down between BPT Trading and Swiss Volksbank..

Tuesday started normally for Mr. Barbonet. His secretary brought in the business journal and a porcelain cup filled to the brim with coffee. His first appointment was bound to be pleasant. An American was interested in buying the shares held as collateral for a 500,000-Swiss-franc loan to a very shrewd Swiss businessman, Mr. Bigi. Mr. Bigi had informed Mr. Barbonet his preference that the bank handle the transaction.

Barbonet would use his vivid imagination, tallying bank fees and costs to be added to the transaction. If Barbonet sweetened the deal, Bigi would also benefit.

Mr. Barbonet, like most Swiss bankers, was not enamored with people who showed up to a meeting without a tie. Girondi was an Italian American living in Southern

Italy with a sordid past. Being a proper Swiss, of the French canton of Vaud, there were many details that could provoke discretion from the banker.

The Swiss newspapers were often riddled with stories about difficulties Switzerland encountered with its southern neighbor, Italy. Usually the stories covered the mafia. For decades, Swiss banks did a brisk business with the Italian mafia. Today, however, it was common knowledge that the Italian American mafia was under attack from the US government, losing its clout, and therefore had become an undesirable element.

If the American wanted Fortissa shares, Barbonet would make him pay dearly for them.

This was the playing field on the cold gray Tuesday morning. I called my mother for prayers and, praying myself, I held the door open for Mr. Bigi as we entered the opulent boardroom.

Ludwig looked twice to see if his eyes failed him. I was shoeless and sitting with my legs bent over the side of my chair.

After a few minutes, two men walked in. One of them, Barbonet, was Ludwig's age, and the other, Patrick, was my age. Patrick introduced Monsieur Barbonet, the president of Swiss Volksbank, Lausanne. Monsieur Barbonet did not speak English. I believed this to be a tactic and that the banker spoke English. Barbonet glanced at me and my shoeless feet and spoke to Patrick, who translated.

"Mr. Barbonet wants you to know that these chairs are precious antiques." Patrick looked at my traipsed legs. I dropped my legs to the floor, winked, and smiled timidly. Right. When was I ever timid?

Patrick spoke American, not English. I assumed that he had attended a US university. Barbonet was average height and build, with articulately combed brown hair. I stared, and he looked away, feigning that he hadn't noticed. He was a professional, with no compassion. His concern was for the bank above all else.

My face put on its best schoolboy attire as Patrick translated Barbonet's words. I held on to each one and understood some French. I often looked at Barbonet, nodding in agreement.

Barbonet turned his gold wedding band, content with how things were proceeding. Patrick offered beverages. Bigi passed; I accepted both coffee and water. Barbonet approved; drinking fluids would make me a moister fillet.

I lifted my coffee. "Here's to you," I said and smiled broadly.

The small talk out of the way, Barbonet spoke again through Patrick. "Mr. Girondi, it appears we have something that you want?"

"Yes, sir," I responded politely.

"We are willing to discuss this matter, of course," Patrick added.

"I appreciate that," I said.

Mr. Barbonet smirked, all ducks in a row. This would be a chapter for the book he planned to write on his life. He wasn't happy that his assistant had studied abroad. Swiss universities and Swiss tact are the finest in the world. He would now demonstrate the latter.

"Mr. Girondi, we assume that you brought your checkbook."

"Yes, sir, right here," I replied as I patted my front breast pocket.

"Mr. Girondi, it is your lucky day. We're willing to sell these incredibly valuable shares."

Barbonet glanced at what he thought was a confident look on Bigi's face, and then pretended to concentrate on data-filled pages. He would strategically attain the highest price from me, and then deal with Bigi.

"Mr. Girondi, will you be paying the amount out of a Swiss bank?"

"That can be arranged," I responded.

"Mr. Girondi." Patrick paused. "Write the check in the amount of 650,000 Swiss Francs to the Swiss Volksbank."

During my silence, Patrick must have contemplated the four years he wasted at Harvard. Waiting for my response, Barbonet's confidence began to slip.

"I'll give you 10,000 for 'em," I said with a broad smile.

Barbonet abruptly left the room. I guessed that he was upset that they had offered me coffee.

Patrick fought to hide a smile. A secretary came to the door and called Patrick outside.

Bigi remained silent. After ten minutes, the Swiss banking team reentered. They didn't smile, offer coffee, or even water. It was war—as if it had ever been anything else.

They spoke briefly between themselves and seemed somewhat confused. Finally, Barbonet nodded, and Patrick spoke. "Mr. Girondi, Mr. Barbonet would like you to know that the Swiss Volksbank has more money than yourself."

"Really? I'm glad we got that out of the way," I said coyly.

"We can buy the shares from you," Patrick said.

I stood and shoved my open briefcase, landing it at the Swiss banker's fingertips; simultaneously, I screamed, "Yes, it's yours! It is all yours! If a 25 percent minority share costs 650, then the majority share of 75 percent for 2.5 million is a steal! Make the check out to Patrick Girondi," I yelled with a huge smile on my face.

I paid 25,000 for the shares.

ℱ

Italian was BPT's official language. I dressed in jeans and offered lunch and/or dinner to employees, who seemed content to be friends with their eccentric boss.

People considered me a nut from the time that I was born. Several times, after I had become wealthy, when people called me crazy, I would explain to them that insane poor people are nuts but insane rich people are eccentric.

It became clear to my wife that I was not interested in normal things. I deplored any kind of shopping. By now we had our own apartment. When she moved the furniture, I never noticed. Once, she painted the kitchen. After a few months, I remarked, "Something's different here."

We got along better when I traveled.

Italy was where she learned to walk and talk. Italian was her mother tongue, but southern Italy has more in common with Morocco than it does with Milano, forget about Chicago.

She appreciated the finer things, and had dreamt of being the wife of a well-to-do man. Though I had been on *The Oprah Winfrey Show* and in *Playgirl*, I lived as someone from Bridgeport, and in Italy fit perfectly as a southern Italian. She felt betrayed and worst, deceived.

I loved Altamura and southern Italy. When I traveled, I couldn't wait to get back. Twice a week, I played soccer with my new buddies, learned Italian card games, and laughed and joked the whole time that I hung out at my new Totó club in the town center. The club was named after Italian actor/poet/philosopher, Antonio de Curtis, Totó, Italy's prince of laughter.

A retired police (Carabinieri) commander named Antonio Arcella became my close friend, consigliere, and in time a father to me. The Carabinieri are devout Catholics, devoted to the "Blessed Mary." Antonio dabbled in real estate and lived in Modugno with his wife and daughter. We began investing together. Antonio kept the books. Zio Mimmo, the uncle who had raised Lucrezia, took the place of Lucrezia's father, and he and his wife, Zia Chiara, became Santino's substitute grandparents.

I traveled in tranquility, knowing that my family was in good hands.

By the time Lucrezia was twenty-two, she had one child and another on the way. She missed much of what life in a big city offered. We rarely conversed on the subject, and I assumed she'd eventually get used to the situation.

Three ultrasounds confirmed we would have a daughter. I wanted to follow tradition and honor Ma by naming my daughter Sara. Lucrezia wanted to name her

Aqualina. After all, I'd had my way with Santino. Aqualina was, to me, a crazy name, and Ma didn't even have a distant cousin named Aqualina.

The fight escalated. In the heat of discussion, I rushed my wife, placed my hands over her stomach, and prayed. After a few moments, I walked out of the house and went to the town cathedral, completed in 1196. "Please, Lord, do something to lift this problem from my family," I pleaded.

A few days later, on December 20, 1991, the doctor pulled my daughter out of the womb, shocked to see a long penis. The Lord found it easier to change the sex than Lucrezia's mind.

I rejoiced and felt comfortable with my overall situation. Could you blame me?

Following tradition, Vincenzo was named after Lucrezia's father. Vincenzo is also the name of my own Uncle Vince and Saint Vincenzo de Paoli is the patron saint of the poor. I couldn't have been happier with the name. Lucrezia was incensed that I had gotten my way again. She didn't believe that I could change the sex of the baby—or at least she was fairly certain.

There were nine Vincenzos in Lucrezia's family. They all had nicknames. I gave my son the nickname Cenzino.

Santino had a strange maturity about him and was never jealous of Cenzino. Instead, he knew that he was the big brother, and had a generosity toward his little brother, evident even when he was just a year old.

Santino was full of energy, yet astute, a picture of health and wisdom. I had been blessed by the Lord and Grandpa Santino.

Like everything else and like all other probes, the FBI floor investigation ended. All of these public eye-catchers burn bright and then fizzle.

As a result, however, there was a mark next to my name on government computers. At customs, they held me up for hours. Some of the questions were very astute.

"How many bags of drugs do you have in your suitcases?"

"How much counterfeit money have you brought with you?"

If you doubt me, or have any trouble whatsoever believing me, you watch too much American television.

Chapter 14

Paradise Lost

I n September 1992, Santino was pale, lethargic, and diagnosed with Thalassemia, a fatal blood disease. Thalassemia has similarities to its cousin, Sickle Cell Disease. I was confident there had been a laboratory error, but I researched the illness anyway.

Fifteen percent of the coastal people of southern Italy, including Sardinia and Sicily, are carriers of the Thalassemic trait (Mediterranean Anemia or Cooley's Anemia). Mosquitoes carried malaria where stagnated water was common through the Mediterranean, into the Middle East, India, and China. Thalassemia is believed to have genetically evolved to protect people from malaria.

My wife and I were carriers. Grandpa Santino had handed me down more than olive skin. When carriers of the trait have a child, there is a 25 percent chance of passing the defective gene from both parents to the child. At this point, he or she is not a healthy carrier, but has the disease.

Hemoglobin is a protein in our red blood cells that carries oxygen to all the organs in our bodies. Until the first year of our lives, our bodies contain only fetal hemoglobin. At that point, a switch occurs, and our bodies begin to run on adult hemoglobin. Thalassemia prevented the production of adult hemoglobin. If the diagnosis was confirmed, Santino's life was in jeopardy.

Within thirty days, the diagnosis was reconfirmed by a half dozen centers.

The drug industry historically invested very few resources in curing rare diseases, as it is perceived that there will be limited or no profit in doing so. The afflictions are so rare that they are orphaned by the drug industry. Both Sickle Cell Disease and Thalassemia are rare diseases. To be considered rare, the disease must afflict fewer than 200,000 people in the US and fewer than 250,000 people in Europe.

When the first doctor explained the sickness to us, she did so with the gentleness of an aluminum baseball bat. I suspected that she may have watched some videos on "hard love." She was an Altamurana doctor named Cinzia, a friend of a friend and medical intern at the Thalassemia Clinic in Taranto, a city about forty miles from Altamura. She brought a Thalassemia pamphlet that further explained the sickness.

In those days, Thalassemics would commonly transfuse blood every twenty days, were hooked up to pumps for twelve to sixteen hours every day, and rarely reached their twenties. When parents realize that they have the risk of birthing a Thalassemic child, they do an amniocentesis. In case of a sick fetus, the woman usually aborted.

After a blissful youth, I wanted to solidify a base for my descendants. We were off to a rough start.

My thoughts turned to visions of diabolic self-destruction. In my living nightmare, my most beautiful blessing was turning into my most dreaded curse. I was vulnerable and literally helpless. There wasn't a thing I could do to stop the terror.

My wife crumpled into her cousin's shoulder, wailing, blubbering, weeping, and gnashing teeth. The profound pain reached back to biblical times.

I physically flinched at the thought of not having Santino. I had to see him. The need could hit me without warning; one time, I left the grocery store, ran home, and flew up the stairs to the apartment. I had to hold him. He was my world, my life. I left the door open and rushed in.

"What happened?" Lucrezia cried in a grief-filled breath.

"Where's Santino?"

"He's sleeping. Don't wake him. He needs his rest," she said sternly.

I barged into the children's room. Cenzino was sound asleep in the crib with Santino. I grabbed Santino into my arms, weeping silently. I squeezed him too hard and he awoke. Through blurred eyes, I stared. He returned my gaze and smiled ever so slightly. I cried even harder and squeezed him into my shoulder, hiding my face from him.

At that moment, a blessing came sailing into my head. It was a lifesaver. A life-changer. *What if we had discovered the disease while Lucrezia was pregnant?* I was glad that we hadn't known. No pain could compare to the thought of not having Santino.

Ironically, our Italian bloodline, which had made his life possible and brought so much beauty into our lives, was now putting his life in jeopardy. Unfortunately, there was absolutely no chance of dodging the bullet. Santino's diagnosis had been confirmed and reconfirmed.

In Bridgeport, the news spread like wildfire. Across the globe, friends rifled through medical books and the internet, and made appointments with hematologists to seek help for us.

The Italian health system is an extension of the family. Children of doctors frequently become doctors. Patients pick their physicians, who are expected to make house calls. No doctor is allowed more than 1,500 patients. Salary is around 40,000 a year (add free healthcare, schools, and universities; little risk of lawsuits, and no real estate tax on primary residences; earnings are realistically much higher).

Italian hospitals have more experience in Thalassemia than US hospitals, where only 2,500 cases are scattered throughout all of North America. Dr. Rino Vullo of Ferrara was a world-renowned Thalassemia specialist. His center, Santa Anna Hospital, was possibly the best-equipped Thalassemia center in Italy and the world. Ferrara is in northeastern Italy. Because of the Po River and emigration from Southern Italy, Ferrara has a large number of Thalassemic patients.

Vullo's gentle strength calmed us, but he presented us with an unsettling situation. Each and every one of our children had a 25 percent chance of having Thalassemia. Our little Vincenzo also had a 25 percent chance of having the disease.

Lucrezia sobbed, "Cenzino, Cenzino!"

We remained in Ferrara with Santino. The aunt and uncle who had raised Lucrezia as an infant, Zia Chiara and Zio Mimmo, brought our infant, Vincenzo, to a medical laboratory in Altamura. Blood was drawn and sent to Ferrara. In a few days, we would know if our second son was also afflicted.

Italy's clan mentality and skepticism toward the state helped me feel right at home, but I wasn't in Bridgeport, where street smarts fixed things. Thalassemia was a whole different world. Still. I'd been strangled, shot at, skated more than twenty arrests, made it through an FBI witch hunt, and was a high school dropout that went from the docks to trading and big money.

Big money means big influence. I would see my son cured. How hard could it be?

I lay on the hospital bed next to Santino and thought of Uncle Rory, Judge Stokes, Big Mamma, Compare Ciccio, Mr. Dicecca, and Joe Horvat. I had a responsibility to each of them. I began scribbling notes and hearing music.

Professor Vullo interrupted the music.

Normal hemoglobin for a male, he said, is twelve to sixteen. Santino's was seven. His body was under stress. Vullo recommended that we evaluate giving him a blood transfusion.

There were no tests for AIDS or Hepatitis C back then. The blood banks were sprinkled with tainted bags and stories of infected victims were commonplace. Terrified,

I asked for time to consult other specialists. He conceded and gave us information about Dr. Susan Perrine of California, who was experimenting with fetal hemoglobin enhancers (Butyrates), which raise a patient's hemoglobin. Raising Santino's hemoglobin would help to avoid transfusions.

Santino was markedly less active than he had been a few months prior; however, only someone who had lived with him would notice this.

A few days later, Vullo pointed out that Santino was functional, his body adapting to the lower hemoglobin. This bought us some precious time. Santino's physical appearance continued to worsen at a hemoglobin of seven; however, it seemed to me that Santino allotted his energy, playing and adapting his life to a somewhat normal existence.

The following day, thinking only of Cenzino, I arrived at Vullo's office. We would now know if Cenzino was also afflicted with Thalassemia. Dr. Rino Vullo noticed me in the doorway. He stood and his smile told me that Cenzino was not afflicted. I kissed Dr. Vullo, and hugged him tight so as not to yell out with joy.

Focus rose from devastation. I wrestled with the scene of me experiencing untold joy in the glaring face of Santino's tragedy. It was a movie in my mind, and like any good Capra film, it would end happily.

While in Ferrara, we met Thalassemic patients with flattened faces and dark, yellowish-brown skin. Smooth face bones pushed out because bone marrow worked nonstop. Iron from transfused blood changed skin color. Many patients died from iron overload in their main organs and never made it to their teens. A new iron chelation drug, which helped patients discard toxic iron delivered in transfusions, was invented by Tisravno. Unfortunately, the Tisravno drug, FeeralX, was administered by subcutaneous injection. The injection lasted 16 hours a day, everyday. The medicine was extremely painful to administer and though simple to produce, incredibly expensive.

A bone marrow transplant could cure Santino, but there was only a small chance of finding a match and risk of mortality. From Ferrara, we had arranged for Santino to be registered in the bone marrow and stem cell banks in the US and Europe.

A struggling Calabrian (woman from Calabria, a southern region in Italy) mother slept next to her son's bed. I stuck two million lire (a thousand bucks) into her purse, donated ten computers to the center, and left to meet Dr. Guido Lucarelli about a possible bone marrow transplant.

I had spoken to Dr. Guido Lucarelli by phone. If we found a match for Santino, Lucarelli put the mortality risk at 10 percent. That made chances of survival 90 percent. If Lucrezia, Cenzino, or I were compatible, or if we found a match in the donors' bank, the situation would be resolved. For now, I put the 10 percent mortality out of my mind. We could cross that bridge if there was a compatible match for Santino.

We packed our bags hurriedly, and loaded them into our Fiat Duna station wagon. The car was basic white, with roll-up windows and without air-conditioning. I bought it new for around $7,000 in Matera, a town in Basilicata ten miles from our own town, Altamura. It was a humble man's car, perfect for an American who didn't want to attract attention in southern Italy. It ran like a charm.

Lucarelli's Muraglia Medical Center was in the town of Pesaro, in the state of Marche on the Adriatic Coast. Lucrezia's cousin Enza, her fiancé, Peppino, and our second son Cenzino arrived at the coastal town hours before we did. It was early November, and the cool winds had already begun drifting down from the Alps, assailing anything and anyone in their path.

We exited the expressway. As I wound through the tiny streets, instinct had me sizing up Pesaro, a town of 95,000 inhabitants. As we drove, I mentally counted the number of florists, bars, churches, and benches. I looked for litter and graffiti. I guessed the years of construction of the buildings and noted the maintenance of them and the details of the roofs, walls, and windows. Each of these things told me a little something about Pesaro. Putting them together would help give me an idea about the people.

Like all Italian towns, Pesaro was distinct and steeped in millennia of antiquity. After a few kilometers, I stopped the car in front of Hotel Nettuno on Via Treviso. Nettuno was the ancient Roman god of the sea and earthquakes. Things fit somehow, the word Thalassemia came from the Greek word, Thal, meaning sea. My family was looking to retrieve our lives swept out to sea and find an end to the earthquake tremoring the ground under our feet.

The following day, Cenzino, Lucrezia, and myself drove the car to Via Cesare Lombroso, 84. Cesare Lombroso was a famous Italian physician from the 1800s who taught that criminality was an inherited trait. I have many friends and acquaintances who would gladly attest to Lombroso's belief. Some would do so proudly. At any rate, this was the address of Ospedale Muraglia, the place where we were hoping to resolve our family's terrifying predicament.

Doctor Guido Lucarelli was a tall, charismatic man with long, curly brown hair. His smile could charm a mother lion whose cubs had been threatened. His voice could calm a tsunami. While his nurse drew blood from each of us, he articulately explained everything he believed relevant to our situation. Test results would arrive in three days.

Lucrezia's arm and hands had broken out in a rash. Enza and her fiancé Peppino did their best to cheer Lucrezia and myself, but that was a tall, tall order.

Santino was unshaken by the day's events. He was one of those everything-will-work-out three-year-olds. The days sauntered by, as gray as the Adriatic sky. The clouds reflected their dismal color onto the waves, and it seemed that the test results were already known by all, including the wind and the sea.

On the third day, Enza and Peppino brought Lucrezia shopping. We all knew the results were due. It was a firm, unspoken agreement that Lucrezia would not be present when the envelope was opened. Shopping may have been a pastime I knew little about, but I was ecstatic if anything could distract my poor wife from pain, even if it was only for a few hours.

I parked and released Santino from his car seat. I looked at his forehead. The lack of hemoglobin in his blood commanded his bone marrow to work overtime, thus pushing out the flat bones of his face. His forehead and cheekbones protruded. His facial features began to be distorted. The disease marched on.

With a hemoglobin around seven, Santino was weak. I carried him into the hospital, utterly devoted to him. My life and body were on autopilot. I knew what had to be done, and I cleansed my thoughts and did my duty. Duty. "No man should ever do less or be expected to do more"—it's one of my favorite quotes, from Robert E. Lee.

Once in the hospital, I had already memorized the way to Lucarelli's office. As a runner, I had long since acquired a knack for such things. The door opened with the force of my soft knock but no one was inside.

Santino and I waited for the doctor in a small room, with nothing to do but gulp down the disinfecting aerosol. To distract my thoughts, I concentrated on the odor, which gave my mind the perception that I was slugging down gallons of water from a chlorinated pool. I scanned the room for other diversions. There was a large crucifix over the doorway and a statue of Mother Mary in the corner. My eyes continued to investigate and they rested on a framed picture of Nettuno.

The god was present here and seemingly everywhere in the town: painted on the murals in the street, printed on menus, sculpted into fountains by the park. And now here he was, where we awaited the judgment of my oldest son. Maybe it was too late, but I prayed. Seeing his image, the trident, the mad waves, made me wild with hope for a moment. Maybe this was only a storm, and all things would pass and be triumphed over.

I cradled little Santino and tried to teach him a word. *"Il mare."* At the moment, talking to him was the only way I knew not to be grim.

My cell phone rang. It was Dirken from my office in Chicago. He choked up as he relayed to me that there were no compatible matches for Santino in the bone marrow banks of the United States and Europe. Lucrezia, Cenzino, and I were not registered in the banks. We represented the best and only chance of compatibility. If one of us was a match, Santino would receive a bone marrow transplant and be saved.

Jesus, Mother Mary, Nettuno, please . . .

We heard steps in the hall. The doctor appeared in the doorway. He didn't even have to speak—I could see it on his face. It was fortunate that my wife was not present.

The next few minutes passed in a fugue. Maybe it was the chemicals in the air, maybe it was the madness of my life. I sped through the hideous, blank corridors with Santino in my arms. Someone could have easily thought I was his kidnapper.

I opened the back door and secured Santino into his car seat. When the buckle clicked, I felt my face convulse. What was the point? He would have no chance in this life.

Chapter 15

Nettuno

I sped away in my Fiat Duna. As I drove, I didn't notice streets, cars, or rain. The wipers were clearing the windshield, but I had no idea who had turned them on. I didn't care about the speed limit. My lungs still seemed to be full of the air from the hospital, the place where the death blow had been dealt. I just had to feel something different. I opened the windows. The smell of seawater and salt entered.

The burst of wind was only a momentary distraction. As we cruised on, I tried to shut out my thoughts, having to focus on the task at hand. Get from A to B. Drive it off . . . but in the snarl of roads, I kept glimpsing flashes of the Adriatic. Nettuno again. I remember once telling my wife that I thought the Adriatic Sea looked like liquid emeralds, but today it reminded me of the skin of a dying man, of someone about to vomit. Nettuno was famously temperamental, just like his waves.

I parked the car by the sea. The golden beaches looked as if they had been turned to ash. Maybe it was the deep shadow of my thoughts. I was in a trance, not wanting to acknowledge the awful deliberations that were rippling under the surface.

I turned and looked at Santino. His face was calm and warm. He had Grandpa Santino's blood in his veins. This was not his first trip to the beach. Like all good Italian infants, he got his share of sand and golden sunshine.

It was all so unfair! My mind took me back to the beginning, to the diagnosis.

I recalled, again, that I had been in Germany at our trading offices when Lucrezia called. Santino was pale and lethargic. I reluctantly agreed that he should get his blood checked. The following day, Lucrezia called crying: Santino was diagnosed with Thalassemia.

Santino would have to transfuse blood every twenty days, and be hooked to a pump sixteen hours a day, to get rid of deadly excess iron coming from the transfusions.

"He'll be dead by the time he's fourteen," the doctor had said.

I opened the back door of the car. My body seemed to know what it was doing, but my mind was not privy to its actions. I felt like I had been thrown off one of the cliffs bordering the sea and I just had to wait to land. The drizzle was giving way to a steady mist, which seemed to strangely echo my inner state. It was difficult to see the street from where I was parked, but the roar of the waves left no doubt that some short footsteps away he was waiting for us. Nettuno.

I removed Santino from his car seat. He watched me as he always watched me. As I lifted his tiny body, I felt withered and rotted. The gray of the sea was the answer. No more pain—no torture for my son. Nettuno would be our savior, delivering us from reality.

I walked to the beach with Santino in my arms, my steps slow and steady. I kept going until I felt water enter my shoes. The hills that surrounded the coastal town receded and moved toward us. We were captured. There was no turning back.

I continued. The water was up to my knees.

I moved in farther. My pocket was filled with money and handwritten addresses and phone numbers. They wouldn't be of much use to us anymore. I felt the water cuddling my stomach.

Santino stared at me warmly as the water began entering his shoes and wetting his clothes. His eyes opened and closed, as though processing this new universe of water, the majesty of it.

We were completely alone. The greens and blues of other days had just been a mirage; the skies were gray; the Adriatic was gray and without temperature. I couldn't tell if it was ten or ninety degrees. I looked ahead of me, and even the sea passage was gray. I couldn't help but wonder: had Nettuno painted the whole world of Pesaro gray for our arrival? Santino's eyes were the only thing not gray. They were a deep, warm brown, and they were calm. He was calm. His gaze was tranquil as he looked at me steadily. Santino didn't even look around. It was as if I was his whole world. The waves, the mist, the wind did not faze him.

He trusted me. If I was in, so was he. I was tranquil, and so was he. Can there be further testimony to loyalty?

We proceeded slowly, my feet traveling over the sandy sea floor. Funny, I was born on the South Side of Chicago and was going to die in Pesaro, a town of 95,000 people, hundreds of miles away from any place that no one in Bridgeport had ever heard of.

Bridgeport. A memory came to mind—when my father told me he wasn't my father.

What made him say that? Was it true? Did it really matter? I had so many other fathers to lean on . . .

Scenes exploded in my head. I was being attacked by Sarge, the German shepherd my father had trained to discipline me and my brothers. I remembered the Old Man throwing a television on top of me and a toaster through the window. Thank God for Grandpa Santino, who had been a warm and kind figure. I remembered the miracle, Santino had been born prematurely, twenty years later—on the same day that Grandpa had died. Grandpa . . .

As a youth, I often wondered what kind of father I would turn out to be. As the current pulled us farther in, a thought smashed into my mind, interrupting its walk with Nettuno: I was Santino's father and he was my son. Santino was a lion. Didn't he deserve the same chance to fight as I had? To escape his own peril?

Maybe he was a better fighter than I. The obstacles I had encountered were nothing compared to what he would be up against; but certainly he was a better man than I. There was a whole life to be lived . . . Santino deserved that . . . and I needed to be around to protect his passage.

But what could I do? He would have the disease. He would suffer. He would be compromised. What kind of assistance could I offer? As we moved farther into Nettuno's grip, other thoughts began to erupt from my ruptured mind.

I had accumulated millions in assets. I could sell what I had and spend it on doctors, clinics, companies, and research. I could begin studying. Deep down, and always, I was a shoeshine. There wasn't a bar or a hospital or a research center that I couldn't scope out if I tried.

I'd do everything to see that Thalassemia would be defeated and my son cured. Christ!—I just needed to get some polish to start. I could afford to buy brushes, and hope. Can you buy hope?

At that moment, Santino's tranquility jolted me back to reality. We were moments away from death, and my son still had not lost faith in me. I panicked as my foot unsuccessfully felt for the sea bottom. I had gone too far. My reconsideration had come too late.

I tried to hold my balance as I fought to move closer to the shore. The current had pushed us out beyond the safety of the low waters and now Nettuno was pulling us toward the sea. I held Santino tightly and swung my arm. My shoes were working as anchors.

My eyes darted and fixed on Santino. His face gave no notice or understanding of my struggle. My face formed a grin. I would not betray his confidence, not now, not ever. The next moments would decide, and as Girondi men, we would accept our fate.

I wished I hadn't worn ankle boots, but there wasn't much I could do about that now. I lunged again toward the shore, hoping my arm could expand like some cartoon character and grasp it. Santino was now completely submerged, except for his bulging face and forehead. He began to cough, the water entering his tiny lungs. I lunged again, raised my feet, and kicked. I hoped that I was making progress, and after several more strokes I tried to touch down. Nothing.

Santino's coughing was interrupted only when his face was submerged. Unfortunately, making my way into the water, my mind had been almost blank. I gauged the distance to the shore and reflected, trying to recollect my steps to formulate a strategy.

I concentrated, my mind began cooperating, presenting me with solutions. The waves were violent. Releasing Santino as I unlaced my boots was not practical. My brain began retracing my trip into the abyss. Click. I was confident that I was within a few yards of being able to set my feet on the seafloor. I calmed, hoping to recuperate my energy. I'd spend all of my remaining stamina making one last push. If my calculation was wrong, we were dead.

Santino choked. He had swallowed a considerable amount of salt water. I lifted his head, and his peril supercharged me. I grunted out as I lunged, kicking and releasing myself from the sea's grip, confident that I was moving toward the shore. After almost a minute, I let out one last grunt as I made what would be my last attempt to save life. I struggled harder than I had ever struggled.

When my energy was depleted, I pushed again but there was no grunt and my feet fell beneath me. They were no longer under my command. Exhaustion now controlled them and they lowered. Thoughts filled the eternity as I waited for the final verdict.

I had been spared by the chain of the Olive brothers and the bullets at the Star Bar and in my apartment on 38th street. Would I be saved yet another time? Did I deserve to be saved? Would my condemnation dash the hopes for not only me but also Santino?

My feet continued to drift lower. Suddenly, I felt something and hoped that it wasn't my imagination. I pushed down, toward the abyss of life and was saved by Nettuno's sandy floor. I breathed in and soared through the liquid death we had eluded. Energized by focused hope, my feet floated over the sand and rocks beneath us.

The decision had been made. I had no idea what I was in for, but I knew that by walking out of the water I was agreeing to enter a race—the race of my life.

Until that day, I had never set goals and or pursued them. I had walked along, instead, doing what I thought made sense, was right, and reacting to the circumstances. I now felt, for the very first time, that I was focused. I would cure Thalassemia.

By what I had read until then, I knew that Thalassemia was a cousin to Sickle Cell Disease. Both are the result of a defective beta-globin gene. I fantasized that they could be cured by the same therapy. This would be a supreme blessing; I'd cure them both. I was born for this. My son was Santino Girondi; and whatever this meant, and no matter who I was or am, one day we would honor Joe Horvat from the dock, Ma, Uncle Rory, Big Mamma, Judge Darren Stokes, Zia Anna, and all of our fathers and mothers. We'd find a cure.

I'll never forget Santino that day. It was he who carried us back to shore. I had nothing to do with it. He wasn't yet three years old and he had already saved something much more valuable than life, the only eternity we can ever possess; he had saved my soul. I started the Fiat Duna station wagon and drove Santino and me back to the hotel, named for Nettuno. I took a breath. I knew then that it would be a long and arduous voyage, but thanks to Santino, the wind was now at my back. I still wonder to this day, *Was Nettuno attempting to kill me or did he save me?*

We headed home. Lucrezia sobbed as the car made its way down the Adriatic coast.

"Please, Lucrezia," I said, "Santino has a chance. Patient organizations are working hard. We'll join them in the fight and see about Butyrate, the experimental medicine of Dr. Susan Perrine."

The battle line had been drawn.

When we traveled, we were in uncharted waters. Would altitude affect Santino's hemoglobin? How would he hold up on long flights? No one could respond to our concerns. No one knew. Santino handled the trips without incident, and never once protested or complained.

Chapter 16

Medical School

On the voyage to the US, I read hematology books bought at university stores in Ferrara and Pesaro. Remarkably enough, I understood what I read. I constructed a list of heads in the Thalassemia field. Dirken ran back and forth to the library at the University of Chicago, sending me the latest relevant medical articles in miles and miles of faxes.

In Philadelphia, we met Dr. Allen Cohen, a gentle, experienced hematologist. Most of his patients were afflicted with Sickle Cell Disease. Sickle Cell primarily afflicts people of African ancestry; Thalassemia, mostly people of Arab or Asian ancestry.

Dr. Cohen's teaching picked up where Vullo and Lucarelli left off. Santino's hemoglobin was 7.3. Cohen agreed that we had time to check Perrine's Butyrate therapy.

We met in New York with Dr. Tirelli of Weill Cornell. Tirelli emigrated from Italy in the sixties. He strongly held that the doctor was the doctor, the patient the patient, and the parent the parent. Our ocean of conversation had a comical undercurrent as we switched in and out of languages, attempting to determine if my Italian was better than his English or vice versa.

Dr. Tirelli ended the visit with a strong message that I wish my wife had not heard. "You live in Italy and there, you have what you have here. You are only wasting time and will damage your son with this unproven experimental concoction."

He supplied us with the name of the head of hematology at the University of Bari and recommended (ordered) that we leave for home, immediately.

Walking into a bar with my shoeshine box, I examined the place, figuring out a strategy in a matter of seconds. I could tell by a guy's look what my likely reception would be, how much he'd pay—which is not to say that I didn't catch a couple of slaps along the way . . .

When I walked into any hospital, I sized it up. I read who the donors were. I smelled it, I saw the colors of the walls, the people in the halls, the number of rooms in a department, the number of empty beds, if the water machine worked next to the pop machine in the visitor waiting area, if they had a McDonald's in the atrium poisoning kids so the hospital would get healthy donations. *If you let us feed this tainted food to your patients and their visitors, we'll donate.*

Needless to say, doctors have their own agendas, and they themselves, aren't necessarily the sharpest knives in the drawer. From New York, we headed home to Chicago, where I continued studying. Lucrezia was confused. I hadn't graduated from high school. How was I ever going to grasp books that were meant for college students and doctors? Shouldn't I get my diploma first?

Published articles measure a scientist's worth; the more publications, the higher his value. I went through Dr. Perrine's research articles; she collaborated heavily with Dr. Fanny Tifo, also a researcher/doctor at Ontario Children's Hospital in Toronto.

Tifo and Perrine's names were, generally, either the first or the last referenced in their many medical publications. This meant that they were the big cheeses. As I made my way through the medical maze, I realized that egos were often more critical to research than the research itself.

Medical scientists dream of saving humanity. It certainly must become complicated for them, as the patient becomes an instrument of progress toward the Nobel Prize.

Research costs lots of money, especially since all hospitals and research centers take a lion's share of donations aimed at a disease for the overhead of the institution, safeguarding executive salary and bonus. Management compensations skyrocketed in the US over the last forty years as healthcare became an industry.

My dear friend Dr. Lucio Luzzatto says that in his experience in Italy, mixing private entities with state-run healthcare usually meant converting taxpayer money into corporate profit with only disadvantage to the state and patient.

Biopharma published in March 2020 that the median cost of bringing a drug to market is $985 million. One of the arguments biopharma companies make for the high cost of a new drug is the expense of drug development. What they excluded to tell us was that often ridiculous executive compensations and the profits of financial funds and investors are often a part of this somewhat mysterious and ambiguous number that encompasses drug development.

Perrine and Tifo worked with grants from the American and Canadian National Institutes of Health and Sickle Cell Disease and Thalassemic Foundations. Dr. Susan Perrine had five patients on her lifesaving elixir and as a result was featured twice on CNN.

I spoke to Dr. Perrine several times by phone. She wasn't quite sure when she could get us on her schedule. Dr. Tifo had a Thalassemic patient doing well on Arginine

Butyrate. Priorities tempered by knowledge, I purchased tickets for three to Toronto, where the Bungaro family, Lucrezia's relatives, made us feel right at home.

Tifo was thirty-five, attractive, and extremely friendly. I assumed that she had heard that we wrote checks. Her patient, Rita, was of Italian descent and had a base hemoglobin of four (normal hemoglobin for a female is eleven to fourteen). Rita needed lifesaving transfusions; however, her body rejected foreign blood.

On IV (intravenous) Arginine Butyrate, from eight to twenty hours a day, every day, she maintained a hemoglobin of nine. With five points, Santino's hemoglobin would be twelve. He'd have no disease symptoms, and would be saved from transfusions, at least until we figured something else out.

We arrived the following morning. My hopeful feelings didn't quite compensate for Lucrezia's nervousness. To avoid a foreseeable unfortunate incident, Tifo showed us Rita's picture. Seeing the flattened facial disfigurement, imagining that Santino would someday look like this, Lucrezia cried hysterically.

I remained cool. My face lacked emotion. This, and other things helped convince Lucrezia that I was only concerned with Santino's health, which meant being victorious. I was obsessed with winning. Stranger still, I was always reading medical material, yet I was skeptical of doctors. Who did I think wrote the articles?

I drove Lucrezia back to be with her relatives and I arrived at Tifo's office at 11:30 for the noon meeting. While waiting, I spoke with the receptionist. Receptionists make appointments and orchestrate billing and prescriptions. In certain circumstances, they are far more important than the doctors they work for.

Dr. Tifo suggested that Rita and I have lunch together in the hospital cafeteria.

Rita's voice was sweet, and sounded younger than her twenty years. She hoped to draw and save her own blood for subsequent transfusions needed for facial surgery, but in the meantime she accepted God's will. The words "God's will," said with her soft voice, inadvertently echoed off the walls of my cranium for days.

"What do you do with your spare time, Rita?" I asked.

"I love to listen to music," she softly responded.

"Me too, honey," I said as I looked into her eyes. "I'm not a good singer, but I love to sing."

Rita smiled.

I wrote a check, bought a stereo for Rita's hospital room, and gave her a CD containing me crooning my favorite songs. With all she had been through, I figured she could handle my voice.

Years later, Dr. Tifo was a hero on *60 Minutes*, and two years after, the protagonist in a book about how sabotaged data resulted in the deaths of dozens of patients.

Today, the internet is rife with stories about hundreds of urologists who, *to be cautious*, treat men for prostate cancer instead of an enlarged prostate. *Coincidentally*, the cost of treating prostate cancer dwarfes the cost of treatment for an enlarged prostate.

To sum it up: *If we are not our own doctors, we are bad patients.*

Doctors are health consultants; their opinions are also conditioned by personal factors. Being friendly with office staff was a good strategy. I found out if the doctors were married, broke, had a lover, or were getting kickback lunches or free trips for speaking engagements from the drug companies producing the medicines our patients used. I sensed if they suffered from low self-esteem or if they were narcissistic. Using doctors' and researchers' egos is often critical in developing the most effective medical strategy.

Researchers live in a complex world. Grants are the oxygen of every researcher's life and I've witnessed them being used for everything from test tubes to dry cleaning. When a researcher applies for grant money from a charity, the Food and Drug Administration, and/or the National Institute of Health, his or her proposal is decided on by a board of *peers*.

If Doctor Jones is jealous of Doctor Smith because he was recently usurped at a conference, it's unlikely that you'll get impartiality from Dr. Jones's evaluation of Dr. Smith's research.

If a scientist criticizes or writes a negative editorial about a colleague's work, what possibility will there be of their grant being funded when the tables are turned? As a consequence, researchers rarely openly challenge one another.

The halls of the relationships between researchers and research centers are lined with greed, ambition, and jealousy. The hatred that many commonly have for each other was shocking, even to me.

Conferences are open battlefields. Presentations are canceled and rescheduled based on radical alliances. Because of politics and greed, critical work is often relegated to the end of the conference in Utility Hall "Z" when 70 percent of participants have left (after the conference, it will be turned back into a storage room) while less significant research presentations are given in Convention Room A, at ten a.m. on the second day when ninety-nine percent of participants are present.

Consequently, medical journals are full of half-truths, tainted data, and even outright deception. Objectivity is a more endangered species than a forty-year-old virgin; but as long as I feigned my beliefs, which I did religiously, the medical community dealt with me readily—though that does not mean they readily accepted me.

I forwarded articles and research news to doctors, parents, and patients. To some, I became a trusted consultant and confidant. Research became my life, but I could not afford to forget that trading funded research.

Flexibility was the most important requirement to navigate these waters. I met award-winning scientists who couldn't be trusted and laboratory technicians who were absolute geniuses.

Earthly accomplishments and titles are not an accurate measure of a man.
—Robert E. Lee

I was reckless and would surely crash. Lucrezia, obliged to protect Cenzino and herself, gladly let me drive solo. We slept in different rooms and ate at different times. As the space between us widened, intimacy became rare, and I'm an intimate guy.

The curdling disharmony did provide for some personal advantages. At any rate, a lucky punch had landed me on the exchange. Could a lucky punch save Santino and, consequently, my marriage?

We were in the early '90s and daily newspapers throughout the world were filled with articles about AIDS and Hepatitis C decimating the gay population. Most articles failed to mention the slaughter of Sickle Cell Disease and Thalassemic patients due to AIDS and Hepatitis C–tainted blood.

For the Sickle Cell Disease and Thalassemia patients who chronically transfused, it was a numbers game. If a patient transfused ten times in a year, he had a ten times greater chance of catching a virus. We desperately hoped that Butyrate would save Santino from transfusions.

I got extremely annoyed when people spoke of my crusade as "valorous." I fought for Santino like you would for your child. I was only doing the minimum of what a parent should. The real heroes were my brothers running Bridgeport and BPT Trading.

My lifestyle changed dramatically. The less I spent on things I didn't need, the more I had for the one thing I needed: research. A man prioritizes life. Santino's clock was ticking.

Santino's spleen ate many of the flimsy blood cells he was capable of making, mistaking them for viruses, pulling his hemoglobin even lower. Each day, I nervously measured, as his spleen grew, occupying more and more space in his tiny stomach. We anguished as his hemoglobin went from seven to 6.7 to 6.5 to 6.7 to 6.3 to 6.5 to six to 5.6. His physical activity halted, his stomach bloated, his skin turned white, and his skull expanded noticeably. This was a result of his abnormally low hemoglobin. His organs were being asphyxiated without oxygen. We rushed him to Children's Hospital of Chicago.

I thought about Rita as I completed the miles of insurance forms. After a few hours, we sat with a hematologist.

The doctor was younger than forty. His demeanor was like a detective's. He talked like he was interrogating me—and I think he pulled that attitude because he surmised I was the one responsible for the state of my son's precarious condition.

"Where is your son being followed, Mr. Girondi?"

"My son has several doctors who are involved."

He cleared his throat. "Really?" He tapped a pencil against a white notebook. "I'm amazed that one of these doctors did not transfuse your son weeks ago."

He looked into my eyes. I felt like I was a fifth grader in the playground. If he didn't have glasses on, I might have cracked him right then, but he did and we'll never know.

He continued to stare, with the look of an angered policeman. "If you do not transfuse your son immediately you may be responsible for," he nodded, "his life."

Lucrezia knew that he meant death. She sobbed.

I nodded. "All right, doctor, we'll transfuse our son."

At the moment, it seemed like the only logical option. Lucrezia sobbed even louder. I tried to unravel Santino's journey for the doctor as he drew blood from Santino's arm. We were obviously Italian, but the doctor never imagined Jehovah's Witnesses in Italy. Jehovah's Witnesses believe it against God's will to receive blood. At any rate, he'd see to it that the Department of Children and Family Services would be brought into the case. He whispered to a nurse to contact a hospital social worker before leaving, saying, "It was unconscionable to allow a child to suffer in this manner."

Lucrezia observed the doctor's contempt. She knew that he judged her unfit. None of this was her fault. I had created this situation and called all the shots, as things went from bad to worse. Angry feelings for me built up within her. She tried to look away, but her stare returned again and again to Santino's growing forehead. The poor woman, the mother of my children, was ready to collapse.

After forty minutes, we were brought into a room where the same doctor was sitting with a needle in his hand. As he probed Santino's tiny fist, I explained that doctors always used the veins in his arms. He completely ignored me, finally reminding me that Children's Hospital of Chicago was a premier center and that he was an experienced doctor. I doubted the veins in Santino's fist noted either fact.

After twenty minutes, and dozens of attempts, things were unchanged, except that Santino's hand was swollen and bloodied, he was screaming in pain, and the doctor was profusely perspiring. Still he was relentless. Lucrezia stared out the window and the teary-eyed nurse assistant suggested that she try. The doctor flatly refused.

Santino, far wiser than his three and a half years, glanced at me. His tearful eyes spoke to me as they had in the Adriatic: *Dad, I want to go along with you on this, but he's hurting me. When are you gonna get me out of here?*

Dripping in sweat, the doctor raised his hands and announced that he needed a break. We were escorted to another room. I called Vullo, Cohen, and Perrine. All three of the doctors believed that Santino's low hemoglobin did not represent an immediate life-threatening situation. They all agreed that in view of the situation and for Santino's benefit we should leave and get on the Butyrate therapy as soon as possible.

We left the room and walked out of the hospital, refusing to wait for the doctor, the social worker, or the police. None of this made sense to Lucrezia, who as the mother of two children, began thinking about how she would protect them from my insane quest.

For weeks after, each time I viewed my son's swollen hand, I thought of arrogance, one of the many faces of medicine.

If someone goes to a hospital and is satisfied with the treatment, he or she will likely refer the hospital for anything from a broken thumb to lung cancer. Likewise, if someone goes to the Mayo Clinic and has an unfavorable experience he or she will likely, quietly or loudly, say things like, "I wouldn't send a dog to that place."

Every medical center on the planet has situations that it wishes had never happened. More and more, medicine and medical centers are driven by profit. Some have become parts of publicly traded companies or financial groups. Marketing drives revenue. "I went to a doctor and he examined me and said I would die. I went to the US Cancer Corp and I'm living."

In 1997, the FDA first allowed the practice of direct-to-consumer advertising, and since then, the number of pharmaceutical company-sponsored TV commercials and prescription drugs has skyrocketed. The United States and New Zealand are the only nations in the world that allow for direct-to-consumer advertising for pharmaceuticals.

With billions in profits going to the pharmaceutical companies and their executives, it is still the taxpayers who foot the bill for the majority of the research done in the US through the NIH and FDA government-funded grants. Doctors and researchers use these taxpayer resources and make inventions. The research center executives are in cahoots with the pharma companies and fund managers. The centers sell off the resulting taxpayer-funded intellectual property to the same fund managers and pharmaceutical companies for pennies on the dollar.

These technologies become lottery tickets for the fund managers and pharma executives as eventually, one of the products which they paid almost nothing for could rake in millions or even billions in pyramid-building IPO's and eventual products.

Researchers themselves have been caught stealing their institutes' inventions and moving them into their own private companies. It's almost always settled out of court, as eventual embarrassing headlines would mean a drop in private donations and/or eventual government grants.

In *The Billion-Dollar Molecule*, one of the many books I read, the founder of Vertex raised millions before one microscope was pulled out of its carton. Medicine is not only about a bunch of nice people trying to cure.

Before leaving for Oakland, Lucrezia and her sister Pamela visited a top divorce attorney, who made a courtesy call to me. Lucrezia claimed that I was ripping the family apart because I would not accept Santino's sickness and that she was growing desperate to find a solution to save Santino and our family from my madness.

We traveled to Oakland, California to begin Dr. Perrine's Arginine Butyrate treatment. We rented an apartment. Santino's therapy, which was intravenous, required him to be hospitalized. Lucrezia and her sister slept in his room. I was with him during the day. One morning, Lucrezia and her sister got to the apartment only to discover that it had been ransacked. It wasn't the only way we got robbed in California.

Dr. Susan Perrine, the inventor of Arginine Butyrate, a fetal hemoglobin enhancer, was single, childless, and enamored with Santino. Our mutual love for him instantly bound us. We spent hours and hours and even full days together in her laboratory. I absorbed everything I could.

When Lucrezia became aware of my dive into the research world she reminded me that I had no formal training and was in fact, a high school dropout. She didn't have to remind me; had I spent four or five years going to a university, I may have never been able to learn and digest all of this. *One learns from studying books, one exceeds from studying life.*

Within weeks of our arrival, Oakland Children's informed Dr. Perrine that the quantities of Butyrate being produced in the hospital laboratory were larger than the hospital insurer allowed. The CEO forbade further production on the premises.

Santino's lifeline was in peril.

I began interviewing possible manufacturing partners, acting as my own attorney and accountant. After all, what books did they read that I couldn't? I was introduced to and quickly impressed with Walter Hayhurst, a smooth-talking Texan pharmacist. Within weeks, Emerging Pharmaceutical Technologies (EPT) was born.

Soon, Walter; his wife, Sandy; Dr. Perrine; and I were joined by a fifth musketeer, Jim Remenick, an attorney with the legal firm Baker and Botts. He believed in the project and did hundreds of thousands of dollars in free patent and other law work for Dr. Perrine, our Joan of Arc.

Jim—a good friend to this day—recently recollected how we met almost thirty years ago. One weekend, Jim had a three-hour layover in Chicago on his way to see Dr. Perrine in California. I gave Jim a call, "Hey, are you Jim? I wanna talk to you. I'll pick you up at the airport." Jim recalls I arrived in an '80s boxy station wagon, dressed in a shirt with sleeves cut off, white-framed dollar store sunglasses, old jeans, and flip-flops.

We pulled up in front of an Italian restaurant called Agostino's. Jim was disappointed when he saw the CLOSED sign. I tapped on the window; Agostino opened up for us and made us lunch. Jim says that he never had a finer Italian meal. He was surprised that I never mentioned a word about business and got him back to the airport in perfect time for his connecting flight.

Walter provided money, knowhow, and supplies; I provided money, strategic input, and public relations. Dr. Perrine supplied the Butyrates. EPT funded the construction of an Arginine Butyrate plant in the Bahamas, where the Hayhursts had been collaborating with pharmacists for years. Santino would be able to start on the therapy in the spring of 1993.

Researchers and businessmen are strong-minded people. From the beginning, to curb conflict and keep the project moving, I often had to take two sides of the same argument.

I believed that trying to help Santino was the sincerest way to demonstrate love to Lucrezia. Somehow, she seemed less than awestruck, as I went from researcher to pharmaceutical producer. I didn't much heed her views, but I was acutely aware that less than 25 percent of the world's population have an HLA-compatible donor for an eventual transplant, and needed her to produce a suitable sibling for Santino. EPT was just a backup plan.

Impregnating someone who thinks you're a few eggs short of a dozen is challenging, but voilà, she was pregnant with our third child. We did an amniocentesis. Fortunately, the fetus was healthy, but unfortunately, not a match for Santino.

Hopefully, number four would be different . . .

I rocketed between trading and Santino's project in the US and Europe. I went through money faster than I was able to make it. I'd readily go bankrupt doing my duty, and many started to believe that I would.

Most parents, at one time or another in their lives say, "I'd do anything for my child." I was blessed; I could actually put these words into action.

Joe Feldman coined the phrase, "If things get really bad, we'll open a beef stand."

Lucrezia's allegations grew like flies on dogshit and they weren't all unfounded. In summary, I was an uneducated, uncultured, criminal madman, flying the world over to save the only thing that was important to me: Santino. I neglected the rest of my family and the only possible end results were bankruptcy and family destruction.

Always the Franciscan, I was only following the parable about the shepherd abandoning ninety-nine sheep to find the one that was lost. As a consequence, I spoke and met weekly with dozens of researchers, foundations, companies, and parents. I would make it up to Lucrezia after Santino was safe.

What does not kill me, makes me stronger.
—Friedrich Nietzsche

Leaving Lucrezia to sort things out would make her stronger, and eventually she'd join me to conquer the intruder. But for now, life together was toxic. My sons, friends, compari, writing, and music were antitoxins. Singing, more than most things, helped discharge poison.

In April, the Aliquò family arrived in Oakland for the Butyrate therapy. Enrico, their son, was Thalassemic and Santino's age. Enrico's father, Luigi, was the owner of a successful office equipment distributor in Florence, Italy. Luigi's wife; Enrico's mother, Angela; and Luigi's sister, Lucia accompanied Enrico and Luigi to Oakland. The Aliquòs also slept in the hospital with their son and not in their rented Oakland apartment.

Many of the children in the ward were abandoned AIDS victims. The dark hours were filled with screeches and screams. The Italians went room to room, quieting the children. Had they not been able to be there for Santino and Enrico, they imagined that other mothers would do the same for their children.

Initially, the help was welcomed, but soon the head nurse discovered the situation and intervened. "If the children get accustomed to attention, it will be impossible for the nurses to cope in a realistic manner after you leave. Please stay in your own rooms." She was not about to have patients ruined by warmth on her watch.

Dozens of blood draws and tests are normal for patients on experimental therapy. There are hours and hours of void in the hospital. In Lucrezia's spare time, she flipped through magazines and television shows. They all delivered the same message: "Your happiness is the most important thing. If you're not happy, your children, and the people who love you cannot be happy."

Of course, the journals, magazines, movies, and show authors are trying to convince you to buy their brand or their sponsor's brand of tampon, eyeliner, or car. I'm not sure that we consciously evaluate this when digesting their content. And I really believe it bunk that one should consider your personal happiness to be more important than the next guy's.

Lucrezia was the mother of a sick child, married to an unstable man. In November, she'd give birth to her third child. She couldn't catch a glimpse of *her* happiness with a telescope.

Back in Bridgeport, the wives of the 26th Street bosses said Novenas. Their husbands asked their doctors for information. The secretaries at the 11th Ward Democratic Party assisted Marianne Meehan, the director of the Valentine Boys and Girls Club, to do a fundraiser for Thalassemia.

Lucrezia believed in privacy. She was fearful that Santino would be judged negatively. She was not ready to share her grief with friends, let alone a whole neighborhood.

> *A sick child either binds a family or rips it apart.*
> —unknown author

One of the spleen's purposes is to clear out viruses. Without a spleen, a bacterial infection could end Santino's life. Any splenectomized child under ten must report to a hospital in the event of a fever. Santino's spleen continued to devour much of the little hemoglobin he produced. Dr. Perrine favored giving Santino a partial splenectomy, which would stop the spleen from demolishing his hemoglobin. Once on the Butyrate therapy, Santino would make normal cells and the piece of spleen that was left would return to doing its job as a filter against infection. In the long run, he would be safer and healthier.

Most of the doctors I spoke to about the situation disagreed with Perrine, believing that doing a partial splenectomy would only prolong the removal of the remainder of the spleen. In their opinion, the risks of a second surgery outweighed the benefits of Santino holding on to his spleen for what they thought would be only another year or two.

It was not a life-or-death decision; Dr. Perrine would be Santino's primary caretaker, at least for now. Santino was scheduled for a partial splenectomy and at the same time, the surgeon would install a catheter into a main heart artery, facilitating the administration of the future Butyrate medicine.

The morning of the surgery, Lucrezia was in pieces. I wanted to be strong for her. She seemed to read this as arrogance or indifference. I just couldn't get anything right.

The rolling bed arrived at six a.m. We followed it down the hall, onto an elevator, and finally to the terrifying "doors of hope," where our son would meet masked people with knives. Signing the anesthesiologist waiver papers reminded us that not all children make it back through those "doors of hope" alive.

Since a *partial* splenectomy was an experimental procedure, our insurance company would not pay for it, and the hospital had limited liability. We signed without reading a word and were told that the procedure would take less than an hour.

The doctor slipped a mask onto Santino's tiny nose and mouth. He glanced at his mother, then at me. Santino's face was calm, but a little tear ran down the side of his face as he was rolled away.

We waited silently for more than an hour and a half. A nurse with the demeanor of a marine entered the waiting room. "There have been complications," she said. "I really can't tell you anything else now."

Bitterness devoured Lucrezia. She started to cry. I tried to console her, but she shoved me away. Had we just listened to Professor Vullo and transfused our son, Santino would not be in the operation room. A heavy silence fell over us. I could not have uttered a word if I wanted to.

Another hour and a half passed. It could have been a minute or a day. Finally, the marine arrived and took us to see Santino.

Lucrezia gazed down at her son. I expected her to gasp or shudder, but she was silent and still. It didn't even seem like she was breathing. I gazed at our oldest child who was unconscious, with five lines connected to him.

After less than a minute, we were ushered out. I was baffled; we were told that a partial splenectomy is an uncomplicated procedure. This was not supposed to happen.

Ten minutes later, we followed as Santino was rushed to the Intensive Care Unit. Outside the ICU, the dark-skinned, African operating doctor arrived. "Your son's spleen was the size of a small football," he said. "We cut him open from his navel to his backbone on the left side. It was extremely difficult to control internal bleeding."

Lucrezia gasped.

The doctor continued. He seemed to be in no mood to explain. "I put him in the ICU so he has the most attentive assistance. The Mediport was safely inserted into his chest cavity."

We thanked him (I'm not sure why), and he disappeared down the hall.

After over an hour, I rang the ICU bell. A nurse answered and suggested we get coffee and return. It was noon. The big lunchroom was full. We sat near the window with the Aliquò family.

They asked about Santino. "*Sta bene?*"

"He's fine," I answered.

Tears streamed from Lucrezia's eyes. Our son was in grave danger. I responded as if I didn't even care. "*Che cazzo dici!*" (What are you saying?!) she screamed.

She stood to leave. Angela and Luigi's sister, Lucia, coaxed her down and attempted to console her.

Lucrezia and I took turns in the ICU, sometimes for eight hours, sometimes for two. We synchronized our stays in a way that made the most sense. I arrived, she left, and vice versa. Then, as if this all wasn't enough weight for Lucrezia to bear, the rash which had been mostly on her hands, became a full-body rash. The insightful dermatologist at the hospital told her that it could have something to do with stress.

In the ICU, coded data stickers were tacked onto the board next to Santino's bed. Three cotton swabs were twenty-seven dollars. An aspirin cost seventeen dollars. Oxygen tubes, which were (conveniently) changed daily for hygiene, came in three pieces with three stickers. The complete kit cost over $500. When the board was filled, it was delivered to the bookkeeper and replaced.

I slept in a chair next to Santino and woke each morning to a completely filled board. One night, purposely sleeping lightly, I observed a nurse filling the board with stickers that weren't ours. She explained that she had incorrectly assumed Santino was insured, and in an act of kindness, gifted us tags from uninsured patients.

Eventually, the insurance company picked up what was deemed conventional therapy. Doctors helped push some of the experimental therapy over, but even after their creativity, our bill was over $70,000 for 30 days in the hospital. Our medical system has become a vehicle for organized crime.

One morning, an older nurse aide arrived to change Santino's bed garments. I smiled tightly and watched Santino's eyes flare with pain as she briskly loosened the sheets. The tube in his mouth did not let out a sound, but tears streaked his face. As I stood, he raised his arm.

"Don't you try to hit me," the nurse snapped.

"Ma'am," I announced.

"Don't you 'ma'am' me, I know my job. Your boy here is spoiled and he better learn."

"*É quasi finita*" (She's almost finished), I whispered to my son.

"If you foreigners don't like it here, why do you come?"

I just stared.

"Goddamn Mexicans," she said as she turned away.

If I lodged a complaint, she'd only deny everything. We'd be labeled difficult, and Santino would suffer the consequences.

Santino was finally released from the ICU. By the time Santino arrived back to his room, Angela, Lucia, and Lucrezia were well-acquainted. Lucrezia explained the typical, hectic American lifestyle, but the Italians still didn't understand why other parents rarely visited their children.

Dr. Perrine had promised the Aliquòs that hospital bills would be covered by grants, yet every day, five or six hospital invoices arrived at the Aliquòs' Oakland apartment.

In Italy, healthcare is provided to each citizen as part of the Italian Constitution. The government oversees healthcare, and each citizen has clear, spelled-out rights. Hospitals are generally dismal, but in Oakland—and, Luigi assumed, elsewhere in the US—hospitals were bright and colorful.

Luigi, as most Italians, loves the US, but he was beginning to sense that giving the patient good care in America wasn't nearly as important as making them *feel* like they had gotten it. This might partially explain why the US ranks 33 out of 36 of the most advanced nations (OECD) for infant mortality and why Americans live almost four years less than Italians who spend a fraction of what the US spends on healthcare. Many US doctors point to Italy's superior diet as the reason for the 5 percent difference in life spans. The low mark in infant mortality is explained away by blaming mothers who take drugs during pregnancy.

In the US, healthcare is an industry. Over the decades, Italy has experimented with involving private industry with the public system. Doctor Luzzatto, a prominent sage who once served as the Chairman of the Ethics Committee for the American Society of Gene and Cell Therapy, has vast experience in both the Italian and US systems. He claims that in his experience, mixing public and private sectors in medicine is almost always disastrous for patients.

"Italian healthcare is in the hands of experts driven by vocation, not greed," Luigi explained.

The Aliquòs were also realizing that the US is far different than how it's depicted in popular American television shows. Their apartment, like ours, had been robbed—twice—and Oakland was statistically more dangerous than any city in all of Italy, or in all of Europe, for that matter.

Statistics—one of the only arms left to combat false perception. Unfortunately, the corruptorations have become experts at manipulating statistics.

Enrico's medical records had been meticulously translated into English by Luigi's niece, who spoke five languages fluently.

There was one major fact that soared above all of the hundreds of lines and thousands of numbers. Enrico was allergic to the Kell antigen. If he transfused blood containing Kell, his immune system would go into attack mode and could literally kill Enrico. He transfused the day before he left Florence, hoping to be on the Butyrate therapy before a US transfusion was necessary. I alerted Dr. Perrine, who said she knew about the situation.

FDA regulation required patients on IV experimental therapies to be hospitalized. I wasn't certain where our permanent home would be, but my son would not live in a hospital even if it was free, and this one cost over $2,000 a day. Each month in the hospital meant $70,000 less for research.

It was critical that Santino had a treating doctor in his hometown when he eventually returned. Dr. Cinzia was the doctor who had delivered the pamphlet to us when Santino was diagnosed and though she had a strange bedside manner, was willing to take the trip to the US. I paid travel expenses, living expenses, and a salary to Dr. Cinzia. Also, with seven thousand Thalassemia patients, Italy would need its own Butyrate expert.

Months prior, Rino Vullo had introduced me to Dr. Nica Cappellini of the University of Milan, and though our communications were by email and phone, I felt that we had forged a strong relationship.

While a student at the University of Milan, Nica fell in love with one of her professors who was twenty-five years her senior. They married and raised two children. It reminds me of the line from the film *Disclosure*, when the street-savvy female attorney says that she was sexually harassed at her office until she married her boss.

Dr. Nica Cappellini shared my view about the possibilities of Butyrate. I hoped that she would help Cinzia gain entrance to the Milan University School of Hematology. Milan is an hour and a half plane ride from Bari. Cinzia could fly home to tend to Santino when needed.

Dr. Cinzia was somewhat attractive but hadn't the slightest idea how to use her femininity to charm. She eventually rubbed everyone the wrong way, including the person responsible for teaching her about the Butyrate therapy, Dr. Perrine.

Preservation of a patient's veins is crucial for long-term therapies. Santino would not use his Mediport until he began the Butyrate therapy. Getting a needle into the vein of a young child is an art. Some nurses had it, others did not. Those who had it were calm and cheerful. Enrico and Santino grew attached to them, only to have them changed the following day. Having the same nurses who easily accessed our children's veins would be better for all involved.

I tactfully approached the floor supervisor, who listened and quickly responded, "Mr. Girondi, the Italian families are always with their children. They are low-maintenance patients. If I give this assignment to the same nurses, I'll have problems with the other nurses, who have to constantly tend to the high-maintenance patients. I hope you understand."

Unfortunately, I did.

I flew back to Chicago looking to make some needed funds. Time was lapsing, and I did not want Santino's stay to be interrupted because of economic issues. The only remnants of the FBI investigation were the harassment that I received in airports when I arrived from overseas and my company and my person being audited each year by the IRS.

In my absence, Dirken Scott went to Oakland to be with my family. Lucrezia was full of kind comments about the "father of the year," who would send a substitute when his family needed him most.

Everyone loved Dirken. Dr. Perrine wanted to fix him up with her sister.

Chapter 17

Enrico

As with all Thalassemic patients, Enrico's hemoglobin fell. Dr. Perrine informed his family that Enrico needed to be transfused. He would then, in a week or so, begin the Butyrate therapy. I again relayed Luigi's concern about a possible allergic reaction to Kell. Dr. Perrine assured me that Oakland Children's Hospital was a research center and one of the best children's hospitals in the nation. The family and I should not worry.

Three days later, Enrico's immune system went into attack mode. He had been transfused with blood containing the Kell antigen. His life was in immediate danger. He was moved to the ICU.

Oakland Children's Hospital used every indicated drug in an effort to stop Enrico from auto destruction. The parents took turns in the ICU. The other Italians prayed. In desperation, Dr. Perrine called me, crying. "Enrico's body's reaction against the Kell intruder created hemolysis. If we can't restrain his autoimmune system, Enrico will die, Pat."

I was speechless. What could I do for Luigi and his family?

The news echoed off the hospital walls. Someone had screwed up the blood exam. The administration was incensed. Accidents like this happened less often before the hospital laboratory downsized. The child's death would mean an expensive lawsuit and lost funding. This would negatively affect the research program, and eventually bonuses and job security.

One day brought reason to hope, the next stole it away. This went on for weeks.

Luigi was in constant contact with Dr. Lippi, Enrico's doctor, in Florence. The family decided, as most Italians would, that if Enrico was going to die, he would die in his own land, in his own room, in the bosom of his family.

Perrine was sure that the twenty-hour trip home would certainly kill the child. The Aliquòs decided to return home anyway. Perrine called the Department of Children Family Services, but Enrico was not a US citizen. It was a complicated situation. There was not enough time to prevent their departure. The Aliquòs returned home without even one dose of the sacred Butyrate medicine.

In Florence, Dr. Lippi struggled to manage Enrico's precarious situation; Luigi's absence created personal business issues. Adding to the family's torment, Oakland Children's Hospital invoices, which amounted to over $250,000, arrived at their home daily.

"How could they have the nerve to charge for almost killing my son?"

I suggested an attorney, who offered to file suit on contingency.

"Suing will not buy my son's health, and I'm sure that the error was not intentional. It would be wrong to sue." Luigi hesitated before continuing. "We were told that there was no sense in getting US insurance because the treatment was experimental and covered by charitable grants." He paused again. "This is all destroying my family."

It seemed equally wrong to pay for life-saving treatment, administered to Enrico as a result of a laboratory error. Unfortunately, hospital executives insisted on immediate payment for all the non-experimental therapy that Enrico received, including the hundreds of thousands consumed fighting "Kell."

The administration was incensed and pointed to infractions against hospital rules committed by Dr. Perrine. They demanded that she pay for Enrico's bills out of her grant money. The battle raged, and it became evident that if Dr. Perrine was forced to pay Enrico's bills, she'd have no funding left for Santino's therapy.

Legal experts investigated how the hospital could strike out at the Aliquòs. After all, it had been their choice to seek care. It was only correct that they pay for services rendered.

I spoke to Luigi daily. Enrico's situation was a roller-coaster ride. I couldn't sit back as they also anguished over this financial predicament. Trading had been profitable. I returned to Oakland and walked unannounced into the hospital president's office. "If you don't stop sending bills to the Aliquòs, I will personally orchestrate a lawsuit on their behalf," I threatened.

The matter was buried and Santino recovered from surgery. Lucrezia left for Chicago and Sandy and Walter Hayhurst flew in from their home in Denver to stay with us in Oakland.

When someone asked me to comment on Walter Hayhurst's character, I replied, "He's the kind of a guy that prays even when no one's watching."

Eventually, Enrico recovered, and the Aliquòs had a third, compatible child. Professor Franco Locatelli, of Bambino Gesù Hospital in Rome, performed a bone marrow transplant. Today, Enrico is a petroleum technician and free of Thalassemia, living with his family in the hills above Florence.

With hard feelings over the Aliquò situation, the hospital was a war zone. I'm not sure if they were related but there were fistfights, vandalism, and break-ins. Dr. Perrine was repeatedly harassed and even locked out of her laboratory. In the tense environment, Santino finally began the Butyrate therapy and out of the ashes of the war-torn medical center, Santino's hemoglobin stabilized and miraculously began to climb.

We met daily with our heroine, Dr. Perrine. Together we were determined to do what we could for our Sickle Cell and Thalassemia patients.

Santino's hemoglobin rose from its lowest of 5.6 to 7.7. We were euphoric. The next number was 7.8—we rejoiced. Dr. Perrine wrote another article to submit to various scientific publications and quietly began negotiating with several research institutes, interested in signing a well-published researcher with media notoriety. Boston University, in particular, seemed dedicated to winning her to their prestigious faculty.

I knew that after a splenectomy, it was normal for the hemoglobin to jump. What was left of Santino's spleen was in shock and no longer suppressing hemoglobin. I kept my thoughts to myself and was finally convinced of the power of the Butyrate therapy when Santino's hemoglobin skyrocketed to 9.8.

Together, our team had been granted a miracle. Santino's energy level was high, and he would avoid transfusions and the risk of hepatitis and AIDS indefinitely.

Dr. Perrine was again a guest on CNN and several other televised programs. We were only too happy to support her efforts.

Lucrezia saw various dermatologists in the US and took their various described remedies. Finally, the rash disappeared everywhere but on her hands. She wore gloves to hide her fish scales–like skin.

Things at Oakland Children's seemed to worsen. One afternoon, Dr. Perrine was visiting Santino when two screaming executives assailed her, all but dragging her out of the room. My wife wasn't present for the show, but at times like these Lucrezia's point of view was easily understood.

The following day, Dr. Perrine arranged for Santino and me to be moved to the experimental therapy ward at San Francisco General. Things there were loud and interesting, with AIDS victims strolling in for their cocktails at all hours of the day and night.

Santino was hooked to a pump, often for days on end. He did not once fuss, complain, or demonstrate discomfort. His courage gave me courage.

Dr. Perrine spoke hopefully about Isobutyramide, an oral version of Butyrate. I daydreamed about Santino going to school and his mother reminding him to take a spoon of Isobutyramide before he walked out the door. I had to know if Isobutyramide would work in Sickle Cell Disease, Thalassemia, and Santino.

The medical expenses weighed on me like bags of cement and I began quietly gathering equipment for a move to Italy. There, Santino could do the therapy in his own home at a fraction of the cost. Lucrezia returned to Altamura to prepare for our arrival.

One night, Dr. Perrine entered Santino's darkened room. Without turning the light on, she gently sat on the bed not wanting to wake Santino. "Pat, Oakland Children's Hospital sold Isobutyrimide to Rezac Pharmaceuticals. The drug will be shelved forever," she muttered, her whisper laced with pent-up anguish and tears.

Drug companies hire marketing firms to brainwash the public and convince venture capitalists. Once the venture capitalists are invested, they pawn part of their investment off to investment banks, brokerage firms, and finally the public. At each step, the shares and/or units become more and more expensive. It's a pyramid scheme that in a rising stock market usually works well.

Isobutyramide was a derivative of Butyrate. Butyrate had been safely administered to humans. Having a drug that had safely been in humans, with application for Sickle Cell Disease, dressed up the Rezac portfolio nicely.

There are 2,500 Thalassemic patients in all of North America. There are over 100,000 Sickle Cell Disease patients in the US alone. I looked at the situation from all angles, like sizing up a muddied boot before shining it. Rezac was a newcomer. The founder, a renowned researcher, raised money and bought a portfolio of patents, doing what the industry calls "filling a pipeline."

Mr. Provenzano was an officer of Rezac Pharma in Cambridge. We hit it off. He confirmed that Isobutyramide was a filler, valuable because it was a derivative of a drug that had been in humans. It was also extremely helpful that it was patented with an application for a therapy for Sickle Cell Disease.

Drugs that have been dosed safely in humans are valuable because garnering toxicity data is the most expensive part of drug development. Sickle Cell Disease had been highly politicized. Rezac hoped to cash in on this strategic chip down the road.

Provenzano explained that many pharma companies pick up a drug that could be used to treat cancer, so that they can throw their hat into the cancer grant arena. If they win funding, they weigh their options. If they don't, the medicine is abandoned.

Mr. Provenzano appreciated my situation and if I was willing to meet him at Bottoms Up with a bag of $40,000 US currency, he would make sure, personally, that Dr. Perrine would get her medicine returned to her. Understandably, Mr. Provenzano was not willing to risk losing his job for nothing.

The strategy had a flaw. If the scheme worked, the drug would go back to Oakland Children's Hospital. Dr. Perrine was likely on her way to Boston University. Rezac could not stop me from using the drug outside of the US. I nixed the meeting with Provenzano and decided to invest the $40,000 setting up for clinical trials in Europe.

I instructed Dr. Cinzia to photocopy anything and everything that she could get her hands on. She would then head back home to study for the hematology school entrance exam. Altamura would have its own Thalassemia/Butyrate specialist.

On her way back, Cinzia, carrying forty pounds of Butyrate data, stopped in Chicago. Dirken picked her up at the airport and drove her to our offices. Leaving her baggage with Dirken, she left to see the city.

I informed the growing team that Santino and the Arginine Butyrate/Isobutyramide project would move to Italy, where he would do the therapy until a better solution was found.

I met with medical equipment representatives and bought an Abbott 5000, the same pump Santino used in the hospital. Abbott pump kits were eighty-five bucks a piece if bought in bulk. Nurses began dropping the kits and other supplies off in our room. I shoveled them into my backpack and hustled them out when I went back to the apartment to shower.

Hoping to turn me into an expert at administering Santino's therapy, hospital staff held class, educating me on how to deal with air in the line, keeping everything sterile, times to change, and how to change the kits. Because of the proximity to his heart, it was critical to keep Santino's Mediport sterile. An infected port could be fatal.

I liked the treatment part of medicine. It was practical and easy to understand.

For efficient delivery, the Mediport, inserted during Santino's partial splenectomy, was connected directly to Santino's heart. A needle pierced Santino's chest skin into a hard, hollowed rubber ball inside the device. A sterile tube hung off the needle, where a tubing from the pump was connected to administer the Butyrate. Though the Mediport device was under Santino's skin, it was very evident where the center of the ball that needed to be perforated was.

The needle was hooked and over an inch long. Seeing it, patients panicked. For this reason, they were often sedated when changing the needle. In most cases, the procedure was performed by surgeons. Abbott suggested changing the needle every three days. In Italy, if I could not change the needle, Santino could not continue the therapy.

I was surrounded by four nurses. They'd be fired if the administration discovered what they were doing. I tried to soothe Santino, telling him exactly what was going on.

I felt certain that the best strategy was the one that shortened the anguish of anticipation. I remembered, I was nine, maybe ten, when in a fit of rage the Old Man threw a television on me. The toughest part was the seconds between when he raised the set and when it struck me.

I pulled the needle out of the pack. Santino broke into tears. The nurses held him as I aimed for the Mediport. I couldn't let my son down. Santino jerked and the needle missed the rubber and went into his flesh.

He screamed, "No, Pà, no!" I looked at the nurses, one by one.

I said calmly, "I have to do this at home. None of you will be there. Susan (the nurse Santino was fondest of), you stay with me. The rest of you, please leave."

I avoided looking at Santino. I wanted him to be distracted. The nurses didn't have time to find the request strange. While they were still present, and while Santino's attention was still diverted, I plunged the needle into his chest and bullseye, into the center of the rubber ball, under his skin. The needle was changed; Santino was calm and a step closer to home.

The US is filled with some of the most wonderful people on the planet.

By the time we left for Italy, the Bahama-made Arginine Butyrate produced by the Hayhurst, Girondi, and Perrine Company, EPT, was being shipped to patients in different parts of the world. It was all rather remarkable. From what was published by the drug companies, this should have been a near-impossible feat costing at least tens of millions.

Arginine Butyrate is diluted in sterile water. This does little to alter the sulfuric acid smell. Within a month, we were in the middle of a production crisis. The rancid smell was unpleasant for neighboring residents and tourists. Only through a passionate plea with town representatives about Santino, and assurances of the eventual benefit for Sickle Cell Disease patients, was Walter able to convince the Bahamians to allow manufacturing to continue.

We moved into Lucrezia's parents' condominium. It was twice as large as our first apartment. It was a joy watching our sons eating, sleeping, and playing in their own home. But, watching Santino running around with a tube filled with blood protruding from his chest drew up other emotions not easily described. If the cap were broken or removed without us knowing about it, he would bleed to death.

Grandpa Santino and Ma at her wedding, Chicago (c. 1960).

Armour Park cookout with the boys, Chicago (c. 1985). *Photo credit: Ricky Gallo*

Statue of San Rocco at inauguration of Centro Medico San Rocco, Altamura, Italy. Sons from left, Santino, Mariocarlo, and Cenzino (1998).

Dr. Franco Locatelli, Vito Cilla, Maria Colavito, Altamura, Italy (c. 1998).

Knuckles Ciacci and me at Italian Telethon event, Chicago (2001).

Joey Feldman and me, Chicago (2001).

Cal, me, Derek Holmes (Big Mamma's Son), Chicago (2001).

Me with the gang raising money for research
Included, Rasheda Ali (Muhammad Ali's daughter), Tony LaRosa (my brother), and
Robert Pastorelli (actor), Chicago (2001).

Me and Susanna Agnelli, Chicago (2001).

U Maestro and me, Chicago (2017).

Ricky Stanic, my shoeshine partner and life brother, Chicago (2018).
Photo credit: Megan Euker

Me and Ma (2018). *Photo credit: Megan Euker*

Dr. John Tisdale (with Third Orphan Dream Award) and me at the National Institutes of Health, Bethesda, Maryland (2019). *Photo credit: Megan Euker*

Zia Anna Ferri, my second mother, and me, Bridgeport, Chicago (2019).

Me and Megan Euker (Margherita), my dear friend and collaborator, outside Casa Cava Concert Hall, Matera, Italy (2019).

Me, Zia Maria, and family, Modugno, Italy (2019). *Photo credit: Megan Euker*

Me and my bosom friend and attorney Ken Sussmane, New York (2019).
Photo credit: Megan Euker

Calhoun, my mentor, sage, and dear friend (2020).

Megan Euker, installation of her exhibition "The Cure," about the court case, at the International Museum of Surgical Science, Chicago (2020). *Photo credit: James Prinz*

Me and Aunt Vittoria, Boston (2020).

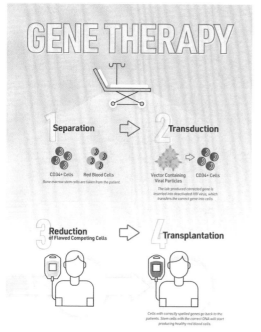

How Gene Therapy Works (2020). *Graphic credit: Megan Euker and TJ Fulfer*

Music Photos

Me and Enzo Matera, Matera, Italy (2017). *Photo credit: Antonio Sansone*

Me performing at Casa Cava wearing the Versace jacket gifted by Vance and Kelly Harris, Matera, Italy (2017).

Left to right: Marco Abbattista, bass; me, vocals; Enzo Matera, guitar; Pat Girondi and the Orphan's Dream concert (2018). *Photo credit: Antonio Sansone*

Pat Girondi and the Orphan's Dream performing at the Blues in Town Fest, Policoro, Italy (2018). *Photo credit: Antonio Sansone*

Me performing at a Pat Girondi and the Orphan's Dream concert, Naples, Italy (2018). *Photo credit: Giuseppe DiMatteo*

Me performing, Rome, Italy (2019). *Photo credit: Antonio Sansone*

Left to right: Antonio Benedetto, bass; Arturo Sanzo, guitar; Enzo Matera, guitar; Giuseppe Chiefa, drums; me, vocals; Nanni Teot, trumpet, outside concert hall, Matera, Italy (2020). *Photo credit: Megan Euker*

Left to right: Enzo Matera, guitar; me, vocals; Pat Girondi and the Orphan's Dream performance (2020). *Photo credit: Antonio Sansone*

Left to right: Enzo Matera, guitar; me, vocals; Alessio Santoro, drums; Marco Abbattista, bass, Blera, Italy (2021). *Photo credit: Project Tuscia*

Left to right: Enzo Matera, guitar; me, vocals; Pat Girondi and the Orphan's Dream performance, Ballets Park Hotel, San Martino al Cimino, Italy (2021). *Photo credit: Project Tuscia*

Lucrezia, justifiably terrified, was back in Italy, a place she didn't want to be, with a rash and carrying a child from a man she no longer believed in. It was nearly impossible for her to get accustomed to wearing gloves as an American dermatologist recommended, and she had no idea what she had done to deserve all of this.

While playing, Cenzino knocked the pump over, and the bottle of Arginine Butyrate exploded. Our apartment and the stairway used by the other condo residents reeked for days. Lucrezia was so embarrassed that she wouldn't leave the house for days.

Our marital relationship improved after I purchased land on the outskirts of town. I traded from my Altamura office and we began planning. "Lucrezia and Patrizio," was chiseled onto a stone and ceremoniously dropped where our new home's foundation would be. It cracked. The builder tried to convince us that the event was meaningless. I don't believe that anything is without meaning.

Women live in the homes much more than men and I believed that Lucrezia would enjoy picking out the marble, cabinets, and room fixtures. I left as much of the decision-making as possible to her. I wanted to have a say in decorating the large room in the basement to hold family parties. She informed me that she didn't want any big parties in her home. She was a private person. One thing led to another and she stopped speaking to me for months at a time. Frankly, the space helped me comprehend that I didn't really have a lot to say to her.

The solitude actually had a calming effect on me, and I believe that it helped reserve my perseverance and strength. The land we were building our home on bordered the Appian Way. The road was lined with boulders stacked up to three meters tall. In time, the wall of silence built by my wife proved to be much harder to penetrate than the Appian Way wall. I was quietly impressed.

Zio Mimmo never said a bad word about anyone. He arrived at my office in the main piazza in Altamura early in the morning, cleaned the windows and the bathroom, emptied the trash, and did whatever he could to make my life easier. He and Zia Chiara looked out for us as their own siblings and my children as their own grandchildren.

Zio Mimmo and I waited for Dr. Cinzia to bring the Butyrate documents. She entered the office empty-handed, insisting that the information was entrusted to her by Dr. Perrine and useful only to doctors. I calmly asked Dr. Cinzia to bring the documents the next day.

The following day, Cinzia again arrived empty-handed. I studied her without saying a word. I sensed a smirk or the tiniest grin on her face. She gained composure and told me that she'd bring the documents only after she had been officially accepted to the Hematology School at the University of Milan.

If Cinzia would help the Thalassemics of Italy, Professoressa Cappellini saw it as her duty to assist in securing a spot. Instead, if she was just another doctor trying to get into specialization school, she'd have to swim with the rest of the fish.

Had she known me better, the opportunist might have known that I would order Dirken to make a copy of the documents while she visited Chicago. This was a test. I had them already. The idiot failed, lost our faith, and never made it into hematology school. I now urgently needed a replacement.

Lucrezia's rash continued and a commarra (her cousin who had been a testimony for her in our wedding) suggested that we speak with Dr. Torre, a physician specializing in treating people with "natural remedies." Dr. Torre lived and had an office in Altamura. He was a few years younger than I, had a strong build, and at six-three towered over almost everyone in town.

Lucrezia was skeptical. She had been to ten dermatologists in Italy and the US. Dr. Torre took one look at her hands and wrote the name of a lotion. We didn't need a prescription and it cost under ten dollars. The rash disappeared in days. I began meeting with Dr. Torre, and was impressed with his overall medical knowledge and eagerness to increase it.

Dr. Torre enthusiastically agreed to get the technical knowledge needed to become Santino's local physician. If an idiot like me could learn this stuff, it would be child's play for him.

Walter and European experts believed that the Abbott kit could be changed every nine days instead of every three days. Abbott Labs was probably not really keen about this. Each week, I changed Santino's kit and needle. It became routine for both of us. Life was good.

An elderly gentleman, Don Filippo lived with his family in an old stone farmhouse in front of the land we had bought to build our home. He walked around in the morning with his lupara (rifle) waiting for a fox, pheasant, or wild rabbit. When he was not carrying the rifle, it sat in his unlocked house. The cartridges were inches away, on top of the refrigerator. So much for gun control.

He asked for the wood from the olive trees that would be cleared. "Of course, grandfather," I said in Italian.

Lucrezia was meticulous with Santino's medication and now that we had a doctor for him, a bit of normality entered the house, if life with a sick child can ever be called normal.

Santino and Cenzino played constantly and searched each other out if one of them was missing. I hired and trained a half dozen Italian traders, including Nicola, a horse butcher who is also my cousin and compare; and my wife's cousin Luca, my godson through confirmation. They began trading with me from my office in Piazza Duomo.

One of the town's feast days is in honor of Our Lady of the Good Walk, *La Madonna del Buon Cammino*. The feast day includes a procession of more than four hundred horses, jockeyed by elegantly dressed riders. They escort the Madonna from her home church, a few kilometers outside of town, into the cathedral in the center of town. The three days of festivities end with an auction of the Madonna's blue and white flag. The winner has the honor of keeping the banner in their home or business until next year's procession. The winning auction price is usually around $40,000.

It always seems to be a holiday in Altamura, and in fact, Italy has thirty-seven holidays, not including local feast days such as Our Lady of the Good Walk, that clutter the calendar.

During the three days of festivities, the streets are clogged everywhere. The smell of roasted involtinis (lamb insides tied together and grilled over wood) fill the air. Lucrezia, like thousands of town mothers, was dressing her children in their best clothes.

The phone rang. I answered, listened for a moment, and hung up and left without a word.

On town feast days, burglars had field days, knowing that everyone would be out at the festivities. Thieves would never rob homes in their own town. Altamuran thieves would rob in Gravina on their feast of San Michele and the thieves from Gravina would rob in Altamura on the feast of La Madonna del Buon Cammino. The Carabinieri would laugh if someone called about a robbery. How would they get through the streets? Most robbery victims called on their families first anyway.

I arrived at Lucrezia's cousin's (Carmela's) house. The entrance door to their condo was locked from the inside, and they suspected that thieves were in the house. Having been summoned was my official welcome to the family.

Italians believe that everyone has a right to live—including bankers, politicians, corporate executives, and policemen whom many consider to be more dishonest than thieves. Violence, however, is taboo and authorities pay little heed to robberies, unless someone is hurt.

Italian victims concentrate on getting their stolen merchandise returned. If a family member, compare, or friend is able to contact the perpetrators, the opposing sides negotiate. Getting police involved actually lowers the possibility of retrieving stolen property. My cousins assured me that the thieves were outsiders. No decent person would rob inside his own town, especially on a feast day.

There is a famous Italian movie about thieves in Rome, upset because families installed complicated alarms, creating hardship for older less technologically savvy burglars. Thieves in all parts of the country went on strike. Police got less work and were laid off. The families of the striking thieves and laid-off police stopped spending. Merchants lost money. Politicians felt threatened. Finally, the government agreed to put a special tax on alarm equipment. Fewer people bought alarms, and the burglars went back to work. Happy ending.

As I looked up at the cousin's third-floor apartment, the statue of the Madonna paraded through town. Priests dressed in festive vestments chanted and sang centuries-old prayers. As she passed, each citizen asked for her blessing.

Many historians claim Italy to be a nation of 500 city-states, each a small nation radically rooted in culture, food, dialect, and traditions. When one's town is at peace, the world is at peace.

Climbing the gutter, I mentally prepared myself for what came next. I wanted to give the thieves an escape route. They'd then run down the stairs, and my cousins would pretend to try and catch them.

I opened the bathroom window, hopped onto the windowsill, and bounced onto the floor. I paused and listened. It was silent. I opened the bathroom door and felt the outside wall, pressing light switches.

Soon, the small crowd heard a yell from above and anxiously looked up to where I stood with a smile on my face.

"*Non c'e' nessuno!*" (No one's home!)

The apartment had been ransacked. Remnants of dried sausage and an emptied wine bottle were on the kitchen table. It's common practice for Italian thieves to eat while they work, occasionally leaving notes commenting on wines, cheeses, and/or salamis.

Southern Italians are survivors. Bravery is likened to foolishness. Parents often go into anxiety attacks when their child goes away to college. By climbing up three floors and entering the apartment, I demonstrated that I was fearless. No one person is perfect, and even if *U Carneveil* was crazy, he was now family.

Our third son, Mariocarlo, was born on November 4, 1993. The builder of our home, Mimmo, became Mariocarlo's godfather. Mariocarlo was named after Mr. Dicecca and Saint Charles, the saint whose name day he was born on. We again tested Mariocarlo, hoping that he might be a match for Santino. He wasn't.

In the middle of our home planning, some genius decided that the Appian Way, one of the earliest and strategically most important Roman roads of the ancient republic, built in 300 BC, should be protected. Any development on the ancient road, in front of our property which connects Rome to Brindisi, a port city in Puglia, eighty miles south of Bari, was forbidden. I figured it was a shakedown.

Many homes in southern Italy are sprinkled with priceless artifacts. The people don't really care much about going to museums. Pieces of ancient walls, vases, murals, and other artifacts become part of personal collections and family knicknacks.

The road bordering my property was of historical value, and the federal government, which was still very sensitive to the murders by the Italian syndicate in 1992 of the Italian judges Giovanni Falcone and Paolo Borsellino, was anxious to penalize infractions of the law. The government felt that they needed to demonstrate to the southern part of the country where the judges were murdered, that they would not back down.

Not a stone on the ten-foot wall in front of my future home could be touched without written authorization from the Archaeological Commission. I'd need a helicopter to get onto my property. Lucrezia was distraught. It seemed like nothing went right. She cried for her son, her unstable husband, unhappy marriage, and now for the home that would likely never be built.

I futilely spoke to various town officials, bosses, and politicians. Lucrezia's cousin Mimmo, a city hall employee, suggested I make an *offer* to the town's building commissioner. We call them bribes in the US, unless you can afford a lobbyist.

I walked into the building commissioner's office. Fiorenzo, the department head, was seated at his desk, in front of a large, open window. He was surrounded by a small group of men. Everything went silent as I entered.

Without an introduction, I spoke slowly in Italian. "If my wife cries again, I'll throw you out this window."

It's not easy to be taken seriously in a country where people yell, point, and curse at each other, only to finish and have a coffee together. My message was understood, but unfortunately, a national archaeologist was now adamant about protecting Via Appia. The federal government was heavily involved and had an iron grip on the situation.

Weeks later, I became a revered guy, when articles hit the newspapers about the disappearance of a 225-foot section of the Appian wall. Officials from various government departments were humiliated and furious. It wasn't possible for 225 feet of a ten-foot-tall wall made of boulders, some weighing tons, to just disappear. The bottom boulders were the size of small automobiles! The press and politicians demanded an investigation.

I was summoned, but I couldn't speak Italian well enough to understand (at least that's what I said), and I was told to return with an attorney. Rumors circulated that *L'Americano* was leaving for America and maybe not returning.

It would have taken bulldozers, cranes, and heavy trucks days to dismantle that section of Via Appia. The Carabinieri (state police) investigated the scene of the crime. Don Filippo, the elderly gentleman, to whom I had given my olive trees, lived with his family in a farmhouse in front of the missing, sacred wall.

When questioned, Don Filippo told the Carabinieri that he hadn't seen anyone dismantling the wall or anything else. The Carabinieri returned the following day hoping to speak to Don Filippo's wife and daughters. Certainly, someone saw something. Don Filippo was walking on his stone driveway toward his house. The Carabinieri pulled their car onto the driveway. Don Filippo heard the car and turned.

"Don Filippo!," the driver yelled out the window, "We'd like to ask your wife and children if any of them saw anyone removing the wall.

Don Filippo fixed his rifle on them. "No one in my family saw anything. Now get off my property."

They weren't silly enough to risk their life for a wall that was already gone.

At the same time, back in the US, the boys from 26th Street were on their way to jail. The film *Casino* shows a good part of their demise. The film stars Joe Pesci, Robert De Niro, and Sharon Stone, demonstrating the downfall of the Italian American syndicate that controlled Las Vegas. Corporate America was now in full control.

Every system is imperfect and full of some great people. One of them is Professor Justice Ford. Justice could take a cell off an embryo and label its HLA antigens.

Hormones stimulate egg production. Extracted eggs are fertilized with the father's sperm. A cell from each embryo is then analyzed. Healthy matches to the HLA-compatibility of the afflicted child are implanted in the mother. The child or children who are born are healthy HLA-compatible donors for the sick sibling.

It was nothing short of a miracle. Of course, conservative politicians and the church were weary of scientists playing God. The topic was a political and theological hot potato.

Lucrezia would be impregnated with only embryos that would create HLA-compatible siblings for Santino, guaranteeing a match and his salvation.

Specialists claimed no long-term side effects from the hormones. Only one, of the many I consulted, indicated that women could have mood swings. Most believed that a mother's focus on saving their child usually made any side effect trivial.

Our first try in Houston was unsuccessful. Lucrezia believed that my attitude—"No problem, we can try again in a few months"—was repulsive. I only paid for the procedure; that was the easy part. I guess she had a point. Wanting to demonstrate my compassion and understanding, I actually allowed her to inject a syringe full of cold water into my buttocks.

The following year, an IVF was scheduled with Doctor Ford at the Community Hospital in Bethesda. I arrived at the end of the cycle and met Lucrezia in a DC shopping mall.

Later, at the hotel room, Lucrezia told me calmly that she wanted a divorce. One thing led to another, and she ended up crying on the floor. The next day, I returned to the hotel and spotted a squad car parked in front. I knew that Lucrezia's father had convinced her to make a report.

It was my word against hers. The coppers gave me a warning. I'm not sure for what, I would never hurt the mother of my children, especially when she was the only one who could give me a compatible match for Santino.

That night, Lucrezia had to take the final dose of HCG before Dr. Ford retrieved the embryos. I told her that she needed to take the whole vial, or five thousand units. She screamed and yelled that she was supposed to take 1,500 units. It was midnight. Texting or calling anyone would have only exacerbated the situation. I injected Lucrezia with 1,500 units. She was supposed to receive five thousand. The whole cycle was trashed.

For the next attempted IVF, she refused to allow me to come and was accompanied by her sister. Again, the cycle failed. An eventual fourth attempt also ended in failure. We spent over $100,000 on the failed procedures.

Searching for funds, in 1995, Dr. Perrine, the Hayhursts, and I visited Saudi Arabia during Ramadan (similar to Lent for Catholics). A decade prior, Perrine had discovered asymptomatic Sickle Cell patients there in the Empty Quarter. These patients had a higher than normal level of butyric acid circulating in their blood and this discovery became the basis of the Butyrate therapy. Heading from the airport to Riyadh, the driver stopped and knelt on a car mat. I knelt and prayed next to him.

I told Santino's story at the end of Walter's presentation. A prince invited me to his home. His Mercedes headed down the immaculate streets of the desert city and arrived at a walled encampment. Inside the enclave was a block-long desert garden and a home with a small edifice next to it.

A male assistant greeted us. Prince Abdullah told him to inform the women that he would take dinner in his den. We entered the nine-hundred-square-foot, plush office. He removed his headwear and offered me a drink.

He was Harvard-educated, with an in-depth knowledge of US history (if anyone can have knowledge of history). In fact, his hobby was studying the US Civil War. We spoke for hours. People are just people, wherever you go, despite what governments try to convince you of.

He offered to donate but was not investing. Did he believe it was a bad venture? Did he resent Americans? He never explained and I never asked, for his reason or for his donation.

Walter's wife Sandy grew up in Little Rock, Arkansas with the Walton family, the founders of Walmart.

John Walton was the son of Sam Walton, the founder of Walmart. As a young child, John Walton's son Lukas was afflicted with Wilms' tumor. Professor Perry Sand, a medical specialist at the University of San Diego, recommended removing one of Lukas's lungs. Instead, the family went to a medical institute in Tijuana, Mexico for herbal therapy. The tumor subsided but the family lived in fear that the cancer would return.

A proven therapeutic effect of Arginine Butyrate was extinguishing Wilms' tumor cells in vitro. John Walton invested $7.5 million, and the company put in Arginine Butyrate and a few other Perrine inventions. Beacon Pharmaceuticals was born.

The Waltons insisted on a retired pharma executive, Art Nieman, as CEO. Almost immediately, Art announced that cancer would be Beacon's primary focus, with an eye on Thalassemia and Sickle Cell Disease.

Having no income, and paying a CEO $20,000 a month seemed ridiculous to me. Compounding the injury, Art leased company offices near his home in Wayne, New Jersey and hired a staff of ten before he even moved in.

Walter, Sandy, John Walton, and I comprised the Beacon Board. Professor Perry Sand was the head scientist. Ronald Troy and Travis Dunn, John's assistants, became Beacon consultants.

John's son's bout with Wilms' tumor and Santino's Thalassemia linked us. I flew in for two board meetings; after that, I figured that the company could find better ways to spend its money.

Chapter 18

L'Americano Risks Wife to Save Son

On December 20, 1995, we moved into our new home. My father-in-law was a very industrious person, but he did not pick up one box or even a lamp. I believe that he was making a statement. *We were not quite out of the woods.*

"You're anxious to make my daughter have another baby," he said to me. "She told me you want to do it using the laboratory so she can have a compatible child with Santino. But doing it that way, she can have twins or triplets. Me and my wife are not returning to Italy to become babysitters," he stated.

I respectfully remained quiet.

He continued. "You're trying to save your son, but in the end you're gonna lose your wife," he added. "If you lose your wife, you lose your whole family."

I couldn't find a flaw in his logic.

At Beacon, Mr. Nieman landed articles in a few small pharmaceutical journals. Salaries, executive bonuses, attorneys, and scientific and research consultants (who all seemed to be friends of Mr. Nieman) were quickly siphoning the pond dry.

Although my involvement with Beacon was limited to calling in for board meetings, I objected directly to Mr. Nieman about what I thought was a faulty strategy. He correctly pointed out that I did not have proper training and was not an expert.

Not wanting to be disruptive, I visited John at his home where I met his wife Christie and his son Lukas. What a wonderful guy Lukas is. I spoke to John about my thoughts on Mr. Nieman and Beacon. He felt it too early to change captains.

Santino was hooked to the Arginine Butyrate pump eight to eighteen hours a day. Dr. Perrine and I lined up more patients to do clinical trials in Italy for both Arginine Butyrate and Isobutyramide.

Clinical trials begin when humans are first dosed with a product. In Europe, experimental medicines can be managed by a local doctor at the patient's risk. In the US, most experimental treatments would first have to be granted permission by the FDA.

There are thousands of Thalassemic patients grouped in large clusters in southern Italy. An Italian clinical trial made sense. Dr. Perrine now officially worked as a professor at the Boston University, School of Medicine. She was known around the world as a ray of hope for Sickle Cell Disease and Thalassemia patients. She was welcomed with a red-carpet reception wherever she traveled and began flying almost monthly between the US and Italy.

Initially, the University of Bari hosted the Butyrate project in their laboratories. It quickly became apparent that this was not a long-term solution. I bought five thousand square feet of offices from Lucrezia's cousin, pulled some political strings, and began building the San Rocco Laboratory (Saint Rocco is the patron saint of incurable disease and also the patron saint of Modugno, my grandfather Santino's town).

Federal, state, and municipal authorities readily collaborated; "Such a good father should be respected." My role as patient benefactor was also a pleasant distraction and helped take some of the sting out of the investigation into the mystery of the missing Appian wall.

Building in Italy is a unique experience and each day an adventure. Despite the complexities of Italy, it's my opinion that they live a quality of life superior to that of any other people I know. They care little about armies and wars, and even less about glory, unless we're speaking of the European or World Cup. Most couldn't tell you who the president or prime minister of Italy was. Their true focus is on family, compari, friends, and of course, *what's for dinner.*

Complaining is part of Mediterraneans' and especially Italians' DNA. A famous Italian saying is *lamenta rende,* which literally means that if you complain enough someone will give you something. So, there you have it! Italy, a nation with an incredible wealth and lifestyle, is filled with inhabitants who are constantly whining.

In Italy, I spread my Robin Hood way of thinking to Altamura, buying toys for orphans and giving support to families in distress.

Altamura's mayor, Vito Plotino, was a force in the local Fascist party. The Fascist party is one of Italy's more than fifty different political parties. There is also a Communist party. The mayor and I quickly understood each other. Simply stated, he would have done anything in his power to help my family. Permits for the building of the medical center were rushed through in days.

On a Tuesday evening in October, I walked into the kitchen and spotted a cigarette butt in the trash. I had never seen my wife smoke. When I inquired, she lit up another cigarette and puffed smoke in my face. I wasn't sure what she was trying to say, but I imagined it wasn't real positive. The poor woman had been through more than many could bear and was suffering greatly. It became impossible to know what would set her off. The boys often communicated with coded face and hand signals, trying to avoid landmines.

For me, this was a very unique situation. I lived in a home with three sons and a woman who readily admitted that she detested me. Fortunately, growing up, I had been molded by unique situations. I was sure that this experience would strengthen my sons and my marriage.

Lucrezia's older sister Pamela, getting over the wounds of a divorce, visited. I hoped that this would help our own situation.

BPT trading profits began to fall and I needed to go back and forth to the trading floors in Chicago to continue the march for a cure. Sometimes I'd spend months there, earning the funds needed for the medical center and research.

Dr. Perrine funneled a constant stream of medical books and articles to me. I paid the salary for Becky Martino, a bubbly Thalassemic patient, to help with the growing administration work of the project.

As previously stated, lifesaving blood transfusions deposit iron in all major organs. A person's normal iron level is under 300. Few Thalassemic patients maintain an iron level under 1,000. Excess iron in the pancreas leads to diabetes; in the heart, heart conditions; in the liver, liver disease; etc. Tisravno's product FeeralX causes patients to excrete excess iron through urine. It costs $35,000 annually in the US and $15,000 in Europe. It's administered by needle, under the patient's skin, twelve to sixteen hours each day. Pain and skin irritation are extreme and patients needed to continue this therapy as long as they transfused (lived). Compliance was problematic, but without FeeralX, iron levels climbed into the thousands. A patient is walking dead at these levels.

In the late eighties, an oral drug called L1 was invented. It had no patent protection. European and Indian patients flocked to buy the cheaply made oral alternative.

Becky was allergic to FeeralX. Her iron level was over 3,000. She was at risk for multiple life-threatening complications. L1 was illegal in the US, but it was my duty to get it to her. FeeralX sales fell, and Tisravno moved to protect the bottom line.

Prior to a Thalassemia Convention at the University of Milan, Tisravno researchers administered L1 to laboratory rats. As doctors and patients filed into the Tisravno-sponsored event, Tisravno personnel distributed pictures of the dead rodents, who died after being injected with the lethal L1. The animals' heads appeared smashed, their bodies twisted and deformed. The unwritten message was that doctors needed to protect patients from L1.

Hours later, at the same convention, in the same hall, Indian (from India) researchers presented their miraculous results using L1, the oral iron chelator, on patients.

Tisravno representatives then schmoozed doctors with promises of research collaboration, sprinkled with comments about India being a third-world country. Tisravno would do everything to protect their turf and buy time to work on their own oral form of the drug, which of course would be patent-protected.

The Tisravno rats were not iron-overloaded. If you gave an iron chelator to any creature that was not overloaded with iron you would be killing the creature, as the chelator, in the absence of iron, eliminates other critical minerals in the body. Fortunately, not all doctors were fooled. Patients in Europe and India permanently switched to L1, and FeeralX was all but eliminated there.

Sadly, the L1 product wasn't approved until almost twenty years later in the US, costing the lives of hundreds of American patients. The L1 story is told in Miriam Shuchman's book, *The Drug Trial*, a must-read for anyone interested in understanding the pharmaceutical industry.

Street smarts and a bird's-eye view helped me recognize hoaxes, good projects, shelved medicines, and products that were not likely to function. It is complex, and certainly not simple separating truth from public relations.

More times than not, patients get the best-financed medicine as opposed to the best medicine.

Art Nieman died in the fall of '97. Beacon coffers were empty. In the midst of the ruins came accusations of misappropriation. Chairman of the Board Walter Hayhurst stepped down. He was replaced by Walton managers Ronald Troy and Travis Dunn (Ronald Troy eventually became the CEO of one of the largest makers of solar panels, a company in which John Walton had a significant ownership interest).

I was trading in Chicago and on a bitter cold winter morning, I received a visit from Emmett, a great neighborhood guy who teaches special children on the far South Side of the city. Each Christmas, he throws a party for his kids. Dirken Scott was often Santa, and our crew frequently helped pay for the toys.

"Pat, my wife has cancer and the doctors at Northwestern University Hospital gave her a month to live. I heard what you were doing for your son, if you ever hear of anything for my wife," Elmer said as he began crying.

I shared Patty's, Emmett's wife's, paperwork with our team. Within a week, she began an experimental therapy at Texas A&M. Eventually, she testified to the US Congress on behalf of the inventor of the medicine that saved her life. Unfortunately, this did not keep him out of prison for selling *illegal drugs*.

There's an Italian saying that goes, "*Fai bene, scordati; fai male, pensaci* ----- Do good and forget about it; do bad and think about (never forget) it."

One evening, while still in Chicago, I grabbed the phone and called Zia Maria in Italy. She answered sobbing. Her father, Zio Cosimo, had died that very second. I was on a plane the next afternoon. The family never forgot my sixth sense, nor did I. My fathers left, one by one, Uncle Rory, Mr. Dicecca, and now Zio Cosimo. A piece of me died and was reborn with the passing of each of these men who had taught me how to live.

From 1997 to 1999, the Girondi family sponsored clinical trials in Italy with Arginine Butyrate and Isobutyramide, collaborating with Dr. Patrick Mazza of Taranto, Dr. Nica Cappellini of the University of Milan Medical School, and Dr. Perrine at Boston University. Arginine Butyrate's potency was confirmed; unfortunately, Isobutyramide, the oral form of the drug, proved to be much less effective.

I had dreamed of Santino taking a spoon of Isobutyramide before going to school and being asymptomatic. Of course, I was disappointed that this was no longer a possibility. In the seminary, I learned the phrase, "Lord, help me change the things I can and accept the things that I cannot change and the wisdom to know the difference." In certain respects, the life of a parent of a sick child is emotionally restrictive. If disappointment takes hold and bitterness or depression takes control, the sickness has other victims, and there's no one left to fight.

The Italian clinical trial cost a small fortune, and we still had no practical oral hemoglobin enhancer. The torturous intravenous administration of Arginine Butyrate eliminated it as a practical alternative. I pushed for Lucrezia to attempt another IVF, guaranteeing an HLA-compatible match. I couldn't understand her delay.

What did our marital problems have to do with Santino? In desperation, I again spoke to her father, who accused me of making a baby machine out of his daughter.

One evening while home in Italy, I noticed redness at the Mediport site. An infection this close to the heart was dangerous. Within hours we were on a plane to Boston University, where Dr. Perrine was now Head of Hematology. The Mediport was removed.

After almost five years of different drug schedules, Santino's hemoglobin fell. It had been a miraculous run that saved our son over eighty blood transfusions with all the damage this entails at a time when blood transfusions were a dangerous risk.

Santino began taking Isobutyramide, the oral form of Arginine Butyrate. Eventually, Santino's spleen grew back and he was once again under the knife. This time, the whole spleen was removed. After the operation and on Isobutyramide, Santino's hemoglobin fell to below 8. His forehead began violently protruding as the disease transformed his facial appearance and all of our lives.

Still hopeful of extending the time before he would transfuse, I sifted through the *American Hematology, Blood, Phenomenon Magazine, Lancet, New England Journal of Medicine, Nature,* and *Science* journals that arrived monthly. I discovered a protocol for an oral hemoglobin enhancer, Sodium Phenylbutyrate, written by Tifo in the *US Medical Journal.* The drug had safely been in hundreds of urea cycle disorder (UCD) patients at higher doses than Santino would take.

At ten pills a day, Santino's hemoglobin shot up to almost 10. Transfusions were again avoided. 100 pills cost about $900. That was $90 a day. The therapy was experimental for Thalassemia and not covered by insurance. Getting reimbursed in Italy was possible, but would require time.

I called the drugmaker Ucyclid Pharma in Baltimore and spoke to the director, Chris Wiech. Chris was the son of the inventor of the therapy, Dr. Norb Wiech. Dr. Wiech was also one of the founding partners/owners of Ucyclid Pharma. I explained Santino's situation to Doctor Norb Wiech. After a week, bottles with the labels ripped off began arriving at my home, at zero cost.

I met and thanked Doctor Wiech, a Notre Dame grad who had a master's in biochemistry from Tulane and a fellowship at Harvard. He had personally attained FDA approval for two drugs. He became my resident bench biologist, unpaid scientific consultant, and friend.

A Crayola drawing from a UCD (Urea Cycle Disorder) patient in his home office in Phoenix, Maryland sums him up: "Thank you Doctor Wiech For Making Me Feel Better."

In Chicago, I raffled my Rolls-Royce to find needed funding. My address book became flooded with names of doctors, patients, pharma people, lawyers, bureaucrats, politicians, mobsters, and even FBI agents, anyone who I believed could someday, someway be of help. I was never alone, whether I was in New Delhi or New York.

I read hundreds of articles and remembered much of what I read, hoping that the information might help someone in the future. Patients with dozens of rare diseases contacted me as I became an expert safari guide. When I was contacted about new situations with patients, I predicated each conversation with these words: "I'm not a doctor, I did not graduate from high school, but I'd like to help."

When I was able to make a difference, the joy was immeasurable. I was Santino's father, a shoeshine, a dishwasher, a street mechanic, a trader, a singer-songwriter, and a health consultant, and born for this.

In Cenzino and Mariocarlo's presence, my wife often said that I only loved Santino. As a consequence, when I was alone with each of them, I confided that they were number one, *numero uno* (I learned this from Midge Botica, my friend Patrick's father). When they discovered that I also told their brothers the same thing, I had to admit that I did this because I did not want their brothers to be jealous of them, telling them the biblical story of how Joseph was sold into slavery because his brothers were envious of their father's love for him.

In 1998, though already in the middle of Clinical Trials with 38 Italian patients using Arginine Butyrate and Isobutyramide, I delayed the official opening of Centro Medico San Rocco to coincide with Lucrezia's birthday, December 13th.

Centro Medico San Rocco was now officially a research and medical center. The laboratory was blessed by Don Nicola, the cathedral priest. There were speeches and countless local and national dignitaries. Sebastiano, my Swiss knight, and Dr. Norb Wiech flew in for the festivities. Dr. Franco Locatelli, today the highest-ranking medical doctor in the entire Italian healthcare industry, attended and became a collaborator.

A ten-foot-tall statue of Saint Rocco kneeling at the bed of a sick child created by local artist Domenico Laterza was uncovered on the lawn in front of the entrance and welcomed with frantic applause.

To celebrate the Centro Medico San Rocco, I gifted to anyone who attended CDs made by my band, Pat Girondi and the Orphan's Dream. Countless guests asked that their CD be signed by me to commemorate the sacred event.

Lucrezia's mood at the gala was noticeably cloudy and distant. *Now I was a musician.* My wife's skepticism grew as I pretended to be everything but what I was, nuts. *Where was I finding all of this money? How were her and her sons going to survive my insanity?* These were some of the questions going through her mind. Believe me, I understood her thinking and certainly didn't blame her for having those thoughts.

Personnel and equipment were in place to keep Santino's therapy organized. Doctor Ferdinando Torre was Santino's physician and point man at the expanding laboratory.

As stated previously, without a spleen, a bacterial infection could end Santino's life. In the presence of any fever, Santino or any child in this predicament needed to be under the immediate care of a physician.

I continued communicating with Rita, the Canadian patient on Arginine Butyrate. People's stares while Rita was on the bus from her home in Guelph to Toronto made for a punishing trip. The FDA and Health Canada obligated a patient on drugs administered by IV to be treated at the center of the clinical trial's Principal Investigator. Rita's principal investigator was Dr. Fanny Tifo.

Rita's parents struggled to convince her to continue the therapy, but Rita decided it was better to die than to get on the bus everyday.

Milly, Rita's mother, wanted to ask the FDA and Health Canada for an exception so the drug could be given to Rita in Guelph. Dr. Tifo claimed that Rita needed to be under her own constant, personal care. Accusations flew. The good doctor accused the parents of trying to kill their own daughter.

Nothing would change for Dr. Perrine, who had no access to Rita in Toronto and would have no access to her in Guelph. Dr. Perrine favored the idea of asking the FDA for an exception.

I called Congressmen Amato, Lipinski, and the Daley organization. I spoke to the guys on 26th Street who contacted other friends and collaborators. Rita got the FDA exception. The drug would be administered in her hometown under a local oncologist.

After Rita's move, Tifo stopped communicating with me and ceased collaborations with Dr. Perrine.

At Boston University, Dr. Perrine had other inventions and Beacon invested more money. Walter and I found additional funds. Joe Feldman and his father; Peter Bellus; the Caputo family in Italy; and BPT traders Sebastiano, Herzig, and Schmidtt from Switzerland all wrote checks.

On my arrival at Ed's Street, Willy Banto, a trader and owner of the bar, called William Milton. William did not forget that I had helped convince him to not buy the soybean thirteen-dollar straddle at the top. He thanked me that evening and his group wrote a check for Santino's project.

I raced back and forth to the trading floors and emptied any profit into the project. Fundraising became a full-time job.

Chapter 19

Navigating Healthcare

I performed whenever I got a chance, and gave CDs to friends and patients. Some were sold for donations.

I dedicated a CD to Lucrezia, intending to gently remind her of the need to have a compatible child so Santino could have a bone marrow transplant. This was still our only shot at salvation. I lived in fear that out of spite, or something that I could not fully comprehend, that she would never do another IVF. Whenever I raised the subject, she would not speak to me for weeks.

In Italy, medical centers were always accredited prior to opening. If one was not authorized by the government, there was no way to be compensated. I needed to open the center for Santino. We were not accredited for government reimbursements, and treated dozens of Thalassemia patients and other patients of rare disease on our dime; tens of thousands of dollars evaporated monthly.

One of my favorite patients was Rodolfo Marche from Triggiano. His parents, Rocco and Maria, never arrived empty-handed. Thanks to them, my family enjoyed the freshest fruits and vegetables.

Rodolfo was allergic to most blood. It was a real challenge for the hospitals to serve him. As a result, he transfused minimally. This kept his hemoglobin incredibly low. Arginine Butyrate was a miracle to him and he responded well, almost completely eliminating the need for transfusions. Rodolfo never walked into the clinic without a smile. He was like a little brother to me. I paid for whatever medical supplies and equipment he needed. Very few things have ever brought me the joy that I received when I gifted him his very own Abbott pump. It was the best five grand I ever invested.

In a strange way, I felt that by taking care of our patients I was also repaying my friends back in Chicago, Germany, and Switzerland who were doing their best to run the Bridgeport-BPT company. My friends in Chicago had the added arduous chore of trying to keep an eye on my brothers Mikey and Paulie.

It seems like I've never had a boring day. While on a trip to Chicago, Santino, then nine, busted his lip. I handed him a towel and we walked to the car. On the way to the emergency room, I called Dirken Scott.

Santino sat quietly, and after twenty minutes of filling out insurance forms, I walked to the receptionist. "Miss, can we get my son in quickly? He's got issues. It's not good for him to be losing blood," I said patiently.

She winked at Santino, who looked at her and then at me.

Another ten minutes passed, and another nurse arrived and knelt beside Santino. "Let's see that cut."

Santino pulled the towel down. His lip was literally sliced through.

"Sir, he's a handsome little guy and you don't want the scar to be permanent. Of course, that's up to you. What insurance do you have?"

"Prudential," I replied.

"Is it an HMO?"

"I don't know what an HMO is," I said.

"Would you like me to call the plastic surgeon? I would suggest it. We wouldn't want to compromise his looks."

"We'll take the plastic surgeon," I replied.

"It's Sunday, and the doctor lives about a half-hour away. The bleeding has stopped. Your son will be fine." As the nurse finished, she winked at Santino, who looked at her and then at me.

After a few seconds she continued. "The insurance will usually cover most plastic surgery. Whether it does or not, it's a good investment, he's such a handsome little devil." She smiled, turned away, and disappeared behind a closed door.

Santino sat quietly. Dirken arrived, and we stood in the waiting room looking out a large glass window into the parking lot. After about an hour a silver Mercedes pulled up. The guard smiled at the man who entered the emergency room doors.

"That's him," I said.

Dirken nodded. I moved toward the doctor.

"Doctor, the patient is right here."

He put his hand up as he walked by, obviously not wanting to be disturbed. I looked at Santino and then at Dirken.

After a few minutes, the nurse returned. "Right this way, sir." We followed her into a draped room. "Put your son on the bed sir," she said.

The doctor arrived, masked, in a white smock. "Nurse, tell the men to leave," he said.

"Gentlemen, please take seats in the waiting room," the nurse said kindly.

"Ma'am, I told you, my son has medical issues. English is not his mother language, I need to be with him."

"Nurse, tell them to leave now. I will not do the procedure with them in the room," the doctor said coldly.

I moved toward him. "Please, my son has Thalassemia. I've never left his side."

He rushed past me, to the door. "I disturbed my Sunday to be here. Find someone else to sew the kid up," he said.

Dirken grabbed me by the arms. "Don't do anything stupid. Santino needs you to be calm," he said firmly.

The doctor sped off. I made a few calls and we took care of things at Loyola Hospital.

Uncle Vince's youngest daughter dated a guy with issues. In a fit of rage he clubbed my uncle with a butcher knife.

Cook County Hospital is a top trauma center. I flew into Chicago and brought my Aunt Alice to the hospital. Uncle Vince, one of the kindest men I ever knew, and Grandpa's only son, was within death's grasp.

I did what I could for my aunt and reminded my sons to constantly pray for Uncle Vince.

The doctors and nurses at the county hospital did a wonderful job. Their dedication and compassion are typical of many wonderful men and women in the US health industry. Thanks to those folks, after some months, Uncle Vince slowly came around, kidding with nurses and dishing out kindness to everyone. He was taken care of nicely, and so was my cousin's boyfriend. He was stabbed to death in his jail cell.

I wrote songs, a book, and screenplays, including a film called *Hodge*, about an eccentric eighty-year-old man. Howie Deutch, the producer of much of Walter Matthau's work, liked the script and wanted Walter to consider the project after the sequel to *Grumpy Old Men*. Unfortunately, Walter died shortly after in 2000.

John Walton's son Lukas was now twelve and doing fine. John was focused on other industries. Ronald Troy and Travis Dunn managed Beacon. John was a gentleman; I'd do my best. I directed and funded the Beacon, European subsidiary dedicated to Thalassemia and Sickle Cell.

Patients and patient families with various rare diseases continued to contact us. Within twenty-four hours, we identified the center of excellence in their affliction closest to them, spoke to a treating doctor or competent researcher, and identified pertinent clinical trials anywhere in the world, asking only for prayers as payment.

My sons and I often went to Lucrezia's relatives for lunch and dinner. In these homes, they saw what love of family was. The boys attended school six days a week, including Saturday. This was actually a welcome gift.

One afternoon when my sons returned from school and were still in their school "grembiule" (obligatory robes worn over their clothes until sixth grade), I put four apples on the table.

"Young men, these apples represent life."

Their eyes filled with curiosity.

"We decide how to live life and how to eat the apple."

I stuffed one into my mouth, chomping away as the juices flowed down my chin. The boys laughed. Lucrezia began banging dishes.

"Some gobble life up, almost not tasting it. Some complain that their apple is red and they wanted green, or that it's green and they wanted yellow. Some wanted a smaller apple, others a bigger apple. Life can be complicated, my sons."

Pots and pans were exploding in the background.

"As time passes, the apple changes. It's discolored where we bit into it. Things didn't go the way we wanted. Some are afraid to eat the apple, thinking there's nothing left after. They shine it with makeup and clothes. They may buy a wig or change wives or husbands." I smiled, walked over to Lucrezia, who was distracted, laid her hair over my head, and for a moment looked like a hippy. The boys laughed. Lucrezia shoved me and growled.

"That's the last time I'm using your hair as a wig," I said indignantly.

"Get out of here, loser," she said.

As she turned, I stuck my tongue out and continued. "Life is a bushel of apples in every color, flavor, and size. Some never really choose, and few realize that life can begin when you finish them."

The boys laughed as they watched my antics, gobbling, spying, and then carefully cutting the apple. I smashed one against the table.

"You're cleaning it up, you jerk!" Lucrezia screamed.

"I will. In life, we must clean up when we make applesauce," I replied.

While I was personally concentrating on Beacon Europe, the Swiss and German exchanges merged. We were now trading both exchanges from BPT Trading of Switzerland. The European operation survived while Bridgeport Securities Group in the US thrived.

At one of the Altamura town festivals, I noticed a guy punching a man who was considerably smaller than he was (my precise size). I wrestled the aggressor to the ground. A town copper showed up and I gladly surrendered the predator. The officer scolded them for fighting on a religious feast day and thanked me. My intervention was duly noted by town people. I laughed inside, that was a change, a law official thanking me. What would be next?

Art Nieman had still not been officially replaced. I was impressed with Dr. Wiech, and thought he was perfect to head Beacon. I set up a meeting in Los Angeles with Lance Rolf, my often-unorthodox wheeler-dealer, or "deal junky."

Lance's real last name was Rofanowski. He grew up in Queens, New York and moved to Los Angeles after college. Lance was impressive. He could talk faster and make less sense than anyone I have ever known. Still, his heart was in the right place, I liked him, and he had raised millions for different funds.

Through Lance I met California attorney Ken Sussmane. Seemingly in seconds, Ken quietly absorbed a situation, then erupted with unique solutions. While the normal person was running to first, Ken was already showering in the locker room.

Lance thought it a no-brainer for Beacon to buy Dr. Wiech's company, Ucyclid Pharma. Beacon would have a product and instant credibility as a drug company. An Initial Public Offering (IPO) would quickly follow, making all Beacon shareholders wealthy.

The purchase price for Ucyclid was $18 million. John Walton was not convinced. Shortly after, Ucyclid was sold to Medisys Pharma for $26 million. Dr. Norb Wiech signed his noncompete with the new owners of Ucyclid and was hired to manage Beacon.

Before his death in 1997, Mr. Nieman had spent $10 million, securing patents from Boston University (BU) and Bar-Ilan University of Tel Aviv. Norb was disgusted with the waste he discovered, and struggled to understand what Beacon actually owned. It seemed nothing was in order, particularly the patents from BU.

Duke Rymt, a Pittsburgh attorney and friend of Ronald Troy, was consulted. Duke was convinced that Boston University had compromised their own patent position and, intentionally or unintentionally, sold to Beacon intellectual property that they didn't rightfully own.

As Norb invented and added other molecules to the firm, Duke Rymt prepared for war against BU.

Centro Medico San Rocco and Beacon Europe heavily depended on Dr. Torre, who *gallantly* refused compensation. Dr. Torre was married with two children, didn't smoke, didn't drink, and seemed to have no vice that I could identify. What he did enjoy was matching wits and challenging me on world events. I cared less about world events than I did about matching wits and personally, wasn't sure what made the guy tick.

Whenever we got together, he jumped, almost not able to contain himself, bashing the US war complex and the hundreds of thousands that the US murdered unjustly. He seemed to almost foam at the mouth when speaking about America's avid support of apartheid. I didn't necessarily see things his way and mostly ignored his provocation.

We had just left the seaside home of a family with a two-year-old Thalassemic child. We had informed them about our center and our vision of what the Thalassemia landscape would likely mean for them in the future.

Before heading back to Altamura we stopped at a restaurant; it was the least I could do. During dinner, the good doctor prodded, "What do you really care about?"

"Curing Santino."

He laughed mockingly, "All parents of sick children say the same thing. They're programmed by the television, the church, and films."

"Programmed or not, I'd kill to save him."

"I don't believe you. Mr. Girondi, you're just like the rest of the people who have sick children. You're not only trapped by the incurable disease but also by your dramatic and romantic ideas of seeing your child cured." After a five-second hesitation he added, "As if there was anything concrete that you could contribute to his salvation."

I changed the subject. I needed the good doctor. He was well-versed in Thalassemia and had begun helping even problematic patients, including Rodolfo Marche. In fact, Torre's collaboration dramatically reduced Rodolfo's trips to see Dr. Perrine at the Boston University.

The following week Santino had a fever. This was dangerous. Santino was without a spleen to protect him from a bacterial infection. Dr. Torre visited and nodded. Things would be all right. I sent Dr. Torre a basket of goodies, wine, cheeses, Tartuffe, etc. as a token of thanks. However, days passed and Santino's fever persisted.

I tried to remain calm, but inside I was panic-stricken. Sickle Cell Disease and Thalassemic patients rarely die of their diseases. They perish because of complications brought on by chronic transfusions, iron overload, which accompanies the chronic transfusion, and viral or bacterial infections.

Dr. Torre did not answer his cell phone. I called his studio. He answered, curtly said that he was busy, and hung up. I called back. He told me that he'd never see Santino again as a patient. I was stunned; going to another doctor would greatly complicate things for my son.

I called my compari. Within thirty minutes, Mimmo, Mariocarlo's godfather; and Nicola, my cousin Antonella's husband, arrived (Lucrezia and I had been witnesses for Antonella and Nicola's wedding). I trusted both of these men with my life; more important, with advising me about how to safeguard my son's life.

Nicola and Mimmo were certain that Dr. Torre felt slighted by the basket. They assumed that the good doctor felt that he was worth far more and that I was purposely mocking him and his efforts. We drove to his office. They warned me about creating problems. I promised to be calm. Santino's life depended on it. It was a scorcher. Nicola and Mimmo sweated profusely waiting for me to return.

I rang the bell and an elderly gentleman let me in. The office was simple. The only thing out of the ordinary was the presence of measuring vials used by chemists on a file cabinet. Dr. Torre looked out of his inner office and grimaced. A moment later, he stood in front of me with a stack of folders containing Santino's medical data.

He shoved them into my upper stomach. "Take these with you" (in Italian).

"Doctor, I don't understand," I said.

"That makes two of us. Now get out of my office," he growled.

"Please, Doctor, Santino still has a fever. You know how dangerous it is for him. Please come see him," I pleaded with teary eyes.

"I don't give a shit about Santino," the doctor snapped.

I threw one punch and leaned to pick up the scattered documents. The doctor was on his back, bleeding from his nose and mouth.

I turned to leave, but out of the corner of my eye I saw him rising.

"I'll take care of you . . ."

He did not have time to finish the phrase.

I put him in a headlock and pushed a test vial against his neck. "I once told you that I'd kill for my son. Would you like to be the proof?" I asked calmly.

His bloodied face went blank.

The elderly gentleman that had opened the door for me crouched next to me. "Please, son, leave the doctor be. Please," the man pleaded.

I dropped Torre's head, placed the vial on a chair, picked up the documents, and left.

On the street, I ashamedly looked at my trusted knights.

"Is he bad?" Mimmo asked.

"He's bleeding, but he'll live," I replied, looking at my shoes.

"Take him to attorney Pasquale Fiorello, behind the newsstand on Via Bari. I'll tend to the doctor," Mimmo said.

Nicola and I headed to the attorney's office.

The doctor, holding a bloodied towel to his face, walked to his car. Mimmo stood in front of the driver's door.

"*Dottore*, I'm sorry for what happened. The American is a bit nervous. He has a sick child," Mimmo said.

"Get away from my car," Torre said, unmoved.

"The American is a bit odd, but he's a good guy. Please don't make trouble for him," Mimmo pleaded.

"The American should have thought about trouble before he attacked me. Now get away from my car."

Mimmo sprinted behind Dr. Torre's car the 800 meters to the hospital. Ten years and thirty pounds ago, he boxed, but now he walked into the emergency room out of breath and soaked from perspiration.

The doctor stood thirty feet away, still holding a towel to his bloodied face, violently waving the other hand, screaming to everyone and no one in particular. "That lunatic they call the American came to my office and attacked me! He must be stopped! Call the Carabinieri!"

Two doctors arrived and walked Torre away. Mimmo grabbed a phone off a desk and punched in numbers.

A busty, angry-looking, Nurse Ratched–type arrived.

"Sir, you cannot use that phone," she said in a stern voice.

Mimmo ignored her.

"Sir! You cannot use that phone!"

Mimmo smiled. "There's already a doctor looking for a room. We wouldn't want to make it a doctor and a nurse. Would we?"

The nurse turned in a huff.

I sat with Compare Nicola in Pasquale Fiorello's office. Pasquale answered the phone. "Your compare," he said to me. I knew that he meant Compare Mimmo.

We could hear compare Mimmo's voice erupting out of the phone. "I see," Pasquale responded. "Don't worry . . . don't worry. When you get a chance, come by, we'll go for a coffee. *Ciao*." Pasquale said as he ended the call.

Without pausing, Pasquale punched in another phone number. "Tomaso, Pasquale. Listen, your client, that idiot Dr. Torre, is at the hospital. *L'Americano* gave him a slap. He deserved it. I'm telling you right now, you better calm him down. If he reports the '*L'Americhein*' (Americano in the Altamura dialect) to the police, I'll have him canceled from the doctors' album." Pasquale's voice raised. "He cannot for any reason refuse to see a patient in need!"

There was a pause. Pasquale listened, hung up, and looked at Nicola and me.

"He's stupid but not that stupid. It'll be fine." Pasquale paused. "Can you take Santino somewhere else? I don't think that it's a good idea to put him under Torre's care after you smashed his face."

The room was silent.

"Go on, go take care of your son," Pasquale said.

"What do I owe you?" Nicola said, reaching into his pocket.

Pasquale smiled. "Owe? Owe? You don't owe anything. It's a gift for Santino." Nicola shook his hand. I went behind the desk and kissed him.

I continued to dream that Lucrezia would get pregnant with a compatible child. The more I insisted, the more she resisted. One day after dinner, she told me, "I might get pregnant again, but you won't be the father."

All that really mattered to me was that the child was compatible.

Back in Chicago, things were not going as smoothly for some colleagues. The FBI tried to snare Ronny Moreno, who had now become a state senator. His wife was convicted and wore a bracelet for a year for what the government called "ghost pay-rolling." Ghost payrolling was a phrase given to paid employees who rarely or never showed up for work.

The FBI, as always, wanted someone that could implicate big fish to create big headlines. I had written checks to Moreno's organization and my name was mentioned in many conversations they listened to during the investigation. I had been in *Playgirl*, on *Oprah*, and in dozens of magazines and newspaper articles; I would certainly make headlines. Big news stories helped FBI agents get notoriety and promotions. A few threw their hats into the political ring after a big investigation.

Agent Weatherspoon was fishing for me. Martin Robin had flipped him onto the hood of the FBI car and frisked him in front of a crowd on Archer Avenue. Martin thought the FBI agent was an outfit guy following him. He should have known better; an outfit guy would not have been spotted.

Weatherspoon was acutely aware that I had skated on the Exchange investigation. He wanted to fry me. He thought that this was the best way to hurt Martin, who refused to implicate anyone.

By phone, in conversations with agent Weatherspoon, I promised ten times to return to the US. The investigation eventually ended and I had not even given an interview.

When the state's star witness was asked to identify Martin, she put her hand on the shoulder of Martin's attorney. That night, there was a party in Chicago and Altamura. In the meantime, the FBI had gone to the workplace of some of Martin's intimate friends. Bosses are leery of FBI investigations. A few of them lost their jobs. Land of the brave and home of the free, and all that.

An alderman with a bad heart, who was also snared in the FBI hunt, didn't want to die in prison. He joined the witness protection program and incriminated Martin Robin, basically swearing to whatever the FBI asked him to.

After Martin's guilty verdict, Attorney Garby called me in Italy. Garby told me the FBI offered Martin a deal if he would flip or lie to help them to trap bigger game. Being a true American, Martin refused. Growing up, I remember the common discipline of most parents. If you tattled on your brother, he got slapped once and you got slapped twice.

There were thirty to forty days before sentencing. Martin had two sons and a daughter. Martin Jr. was 15, my godson Michael was 13, and Jeanie was 9. Martin needed to help situate his kids before he went away. Garby claimed that if I bailed Martin out while he was waiting to be sentenced, IRS audits and hassle from the FBI were likely repercussions.

I hung up with Garby and sat with my sons, Santino, Cenzino, and Mariocarlo. "Fellows, we have a decision to make. A friend is in trouble. If we help him, we will have trouble."

"What kind of trouble?" Santino asked.

"Uncle Martin is going to prison." The kids had met him and knew of Martin's importance to the family. "Uncle Martin needs time to set his kids up and find a place for them to stay," I continued, "he needs bail money. If we send it, certain elements of the US government will not be happy with us."

I looked into my sons' eyes. They were going to be good men.

I sent Dirken with a check to Martin's packed hearing. Garby told the judge that Mr. Robin had procured bail money. The FBI objected. Their demeanor threw the court into chaos.

"Your Honor, if you accept bail from Don Patrizio, a mobster in hiding, Mr. Robin will be in Italy before the weekend," said Agent Weatherspoon.

Garby told me what had transpired. I didn't give any thought to what the agent said but my friend needed to be sprung so that he could straighten things out for his family. The judge ordered Garby to establish proof that the funds I procured for bail were not ill-gotten, proof of how I earned my income, and at least three character references for me. After five days of adjournment, the judge had already received tax returns and letters from priests, friends, and myself.

This is what I wrote:

Your Honor,

I was born and raised in Chicago, have honorably served in the nation's military and now spend a lot of time in Europe due to my son's illness. I have been warned by counsel that I could become a target of the FBI and IRS for helping Mr. Robin but I believe that one of the most important things about being a true American is that you do not turn your back on a friend no matter what the personal risk is.

Patrick Girondi

Martin was released until sentencing. The FBI was not happy.

I petitioned Congressman Patowskus to intervene. I wanted him to use his clout to get Martin imprisoned close to Chicago so his kids could visit him. Years prior, Martin worked for an opponent of Congressman Patowskus. Martin discovered that Patowskus had already printed all of his election posters, bumper stickers, and election cards. Martin recruited a last-minute candidate with the sole intent of changing Patowskus's number on the ballot from twenty-two to twenty-three. Patowskus had to reprint everything. It cost his campaign tens of thousands. As a consequence, low on advertising funds, Patowskus almost lost the election to an unknown Chicago bus driver. The congressman wasn't a forgiving person. As a result, Martin served his time in Leavenworth, Kansas, where it was nearly impossible for his kids to visit.

I, in fact, was audited for the next nine years, and was delayed in customs when arriving in the US, often missing connecting flights. In the various holding rooms, it's written on the wall, "If you believe that your rights are being violated call 1-800 . . ." The State Department.

A few years later when Joe Farrell, my friend and attorney, called, he was warned, "The FBI knows what they're doing and you should be careful about what you, Joe Farrell, are doing representing such a criminal."

Traveling hassles and the audits created economic and emotional damage. They also helped convince me that I'd do nothing differently if I had to do it all over again.

My cousin Ken managed fifteen artists and a small recording studio. He claimed I wasn't the worst singer he had ever worked with. We began putting tracks up and producing some of my own songs.

I only had the time to sing and compose because Dirken Scott and Joe Feldman managed Bridgeport Securities and Sebastiano continued to manage our operations in Lausanne.

Our trading competitors in Germany and Switzerland were gaining experience in the not-so-new electronic markets. Profit at BPT Trading declined. We had already begun tightening our belts when Switzerland passed a law necessitating a banking license for BPT Trading. The license would add another half-million swiss francs of expense in accountants, attorneys, and government fees (the Swiss franc at the time was about .8 to the euro and .7 to the dollar).

Lucrezia paid a local artist to paint her portrait. She posed a few times and he took hundreds of photos. I shelled out €3,000. When it was complete, she excitedly called me to her bedroom. The portrait had her seated with white gloved hands ceremoniously folded on her lap. I was a bit disappointed. The heading read, "Lucrezia of Altamura and Chicago" and not "Lady Lucrezia of Fauntleroy."

We were just growing farther apart, and though I'd never get used to a life without sex, I was getting used to a life without her. Surprisingly, for a few weeks we returned to being a couple. If the portrait had done this, it was a fantastic investment.

A few weeks later, Lucrezia insisted on a trip to Florida with her sister's family. It would be an expensive trip at a moment when liquidity was scarce. She seemingly appreciated my sacrifice and we made a deal; after Florida, we'd go to Chicago, where she'd undergo an IVF.

In Florida, things became combative. I rolled with the punches, not wanting to give her an excuse to change her mind. We left for Chicago but as days passed, it became evident that Lucrezia had no intention of doing an IVF. The trip cost $25,000 and with the Centro Medico San Rocco hemorrhaging and profits getting skinny at BPT, I was in the middle of a liquidity disaster.

The day before our departure to Italy, I walked into Lucrezia's old bedroom at her parents' home. Santino was playing. Lucrezia looked at me viciously.

"Don't touch anything, all the bags are packed," she snapped.

"Get out of here," I said sternly. The sight of her curdled my stomach.

She cowered momentarily and walked out, closing the door to a crack. I slipped a manila envelope into my briefcase.

Alitalia called families with children. I took Santino and Cenzino by the hand. Lucrezia and Mariocarlo followed. The boys wore backpacks. I carried a briefcase full of medical articles for the flight.

At the plane door, two men with Treasury Department badges grabbed me by my arms.

"Mr. Girondi, we'd like to speak with you. You are Mr. Patrick Girondi?"

"Yes, but I'm on my way to Europe. Could this wait until I return?"

"If you don't mind, we'd rather speak now."

"Have it your way," I said.

The younger officer made a thin-lipped smile.

"How much money are you carrying?" the senior agent asked.

"I don't get it," I said sincerely.

"How much money do you have in your possession, Mr. Girondi?" he asked quite seriously.

"If I had to guess, I'd say about two-grand."

Lucrezia looked to the side.

"May we see it?" the senior officer asked.

I reached into my pockets and came out with a little over $1,400.

"May we open your briefcase?"

I nodded, and he placed it on a small stand. On top of medical articles was the book *Napoleon* by Richard Cronin.

"Do you read a lot?" The younger officer asked.

"I try."

"Where's the rest of the 2,000?" the senior agent asked.

"I imagine my wife has something."

"Mrs. Girondi, please place the contents of your purse on the tray."

She emptied almost $400 from her purse.

Passengers filed by, each surmising a sinister plot.

"Do you have money in your bags under the plane?" the senior agent asked.

I purposely hesitated and smiled. "Buddy, I'm leaving my bags unattended for hours and hours in two Italian airports." I smiled kindly. "I hate putting my clothes in there."

Santino whispered. "*Papà, forse stanno guardando per la busta che hai messo nel mio zaino,*" (Dad, maybe they're looking for the bag you put in my backpack).

"*Cheet*" (hush), I said almost silently.

The officers quizzed one another with their eyes. They had to decide if emptying the plane to search my bags was warranted on an anonymous tip.

"Mrs. Girondi, you can put your belongings back in the purse," the senior officer said.

While taking Santino and Cenzino to the airport bathroom, I had moved the package from my briefcase into Santino's backpack. As the plane's landing gear left the runway, I stared at Lucrezia. Her face was blank.

I wasn't sure what had actually transpired, but she didn't do the IVF she had promised to do and if only for that, I knew that she could not be trusted.

Chapter 20

Blood, a Bank, and the FBI

E asy money in the electronic markets skid to an end. I had never worked in my life and did not want to begin now. Work is for donkeys.

Days had turned into weeks, and months had turned into years. Professor Nica Cappellini from the University of Milan, a treasured voice of wisdom, insisted that as Santino approached adolescence, he needed a higher hemoglobin than the Butyrate treatment availed.

Blood was now infinitely safer. There were tests for HIV and Hepatitis C antibodies. Dr. Perrine's Arginine Butyrate and Tifo's sodium phenylButyrate had helped us safely avoid years of transfusions.

Santino and I had a heart-to-heart. Afterward, he began transfusing every twenty days at the Madonna delle Grazie (Our Mother of Grace) hospital in Matera, eighteen kilometers from our home in Altamura. He was now almost ten years old.

According to Lucrezia, Santino's transfusions exposed me as the failed fraudster that I was. She made a decision to protect her children and to even out the score with me for all the anguish. I strongly suspected that the near-miss at the airport with the Treasury agents was the beginning of her retaliation. The kitchen and the bedroom were stringently restricted.

In Matera, I watched the red drops fall into the tube curved into Santino's vein. Each night he was stuck with a needle hooked to a pump that infused the Tisravno FeeralX iron chelation therapy. The most sensible place to lodge the subcutaneous needle was in a patient's arm or stomach. The needle remained in his stomach or arm for twelve to sixteen hours a day. School and almost any kind of physical activity were complicated. Whenever humanly possible, I was by his side. When I was not with him, he dominated my thoughts.

Writing and reading helped my mind defend against life's volleys. I prayed that one day this would all end, for Santino, for all of us. Through it all, I never once considered divorce, which I would have assessed as the greatest of my many failures.

A poem I wrote in this period begins, "Your hate has given me wings and off runs my soul like a runaway slave," and it ends, "I no longer cry for pain, instead I cry for those who have arrived at the juncture sign which reads, life and conditional love. I'm sorry, I can't help you. You may as well strike again."

I had a handle on the research world and needed funding more than ever. Life was about the cure.

Getting the Swiss authorities to grant us a banking license would be infinitely more complicated with an Italian subsidiary. I was sad for the Italian workers, and in particular for compare Nicola, a truly gifted trader. I shut Italy down.

Norb ran the day-to-day operations of Beacon. I popped into Chicago when I needed money. The soybean pit opened like the Red Sea. My colleagues knew where my earnings went.

While in Altamura, I had time on my hands. I spent it with my cronies in the town center at the Totò Club, named after Antonio DeCurtis, a famous comedian from Naples. I was back with my roots, the garbagemen, the laborers, the thieves, and the connivers. Lucrezia knew that I'd end up like this. Bridgeport of Altamura. What a mistake she had made.

The guys at the club loved *L'Americhein* who lost and didn't whine, who won and didn't gloat. Antonio, the owner, was fortyish and drove a garbage truck. Nicola, his son, was of course named after Antonio's father. Nicola asked me to be his confirmation father. I was honored. My family with Antonio's family were now "compari!"

Antonio gave me a book of poems written by Totò. My favorite poem from the book is "Illiterate Heart."

"I took my heart to school to learn to read and write, alas it learned but one word, 'love,' and nothing more."

I enjoyed my buddies. I watched, played, instigated, kidded, and loved. It was not a big money club; if someone lost fifty dollars, that was a lot.

Thanks also to the Totò club, my life outside the house was shaping up.

We continued to find centers of excellence, identify research teams, translate patient data, indicate pertinent clinical trials, and even made appointments with doctors and or researchers for anyone with a rare disease who reached out to us for help.

When asked how they could pay for my kindness, I often replied, "Help someone else."

Home, instead, continued to be a stockpiled ammunition dump. Almost any statement made by me seemed to ignite a small explosion. I feared the incident that would destroy our entire lives; my biggest dread was that Lucrezia would never again do another IVF.

I was convinced that she would change her mind. How couldn't she?

I slept with Santino. When I woke during the night, more times than not I found the needle out of his stomach or arm. The IV FeeralX therapy was just too painful and irritating to tolerate for all of those hours. It was heart-wrenching to find his medicine dripping on the floor. The situation had to be resolved.

I confronted Santino's doctors about the issue. They pointed out that the scientific information on L1 was new and the product, in their mind, was not fully proven. However, in view of the situation, Santino's doctors in Matera switched him to L1, the oral chelator. Though illegal in the US, it was a true lifesaver for Santino.

I found an Italian female psychiatrist who had experience in the United States. Lucrezia and I drove a tense seventy minutes to her address in Tricarico. Once in the doctor's office, Lucrezia screamed for an hour and a half. The psychiatrist said that I would be able to speak at our next appointment. Lucrezia refused to return.

Pharma companies sent representatives to meet me. I was offered the presidency of the Italian Thalassemia Federation. Work of this group and others like them helped guarantee safe blood and iron chelation for my son and all my son's brothers and sisters. I was honored, but decided to concentrate on the cure.

In the late summer of 2000, the new Italian Thalassemia Federation president, Angela Iacono, asked me to investigate an article from *Nature* Magazine. A French researcher, Pierre Shorf at Kragness Medical Center in Los Angeles, claimed to have cured five generations of Thalassemic mice.

I was mesmerized and arranged to meet Dr. Shorf when he visited Rome in the fall. His simple explanation and sincerity made me comfortable. I was sure as I had ever been about anything in my life; this technology was going to cure Santino. Out at sea for so long, this was my first glimpse of land.

In January 2001, I organized the Italian Telethon event in Chicago. Thanks mostly to my friends and family, we packed the Hilton Ballroom with almost a thousand people and raised over $250,000, all of which was supposed to go to the charity of my choice. Sickle Cell/Thalassemia research actually got less than half, but I'm a patient man.

During the days of preparation, I met Susanna Agnelli, the Fiat heiress and a strong and determined woman. We hit it off and she nicknamed me her "pazzo completo" (complete nut). It was a great relationship that endured until her death in 2009.

Altamura continued to be blessed with the presence of One Arm Rico, the boss who had one of the finest hotels and restaurants in Italy. Politicians, movie stars, industry moguls, church hierarchy, and other bosses all did homage to One Arm, visiting him in his Cathedral Restaurant in the center of Altamura. One Arm was a kind sort who would not refuse a favor. He was mythical and no film has ever had a character that even touches One Arm's aura, and I was his trusted friend.

Some members of an old syndicate family from New York contacted me in Altamura. They had heard that One Arm was not in the best of health. Just as important, they knew that their time was up in the US. As a consequence, the New York family decided to purchase One Arm Rico's hotel, businesses, and restaurants.

Cash is still involved with most business deals in Italy. Transactions are done using fictitiously low numbers to avoid government observation and/or taxation. This goes as well for workers, which gives you part of the reason that overall families in Italy are some of the more prosperous on the planet, though they don't necessarily look so good on paper.

In reality, One Arm Rico, Don Enrico to me, was in bad health.

The New Yorkers envisioned making transactions with minuscule amounts, paying the lion's share in cash. Of course, One Arm Rico would be eliminated by natural causes or not before any cash transaction would be made. They also insisted that I be their paid representative in the transaction. Here we were back shining shoes on 51st Street. Deciphering their scheme was as easy as reading a billboard.

I immediately visited my friend One Arm, pleading with him to be cautious. He thanked me and asked a favor of me. He wanted me to contact his son Bernardo, who had left for Florida with his family and $800,000 of One Arm Enrico's cash.

Bernardo nearly wet his pants when he spotted me in Gus's Greek Restaurant in Miami. What did he know?

I was only there to help him. He cried real tears. He never wanted to rob his father and didn't want to stay in America. His wife had talked him into it, threatening to leave him if he didn't agree to move with her and their daughters to Florida.

It was arranged for his wife to be stopped by the Miami police. She was over the ninety-day stay allowed to tourists. The family was shipped home. No New York deal was ever made.

Funding and assisting Shorf's project at Kragness Medical Center became my focus.

When in Chicago, I loved hanging with my brothers and buddies, but needing money for research, I sold my home on 35th Street. Now, when in town, I slept at Dirken Scott's apartment. Dirken loved reading about the Roman Empire and spent hours educating me about Roman life and Roman honor.

Duke Rymt and Beacon sued Boston University for $2.8 million, the loss that Beacon claimed it incurred when the University sold Beacon intellectual property they did not rightfully own.

In February 2001, Beacon's case was called before the Massachusetts Arbitration Committee. I spent my days in the arbitration room and my nights with Norb and his wife Linda, or at my Aunt Vittoria and Uncle Philly's apartment in Boston. It was freezing.

The Boston University attorney had a habit of scribbling notes and tossing them into the wastebasket. I paid the janitor each evening for its contents and laughed over the phone to Santino, "They haven't made a law against buying contents from wastebaskets yet."

In arbitrations, each side chooses a judge and then decides together on a third judge. The mechanics push both parties toward compromise. Duke Rymt did a fantastic job. As a result, Beacon received everything they asked for. John took the money as a partial payment for the over $19,000,000 that he had invested to date.

Drug companies routinely eliminate possible competition by buying up molecules, compounds, and therapies similar to their own. Unfortunately, it's likely that some of these similar inventions would make superior products for patients. This is legal. Bringing L1, a lifesaving drug not available to US patients, was illegal.

The Swiss banking authorities requested an official government-authenticated Bridgeport audit. This was not an easy task for any of us.

On our side, Dirken was responsible. But he had been a security guard when we hired him, and was ill-prepared to deal with accountants and attorneys who called him all day with questions he had no idea how to answer. He never mentioned any discomfort to me, and I guess he just hoped that things would eventually work themselves out.

Life for him was already complicated; his new girlfriend was arrested multiple times for shoplifting, and his mother had recently died.

On March 29, 2001, Peter Bellus called Italy and told me that Dirken hadn't shown up to the office. In all the years he had worked for us, Dirken never missed a day. I immediately called the FBI. A few days later they notified us that Dirken used his credit card to check into an Iowa hotel.

Derek Holmes was now living in Iowa, with Jessica and their three sons, Derek Jr., Kalen, and Marshall. Derek headed out to the hotel, five hours away from his home.

After a few hours, I was called by an FBI investigator. She told me that agents had waited in the lobby to make sure that Dirken was safe and that no one was holding him against his will. She could not legally follow him any farther.

I looked at the calendar. It was April Fool's Day.

I cried, "He's going to commit suicide. Please."

She was sincerely sorry, but could not help further.

Before Derek could catch up to him, Dirken went to the town Ace Hardware and purchased duct tape and fifteen feet of tube. Like a failed Roman general, he paid the price for failure to his brothers and Bridgeport Securities. He was found by a farmer in a cornfield, my music still playing from the stereo. Derek arrived two hours later.

The funeral mass was at the Nativity of Our Lord parish, a block from Dirken's home. Committing suicide is against church law. Some objected to Dirken's services being held in the Nativity of Our Lord Church.

Father James would not allow a eulogy but asked that I say a few words after the service. At the end of the mass, I stood and approached the altar. I turned and faced a tearful crowd. "Many of us have done some real crazy things." I paused, thinking about driving through the fence at Midway and racing the plane. I looked around at some of our troops. "And though he might not have agreed, Dirken supported us and stood by our side. I know of no finer man." I paused again, "And we stand beside him."

I walked solemnly to my pew and sensed that only the sanctity of the building stopped friends from erupting into applause.

Peter Bellus, who had weathered separations and divorce from the same woman twice, was happy to give up trading. He took over Dirken's duties.

I continued to fly around the world like a Ping-Pong ball, concentrating on my most important duty. Now in Dirken's absence, when in Chicago, I stayed mostly with my guy Kevin Dever, or as I call him, Calhoun.

When I'm away, Calhoun goes to the thrift shop and picks up shoes, pants, underwear, and socks for his buddy, "the Italian." He washes my clothes along with his own. He procures toothpaste, underarm deodorant, and razors.

Often, after we finished walking, I took a shower by Calhoun's house. He patiently waited and made comments about how I matched my clothes. Calhoun has several ways to address me, his adopted son. They are, "Hey jagoff," "Hey asshole," and "Uh, dickhead." I'm fond of them all.

Facing a public relations fiasco, Switzerland had set aside over 1.2 billion dollars in reparations to be paid to Jewish families whose assets were taken and held in Swiss banks during World War II. After my sixth trip in as many months to the Swiss capital Bern, trying to convince the bank authorities to give us our license, I called my friend Arnold Courtney.

At the next meeting with the Swiss banking authority, I wore the yarmulke that Arnold had sent. I calmly stated that I had done everything required, and asked if there was something personal that the banking board had against me.

BPT got the license a week later. Wearing Arnold's yarmulke brought good luck.

In Dirken's absence, I spent even more time with Calhoun Dever, and often bragged about his unique intelligence.

Clay Canon was the longest-running chairman of the Chicago Board of Trade, a successful businessman and US presidential representative to Moldavia, Ukraine, and Belarus. I informed Clay that Calhoun had called the NASDAQ crash, the rise of gold, and other major moves in commodities.

"It's like he's psychic," I told Canon.

Canon, who was always looking to make a buck, wanted to meet the wise man in the worst way. After much insistence I agreed to arrange a personal encounter with the financial sage, Calhoun (Kevin Dever).

I picked Canon up in my baby blue '65 Cadillac Sedan DeVille convertible. Santino loved the car, and I promised that when he was cured we'd ship it to Italy. Canon said it was like driving a couch.

We pulled up next to a dilapidated building in front of the old amphitheater and beeped. Canon stared curiously at the setting, and after thirty seconds a beer-bellied man, clad only in his underpants (Cal), came to the door. He pushed his head between two bars on the security gate.

"What are ya doin'?" Calhoun asked.

"Come on out," I said.

"For what?"

"Want to get some breakfast?"

"You gonna eat off my plate?" Calhoun asked.

"Nah," I said.

"You know, you should learn some frickin' manners. You ain't supposed to be eating off other people's plates. Now you can eat off my plate because, you know . . . of who we are."

Calhoun paused and peered at Canon. "Who's dat guy?"

I smirked inside as I glanced at Canon's dumbfounded look.

"I'm Clay Canon, the president . . ."

Calhoun ignored Canon. "You gonna eat off his plate?"

"No Cal, you wanna put some clothes on so we can go?"

Cal looked at Canon, then at me, and disappeared, reappearing after a few minutes wearing pajama bottoms and a dego tee. He unlocked a padlock on the outside of the bars and there was an uneasy silence as he approached the car.

"Well?" Cal blurted out. "We goin' for breakfast?"

Canon sat silently. Cal looked at me.

"Well, what are we waiting for? There ain't no hookers here at this time of the day. Well, not today, anyway."

I looked at Clay Canon. "We ain't lookin for no hookers, are we, Mr. Canon?" I asked.

Cal interrupted. "The last time you came, you gave that pretty, light-skinned coke-head a twenty."

"You ever gonna let me forget that?"

"You ain't screwing up a good thing. I usually get some for a few dollars in food stamps or the rest of a Ricobene's steak sandwich. Hell, a few of them come in the winter just for company."

"Sorry," I said.

"Sorry . . . I thought you said we were going to breakfast," Cal said as he put his hand on the car door next to Canon.

Clay nervously cleared his voice. "I'm Clay Canon." He again cleared his voice. "I'm the President of the Chicago Board of Trade."

Cal looked at me and then at a very skittish Clay Canon.

"So," Kevin said.

Five uneasy seconds passed. "Yes, yes, so. So, I heard, I mean to say that Pat Girondi told me that you called the NASDAQ collapse."

"You had to be an idiot not to see that coming," Cal replied.

"Pat also told me that you called the rise in gold," Canon said with more confidence.

"So?" Cal deflected.

"So, so, I was wondering if you had any more tips. I mean, I am a reasonable man, and if you could lead me to the well we could both drink. If you know what I mean."

Cal looked at me. I shrugged.

"You mean we could make some money," Cal said.

"Exactly," Clay Canon smiled, "exactly."

"What would I do with money?" Cal asked.

"Money, well, we all need money. What is it that you do for a living?" Clay asked.

"I'm unemployed," Cal flipped back.

"Oh, I'm sorry to hear that. How long have you been unemployed?"

"About thirty-four years," Cal responded.

Canon stared.

"I'm gonna make another prediction," Cal said.

Canon was engulfed in anticipation.

"I predict that you'll open the frickin' door so I can get in."

On the way to breakfast, we picked up Mr. Knuckles Ciacci.

Growing up, the Ciacci family, like mine, had been one of the poor families in Bridgeport. There was no way to grow up in the neighborhood without knowing at least one of the Ciaccis.

Pistol, Knuckles, Hiney, Blue, and Ruggero were the five brothers. A few of them did some time in the state colleges, but each one of them was more ethical and honest than most businesspeople I know. Hiney and I formed the neighborhood baseball pony league. Ruggero, a political guy, worked for a onetime powerful city alderman named Rudy Cepak, or "Fast Rudy." Neighborhood rumors had it that Knuckles parked cars, hijacked trucks, and pulled off jewelry heists and robberies. He also dealt in and had a heart of gold.

At breakfast, we were joined by a few neighborhood guys. We all took turns telling and listening to each other's stories. One tale was about a crew hitting chain grocery stores. As a consequence, the store managers kept less and less cash on hand. After a few dry runs, the gang took a break. But, it was summer and the boys needed cash. There hadn't been a robbery in a few weeks, and some store managers stopped paying for increased armored truck service. The crew got the skinny (scoop) from a store employee (that's what they get for paying twelve dollars an hour without healthcare).

One of the crew chopped through the roof with an ax, slid into the hole, scaled the aluminum roof support to the alarm, disabled it, and opened the dock door ("Monkey" was his alias).

It was Fruit and Nuts' first time with the team, and he wanted to make a good impression. He hopped on the fork, drove through an aisle, and went through the separating wall of the front office. He wedged the forks under the safe and broke it from the floor. He drove back through the store and onto the truck. The other guys covered the safe with moving blankets. They were out in under ten minutes.

Couch was Fruit and Nuts' cousin, and he had guaranteed Fruit and Nuts to the crew and was rightly proud. But it slipped by everyone that Fruit and Nuts had made a rookie blunder.

He backed onto the truck. The forks were inclined and it was metal on metal. On North Avenue, Wacko slammed on the brakes to avoid a red light. The safe slid off the forks onto the street.

They left it where it was and drove to Lucky's for breakfast. Fruit and Nuts paid.

Morning DJs all over town laughed about a car hitting a safe on North Avenue that contained more than $150,000 in cash. Most of the crew rolled over in their beds, not getting up until the following day.

Canon said he'd never had more fun in his life.

Chapter 21

Annunziata

My sons were eleven, nine, and eight years old. When in Altamura, each morning, the boys and I had breakfast at the bar and then were off to the fruit market where they worked for thirty minutes before school. My kids were the only children, other than a few of the owner's sons, who showed up to sweep and move fruit around. I wanted to instill in them the good old American work ethic.

Santino worked with the Nish Nash family. Cenzino worked with the Franceschidd family, and Mariocarlo worked with U Pagliaccio. These were all nicknames that the family members went by, some of them for centuries.

Lucrezia followed her mother's habit of making only enough food for each sitting. Waste not, want not. This was against the Italian American culture's habit of putting enough food on the table for three dinners.

At lunch, Lucrezia refused to make a portion for me. If I was really hungry, I'd swipe food off my son's plates. It was no fun for anyone, and it got so we ate at Lucrezia's relatives or the homes of Compari more than at our own home.

Annunziata was an Altamurana in her early twenties, as simple as she was beautiful. She wore no makeup, was five foot five with thick black hair, deep brown eyes, and a body that curved like no woman I have ever seen. I was mesmerized from the moment I laid eyes on her. She of course ignored me. One morning, I offered her a coffee.

"I don't know you," she said.

"I'm Patrizio, *L'Americano*," I replied. I reached to shake her hand.

After coffee, we walked to the women's clothing store that she managed. She loved poetry and philosophy. Annunziata was smart and sincere, a dream.

Whenever I visited and there were no customers, she was always reading something. I loved gifting her books. Certain times, I could not find an Italian version of what I wanted for her, and she'd get through books written in English as well.

I gathered information discreetly. Her family regretted her involvement with the man she dated. People in the town believed that he used and/or sold drugs. Having said that, hanging around with a married man was even more damaging for her reputation and that of her family.

Rosalba, her older sister, confronted Annunziata. Annunziata refused to abandon our relationship. Rosalba was shocked. Was Annunziata involved with a married man?

I was with my sons every day for lunch and home each night by 10:30 p.m. to put them to bed. Annunziata and I usually met for coffee in the morning, then in the afternoon, from 3:30 to 5:00 p.m., and each night, after she closed, at 9:00 p.m. She slowly became inquisitive about where the relationship would go. Routinely, she'd run her nails up and down a book before she'd ask, "Do you love me?"

I pushed Annunziata toward the church, and we often prayed in the cathedral, completed in 1196. We spoke of the lives of the saints who were pillars of my church, my belief, and me.

Sometimes her nail-scratching turned musical. In the middle of her concerts, she'd often pause and laugh, "Do you love me?"

I spotted Annunziata walking toward the car, smiling brighter than usual.

"What's going on?" I asked.

She got in and continued to smile.

"What are you glowing about?"

"I saw your future daughter-in-law today."

Confused, I prodded.

Santino was now almost twelve, and had seen me speak with Annunziata a few times. He went to her store and confided that he wanted to buy his girlfriend, Lucia, a name-day gift. Santa Lucia Day is December 13th.

When Annunziata told me about Santino's visit, I tingled all over. Through all the trying years, I had never really thought that the day would come when my son would have a girlfriend.

Santino didn't know the young lady's size. Annunziata suggested that Santino pass by the store with her. Annunziata would then be able to know the perfect measurement and style that would complement her. Lucia and Santino passed by the store. Santino told Lucia that he wanted to say hello to Annunziata. They walked in, exchanged some pleasantries, and left. Fifteen minutes later, Santino returned by himself and walked out with a gift that Annunziata helped pick out.

That evening Annunziata was giddy and fluttering like a butterfly. We parked and I turned on the dome light. "Patrizio," she said, blooming like a flower.

I stared and smiled.

"Yes? Do you have something on your mind?"

Tears filled her eyes and she quietly nodded. "Patrizio, if you can't convince your wife to have another child, I'd like to offer myself. I will carry you and your wife's child to save Santino. He's so darling."

I stared at her. "Annunziata, it would compromise your whole life."

"He's your son. I love him, too." She stared, smiling broadly.

I gazed at her tenderly. She moved her nails up and down her book. I tried to concentrate on the sound, so as not to be distracted by the significance of her offer.

Later that evening when I brought her home, I parked the car a block from her house. We both quietly looked at each other. I have never felt anything so strong. I placed my hand on her hand. "Grazie," I said.

She smiled tightly, kissed me on the cheek, and disappeared.

Lucrezia would have to agree to give the eggs for the process. It was an incredible moment for me. My hopes sailed. I proposed the idea to my wife without telling her who offered; she flatly refused.

Annunziata was truly disappointed and didn't ask for an explanation. I was distraught but saw no solution. Annunziata knew that my relationship with my wife was strained. Lucrezia's name was rarely spoken in Annunziata's presence. Our time together was incredible, but my conscience continuously reminded me about the restrictions that our relationship placed on her future.

Apart from my family situation, Annunziata didn't like me speaking with other women; she said it made her feel less special. She was wrong to feel that way. I had never met anyone like her.

I did a favor for the family of Mariocarlo's piano teacher, Valentina, who was the same age as Annunziata. Valentina's family invited me for dinner. That evening, Annunziata convinced me to see her before going to Valentina's. After an hour together, she staked a claim, having me drop her off right in front of Valentina's home. She hoped they were watching. Until then, for her sake, I was discreet, even secretive. Now it was actually she who wanted us to be seen together.

I left Valentina's and sent Annunziata a phone message: "*Buona notte.*"

She responded within seconds. "I go home every night at 10:30 so you can be with your children. My boyfriend of six years is now my ex. You leave the home of another woman at 1:00 a.m.?"

The following day, January 5, 2002, Compare Tonino, from the Totò club and I were bringing a bottle of grappa to my friend, Don Mario, the provincial bishop. While I was in the car on the way, Annunziata called to invite me for coffee. I told her I couldn't do coffee and she asked about meeting after lunch. There had to be limits. I was married, the father of three sons, one of whom was sick. I informed her that we would not see each other at all that day.

Did I speak like that because I was going to see a bishop or because of the jealous comments she sent me the night before? I suspect I'll never know.

Tonino, who loved her almost as much as I did, grabbed the phone. "Annunziata, we're bringing grappa to Don Mario. Don't worry, honey, I've got my eye on him."

Don Mario and I spoke about the three new churches being built in Altamura. He knew that I was adamantly against the idea. There were more than enough churches. Italy and Altamura would likely shrink in population in the years to come. He believed that each child should be able to walk to mass and the town had expanded greatly over the past 20 years. He built three new churches.

As usual, we also spoke about the Sickle Cell and Thalassemia research project. When I thought that we had covered the critical discussions, I rose. The bishop blessed me. I made the sign of the cross. He then put his arms on my shoulders and smiled solemnly. "Patrizio," he said, "If I ever had a son, I'd want him to be just like you." It was a special moment for me and my spiritual father.

That day, my three boys and I ate at Tonino's home. Franca, his wife, was a fantastic cook and always made my sons feel wanted. Santino and Tonino constantly teased each other. We were truly happy there.

I daydreamed about Enzo Ferrari, whose biography I had recently read. Enzo was a rugged unschooled man who founded the Ferrari car company. His son Alfredo was his opposite—cultured, educated, and a charismatic engineer who worked in Enzo's factory and was loved by all. When Alfredo was twenty-four years old, he died of Duchenne Muscular Dystrophy. Enzo had a second son with his lover, but remained married to his wife. Alfredo's death sent Enzo into seclusion until the end of his life.

When a man tells a woman that he loves her, he really means that he wants her and the only true love a man can feel is for his children. - Enzo Ferrari

Tonino slapped my arm. "Eat!"

222

I wasn't hungry. It was the first day, while in Altamura, in over a year, that I did not see Annunziata. I missed her. It was good that I traveled often. I, like Enzo, would stay married until I died.

At 3:00 p.m., Tonino, like most southern Italian men, headed to bed for his nap. Tonino's wife, Franca; their daughter, Rosa; their son, Nicola; and my three sons and I had coffee and dessert.

Annunziata was the only woman I had ever really spoken to, other than aunts . . . some of whom were actually Lucrezia's aunts. To this day, women are still enchanting mysteries to me.

I was a married man; it was time for Annunziata to slow down. She, as well, had to get on with her life. I felt a bit guilty, knowing that if Lucrezia had consented to giving her eggs that I would never, ever let Annunziata go. But things were not that way and it was a new year and time for us to begin putting space between each other.

Lucrezia claimed that her going to school in a very different system made it difficult for her to help the kids with their schoolwork. Lucrezia was an intelligent woman. I was curious, but not amazed at her position. Zio Mimmo arrived at Tonino's home to take the boys to their respective tutors to study and do their homework. Afterward, they'd play in the piazza under his careful eyes, until it was time to go home.

At 4:45, I walked up the main street (*Il Corso*) to my office, expecting to see Annunziata in her store. Surprisingly, the shutters were still closed. I grabbed a coffee with a friend and headed back. Certainly she'd be smiling and waiting for me, but the store was still closed and she was nowhere in sight. Annunziata was never late. I became uneasy and walked to the Totò club. Tonino knew what I was thinking. He smiled and then spoke. "You know what the old people say? A woman can pull a wagon train with one pubic hair."

"Yeah, I'll keep that in mind if my car ever gets stuck," I said.

I gazed at the church clock; it was 5:20. I nodded to Tonino, he followed me, and we walked to Annunziata's work. I could see a group of women in front of the store; it was probably Annunziata and other shopgirls, kidding about how she had been late for the first time ever. Not having a meeting with me, she probably overslept. We got closer. The store shutters were still closed. About ten meters from the store, I observed one of the girls crying.

I froze. Could my decision to separate have created tragedy? Tonino walked ahead of me and returned with a solemn face. Annunziata had gone to Bari, with her boyfriend, to pay his brother's attorney. I assumed that the two of them still talked. I felt I had no right to ask anything else. On the way back from the attorney, they got into an accident. The drivers of both cars were dead. Annunziata was injured.

Had I seen her this afternoon, Annunziata would have been smiling in the store. As usual, it was my fault.

Maybe he coaxed her, or maybe she decided to turn the tables on me. Why should I care? I was married with three sons, and that would never change. I thought I should take this as an omen and leave well enough alone. My mind did a few more laps, and I decided I'd go see her in the hospital. We were friends, the best of friends. She sacrificed everything for me and offered to help Santino. Somehow, someway, I would make things up to her.

Tonino left me and walked to the town police station, a three-minute walk from the piazza.

Annunziata knew how much I loved Tonino. She loved him, too, smiling and waving as he passed by in the garbage truck. He'd stop to pick up her empty boxes, and they'd kid about how crazy the American really was. I had recently learned how to Rollerblade, and did so up and down the corso, instigating arguments, teasing, or playing peacemaker.

Tonino arrived, crying. "The car crossed over the line traveling at over 200 kilometers an hour, plowing head-on into the car of a father of four from Gravina. There were no survivors," he said softly.

I didn't believe it. The girls at the shop said that Annunziata was only injured. In such a grave accident, the local police would be involved. I walked to their headquarters, Tonino close behind me. A man stood at the desk with a stocking cap covering his eyes. Felix, one of the coppers, was in the corner wiping away tears. I approached him.

"That's the girl's father," Felix whispered. "What was she doing with that jerk? She was one of the sweetest girls in town."

I sat in my office with the lights off. Santino walked in. "Pà, it's time to go home."

"Tell Zio Mimmo to drive you. Papà has some things to do."

"With the lights off?" he asked.

For years, I had been sleeping with Santino and sometimes with Cenzino or Mariocarlo. Our bedroom had long since become Lucrezia's bedroom. The house was silent and dark. I walked the two flights of stairs to the attic and crawled under the covers with Mariocarlo.

Almost instantly, I heard nails rolling over a book. I thought I was dreaming and looked at my phone. The scratching continued as I hugged Mariocarlo. It made no sense to turn the light on. I knew what was happening. I knew who it was. The rhythmic scratching continued a few seconds and then stopped. I felt obligated to respond.

My mind raced over the universe. There was silence, as if the whole world knew what I was thinking.

"Ti amo, sei contenta mo?" "I love you. Are you happy now?" I asked.

I wasn't sure, but I don't ever remember thinking before saying those words and I have never repeated them to another woman since . . . it's been twenty years.

There was silence. I rolled over and again wrapped my arms around my Mariocarlo.

The town was full of rumors. "They had been arguing. The man found out she was unfaithful, and he killed them both. They had been on drugs."

It reminded me of the rumors about me spread by the FBI. Personally, I paid as much attention to what came out of an idiot's upper orifices as I did to what came out of their lower orifices, and true freedom is not caring what others say or think of you.

One certainty was that had I met her that day, she would still be alive. There was absolutely no doubt about that. My first real friendship with a woman ended with her death.

The next morning, I called Tonino out of the club. "Ask your daughter Maria what I should do. I mean, I don't want to create a problem for the family. I don't know if I should go to the funeral. I don't know what to do," I said with tears in my eyes.

That evening, Tonino came into my studio. "Maria told me that Rosalba, the sister, said that you must go to Annunziata's house this evening."

I had prepared myself for ten different messages. This was not one of them.

The traditional funeral poster with Annunziata's sweet face was on the wall, surrounded by crying mourners. As Maria and I made it up the stairs toward Annunziata's condominium, people moved out of the way, as if they knew it was the right thing to do. I nodded occasionally when someone looked at me.

Rosalba stared at me as she embraced Maria. She left and returned arm-in-arm with her mother, whose eyes were almost swollen shut. "Mamma," Rosalba said, "this is Patrizio, *L'Americano*."

Annunziata's mother took my hand and we walked to a doorway. "Patrizio, this is where Annunziata slept with her sister." The room was simply furnished with two beds. "Annunziata slept here," she said, running her hand over the quilted mattress.

Books I had gifted and a small CD tower peppered with CDs I had given her were on the shelf above her bed.

"You were her hero. She told us about your son. How is he?" she asked.

"Santino's fine, thank you." I smiled reverently.

Some hero, I thought.

People clapped as the casket exited the church. The funeral passed in front of my office. Annunziata had made it to the afterlife.

F

I was still rattled, weeks later, when I got a call from Sweetboy Leone, one of Dominick's captains. Most of Dominick's men were dead, in jail, or on their way to one of the above.

Slim Traino spent most of his days in prison, wishing that tape recorders were never invented. He still found it hard to believe that Twirls was wearing a wire. Why did he tell him to put a meat hook through Jerry's eye? If the FBI didn't have that recording, he might have gotten off the "hook" himself.

Some of the guys miraculously slid through the FBI's grasp.

I answered the phone. "*Pronto*," I said.

"Don't give me that *pronto* shit, Patty, you're a neighborhood guy."

"Hey Sweetboy, how are you?" I asked.

"You know the tune, Patti, you're a singer. They're putting us in jail for running the numbers so the state lottery will be a monopoly, and they threw us out of Vegas so the politicians can sell it to the real outfit, corporate America," Sweetboy said.

I laughed. "That's not how the journalists report it. I guess life's funny."

"That's because they own the media. Journalism's dead." Sweetboy hesitated before continuing. "Patti, they're digging holes in the neighborhood looking for guys missing since Vietnam. Put a uniform on and get a medal for murder. The guys soldiers kill have kids too, right?"

"Definitely, my friend," I said.

"Freeze some jagoff and the government spends 10 million to find out who did it," Sweetboy grunted. "How's the kid?"

"Santino's good, thanks."

"And the other two, I forget their names."

"Cenzino and Mariocarlo are great. What's up by you?"

"Listen, Patti, we love you and your brothers, well, at least your brothers," he laughed.

Sweetboy tried to bring levity, but I knew there was nothing funny about his call. Someone close to me was in serious trouble.

"It was a sin about Paulie goin' away for that bullshit. He makes me laugh, though . . . Stickin' a guy in his own trunk, drinkin' on the guy's money, runnin' a light, and . . ." Sweetboy laughed.

"Your nutty brother tells the coppers that he's movin' and a cat's banging to get out of the trunk."

Sweetboy laughed.

"'Let the cat out,' the copper tells him. 'It will get scared and run away,' Paulie says. The guy in the trunk starts yelling. The copper asks if the cat talks. Paulie looks at him. 'Would you believe me if I told you it ain't a cat?' He breaks me up, dat kid. Lots of tough breaks, but he'll be out soon."

"Sweets, he's a great kid with a heart of gold," I said.

"It's Mikey Fontana, I know you raised him." Sweetboy hesitated and sighed. "He's got a beef, out of respect I'm calling you." He sighed again. "We ate a lot of shit for dat kid. He stiffed us for more than fifty Gs. Cause he's your brother, a neighborhood kid making Bridgeport proud, we let it go. You know he was ranked number nine?" Sweets asked.

"Yeah, in *Ring Magazine*. Thanks for the breaks, Sweetboy, you're a keeper."

"Tell that to the government fairies that won't get out of my ass."

"It's a system of bribery, brother," I replied

"I remember when bastards had decency. RICO and now this unpatriotic Act has turned us into a nation of stool pigeons and cowards."

"Just a corporate tool, but don't get me goin,' Sweets," I said.

"Patty, your brudder Mikey owes the boys from Melrose. You know I hate them guys, but we ain't got the clout. He owes dem a hundred Gs. They're gonna ball bat him."

"What kind of idiots would give Mikey a hundred of anything?" I asked.

Sweetboy laughed. "Real chooches. Your brother gave some story about having money in your Swiss bank. He did fight three champions, Berbick, Barkley, and Qawi. I guess I see why they believed him. Anyway, he's in trouble if he don't pay up."

I glanced out the window as Santino drove away from the house on a scooter.

"You always been a good guy," Sweetboy continued. "The neighborhood loves you and we do, too. The boss bragged about you any chance he got, God rest his soul."

"Thanks, Sweets, I love you guys, too. I'll talk to my brother."

"Hey Patti, before I hang up I want to tell you something," Sweets said.

"What's that?"

"We was all proud when you took your mother's name, but you were one of us before . . . and you'll always be one of us. Dominick laughed for twenty minutes when he heard you told the mayor you'd slap him if he mentioned your name change again. I mean, you are nuts to do that in front of two hundred people at a ward meeting."

"Thanks for the heads-up about my brother."

"Love ya, Patti," Sweets said.

"Yeah, love you too, Sweets."

I got up and looked out the window. Santino was nowhere in sight. Instead, Don Filippo was in front, walking back and forth with his lupara rested on his shoulder.

The more time I spent in Italy, the more I realized how different it was from the United States. I stared out the window thinking about Mikey, Dirken, Chicago, Santino, Switzerland, Annunziata, and Lucrezia.

The next day, I dialed the last number I had for my brother Mikey. Amazingly, it still worked.

"Mikey, it's me," I said.

"I know it's you. You're the only one with the balls to call me at eight o'clock in the fricking morning. What's up?"

"I'll tell you what's up, you rock head."

Mikey interrupted, "Oh, dis is brotherly love, I ain't speaked to you in a month and right off, I'm a rock head. You didn't even warm up, stunad, idiot, dutz, right away, rock head. What did I do?"

"The guys said that you owe Melrose 100 G," I said.

"They're full of shit, it ain't no hundred G.'"

"How much is it?"

"It's shy of eighty," Mikey said calmly.

"Shy of eighty! You goof!" I looked around to make sure I was still alone.

"That's better. I like goof. Reminds me like old times at the house. Paulie gets out soon. You better have a job lined up for him. If you don't, he's goin' right back to the shitter."

"Let's talk about you, they're gonna ball bat you."

Mikey began laughing.

"They ain't got the balls. I'll stick the bat right up their ass."

"Mikey, these ain't like the coppers you beat up."

Mikey laughed. "That was funny, dose coppers. Paulie held their badges and guns, bunch of pansies. You know, all coppers and G men [government men] were sexually abused kids," Mikey said.

"Mikey, these guys could hurt you."

"Thanks for the call. I love you, brother."

"What are you gonna do?"

"I'll straighten it out."

"You ain't gonna straighten it out unless you pay 'em.'"

Mikey's roar was cut up by laughter. "I can't pay my frickin' rent! Dey deserve to be stuck for how stupid they are . . . Letting me go to eighty Gs."

Some nights later, the Melrose guys didn't hear the crackling of the egg shells sprinkled on the stairs leading to Mikey's apartment. Mikey did. He waited patiently behind his bedroom door.

He didn't stick the bats up their asses, but they were lucky to make it back to their cars. They'd have killed him, but dead people don't pay debts, and making an example of him served little. It would only send more clients to online betting and payday loans.

ꟻ

A few days later I received a call from Annunziata's mother. She wanted to speak with me at their home.

I analyzed everything about our conversation. She had something to settle. In Italy, killing someone who dishonors your family is still a thing. I was possibly going to be an honor victim. I suspected that she'd discovered just how close her daughter and I really were. Of course I'd try to explain, but I prepared myself to be stabbed or shot. A man without honor could not be a good father or a good anything.

It was 10 a.m., 3 a.m. in Chicago. I text-messaged my mother, brothers, and friends in Italy, Switzerland, and the US, telling them that I loved them, which in Italy is "*Ti voglio bene,*" or "*TVB.*"

As I walked up Annunziata's stairs, I shut my phone off. I heard rustling as I softly knocked. I didn't have time to ponder further. The door opened, revealing an empty apartment.

Annunziata's mother smiled gently. "Patrizio, please come in." She quietly shut the door behind us. Italians can be dramatic. I imagined her thrusting a hidden knife into me.

"Please follow me," she said.

I surrendered to the inevitable. *What about Santino, Cenzino, and Mariocarlo?* She led us to her bedroom, moved to the dresser, and opened the top drawer. Doesn't every soldier welcome a soldier's death? I gazed as she raised a bloodied object.

"They found Annunziata's purse. The impact was so violent that it was thrown a hundred meters from the accident."

I gazed at the tiny object, and pictured it when it was not covered with dried blood. Annunziata, not a girl for makeup, kept lip balm, maybe a spare earring, and her phone in the purse. As I tranquilly stared at it, I was also relieved.

"They said many evil things about my daughter, so many evil things. Look at what my daughter had in her purse."

She unzipped the tiny keepsake and reached her fingers inside. I watched with the attention of a child. Her fingers slowly exited with pictured holy cards. A tear streamed down her face.

"This is the evil that my daughter carried. These are the drugs and the indiscretions that she committed. They did not know my daughter," she said fleetingly.

She delicately unfolded a yellow paper. "This was in the purse. Do you know who wrote it?"

I took the note. "Christ taught us, the greatest thing that we can do with our lives is to serve others." It was signed, "Your servant."

I had written the note shortly after meeting Annunziata. I knew about the uncomfortable situation with her boyfriend. The Franciscan in me sincerely wanted to help. Other parts of me were concentrated on different aspects.

I looked down momentarily, then raised my head, looking into her eyes. "I wrote the note."

She took it from my hand and delicately placed it under a small jewelry box on the dresser. "Let's have a *caffè*," she said.

Annunziata loved me and my son, and her family loved her. Over coffee, we spoke of Santino's project. It was now also their project.

Research always goes too slowly, but in the blink of an eye it was All Souls Day, November 2nd. It's a national holiday, and families visit cemeteries all over the country.

I got up as usual and helped the boys dress. We were on our way to breakfast at the bar, and then to the piazza. I had just closed the door, leaving the house, when I heard Lucrezia's voice.

"Pat, oh Pat," Lucrezia called sweetly. She had not spoken to me in months, and had never spoken to me in such a sweet tone.

I popped my head back in the door. She was smiling tenderly. "Patrizio, I just wanted to remind you that it's All Souls Day. Don't forget to visit your friend Annunziata," Lucrezia smiled broadly, "in the cemetery."

I was infinitely impressed. She had waited almost eleven months to say this.

Chapter 22

Salvation Has a Steep Price

The markets in Switzerland became illiquid and difficult. I made a deal with Adrian, Giuseppe, and Thommy, traders from Zurich. They took the reins of BPT from Sebastiano and myself. The Zurich traders were young, aggressive, and honest. I made far fewer trips to Lausanne.

Joe Feldman ran the company in Chicago. I raised capital for the Kragness Medical Center project and learned about other research projects for Sickle Cell Disease and Thalassemia. It was all a piece of cake, a lot easier than shining shoes or breaking into a new pit. Generally speaking, these medical people were no smarter than anyone else. Within a short period of time, millions were flowing through my hands and into research.

In spring of 2003, I raced down the stairs and grabbed mail addressed to me on the way to catch a flight to Switzerland. My Compare Vito, Santino's godfather, was waiting in the car. It didn't matter how early, late, or tired they were, Santino and Vito made every trip to the airport.

In Italy, students attend specialized vocational high schools. Santino, thirteen, was in his last year of grammar school, and had decided he would attend chef's school. Santino always loved food and cooking. Cenzino, twelve, was talking about eventually going to the science academy, and Mariocarlo, still eleven, had a few years to decide. I grabbed the mail and scurried to the car.

Five minutes into the ride, I said solemnly, "Turn the car around."

"Did you forget something? We're already late," Vito said.

"No, I didn't forget anything, I'm tired," I said.

I held up an envelope in my hand. "*La Signora* wants a legal separation."

Vito pulled over and he and Santino watched me.

"Pat, it's just a letter from an attorney. Just throw it away," Vito said with a smile.

By now, I was rarely surprised by my children's mother. A private woman, she had skirmishes with relatives, often barring them from our home. She communicated with

231

me, only in verbal animosity. But being the naïve buffoon that I was and truly am, I was still flabbergasted. I didn't see it coming. With all the pressure that she was also under, I guess maybe I should have.

After twenty sad seconds, I said, "I'm just too tired. Things will have to sort themselves out in Switzerland."

Santino put his hand on my shoulder. "Pà, you taught us to not give up. You say that everyone can be successful when the going's good, but only men can make it when things get tough. Don't give up, Papà."

I didn't respond and Vito quietly edged the car back onto the road to the airport. "Don't worry, I'll talk to the *Signora*. Go take care of business."

At that time, before filing for divorce in Italy, a couple had to be legally separated for three years. The Italian system takes into consideration the entire family. If there are children, the family assets will eventually get split up with them. It makes for some interesting deals. Couples can be separated for a long time, figuring things out.

In May 2003, Juventus, the Italian soccer team that Santino and his godfather were fans of, was scheduled to play Real Madrid, in Torino. I made a call to Susanna Agnelli, the day before the match, and she procured the impossible-to-get tickets. We drove over 100 miles an hour to make the event. Juventus won three to one.

Things at home were normal; I was locked out of the bedroom. For eating, I was on my own, and communications arrived weekly from Lucrezia's lawyers. I finally decided to call her bluff.

After ten minutes, I walked out of her attorney's office and engaged one of my own.

In Italy, the church is in the first line of defense. Our parish priest, Don Peppino, visited our home twice. Both times, Lucrezia threw him out. The second time, he actually left in tears.

You were either for her or against her and one by one, she silenced anyone who didn't support her decision.

I flew back from a Thalassemia meeting in Palermo, and rushed to the courthouse to find Lucrezia, her attorneys, and my attorney standing in front of the judge's chambers.

"I trust that you're looking out for the welfare of my family, as I will be," I said to Lucrezia's attorneys as I shook their hands. They looked at me with odd expressions. I could have easily socked both of them and probably should have. *Our civility has become so inhumane.*

Attorneys were instructed to wait outside. Lucrezia and I entered the silver-haired judge's chambers. He sat behind an antique wooden desk, in a dark suit with a red tie. He smiled softly.

"You do speak Italian?" he asked.

We nodded, he motioned, we sat. He rubbed his chin. "I have studied your case carefully."

Lucrezia stared, I nodded slightly.

"I understand that you have a sick child. I have four children of my own. I can only imagine the pain." He hesitated. "Mine is not an easy job. The world has changed dramatically. Advancement has helped and hurt . . . My duty is to your family, to your children. Do you understand?"

We nodded. He said he'd uphold the family. I was used to hearing judges say that they would uphold the law. I had never been in divorce court anywhere. I wasn't sure what to expect. The case was atypical: two US citizens living in Italy and a sick child. I just assumed that the judge believed that the uniqueness of the situation warranted handling our case differently.

"You have a sick child and two other sons. It seems to me that you need to be unified." He then looked at Lucrezia. "Signora, I do not understand your request for separation."

Lucrezia was not prepared. The judge was supposed to tell her how much money she got, order me out of the house, and give me visiting days. Lucrezia regretted not listening to her sister, who told her to get caught cheating on me. With my "goofy" code I'd never accept being betrayed.

"I beg you to reconsider," the judge concluded.

The last thing her sister told her was, "If all else fails, cry." Tears flowed and soon Lucrezia was sobbing.

The judge calmly raised his hands and looked at me. "Signore Girondi, I cannot force your wife to live with you. Draw a line down the middle of your home and build a wall."

A volcano was erupting in Lucrezia. *What the hell was this old man talking about? Drawing a line down the middle of her house! He was a raving lunatic.* Her gasps subsided momentarily as she grasped the situation. "But we have a *cupola*! It will be divided," Lucrezia cried.

"I guess it will, but your children will be able to see their father when they want. I value this over the *cupola* of the Pantheon."

The judge stood and motioned us toward the door.

Lucrezia moved toward the judge. "Your Honor," she said.

It was like the scene from *The Godfather* where Carlo, the brother-in-law, admitted that he set Sonny up to be killed.

The judge raised his hands, palms to the front. Lucrezia stopped in her tracks. "Build a wall down the middle. Do not move one stick of furniture, don't pick a towel up," he said.

Santino's illness had unrooted Lucrezia from the life she'd imagined.

After, Lucrezia and her attorneys were huddled in the hall. Antonio was thirtyish, blonde, tall, and handsome. Giulio was a bit older, with dark skin and dark hair. I walked past and winked. This was not the US, with tens of thousands in economic stimulus going to judges, attorneys, psychiatrists, attorneys for the children, psychiatrists for the children, and child counselors. I was enormously satisfied that my children would go through the next phase in Italy, where the intent was that my sons should not suffer for our sins so that attorneys could make money and judges get donations for reelection. There was none of that Tuesdays and every other weekend crap.

We had separate marital property in Italy and a prenuptial agreement in the US. The Italian courts saw five people, three of whom were minors. Lucrezia was livid. This backward country looked out for her children, when that was her job. My business partner, Antonio Arcella, attempted to speak with Lucrezia as a father would. He agreed that I neglected her, and that I was peculiar, but things hit a wall when the topic of Santino arose. It was unthinkable that she would not make absolutely every attempt possible for her son. She threw him out and concentrated on the "war of the *Cupola*."

I call myself things like peculiar, goofy, etc. As a Fransiscan, I am taught that we are all wretched sinners and no better than anyone else. I love thinking of myself honestly, the sinning idiot that I am. It keeps me grounded.

The cupola is a one-hundred-square-foot dome on the roof, three stories above the main room, with an image of a guardian angel etched into it. Cutting the home into two equal sections meant cutting the cupola in half. After tough negotiations, Lucrezia conceded a door in a back hallway, allowing the boys to move freely without going outside. At her insistence, the door was steel-plated with no handle on my side.

In the request for separation, it was stipulated that I was an alcoholic and violent. That's pretty much standard in divorce cases. I think the security door helped convince herself of these things. I gave up some space and the cupola remained on her side of the wall. I didn't much miss the stained-glass angel. He had been sleeping on the job anyway.

In true form, after the wall was up and the cupola safe, workers moved a two-hundred-pound bookshelf in front of Lucrezia's side of the door.

My ex-father-in-law sent letters to his brothers and sisters, asking them to no longer welcome me into their homes. Zia Caterina said that she only turned out dogs, and that my sons were blood; as a consequence, I, as their father, was also family and welcome. Thanks to Lucrezia's relatives, my failure at being a husband did limited damage to my sons, who just went on with life.

Papà was just on the other side of the wall. Life was good.

The taxpayer is the major sponsor of research in the USA, through government and not-for-profit-funded grants. Researchers spend years of their lives applying for the billions of dollars doled out annually. Committees at the FDA (Food and Drug Administration), NIH (National Institutes of Health), and hundreds of not-for-profit organizations award the grants as they see fit. Politics are often the main factor when divvying out these crucial chips.

During the Bush years, hundreds of millions were diverted from cancer and other diseases into anthrax vaccination research.

According to Pierre Shorf, his brainchild, the beta-globin gene vector, was ready for clinical trials (to be tested in humans). Billions of beta-globin genes would be encapsulated into billions of disarmed HIV viruses (they would now be labeled "vectors"). The vectors would then be incubated with, and hopefully insert themselves into the patients' stem cells. The stem cells containing the beta-globin gene vector would then be infused back into the patient, who would now express the needed beta-globin gene. If the scheme worked, Santino would be cured. Friends and I had written checks since I met Pierre in 2000, but in late 2003, Kragness Medical Center informed Shorf that they would halt funding. Without a corporate sponsor, the project was dead.

Norb Wiech contacted several pharmaceutical companies, who regarded gene therapy as unproven, and scientific folly.

I spoke to Sergio Rato, president of Thalassemia International. His son Diego is about eight years older than Santino and also has Thalassemia. Sergio's organization was funding Redunt, a French company working on a similar vector for the same diseases, Sickle Cell and Thalassemia.

Asman Temple, the Redunt researcher, and Pierre Shorf, were French nationals and former academic colleagues. Pierre claimed that years ago, Asman had created a mutant vector of the wild-type, natural beta-globin gene that Pierre had discovered to get around trouble with eventual patents. Asman Temple lived in Paris and Massachusetts, where he was a professor at Harvard University.

Redunt had just received $12 million from pharmaceutical giant Nathaniel and Nathaniel, to support research in Asman Temple's beta-globin gene vector. It seemed absurd that Nathaniel and Nathaniel, or anyone would invest in the mutant gene, Redunt vector.

Brett Galen, the new CEO of Redunt, and I had breakfast near Harvard. Guys from the neighborhood would have left with the forks, knives, and spoons; they were real silver. We saw advantages in managing the projects jointly, but eventually the scheme fell apart. He was likely irked by my statement that executive compensation should be minimal and based on long-term results.

Most CEOs I've known are Ivy League grads. The more of them I meet, the more I admire the US employee. Despite the modern US CEO, we have a lot of successful companies.

A Ford executive once told me, "Don't fault the unions for American automakers' problems. Blame the executives who chose short-term profit over quality, making gas-guzzling junks and the Vega."

Wanting to have all our bases covered, Sergio Rato continued funding Redunt. When we were confident of which vector was better, we'd concentrate on one.

In 2004, the Orphan Dream band released *Orphan's Soul*, my first CD, finding my soul through the "orphan disease."

As stated previously, orphan diseases are rare afflictions with small patient populations. For that reason, the drug industry devotes few resources to curing them. They were so rare that they were orphaned.

The CDs were sold on CD Baby and Amazon. My buddy Derek Holmes bought two hundred of them and gave them away at business events. Money from all sales went toward research.

I flew to Jackson Hole, Wyoming, to pitch the gene therapy project to my partner John Walton. Christie, John's wife, and Lukas, their seventeen-year-old son, made me feel right at home.

That evening, John told Lukas's story. His son had been near death with Wilms' tumor. Thanks to the medical institute in Tijuana, Mexico, and Christie's diligent work keeping him away from processed foods, Lukas, was a healthy, strong young man.

Watching Lukas, it was hard to believe that he was the same boy from whom medical specialists wanted to remove a lung from years prior. I told some of my own stories and the evening was full of laughs. Christie, Lukas, Santino, John, and I were bound more than ever by parental love.

Under Norb (I called Dr. Norb Wiech Uncle Norby and his lovely wife Linda, Aunty Linda), Beacon filed twenty patent applications on original molecules, with cancer and non-cancer applications. Still, Lukas was healthy, and John was heavily invested in the solar industry. John and his partners, Troy and Dunn, passed on the Shorf project.

With no alternative, Norb and I founded Beta Gene Company (BGC), a Delaware corporation headquartered in Chicago. I was the CEO, Norb the president and head scientist.

Brad Wolf, an attorney friend of Norb and soon mine, began contract negotiations with Kragness Medical Center. Brad knew about rare diseases—he had one. Ceradase, the medicine he needs to live, costs $500,000 a year. He had recently left a law firm because of economic issues, which were consequences of his pricey medication.

The costs of producing the medicines themselves are often inconsequential. It's the executive and fund compensations that we need to keep our eyes on.

Angela Iacono, the president of the Italian Thalassemia Federation, became the project's Italian godmother. In May of each year, Italy has a Thalassemia Day. To raise funds, they sell orange plants. Some years, a Pat Girondi CD was thrown in with each plant sold (they make great beverage coasters).

I was in Chicago trading when someone yelled into the pit that John Walton was on the phone. "Pat, this is John," he said in his gentle Arkansas drawl. "I really admire what you're doing and Lukas is doing fine. I want you to have the patents from Beacon. I'm going to shut her down."

I hung up the phone and called Norb. The patent applications were mostly for Norb's inventions through collaborations with Nelly Gester and Professors Falo Twist and Pierson Reinst from Notre Dame University, Norb's beloved alma mater. The patents represented $19 million of investment. We rolled them into BGC and hired a firm that specialized in valuations of similar companies. The firm came back with a replacement value of over $50 million for BGC. We discounted it by 40 percent and used a thirty-million-dollar valuation to raise funds.

Thalassemic patients habitually transfuse and are gravely damaged by excess iron that accumulates in their organs from transfused blood. Iron in the heart is especially deadly. Periodic examinations are crucial, and Dr. Cianciulli, a Thalassemic heart specialist at Gemelli Hospital in Rome, was booked months in advance.

Angela Iacono called late one evening. A patient scheduled for a visit the following day had died. She offered Santino the 9 a.m. slot.

Managing Santino's medical issue had become a tug-of-war with my separation. Everything I thought was right, Lucrezia thought was wrong. Mentioning the Rome visit meant not going.

Luckily, Santino slept with me. We left for Rome at 3 a.m. Vito, Santino's godfather, drove. At 8:00 a.m., Santino called to inform his mother where we were, and explained that we had left too late the night before to inform her.

At 9 a.m., I received a call from a marshal of the Carabinieri of Altamura. Lucrezia was standing in front of the marshal's desk, and wanted me charged with kidnapping. I explained the situation. The marshal gave me his kind wishes, and asked that I visit him at the station when we returned. He assured Lucrezia that all was well.

Within an hour, Lucrezia returned and filed two complaints, one against me for kidnapping, and the other against the marshal for not accepting her kidnapping complaint against me.

Brad Wolf dealt with Jane Nunn of the Kragness Medical Center's Industrial Affairs Department. Jane's boss, Dill Pickens, Esq., had to approve any deal. Finally, after sixty weeks of negotiations, on March 4 of 2005, BGC and Kragness Medical Center signed License Agreement 9927. We now owned the worldwide rights to the Shorf vector.

Italy was abuzz with rumors about Pope John Paul's health. Santino, Cenzino and Mariocarlo had all visited him at the Vatican with their schools. They, as the country, loved his soft, kind ways.

The evening of April 2, 2005, I walked into the house. Santino's eyes were glued to the television. I sat down next to my fifteen-year-old son, noticing the transmission from Saint Peter.

"How's he doing?" I asked.

"Not good, Papà. He may go tonight."

I put my arm around my firstborn. "Let's go to bed, son, we can't help him."

Tears rolled down Santino's face. "No, Papà, I want to wait."

After a few hours, my bedroom door opened. "Pà," Santino cried, "he's dead."

We hugged and embraced the loss of the greatest public figure of my lifetime. Many Italian stores stayed closed for days. Few people spoke on the streets. The country was in *lutto* (mourning).

The pope had been a special man, and Italy was a special place. Since I'd arrived in Altamura, three new churches had been built. Back home, in Bridgeport, five were closed in less than a decade.

John Paul had touched Italy and the world. Bari's airport was renamed Bari International Airport–Karol Wojtyla (the pope's baptism name). Two Italian families I know named their children Karola and Karolo. What a strange guy he was, trying to teach us to love others more than ourselves. If the corruptorations ever believed that this kind of silly thinking could actually catch on, I doubt that he'd have lived as long.

I put seed money in BGC and began rounding up investors on the floor of the Chicago Board of Trade. Over a dozen top research scientists attended the first BGC International Conference in Mainz, Germany.

Nelly, Norb's assistant, told friends that the most unforgettable part of the trip was visiting the Mainz cathedral and watching me, the often brash, crude, and uncouth man, kneel and pray in the holy house. She claimed to have felt a rush of energy.

The *Wall Street Journal* published that it took $800 million and nineteen years to get a drug to market. The odds of success were less than 1 percent. Santino was fifteen, and my separation was two years behind me.

Companies like BGC are always in fundraising mode. *Always raise twice the amount of money you need.* This was one of the many rules of thumb I did not adhere to. The more you raised, the more you risked, and the more you diluted investors. I raised funds as they were needed.

Salaries are a start-up's largest expense. Of course, the CEO got a huge chunk. I didn't take a salary. We didn't pay the going rate to anyone. Our collaborators believed in the cause and worked even harder for that reason.

On June 27, 2005, John Walton died in an ultralight plane crash. I communicated with Lukas, figuring it was the minimum I could do for my gentle friend.

In July 2005, BGC sponsored the Protocol Meeting at Kragness Medical Center in Los Angeles. Greek and Italian doctors attended. Dr. Tian flew in from Singapore. Experts were flown in from all over the globe. I intended that our meeting and project moving forward would honor my late partner John Walton and his beautiful family.

Dr. John Tisdale, our principal investigator from the National Institutes of Health, soon became a favorite confidant and friend. Omar Achman was the principal investigator for Kragness Medical Center.

The first day, I called Dr. Aurelio Maggio's hotel room early in the morning, figuring we both had jet lag. Aurelio is a smart and kind Thalassemia specialist from Palermo. With his light, freckled complexion and reddish-brown hair, he's living proof that the Normans invaded Sicily.

We sat on a bench in LA's Central Park. While speaking about the protocol, he boldly interrupted. "Patrizio, do you know why I'm working so hard with you on this project?" he asked.

It reminded me of the time Father Ambrose in the Franciscan seminary explained to me why he became a priest. I was captivated.

"Like Puglia, Calabria, Sardegna, and Campagna, the coast of Sicily is full of carriers of the Thalassemia trait. The pregnant couples make their pilgrimage to my office. We do the amniocentesis exam and wait for the results."

Entranced by Aurelio's words, I paid no attention to the skinny black pigeon that landed on my leg. As Aurelio continued, the pigeon made its way up my arm. Joggers and walkers stopped and watching the spectacle, formed a circle around us.

"The couple lives in agony waiting for the results. I also live their agony. I know that I will possibly give them news that will destroy them. If the fetus is sick, they have two choices."

The pigeon hopped from my legs to my stomach, and chest, and onto my shoulders.

"They can have a Thalassemic child with all of the complications, or they can abort. Either solution is full of pain," Aurelio said.

I concentrated on Aurelio's words. The crowd concentrated on the small, ugly bird.

"This project means that I can offer these couples a third possibility. If the baby is sick, they can do gene therapy and cure the child." Tears formed in his eyes.

A woman interrupted the intense conversation. "How did you train that bird to do that?" she asked.

I looked at her and then at Aurelio. Whatever she was selling was irrelevant. The news put me in a trance. Gene therapy would save the unborn!

The circle around us grew. There were now more than thirty people staring at us. The ugly, winged creature was on my right shoulder and stuck its beak near my ear. I looked into its ugly beady eyes. It gazed firmly back.

My mind jerked, suddenly realizing the situation. "Hey! What do you think I am, San Francesco?" I yelled.

Unlike the rondone in Piazza Duomo of Altamura, the bird was able to fly off. The crowd dispersed. As Aurelio and I headed to the protocol meeting, I had even more kick in my step. Our project would save the unborn . . .

Many things were decided in those crucial, critical meetings, including the age of the subjects to be treated, the scheduled treatment centers in Europe and the US, and the dosage of Busulfan, the chemotherapy preparatory regimen, used to arrest the immune system and make space in the bone marrow before the vector was infused into the patient.

We were a team and by the end of the four days, the basis of the treatment protocol was complete.

Chapter 23

Cousins and Going for Broke

Sickle Cell Disease and Thalassemia are both caused by defective beta-globin genes. They are cousins, and our therapy would cure them both.

The blood of Sickle Cell Disease patients sickles. In other words, red blood cells get distorted into a crescent or sickle shape which clog up the veins, causing severe pain and disastrous complications. In essence, this was another defect to deal with. For this reason, Thalassemia was the simpler target and we would begin there.

Dr. John Tisdale, from the National Institutes of Health, is one of the world's top Sickle Cell experts. John had been present in the protocol meeting of 2005 in Los Angeles. John could have gone on to work for any number of pharmaceutical companies, but decided to dedicate himself to patients by working at the National Institute of Health.

I had been in *Playgirl* with Magic Johnson, and through Derek Holmes, I contacted Larry Johnson, Magic's brother, to continue preparing the ground for attacking Sickle Cell Disease. Larry was helpful, and Magic does great things for humanity.

We were lining things up and hitting on all cylinders. This is how we would do it: remove stem cells from patients, incubate them with billions of copies of the beta-globin gene (our invention), give patients chemotherapy to make space in the bone marrow, and re-transfuse their own modified stem cells back to them (see photo insert, "How Gene Therapy Works").

In the fall of 2005, three out of thirteen patients in France treated with gene therapy for SCID (boy in the bubble disease) developed Leukemia. One of the patients died. The other ten patients were cured of a disease that usually took its victims before their tenth birthday. The world saw disaster, but the French trial only proved to me that we were on the right track.

John Walton's memorial was held a year after his death at a wilderness school in Jackson Hole. Guests were housed in a dormitory. The events were storytelling and experiences of how John's kindness helped others.

The first day, Christie, Lukas, and two of his cousins were joined by me and Santino at the river for a family picnic. Santino enjoyed the Walton boys a lot more than the freezing river water. I watched him playing with his older brother Lukas and their cousins, all linked by parents' love.

Santino amazed me. Most Thalassemia patients eventually cower and get used to a life limiting risk and physical activity. They all suffer from osteoporosis and know that minimal contact could fracture a bone. Santino did it all. He competed in go-cart races, played soccer, and rode his mountain bike through the rugged terrain of the surrounding hills and forests. Santino was a lion of a man, as are his brothers. I guess I'm just a lucky guy.

At John's memorial, Ronald Troy told me of his confidence in my ability to make something good out of the time and resources that had been invested in our project. The right people's confidence was essential for our success.

I was introduced to John's brothers and sister as his partner in the pharmaceutical industry, trying to help my son and patients. They were all encouraging and complimentary. I really appreciated John's sister Alice's free spirit. I left the John Walton get-together supercharged.

Separated life became normal, though I continued to plead for another child, or for the eggs to produce a compatible sibling. Lucrezia ignored the amorous text messages I occasionally sent.

During the three years of separation, from time to time, I was required to show up in court, where I would swear my love for Lucrezia. People often burst into laughter.

"Honey, we're still officially married, should we celebrate our anniversary?"

"If we had sex a thousand times or a thousand and one, who'd know the difference?"

I used patgirondi.com to give patient updates. Writing and performing became my days on the golf course or in the gym. I wrote and entered my screenplay *Blind Faith* into the American Screenwriters competition. The judges had to decide over 3,200 pieces. It was an amusing surprise: I was in the five runners-up.

I kept in touch with my father, the Old Man, Matty, or whatever you'd like. He lived in the building I owned on 28th Street. Ma also looked in on him from time to time.

In April 2006, Ma called me while I was on the trading floor. I drove to 28th Street. He lived in a one-room ground-floor apartment. I walked in.

"He's dead," Ma said.

I grabbed the pistol from the coffee table, put it in my pocket, and walked into the bedroom. He looked like the picture of health as he lay naked in his bed. We had found a tenant in a similar situation a few months prior. It was my belief that both men were victims of a neighborhood cokehead who strangled her lovers while riding on top. I smiled to myself. There were worse ways to go.

The police entered, asked a few questions, and took the body to the morgue. It was obviously a heart attack and a lot less paperwork.

I have this idea that Catholics and all believers should welcome death. This obviously does not mean that we should not preserve life, which is a precious gift. I love people when they're here on earth, and I don't pay a lot of attention to mourning, the big business of funerals, or any of the other theatrics that occur when a person passes from one existence to another. Not all of my brothers and sisters made it to the funeral. I understood perfectly.

My father, the Old Man, Matty was gone. I would honor his life by doing good things for others. What does sulking do for anyone?

Daily communications filled my email. The world wanted to know the latest on gene therapy, and there was no one better to ask. I had a finger on the pulse of most everything going on, and I promptly answered each inquiry.

I read Fanny Tifo's data with great concern. She claimed that L1, the oral iron chelator, dangerously compromised patients' livers. She was a guest on the television show *60 Minutes* as the Florence Nightingale who stood against big pharma.

Santino had been on L1 therapy for years. US patients like our bubbly assistant Becky Martino would die if we didn't get the drug to them.

Sadly, L1, which was produced by the Canadian company Apotek, would still be illegal in the US for years to come, causing the premature deaths of scores of American patients. Eventually (as mentioned before), Miriam Shuchman published her book, *The Drug Trial*, which demonstrated how research in the hands of the wrong people can be very dangerous. In 2017, Apotek owner Barry Sherman and his wife Honey were found murdered in their home. The pharmaceutical business can be a dangerous one. No suspects were ever arrested.

The wheels turned in everyone's lives. Tam Smith, Larry Smith's mother, died of cancer. Shortly after, Al Smith, Larry's dad, was stopped for a traffic violation and beaten by Chicago police. He died two months later.

My economic situation became dire. I had debt, an ex, three sons, and research to maintain. I began borrowing from Peter to pay Paul. They weren't always apostles, but they were mostly good guys, happy to lend a hand.

Trying to stay afloat, I bought and sold depressed real estate on Chicago's South Side. Many of these properties were less than five miles from the pristine Loop, in the center of the city. Some of the lots I purchased were only hundreds of feet from where lots sold for $200,000 or even $300,000.

My bank loved the idea. I'd buy a property for $3,000 to $10,000 and the bank would give me a $30,000 mortgage. This greatly helped liquidity.

Traders, friends, and business acquaintances continued writing checks as BGC's plane moved to the sky. Doctor Christopher Ballas, an incredible scientist and man, became BGC's vector expert. Joshua Bandik continued as our administrative officer.

I visited various fund managers in Los Angeles, and hung out with wheeler-dealer Lance Rolf and Wilem Masters, the CEO of the investment firm Callom Stoke. Jonas Hoffman, award-winning analyst at Callom Stoke, became our staunch supporter, and believed that the technology and our Spartan-like company were on the cusp of greatness.

Different from many Los Angeles wheeler-dealers, Lance really knew the people he spoke of. Once, we had dinner in a room that held five people: Robert De Niro, Steve Wynn, Steve Wynn's companion, Lance, and me.

I shoveled every dime I had into the project. The more I put in personally, the less investor money I risked. After all, Santino was my son. I slept in cars, shared rooms, hitched rides, split cab fares, and often walked to the airport. There was no sacrifice on my end. I enjoyed it all.

Traveling light was essential to saving time and money. I lived out of a backpack. My often-wrinkly clothes demonstrated this. My formal attire, when needed, was from the $99-suit store. I gravitated somewhere between the 1920s mobster and the 1980s pimp look. I believed that being remembered by the independent thinker was more important than disappointing the cookie-cutter managers, who were unlikely to help me or anyone else anyway.

Performing rock and blues concerts helped me cross some pretty rough seas. Pay for my performances was anything from dinner to a check. It all went for research. I sang on *Una Mattina*, Italy's number-one television show, and on Chicago televised programs.

In Los Angeles, I sang three songs on the terrace at a charity event. The group wrote a $100,000 check. "If I didn't sing, would it have been 200,000?" I asked.

Had it not been for Santino's situation, I doubt that music would ever have been so critical, and obviously, I wouldn't be writing this book.

My supporters were more than precious, and whether they sent a prayer or a check, these kind people's efforts and resources had to be respected. BGC demanded this from all of our growing team. This mentality allowed for some creative management.

At home, Lucrezia's younger sister moved from the US to Italy and married. Her older sister visited often, and the three of them filed complaints against me six different times for verbal abuse, or for not informing Lucrezia where I was with my sons. Attention to her sons seemed to peak when she felt that a complaint could be alleged. The sixth time she filed a grievance, a miffed Carabinieri suggested she not do so again. She didn't.

Once, one of my sons forgot keys to her side of the house, on my side of the house. I glanced at them and knew instantly what needed to be done.

Everything was quiet. I sauntered into my old bedroom and glanced at Lucrezia's stately portrait. Her eyes looked directly at me as I approached. I imagined she'd begin blaring, but she remained dignified and quiet. After a few moments, I stepped back. She was far more attractive with a charcoal black mustache.

Leonardo Giambrone, the founder of the Italian Thalassemia Federation, and another father like myself, was in Lyon, France, being treated for stomach cancer. I made the trip, and before I left his side, he asked me to promise I would do all I could to see his son and all of the Thalassemics cured. I promised. He died two days later.

In 2007, I received communications that Redunt had treated three E-beta patients as compassionate cases in Paris. Compassionate case patients are those who refuse or do not respond to traditional treatment. He or she is allowed to be treated with experimental medicine even before it is approved by government agencies.

The vector used was made in Indiana. Dr. Christopher Ballas, BGC's vector expert, assisted in the production.

Our experts studied the situation; Redunt's choices seemed to be far from coincidence. E-beta Thalassemia is a mild form of the disease. Many E-betas outgrow transfusion dependency and 85 percent of the patients in Europe and North America are Beta Thalassemics, not E-betas. French rules are more flexible. Redunt saved time and money not conducting the trial in the US under the FDA.

Redunt used unfiltered vector in quantities that would likely compromise patient health. They used myeloablation (a chemotherapy regimen that kills all bone marrow), completely knocking out patients' immune systems, and leaving them in perilous straits. Many specialists believed that conducting the trial was immoral, others believed that it was a sham, and still others believed that it was a trial conducted exclusively for financial gain. I did meet some who held that it was a necessary "ends justifies the means" maneuver.

An Indian doctor from New Delhi wrote in a Thalassemia blog, "Treating patients with the mildest form of the disease with experimental living virus particles and myeloablation was criminal."

Possibly the worst part of it all was that Temple, the aggressive researcher, successfully convinced many that he had cured Thalassemia. This helped make the roller coaster of hope which patients and their loved ones ride even more torturous. E-beta was just a very mild form with very few afflicted patients. Saying that he had cured Thalassemia was as untrue as it was misleading. And even if Temple had cured an E-beta patient, there was not a lot of reason to believe that the same product would cure the prevalent, more severe disease that Santino and his brothers and sisters had.

Patients get a boost in hemoglobin after doing chemotherapeutic drugs. Many Sickle Cell Disease and Thalassemia patients take Hydroxyurea regularly, to help sustain fetal hemoglobin. Myeloablation was a likely reason for at least part of the patient's increase in hemoglobin.

Our own Dr. Ballas felt that Redunt's move was tactical. Even modest success in a clinical trial usually opens funding doors. Nathaniel and Nathaniel's $12 million had been spent (squandered) by its executives and founders on their own salaries and expense accounts. Different from us, they suffered from a desperate lack of resources. Desperate people commit desperate acts.

Although Dr. Ballas and other experts firmly believed in the superiority of the more natural BGC vector, our project was viewed as being riskier now that a competitor was in patients. Many companies in our position would have thrown in the towel, but our investors were undaunted. They were in for the cure. Besides, Redunt may have been first in patients, but their vector obviously needed modification, and we had a superior product. I wasn't the least bit worried. They had cubic zirconia and we had the real thing. Only fools would try to pass off one for the other.

Another stark difference in management styles was that Redunt was secretive, whereas we insisted on clear communication. Many began to cheer us on and support our project. Raimondo Culatto, a patient's father and accountant from California, appreciated our spirit and became a critical part of the team.

After seeing the inefficacy of Redunt's vector, the French debacle, and after donating more than $500,000 to the Temple product, Sergio Rato and his team abandoned Redunt and put their support behind BGC and the Kragness Medical Center product.

While working feverishly on the RAC (Recombinant DNA Advisory Committee) submission for the FDA, Norb's demand for precision and efficiency clashed with Pierre's hectic schedule. SickleThalgen (our trademarked name for the beta-globin gene vector invented by Shorf) was BGC's only product close to entering clinical trials. Pierre, instead, was working on a half dozen other projects, and desperately needed money to keep his laboratory functioning.

Kragness Medical Center was obligated to procure research data notebooks to BGC. A research notebook is kept by a scientist to keep track of his or her research. They are the Holy Grail. Assuming the researcher was honest, everything is in the notebooks and Pierre was uncommonly honorable. We needed to begin communication with the FDA. This would not be possible without going through the notebooks and detailing each and every line. The notebooks were crucial. I can't stress this enough.

Norb made frequent trips to Manhattan, only to return angered and empty-handed. I put on as much pressure as I believed possible without jeopardizing relationships and the venture.

After a lot of grueling work, BGC was accompanied to the RAC committee at the National Institutes of Health on June 20, 2007 by doctors Christopher Ballas, Patricia Giardina from Cornell, Nancy Cuttings (Pierre's wife), Pierre Shorf, Omar Achman from Kragness Medical Center, John Tisdale of the National Institutes of Health, and pediatric transplant expert Dr. Oscar Rays. The group was a powerhouse of knowledge and prestige.

Fourteen deep years after Santino's diagnosis, I was callused. Fourteen years in the research business, I was humbled to be affiliated with some of the top doctors and researchers in the world. Still, I needed to continue digging and the calluses were a blessing.

Drew Norte, Redunt's new president, attended our FDA RAC meeting. He confirmed that his company was strapped for cash and plagued by infighting. I told him that I was always open to new ideas and collaboration.

Days later, an official letter arrived at the BGC offices. BGC secured approval from the FDA Recombinant DNA Advisory Committee (RAC) to proceed toward clinical trials for SickleThalgen. We were the first company in the US to receive this award of authorization for gene therapy. It was the greatest day of my life. It was moving and wouldn't have been possible without the selfless sacrifice and work of many. I didn't remotely deserve to be in their ranks but I still cried with joy.

Christie Walton, Sergio Rato, and Raimondo Culatto were not physically at the RAC meeting, nor were they with me as I read the FDA communication, but their constant presence was critical, and they also celebrated a win for our united family.

Dr. Ballas and I pushed ahead, using experts, including but not limited to Drs. Giardina, Perrine, Cappellini, Tisdale, Marsk, Kemp, Maggio, Shorf, Cuttings, Rays, and Drs. Persons, Grey, and Sorrentino from Saint Jude.

BGC worked on a leather shoestring. Some researchers, such as Dr. Martin Tenniswood, actually took money out of their own pockets to assist. Other companies spent tens of millions on what BGC took a hundred thousand to do. Think of it this way. A company annually compensates $5,000,000 to its CEO. They have a budget of $20,000,000 to spend on two research projects. In reality, it's already down to $15,000,000 and that's not counting the CEO's other minions, like the board and/ or staff. After that, you must tag on offices, travel, dining, and bonuses. By the time the hogs are done, a $20,000,000 research budget could easily end up with less than $1,000,000 going to research.

The weak CEO is forced to pay ridiculous sums to his board. Board members making $25,000 a year will be less hesitant to stand up to a dishonest and or feeble-minded captain than a board member making $200,000 annually.

The dedication of our team was responsible for our success, not quality-cutting, public relation schemes, or maneuvers aimed at bilking investors.

Santino was still transfusing after almost fifteen years of being diagnosed (he was diagnosed in October 1992). Looking back, I had thought that by the time he was six he'd have been cured by a bone marrow transplant and/or another therapy. I could have and should have done better. Lucrezia was not all wrong, certainly. Who was I to think that my input could make a difference?

I concentrated on the future and I believed that we were on track to cure Santino and all his brothers and sisters with Sickle Cell Disease and Thalassemia.

In August 2007 Jolee Mohr, a thirty-six-year-old wife and mother from Springfield, Illinois, died of complications related to an experimental gene therapy called AAC94. Her death was a tragedy for her family and a disaster for the gene therapy world. My computer lit up like a video game. Many sought my interpretation of this development.

I wrote a letter of reassurance to patients and investors, and secured $300,000 in financing from Phi Stamin, a large Italian pharma company founded by the Vari brothers. I met Phi Stamin executives Bruno Mauri, Leroy Gertz, Herman Maily, and the founder, Alessandro Vari himself. Phi Stamin had already produced seven orphan drugs, and had an annual income of over one billion dollars. Eventually we would need a commercialization partner. Phi Stamin would be perfect.

Usually drug companies taking advantage of the 1983 Orphan Drug Act targeted diseases with tiny population bases. SickleThalgen targeted Thalassemia and Sickle Cell Disease. Between the two diseases, there were close to two million patients worldwide, making SickleThalgen the most important gene therapy project in the world. Our research team was top-notch. We were hitting our goals. Many companies who had far less than BGC were doing IPO's and reverse mergers.

Lance Rolf wanted to follow this strategy for BGC. When companies follow this strategy the money changers enter and often, greed controls destiny. We stayed independent.

As the project grew, I spent more time on the exchange floor in Chicago, meaning I spent less time at home. Lucrezia said to some that she did not believe in research, or so I was told. If this is true, they likely misunderstood. She probably meant that she didn't believe in me. Despite tragedy and doubt which plagued the camp, the scientific community made great strides. Our patients were living longer than ever. A few made it into their forties.

In my absence, there was an ever-present safety net around the Girondi family, made of compari, relatives, and friends. Santino was in his second year of the five-year, chef/hotel high school, which prepared young people for a career in the restaurant and/or hotel industry. Santino, as his father before him, wasn't always the best-behaved kid. I'm not sure if he was bored or just wanted to have a bit more fun than his professors afforded. In my absence, Vito, Santino's godfather, stepped in to assist and made many trips to speak to the professors, who were kind and more than willing to collaborate.

In 2008, *Orphan's Journey* was released. The album was produced in Italy by a wizard named Giordano Mazzi. Giordano collaborated with some of Italy's finest and best known musicians. He also worked for the car company Ferrari, producing musical CDs using excerpts from Formula 1 races and sounds from the mythical car. There were many things that I admired about Enzo Ferrari. It felt good to be linked to him through the music in my Orphan's Dream project.

BGC owned the Beacon molecules, but we needed to be focused on our main project. Professor Martin Tenniswood, from the University of Albany, was enthusiastic about 1521, one of our patented molecules. He believed that it could be an effective drug in fighting hormonal breast cancer. 1521 had two important publications, and Martin used his own resources and ingenuity to get the drug into animals. Martin became a friend. You couldn't do anything but love him once you knew him.

In the summer of 2008, BGC anxiously awaited the results of the titer experiment. Titer is the percentage of human cells that the vector entered. The higher the titer, the more effective the therapy.

I was at the sea with my sons when Dr. Ballas called. "Hi Chris, how's it going?" I asked.

Dr. Ballas did not answer.

"All well, sir?" I asked, timidly fearing the answer.

"Not really," Chris said softly.

This was not like Chris. He was always warm and cheerful.

"Our titer data results do not match Kragness Medical Center's results," he said.

I was afraid to ask. "How bad are they?"

"They're disastrous."

I looked at Santino. My mind sighed. We were again being pushed out of the port. I felt like I had been punched in the stomach, right in the center, just below the ribs.

Chris continued, "There's no way we can treat patients with such an inefficient vector. We'd be doing what Temple and Redunt did."

I was floored. *Was it time to throw in the towel?*

Some put research above single patients. The thinking goes, *If we lose a few sick patients, but with what we learn are able to cure hundreds or thousands of others, are we not obligated to do so?*

I've had this conversation with doctors and researchers dozens of times, even if they didn't realize it themselves.

I spoke very few words over the next hours. The logical thing to do would be to quit. I thought of my son, all of my sons and daughters, and my investors. I imagined myself at the blackjack table. The dealer had a face card showing; I had 15 and the rest of my chips were riding on the bet. For those of you who don't play blackjack, I was in an uncomfortable situation.

I prayed and asked my mother to round up her group of family and friends to pray. I made a dozen calls and had some tough conversations. Dr. Ballas, National Institutes of Health's John Tisdale, and Saint Jude's Derek Persons, agreed; patients should not be treated, now or ever, with such a low titer.

It was my partner and friend, Joe Feldman who helped me decide. "If you're in, I'm in," he said. "We must cure Santino."

Joe might not have known it, but he had just thrown me in the air, as I had thrown the rondone in the air years ago in Piazza Duomo of Altamura. He saved me and the project. Before slamming to the ground I began moving my wings and flying once more. The team would have to find a solution for the titer situation and I would find the resources needed to do so.

After other conversations, just hours later, I was ecstatic. The decision to continue was enthusiastically supported by our warmhearted investors.

Close to where we lived, a neighbor had set up a doghouse for the pit bull that hung around on the street outside of her house. We got home from the sea only to discover that one of our dogs had been killed by the dog.

I called the dogcatcher, who told me that he wasn't paid enough to be capturing pit bulls. I tried to run the dog over, and then smashed into his house while he was sleeping. He ran away and I damaged my car. I stuck needles and poison into meatballs, but he outsmarted me and wouldn't touch them. Finally, I went to see a friend.

Agatino was a great guy and in charge of the mob in Taranto, a town about an hour from Altamura. I had recently advised them to not buy a load of Kuwaiti dinar. It proved to be good advice. I was endeared to many of Agatino's gang, in one fashion or another.

Agatino knew that I had issues with my ex and found the story about killing a pit bull a bit farfetched. He walked to my car and pulled the pistol out. "*Americhein*, if you want, I'll come and kill the dog."

"Nah, it's my responsibility."

He sighed. "Promise me that you won't do anything crazy?"

I smiled and he handed me the pistol. Santino and I did some target practice, and the pit bull quandary was resolved.

I was again a guest on Italy's number-one television program and performed in Assisi at Serafico with Al Bano and Andrea Bocelli, two of Italy's top performers. My song "It's Your Time" was honored by The Giffoni Film Festival. I only hoped that awards or recognition would lead to resources.

I traveled to a medical center in Thessaloniki, Greece, affiliated with Gustus Antypoulos of Percy University. Dr. Antypoulos was a much-respected Thalassemia specialist aligned with Redunt and or any other company who offered hope for his patients. I reasoned with the good doctor, and he also threw his weight behind BGC.

Obtaining stem cells from patients is a tricky and painful ordeal. A needle is inserted into the hip bone to get marrow. A higher volume of stem cells means a more efficient transplant and an eventually higher hemoglobin. A better method of procuring the precious stem cells needed to be found.

Angela Iacono and I went to visit the Italian Telethon director, Samuele Prete. Let's say that telethon could get two birds with one stone, putting their name on our great project and repaying me for Chicago. Two days later, Telethon announced that we had won a $500,000 research grant for our French, Greek, Italian, and US stem cell mobilization trial.

With the support of Joe Feldman, my longtime friend-partner, and others, we survived. I left for Chicago, where, among other things, I began recording my third CD, *Orphan's Hope*.

Chapter 24

Soybean Traders Save Gene Therapy

Going back to the soybeans trading pit was always a homecoming. Many of the regular traders and brokers were BGC investors. I loved the guys, Jay, Teddy-Jimbob, Mark, Greg, Larry, Brendan, John, and Kostas, a Greek trader who came to the States as a waiter on a cruise ship. They were supportive, even though they themselves were in a David/Goliath scenario. It was them against the programs and computers owned by the banks. Floor traders were gladiators, battling on the planet's last open outcry floors where Goldman, J. P. Morgan, MF Global, and others entered, pushing the markets around, taking huge exposure and consequently murdering the little guys.

When the bank's risky behavior brought them to the brink of bankruptcy, the taxpayers bailed them out. The gladiators didn't have that luxury.

Always the peacemaker, as soon as I landed, I was asked to intervene; the largest trading group was making war against the largest broker. I analyzed the situation and quickly settled the dispute.

In October 2008, I was driving in Chicago when the phone rang. I knew 813 was a Tampa area code. I smiled, knowing it was my little brother, Derek. He told me his mother had died. The funeral was on 50th and State.

It was a cold, sunny morning. I walked into the church. As I removed my hat, I spotted my old boss, Abe Birch. The service had not started, and I walked to where he was standing with others. He didn't recognize me until I asked him if he needed algebra lessons.

"Pat? Pat, is that you?"

"It is, my friend," I replied.

"Pat, we're all so proud of you. Oprah Show and all." He smiled widely.

"Thanks," I replied. "Abe, I always wanted to make it back after the military, and it's my fault." I fidgeted, feeling genuinely embarrassed that I hadn't done so. "Abe, what does Ryan Banks do these days, do you know?" I asked.

"He's a Chicago police officer," he said.

I nodded. "You are all a part of my success." I hesitated. "I want to especially thank Big Mamma. She saved me a dozen times."

Abe watched me curiously.

"Do you know where she lives? Do you think she may come today?" I asked anxiously.

Abe looked down and smiled tightly. "She's here."

My wide smile straightened as he nodded toward the casket at the front of the church.

"That's her," he said. "This is Big Mamma's funeral."

In the hospital kitchen, all of the women wore large white smocks and heavy, meshed nets over most of their faces. For all those years I never had the slightest clue that Derek's mom was my Big Mamma.

I made two trips to Memphis and met with Drs. Persons, Grey, and Sorrentino, gene therapy specialists at Saint Jude. I loved Dr. Persons. Whenever I visited, we went to the rib shack by the hospital. I got up and talked to everyone. I offered lunch for many and a few times belted out a few songs. Dr. Persons's favorite was "Divorce Blues."

"I walked out the courtroom and handed her the check! It's made of rubber, the whole thing turns my stomach . . . Divorce is a big money game, aw the attorneys they love it all. They charge you frame to frame and on their weekend boats with your money they have a ball!"

Saint Jude has an incredible presence; no child pays a nickel to be treated, and the center has a growing importance in the gene therapy field.

As a kid, I remember watching reruns of *The Danny Thomas Show*. Danny was a devout Catholic. When he was struggling, as many Catholics do, Danny invoked the intervention of St. Jude, the patron saint of lost causes. Danny tells the story that he prayed to St. Jude, asking, "Please, please, give me a sign to help me find my way in life—just a sign that I'm going in the right direction, and someday I'll build a shrine in your name." Then he took seven of the ten dollars in his pocket and put it in the collection basket.

Whenever I think of St. Jude, I think of all the good that Catholicism, used correctly, has done and can do. I am proud to be a fellow devotee with Danny Thomas, and when I visit St. Jude I make sure that I rub the nose of the Danny Thomas sculpture in the hospital hall.

I gave a performance at Chicago's Harris Theater. As always, it was a blast to be on stage, to perform, and to speak about my project. My four months in Chicago helped me find another $500,000 for research.

I left Chicago for Switzerland, where a wealthy Italian, Leonardo Franco, bid $3.5 million for BPT Trading. Selling her would relieve a boatload of pressure.

Alessandro, one of the Swiss authorities who gave me my banking license, was now working for BPT auditors Coopers & Lybrand. He gave me a ride from Geneva to Lausanne one evening. I noticed the rosary hanging from his rearview mirror. "My mother is devout and prays the rosary as well, Ale," I said.

He looked at me with a contorted face and swerved to miss a car. "We, I, I thought that you were Jewish," he said.

"I am. As Christ said, 'we're all brothers.'"

Unfortunately for me, the banking authorities refused Leonardo's application. Finding no other offers, and after much turmoil, I closed BPT and gave the license back to the authorities for free. It may have been worth millions to someone, but it wasn't to me, and I didn't have the necessary time or resources to search for buyers. I concentrated more than ever on research.

It was very difficult to be away from my sons, and I longed for a simpler life. Santino was already eighteen. The average mortality for patients like him in 2008 was twenty-eight, though as I previously stated, today some patients make it into their forties. Frankly, this was of little solace to me, and I flew ahead, sometimes directly into storms.

Becky Martino was one of the patients who had survived on L1 smuggled into the US. She was Dr. Perrine's closest friend and our clerical assistant. She died on December 26, 2008. She was thirty-eight. It was cold, windy, and rainy for weeks.

I was getting used to being single, and I was confident that Lucrezia would not change her mind. I frequented women, but never introduced any of them to my sons. Santino's project could not afford distraction.

Zio Mimmo, my Italian father, died. My sons and I were crushed. Countless tears fell. I drew strength from his absence to fight for Santino and all of Santino's brothers and sisters. I owed Zio Mimmo this. He loved Santino, Cenzino, and Mariocarlo with all his heart.

While a guest speaker at a Financial Forum meeting in Italy, I was asked what advice I gave families about what they should do with their savings. I responded that they should pay their debts. I then criticized banks and financial institutions for turning the markets into Las Vegas–like slot machines for profit.

My holidays were filled with Lucrezia's relatives. *L'Americhein* had become godfather through baptism and confirmation, to many in the family; *L'Americhein* had given counsel and comfort. *L'Americhein* did not turn his back, and many decided to not turn their back on me.

I galloped between Cervello Hospital in Palermo, San Matteo Hospital in Pavia, Bambino Gesù Hospital in Rome, Kragness Medical Center in Los Angeles, Saint Jude in Memphis, National Institutes of Health in Bethesda, the Molecular Center in Greece, and other centers, coordinating goodwill and synergy.

The relationship with Jane Nunn, our direct contact at Kragness Medical Center's Industrial Affairs Department, was a positive work in progress She understood the pitfalls and difficulty of research. She also appreciated that the vector was not ready for clinical trials, as Kragness Medical Center had originally claimed when we entered into the 2005 agreement.

According to the 2005 contract, BGC owed Kragness Medical Center a $400,000 payment for the Sickle Cell Disease part of the license. Kragness Medical Center allowed us to delay the payment until the Thalassemia clinical trial began.

I spent investor money more carefully than I spent my own. Pierre complained from time to time about scarce funding, but I never met a researcher who didn't. They're passionate about cures, but statistically, most of their ideas are destined to fail. We had to keep our eye on the ball and the train on the tracks. We didn't want to be one of the thousands of failed projects. We got as much as we could from everyone in the project; this included Kragness researchers.

The BGC team labored, and by the end of 2008, the titer had improved dramatically. It was a team effort and the final product came about by making fifty-five experimental variations of our original vector. During the ordeal, Dr. Ballas also invented a unique way to use an existing nano-filtering system. This BGC knowhow was exclusive to the BGC vector and new to the world. Because of the fifty-five modification attempts, our vector became TNS9.3.55.

Using my growing notoriety, I performed and was a guest performer-speaker at dinners or anywhere I could muster even a minimum amount of support. I was contacted by patients and patient family members from all over the world. Emails arrived from Pakistan, India, China, and Africa. My family was Muslim, Jewish, Christian, and Hindu. I repeat, as a Catholic I believe that we are all brothers and sisters. When referring to any kind of spiritual connection, I spoke of the force of good that links us all. In my communications, I addressed patients and their kin as "my dear family."

We established the Orphan Dream Foundation. Over the years it has assisted many folks with rare diseases and has accumulated over a thousand patient communications. The foundation functioned using word of mouth and the internet. Their support helped me much more than I was able to help many of them.

Doctor Lucio Luzzatto, a top professor in hematology and respected authority in the field of gene therapy, was the former Chairman of the Ethics Committee for the American Society of Gene and Cell Therapy. Dr. Luzzatto had worked at Kragness Medical Center for ten years, and had actually been the person that hired Dr. Pierre Shorf for KMC.

With Dr. Lucio Luzzatto's assistance, we resolved a critical problem for a Romanian mother whose son was afflicted with G6PD.

She sent this note: "Did somebody tell you that you are an Angel sent by GOD to give us hope and peace? And if somebody has told you already, let me tell you again."
—Maria Trian

My brother Paulie was back in jail for carjacking. My brother Mikey put down the gloves and became a city worker. After a few months on the job, bricks fell on his head. Mikey limped around with a cane and spoke with a speech impediment. Suing for disability, his attorneys claimed back damage and mental impairment. The city medical examiner asserted that Mikey was already mental when he came to work a year earlier. This was not fair. Mikey, as many other neighborhood personalities, fell into the neighborhood talk when comfortable. I as well can perform in the language and have entertained more than a few when doing so. "Dese, dems, dose guys got dere heads busted . . . sort a ting."

At court, the city's legal firm demonstrated hundreds of pictures and a film of my brother Mikey dancing with two women and speaking normally (as normal as he can speak) just a few weeks before his final court date. Mikey's legal team claimed that he was entrapped, which he probably was. He still lost the suit and was penniless. Months later, Mikey was arrested, accused of being the muscle for a gang of Chicago drug dealers. He avoided jail time, but it took a toll on his life, as he went from being a world heavyweight boxing contender to being broke and broken. He took pills for his headaches and another half dozen conditions, washing all medications down with vodka.

Most assumed that Mikey not going away to prison meant that he had collaborated with the dark side (the government). I knew that lecturing was not useful, but I arranged to pick him up for breakfast on Saturday morning. I was going to ask him what he thought about the idea of moving to Italy with me. Three days before our scheduled meeting, on Thursday, a woman showed up at Mikey's mother's home and gave Mikey a package. Inside the package was what they call a hot dose (of drugs).

We got together on Saturday. At his funeral.

Some believed that the hot dose delivered to him was revenge from the gang members he ratted out. I hurt all over; a great brother I had been. Paulie was in jail, Mikey was dead. I tried to concentrate on the serious things in life: research, family, friends, and music. I made a few videos and continued to sew everything into one project.

It seemed that the best way for me to deal with my brother's death and the complexity of life was to make it simple. Every single facet became a venue for, a path to, and support for the project. The music, the writing, the performances were all aimed at finding resources and awareness for and about orphan diseases. Many songs were specifically written about patients and families.

One evening, my brother Bobby called to give me his final goodbye. Bobby had been married for almost twenty years. He and his wife had a fourteen-year-old daughter, Jasmine. His wife left him, and he decided to commit suicide. I had some flashbacks about Dirken and how I was not able to help him. I would not fail my little brother. The story is depicted in the book *Tortured Souls* by Tom Finley.

I told Bobby to come to my apartment at 31st and Shields. Bobby never disobeyed his big brother, and if he had, I'd have gone off and found him. I took a gun away from him and we spent the next few days together. Bobby had never laid a hand on his wife or daughter, but his soon-to-be-ex told the police that she was fearful. Bobby was a hunter and had guns.

The police confiscated his weapons. Bobby lodged a complaint.

Days later, plainclothes police trapped him in a parking lot and beat the hell out of him. After they were done, of course, they charged him with assault and battery. Consequently, Bobby lost his job. My buddy Knuckles Ciacci had a few lots close to the Loop. He hired Bobby to park cars.

While still in Chicago, I received a communication from my friend and Thalassemia patient, Rodolfo Marche, inviting me to his wedding. He hoped I'd sing a few tunes, but unfortunately (fortunately for him; why start a marriage off like that?), I was not in Italy on the date of his marriage. Still, Rodolfo getting married was a wonderful celebration, demonstrating perseverance and the courage to hope on his part and the power of love on the part of the woman he was marrying. Rodolfo was thirty-two.

I prayed that Santino would also live to celebrate marriage to a woman he loved.

Sam Salman is an Iranian Jew whose clan was exiled with the Shah. He had gone to school in London, but eventually his family ended up in the US. He is everything I am not: educated, charming, articulate, and groomed. In February 2009, Sam became the president of BGC. Like myself, Sam did not take a salary.

Dr. Christopher Ballas continued pushing the project forward with Dr. Shorf; Dr. Shorf's wife, Dr. Cuttings; and BGC-employed scientists working in the KMC laboratories. Over the years, BGC helped to orchestrate the transfer of dozens of researchers and research academic students into different laboratories around the world. Most often, a disease foundation was more than happy to sponsor the visiting scientists. They liked the idea of seeing how their money was spent. This was extremely efficient for everyone. BGC was one of the first entities to use this strategy of mobilizing researchers and academic research students.

I became friendly with Pierre's lab team, people from Poland, Italy, and Greece. With the titer dramatically increased to an acceptable level, BGC contracted the Research Center of Philadelphia for the eventual vector manufacturing. Production would cost a million and a half dollars.

Sergio Rato and the Thalassemia International Foundation came through with $300,000. The rest of the needed funds would come to BGC from trading, Joe Feldman, the Culatto family, and mostly soybean traders.

"No man is a failure who has friends." - from my favorite film, Capra's *It's A Wonderful Life*

On May 15, 2009, my dear friend and supporter of research, Susanna Agnelli, died in Rome. She would be greatly missed by many.

Street Factory Music, my small label, named me "Independent Artist of the Year." My music was carried on iTunes and a dozen other music sites. I met a twenty-four-year-old Italian beauty queen. My sons were becoming fine men. Vector went into final production.

In June 2009, the FDA sent out an alert to all projects in or approaching clinical trials for gene therapy. The only E-beta patient successfully treated and cured by Dr. Temple at Redunt had developed clonal dominance, often a precursor for leukemia and or other cancers. Clonal dominance occurs when only a limited number of cells are producing all or a majority of the gene being expressed—in this case, beta-globin.

Our scientists felt confident that the sad situation was created because Redunt, in an effort to get around infringing on the Shorf-BGC vector, used a mutant transgene. This gave us even more responsibility. With a safer product, we were now the only game in town.

After Obama's election, it seemed a foregone conclusion that Chicago would get the 2016 Olympics. I continued to buy depressed real estate on the South Side. The bank financing helped me and BGC to stay afloat. When Chicago won the Olympics, we'd be in the chips.

In October 2009, Rio de Janeiro was chosen for the site of the 2016 Olympics. My hopes of cashing in were quickly dashed. Bids for the properties on the South Side dried up. Making things worse, the insolvent city of Chicago, desperate to find funds, raised the fines for violations such as grass-cutting, trash, lack of fences or signs, from $50, to between $600 and $1,000 a violation. After making this genius maneuver, the city hired hundreds of revenue agents to begin walking the streets with cameras at 6 a.m., seven days a week.

Initially, I sent crews to cut the grass on my many parcels. Some of the workers were beaten and their lawn mowers stolen. Required signs and fences barely lasted a day. It was impossible to check 150 properties for garbage. Some reported that revenue agents, in an effort to get promotions, carried rubbish in their own trunks, unloading it onto properties and then taking pictures of the violation with their city cameras. All it took was a picture of your property with a pop bottle on it. There was no defense. They had the picture with the date and time of infraction.

When victims showed up to contest, city employees acting as judges shut them down. "We have the picture. Pay the cashier."

Investors were no longer willing to run the ticket gauntlet created by the town hall jesters. Thousands of lots went up for sale. Some desperate owners paid people to buy their debt traps.

If the city politicians wanted to close the municipal deficit, they should have made the tickets $6,000,000 instead of $600. The people who live in those areas where most of my properties were could afford $600 as much as they could afford $6,000,000.

As strange as it may sound to the rest of the world, Chicago—recently voted one of the more livable cities in the US—has property less than five miles from the center that you can purchase for free.

Chapter 25

Gluttons Turn Healthcare into an Industry

I picked Santino up from the chef academy, the day before Easter break. He announced that he was done with school. I pleaded, trying to convince him to change his decision. "Pà," he said seriously. "I made it one more year than you did." The discussion ended.

Despite past setbacks, the world was waking up to gene therapy. Where there was hope, there was promise. Where there was promise, there was profit. Until recently, we had been wandering alone in the desert, but now we had company: bankers. In March 2010, Stair Seven LTD bought Redunt, BGC's only competitor, in a $35 million deal.

I was confused. Our vector was a better, safer product, and no one had even contacted us. It made no sense from a patient's perspective. It made less sense from a business perspective. Stair Seven LTD was founded in New England by Ivy League guys. One of the founding captains is Garth Sacher. Garth's father, Nat, is an important leader from recent pharmaceutical history.

If Stair Seven had paid $35 million for Redunt, the BGC vector had to be worth ten times that, according to Bruno Mauri of Phi Stamin and other pharmaceutical executives.

BGC attracted other possible partners, and I had weekly conversations with interested entities. The idea of having money for real hotel rooms was lackluster. Growing up and moving around, beds were different wherever you went. Some were comfortable and some were not. The floor was always the same, and I preferred it to a strange mattress much of the time. Over the years I had grown fond of sleeping in rent-a-cars and loved subletting rooms in Los Angeles from John Paul, where I slept in a bunk bed in a room with three strangers.

John Paul told me I was the only guy he knew of to ever bring home a guest. I found her at the Plaza El Segundo Shopping Mall. She was an exotic, Korean-Trinidadian beauty leaning on a rail, looking down at the floors below. I was listening to one of my songs, "Living Without You." *Yeah I can't take it now, the thought, of living without you.*

I moved in. "You're not going to jump, are you?" I asked.

That evening, Serena accompanied me to dinner with my friend, screenwriter Brian Lantz, and a few other Italian American guys. During dinner, Serena was completely involved. One might think that we had dated for months.

After, we went to my sublet bunk bed (you never get too old for bunk beds). My roommates didn't make a sound, either sleeping or enjoying the entertainment. It was a romantic night for Serena and myself, and a first that John Paul knew of.

When John Paul was booked, I stayed at the Porter on Main Street in El Segundo. The rooms all had four lights above the door inside of each room. If the four lights were lit, it meant that the four bathrooms on the floor were occupied. You had to hold yourself, go to another floor, or use the room sink.

It was June 8, 2010. I was in Boston to attend a meeting with Stair Seven LTD. I woke up on the couch of my Aunt Vittoria in Cobble Hill Senior Apartments in Somerville, Massachusetts.

Uncle Philly, Aunt Vittoria's husband, had died in 2005. She and our people came from Puglia. Uncle Philly was from Sicily. In Italy, theirs was considered a mixed marriage. To Aunt Vittoria, the "til death do us part" thing was just the beginning. It was 2010, and from the way she acted and talked, I still waited for Uncle Philly to walk out of the bedroom with her.

Aunt Vittoria moved quietly in her cluttered kitchen, not wanting to rustle her favorite nephew. There was little risk of that—I had been on my phone since 5 a.m. I sat up.

"Oh, I'm sorry, honey, did I wake you?" she asked, in the thickest Boston accent anyone ever heard. I mean, she not only eliminated the R when she said "car," she replaced it with thirty-five 'Hs.'

"No, Aunt Vittoria, I've been awake. I already spoke to my sons."

"How are they, honey? How's Santino?"

Most family members had a soft spot for Santino. He was named after Grandpa and Thalassemia, the blood disease that afflicts him, has origins in Italy. In a strange way, the disease was their link to the old country.

"Great, Aunt Vittoria. He'll be cured soon."

"Oh honey, I'm happy." She visibly concentrated. "You've been working so hahhhd, so many years. Uncle Philly was proud. He was willing to bet anyone that you'd find a cure."

Her statement warranted concern. Uncle Philly loved the ponies, and I adored him. But he couldn't pick the winner in a one-horse race.

Salman, our president, is a quiet guy. His car was meticulously cared for, and he is meticulous in all things. As an Iranian raised in England, he had the politeness of an exceptional Boy Scout, and carries himself as I believed a Persian king should.

I gazed at Sam's sharp business attire. If I attempted to imitate him, I'd be an imposter.

My attitudes about business sometimes aggravated Sam. He admired the captains of industry. I carried high consideration for the French novelist Balzac, who said, "Behind every great fortune is a great crime."

In the car, I asked Sam to say only things he would say if he was recorded. He promised that we wouldn't be. I guaranteed that he was mistaken.

My mind traipsed over the past as I mentally prepared. In 2003, I was caught off-guard when Kragness Medical Center abandoned Shorf's gene therapy project. Uncle Norb Wiech and I found no pharmaceutical companies interested in the crazy project. *Gene therapy was still science fiction.*

I could have done a deal with Redunt in 2004 when Brett Galen was CEO, but our team was concerned about their product.

In 2005, Uncle Norb and I founded BGC and bought the Kragness Medical Center technology invented by Dr. Pierre Shorf.

In 2007, our competitor, Redunt, treated three E-beta Thalassemic patients in France. One of the patients almost died. One patient was (supposedly) cured. I was more than skeptical. E-betas generally have higher hemoglobin levels, meaning a milder form of the disease. Beta Thalassemia patients, like Santino, represent 85 percent of patients in Europe and the US.

Stories about cures are very popular, and it often seems that even the scientific media cares little to know the truth as long as their article gets clicked on by readers.

In 2008, we were close to ending the project. Our titer (product efficiency) was disastrous. Instead, a courageous decision made in great part by Joe Feldman and our investors sent us back to the drawing board.

Our reservations about the Redunt vector were substantiated. In June 2009, the clonal dominance incident with a Redunt patient damaged the entire camp, causing a halt to all gene therapy trials.

Stair Seven LTD bought Redunt anyway. Love can make us blind; add stupid, when speaking about greed. To many financial firms, it was all about finance. Buy a product, spread propaganda, raise funds, spread more propaganda, IPO, more propaganda, sell your shares for profit, ditch the company, and let the chips fall as they may.

Of course, the first bankers in are long gone before any of the companies fail, getting away with the loot and suffering none of the consequences created by their avarice.

Stair Seven LTD was now sitting on $35,000,000 of bum dope. A few weeks ago, Stair Seven LTD sent their medical advisor, Doctor Ronan Wright, to Kragness Medical Center. He told the KMC executive, Dill Pickens, that the BGC vector was superior to their own and that Stair Seven LTD wanted to buy it.

Some days later, I received a communication from Pickens, stating that he had personally spoken to Stair Seven LTD, who were interested in purchasing our product.

When I told Bruno Mauri from Phi Stamin that Kragness had met with Stair Seven LTD executives to talk about the BGC vector without BGC being present, he was disturbed. "It was extremely dishonest to do such a thing," he told me.

BGC was a small fish swimming with sharks. Bruno Mauri believed more than ever that a BGC/Phi Stamin joint-venture would be a great solution for everyone involved.

Stair Seven LTD partner Garth Sacher was the son of former CappasL Pharma Chief Executive Nat Sacher. Garth graduated from Yale. Garth Sacher's wife graduated from Princeton. Her father was founder of Carco Partners, a venture-capital firm in Cambridge. Garth and his wife's merger (marriage) was announced in the *New York Times*.

I, instead, had helped to commandeer Kragness Medical Center's research from the bench to the production of the world's first multi-patient production batch of gene therapy; doing so on a fraction of what typical pharmaceutical companies would have spent. Of course, Sam, our president; Dr. Ballas, our vector specialist; I, and a host of others were unpaid or minimally compensated. Most pharma companies, even start-ups, begin with millions in executive compensation chained to their leg. It's modern capitalism, the dribble-down economy.

The rewarding of mediocrity is a reason why society is coming unraveled.

Because I have no formal education, most argue that my personal achievement is luck-driven. I don't disagree. I'd say that earthly achievement is greatly determined by luck. Had Oprah Winfrey been born in Bulgaria, I doubt that she'd have become a media mogul.

Others claim that hard work and *genius* is responsible for success. After getting to know some top CEOs, I can say that they, to a great extent, are folks born on third, convinced they hit a homer. There are, of course, exceptions to the rule.

My meeting was with Garth Sacher and Rip Sarfel. Scientist Rip Sarfel got his PhD from Yale, and a BS in Biochemistry and Microbiology from Berkeley. He completed a postdoctoral fellowship at Dartmouth. Earl Lein of Stair Seven LTD was a last-minute surprise.

I Googled him as Sam Salman, our president, and I drove to the Stair Seven LTD offices in Cambridge.

Prior to Stair Seven LTD, Earl was chief business officer of Stanlo Pharmaceuticals. He led the sale of the company to Rolexgen. He held executive roles at IBM, Nius Pharmaceuticals, and ChenX Laboratories. He had an MBA from Cornell, Master of Science from Rutgers, and a Bachelor of Science from Harvard.

All these important folks were attending a meeting with Sam and I in Cambridge, an interesting town of 105,000 named in honor of the English University of Cambridge. The town is home to Harvard, MIT, and is a Puritan Theology Center—how fitting.

I wasn't sure what all the letters after these guys' names meant; but I didn't feel intimidated, overpowered, outgunned, or out of place. Some say that I'm too stupid to feel those emotions, but a half dozen prestigious research centers and a dozen top researchers were collaborating and pushing our project forward. I also trusted Sam's instincts and intelligence, and he estimated that our product was safer and 5 years closer to being approved for clinical trials in patients in the US than Redunt's. I was relaxed, in the driver's seat.

It was a beautiful day. As we drove, I noticed our surroundings, but my mind was swirling. Santino was now twenty. He was a handsome, generous, charming, witty, fun-loving man. He had a few girlfriends but nothing serious. He was also quickly arriving at the average age of mortality for people with his affliction. He didn't pay it any attention. I know this is the third or even fourth time you'll have read this, but Santino is a lion of a man.

Through the years, I often thought of leaving critical meetings with prestigious colleagues, laughing my way out and screaming like a lunatic, "it's all about love!" I've been told that this is the anthem for cowards who fear truth. In fact, love's importance, admitted by very many, is trusted by very few.

I thought to myself, *now that the bankers knew that medicines could create incredible wealth, things would drastically change.* And they have; the game has been modified such that it should no longer be called baseball.

The building was modern, large, and shit-brown. An attractive woman greeted us. I accepted water and coffee. The meeting room was large and basic. The conference table could have sat hundreds and the microphone could have been in a trillion places.

Reliving the past often helps with the rebricking of the "yellow brick road."

I thought about something that happened when I was sixteen.

We took the tires off the '66 Bonneville on 63rd Street. It was 3 a.m. on a Chicago winter's night. We moved them into my '65 Pontiac LeMans. The owner calmly approached us.

"Hit him in the head, before the police come!" my accomplice screamed from the other side of the car.

I approached the presumed owner. "Get out of here, before you get hurt," I said.

"Those are my tires," he said coolly.

"They *were* your tires," I rebutted.

"Hit him!" my cohort in crime screamed again.

"Son, you're going to give me my tires back."

He was forty, in good shape, and solemn.

"Your life's worth more than these tires, mister," I said calmly.

He moved within a few feet and remained calm, his hands at his side. "Son, you're going to give me those tires," he repeated with the serenity of a corpse.

"Hit him!"

I raised the tire iron. It was my moment of truth.

"Hit him and let's get out of here!"

I watched the owner. He watched me.

I threw the tire iron to the ground. It bounced off the iced asphalt.

I never thanked the guy, but his courage changed my life forever.

Back in the shit-brown building, my thoughts were crowded by the traders on the floor who had written checks before there was an account to deposit them in, and guys like Joe Feldman who did the right thing even when it wasn't the smart thing.

I felt the strength of the prayers of my mother and her prayer group. I needed to feel them; this was possibly the most important meeting of my life. Even Grandpa Santino was there.

All Sickle Cell and Thalassemic patients are Santino's brothers and sisters. Mine was a boundless honor for all of my family. My thoughts erupted into that kind of high you get when you know you're on the right track.

I heard the door opening. It was time.

I knew that Garth's father had been a professional tennis player and that Garth also was a master at the game. He walked in. I sized him up, but knew better than to judge a book by its cover. I stood and shook Garth Sacher's slender hand. We exchanged niceties. The meeting began.

Initially, they blew smoke up my ass, "Father of the year." This was about patients. Serving them would solve everything else.

Earl Lein entered and sat at the far end of the table. The projector screen lowered, demonstrating the data of a so-called cured patient. I had read the book already. I wasn't impressed then, and seeing the data on a larger screen didn't change that.

Rip Sarfel, their scientist, knew our product and claimed to have great respect for Pierre Shorf's work. He almost got giddy about it, but the chain of command silenced his enthusiasm.

I asked if they knew the difference between Beta and E-beta. Garth moved but couldn't dance. I asked if the (so-called) cured patient had taken Squibb's Hydroxyurea, a drug that raised hemoglobin in many E-beta patients.

Silence isn't always golden.

Earl Lein claimed to know absolutely nothing about our product. If he was lying, it was disrespectful. If he was being truthful, there should have never been a meeting.

I calmly closed the session. If they were willing to proceed with our product, we were interested.

I sent Stair Seven LTD a follow-up email from the car. I suggested that they change their company name, which was sullied by the French trial, and abandon their product. Always wanting to put a positive spin on things, I added: "If there are future meetings, please continue to order the delicious ciabatta panini."

Before boarding the plane, I read a communication from Rip Sarfel. "Pat, great you could make it today. Great to meet you and Sam. Please work with Garth and Earl for the next steps. Best, Rip Sarfel"

The encounter bolstered my faith in our project. If these guys were the cream of the crop . . . if this was my competition . . . if these were captains of industry . . .

Dill Pickens of KMC heard that the meeting with Stair Seven LTD and Redunt had not gone as he hoped. In a letter to me on June 10, 2010, he wrote. "We're lucky to have you on our team. It's Stair Seven's loss."

Within months, Stair Seven changed Redunt's name to VulturX Pharma. Garth took the reins of VulturX, insisting that his underlings call him "Chief VulturX." If that wasn't irritating enough, he also wore only orange gym shoes to work. I wasn't sure where the name VulturX came from, but vultures do have orange flesh caruncles on their beaks.

When I returned home, RAI, the Italian television channel, invited me to sing a few pieces from my latest album and give an update on the upcoming Thalassemia clinical trial.

While in Foggia, Italy, visiting a friend's office, I recognized the face on the front of the Italian magazine *Panorama*. It was Leonardo Franco, the unsuccessful buyer of BPT Trading, in Switzerland. The cartoonist put horns on his head. He was presently in prison for defrauding hundreds of millions of euros from investors.

Clinical trials were scheduled to begin, and 2010 would be the best year of our lives. I decided to visit Rodolfo Marche and his new bride. I dialed Rodolfo's house in Triggiano, hoping to have a coffee and deliver positive news. Maria, Rodolfo's mother, answered.

"Maria, it's me, Patrizio, *L'Americano*. I'm close to Triggiano. I'd love to meet Rodolfo's bride and get a coffee. What do you say?" I asked.

There was a long silence.

"Patrizio. Rodolfo died of heart complications two months ago. We couldn't find your number . . ."

Maria began crying and hung up.

I couldn't believe it. *Vaffanculo*! I pulled over; I couldn't drive.

A few days later, I snuck away to La Baia Dei Faraglioni, the five-star resort tucked into a mystical cliff on the Adriatic Coast in northern Puglia. Standing two hundred meters from the shore are two tall rocks, growing out of the sea. At night, as the moon reflects off the waters, they seem like centurions guarding the ancient coast.

My first morning, I swam out and climbed up one of nature's statues. Laying on a rock ledge about fifteen feet above the water I concentrated on Becky, Rodolfo, and all who had lost their lives to Sickle Cell Disease and Thalassemia.

I needed to focus. I absorbed the sun and shifted my thoughts to some of life's many pleasant surprises. Recently, my Orphan Dream band won the Video of the Year Award in Italy for the song "Living Without You." I was named "One of the most important people from Puglia in the world." Two of my songs were used in an Italian award-winning film *Focaccia Blues*. In Rome, I accepted the Golden Globe trophy with the film's producer and director and thanks to the Italian Golden Globe Award, I walked the red carpet at the Egyptian in Hollywood.

While in California, I spent time with Brian Lantz, the BGC investor and screenwriter who had written three Hollywood hits, *Scott Pilgrim*, *Factor X*, and *22 Jump Street*. I attended a dinner where I became friendly with Jacqueline Bissett, Jon Voight, and Joe Mantegna, all of them sensitive folks and possible supporters for our cause.

It would be a great summer; we had ten scheduled concerts. These, however, were nothing compared to the excitement I felt about the upcoming SickleThalgen clinical trial.

F

A boatload of tourists began circling. I stood, sang my song, "Living Without You," and then dove headfirst into the sea. The boat erupted into applause and cheers. I looked at the sun and felt Becky and Rodolfo smiling at me.

India has more Thalassemia than any single country, with an estimated 10,000 new patients born annually. For years I had communicated with patients in India and had befriended many.

Aarush Patelni lives in Agra, India. His daughter, Brinda, has Thalassemia. Brinda is a dancer. Neither she nor Santino are Thalassemics, but people with Thalassemia. I decided to meet my family in India and focus on the strategy of getting my brothers, sisters, and children cured there.

When I arrived in New Delhi, it was 110 degrees. The Patelni family paid for my stay at the Hyatt by the airport. Each morning, I walked through the dirt streets in the neighborhood behind the hotel. The heat caused many to sleep on their porches, or even on cardboard boxes laid on the streets. They may have been economically challenged, but they were certainly not poor. There was an energy there I had never experienced before. The families were up and about, drawing water from fountains and combing their children's hair.

I returned in the evening, smiling and nodding to many who greeted me. No one there ever asked me for anything, and a few offered me candy and or water.

The days in New Delhi were filled with meetings. Several households made great sacrifices, and traveled hundreds of kilometers to meet the American who called them family.

Aarush introduced me to Advika Nutti, who had lost a child to Thalassemia. She was now the president of India's National Thalassemic Organization.

Aarush, Mithu Sen of Phi Stamin, and I arrived at the Lok Nayak hospital in New Delhi. Mithu's presence, as an important member of the Phi Stamin team, demonstrated their continued support and interest.

The Indian Thalassemic Board seemed rigid and suspicious. Each member emotionlessly announced their names and roles. It was then my turn.

"My name is Pat Girondi. I am the father of Santino Girondi and the founder of BGC, the sponsor of the Shorf therapy."

The ice broke a bit when a board member told me that the patients enjoyed my music. The levity of the comment appeared to annoy President Advika Nutti. "You have traveled a long way, and surely have some sort of expectation," she said.

"I have received many kind letters of encouragement, warm wishes, and prayers from the Indian people. I came to give thanks and ask you to continue to send them." I looked at each one of them before continuing. "My mother is a devout Catholic. We believe in the power of prayer. There have been many times that I thought that I would not make it through the night. There have been many times that I had given up hope. Your prayers saved me. I am no one in this project. Dr. Pierre Shorf is the researcher responsible for this hope. I am only his humble assistant."

They were engaged; Pierre Shorf's research was well known by the Indian Thalassemia community. Dr. Pierre was looked on favorably.

"Did you see what those butchers did in France?" asked a patient's mother/board member.

I grimaced. The message was powerful. The Indian organization was infuriated by what they assumed was a choice made by Redunt/VulturX in 2007, to treat patients using unfiltered vector and myeloablation. They felt that VulturX placed financial goals above patient safety.

At the end of the meeting, I was accompanied to a room where patients were transfusing. I smiled and nodded. A few patients asked me to sing. The doctor that accompanied me told them I was there on a scientific/business trip. Before he finished, I began singing "Living Without You," followed by "Little Sister," and finally "Fire in the Show."

Though there was no accompanying music, the patients kindly applauded. I bowed. India was also home.

I left for Cyprus, where the International Thalassemia Alliance (ITA), part of the World Health Organization (WHO), representing sixty-two nations, was conducting its annual meeting.

I spoke of the Shorf therapy, and of hope, in a professional manner. I actually surprised myself. The room of dignitaries stood and applauded and I was handed a much-undeserved award; after all, I was just Santino's father, and was only trying to do my duty.

For all the work they have done, for decades, for my son and his family, it should have been I giving them an award.

I will never forget the kindness of my family in India or Cyprus.

271

It was August fourth in Altamura, and the sun was openly making love to the whole city. Tourists were peeking around every corner. The cathedral, completed in 1196, stood brilliantly as an architectural marvel and local keeper of the covenant between the Altamuran people and Christ.

Wearing yellow smiley-face sunglasses, blue shorts, and my favorite I-don't-give-a-shit-if-it-looks-stained T-shirt, I solemnly zipped back and forth, up and down the Corso on Rollerblades. I was gathering gawks from visitors and smiles from fellow compatriots and friends who were playing cards at Club Totò, in the corner of the piazza.

I Rollerbladed with earplugs, listening to tracks of my third album, *Orphan's Hope*. No one could possibly understand what music had become, for my voyage, for my heart, for my stability.

It was a big day. That morning, the gene therapy vector, which was a culmination of eighteen years, all of my soul, and all of my cash, was being picked up at the Research Center of Philadelphia (RCOP) and delivered to Kragness Medical Center. Today. Earphones kept my enraptured, fantastic thoughts from spilling and shattering the antiquated stones under my hard-rubber wheels.

Later, at 3 p.m., 9 a.m. in Philadelphia, my mind was fixated as if on some sort of hallucinogen. In this state, I could have understood the lyrics to The Doors' "Light My Fire." For the past nights I lay awake, carefully going over each step of the delivery.

Forty-six hundred miles away, a half dozen tense, white-smocked scientists waited around the RCOP Institute, having toiled almost two years to construct the precious cargo. Spotting the FedEx Custom Critical truck entering their facility gate, they jumped into action.

The merchandise was the world's first commercial batch of gene therapy vector for Sickle Cell Disease and Thalassemia. It had to be held at minus-eighty Celsius. It cost thousands to transport, millions to produce, and if successful would be worth billions.

The driver flashed to the Philadelphia International Airport. The package was zipped on a direct flight to Los Angeles International Airport. There, another specialist rushed the treasure to the Shorf Laboratory, on the tenth floor of arguably the country's top research hospital, Kragness Medical Center, on 137 Skame Drive, Los Angeles, California.

Shorf and I had become as close as he let anyone get. Researchers are known to be secretive, even with their own spouses—especially with their own spouses. It was hard to picture this tall French doctor with boyish looks walking gloriously with Curie and Einstein, other Nobel-winners, but if we were successful, this was the likely outcome. His technology would be the cornerstone of curing dozens, or even hundreds of genetic diseases, saving millions of lives.

Like most history-changers, Shorf's concept was electrifyingly controversial. Our drug was the battleground between science and faith (which usually means old money and new money). Clerics and conservative politicians claimed our technology could be exploited to create generations of superhumans. Creation is God's exclusive campground, and gene therapy tampered with His will (capital H)! The fear had been so tangible in 2001, that President Bush made it a criminal act to use federal funding for stem cell research.

It was part of the battle, to lobby politicians, create the medicine, and start testing in humans. All of this began with Santino, my twenty-year-old hero whose charm was trumped only by his courage. Santino was diagnosed when he was two and a half years old. In eighteen years of therapy, operations, and compromises, he never let a disparaging word slip out. Santino's a natural. *I Rollerbladed over stone; he Rollerbladed over life.*

Many patients don't make it to twenty, and for those who do, the burden of battle weighs substantially. Iron from hundreds of transfusions damages all major organs. Some patients drop dead from heart attacks at twenty-two or even eighteen. Shorf's potion, which within hours would be safe in his lab, was our best chance to keep my son alive.

Today was also gargantuan for Shorf, the terrified inventor who was acutely cognizant of our only competition, VulturX. I was not overly concerned. Their drug was less natural. It created a halt to all gene therapy clinical trials worldwide in 2009 because of clonal dominance. Clonal dominance is a precursor to cancer. I was certain that our Ivy League financiers had blown $35 million on a wooden nickel, bum dope. *But, I guess my assumption depends on one's goal.*

Shorf's fright of VulturX capped any formal jubilation for the arrival of the magical elixir. I understood his fear, but thought panic was unwarranted; I mean, no one in their right mind sabotages a better product, and along with it, the hope of millions of Sickle Cell and Thalassemic patients all over the world.

Anyway, I was seasoned by shoeshining, street life, and encounters with the legal system. I could protect Santino's interests against a bunch of Ivy League economists.

The cargo was so valuable that it had to be delivered as two parcels. The second shipment would arrive in September.

Later, in August, it was front-page news in the *Wall Street Journal* that Dr. Ian R. Koke would be leaving Koenig to become the CEO of Kragness Medical Center. I was encouraged, as Dr. Koke was young and dynamic. Some mentioned that Koke wanted Kragness Medical Center to become a top gene therapy center. There would be a believer at the helm.

Koke was right to believe. The prestige and credibility that would come from treating patients with gene therapy developed at his center was priceless and, Thalassemia, by far the largest disease population ever treated with gene therapy, would be worth billions in royalties.

Finally, on September 17, BGC delivered the second load of vector to Kragness Medical Center. They were now in possession of enough vector to treat eight to ten patients.

Congratulatory notes arrived from around the world. Omar Achman, Head of Pediatric Bone Marrow Transplants at Kragness Medical Center, and Principal Investigator, would be treating the first patients. In an email communication, the kind Syrian doctor wrote that the first patient would be treated soon.

All of my money was tied up in the company. I was living on the other side of a wall from a woman who no longer respected me. I had no savings. During my last trip to the Chicago Board of Trade in 2009, I broke even after two months of trading. Earnings on the floor had dried up. I lived off loans from friends and was looking to open a beef stand.

Ma shrieked. Pinned, her airborne feet dangled.

"Tell the landlord to call the police!" she exhaled in broken gasps.

Another punch landed. "If you go anywhere, I'll kill you," my father said.

In red-splattered underwear, I walked to the hall and sat on the top step. I placed my head in my hands, tears rolled to the top of my lip, as Ma's sobs battled my fear.

I relived this scene all of my life. Finally, standing up for my mother's grandson Santino, I stood up for her. I dashed off a letter of appreciation to all involved. Santino would soon be cured. It was time to begin the fourth CD, *Orphan's Hope*. I was truly a blessed man.

Chapter 26

That's What You Think

In September, 2010, *Nature* magazine published an article, "Gene-therapy Hope for Beta Thalassemia Patients."

The article claimed that a patient was cured by the VulturX product.

The article did not disclose that E-beta patients are generally the least sick and are certainly not representative of the Thalassemia population. The article missed the fact that the patient had developed clonal dominance, a precursor to cancer and that this event caused the FDA and France to issue a halt to all gene therapy clinical trials in 2009.

The author also failed to mention that the treated patient had suspiciously high levels of fetal hemoglobin and that the use of Hydroxyurea, a chemotherapy medicine, or the gene transplant preparatory chemotherapy medicine Busulfan, used in the therapy, could be a likely reason. Obviously the author thought these details did not merit publication . . .

ϝ

Many believe that academic centers get better treatment from regulatory agencies, such as the FDA. I wanted the path of least resistance. We were finishing up the clinical trial agreement, naming KMC and NIH (National Institutes of Health) as sites to treat patients. KMC would also be the sponsor, but BGC owned the product and rights to the data. We would be in patients soon.

The Clinical Trial Agreement had been red-lined and was ready to sign. KMC and BGC agreed that the contract would be completed on October 18, 2010. On October 17, Sam called and told me that Kragness Medical Center (KMC) had canceled the meeting for the next day.

On the 18th, I received a call from KMC executive, Dill Pickens. He said that there were some important things to iron out before the Clinical Trial Agreement was signed. I flew to Los Angeles, not wanting to risk a thing.

I arrived at Dill Pickens's office on the morning of October 19th. Mr. Pickens demanded that BGC deposit a $4,000,000 up front payment for the ten patients who would eventually be treated before clinical trials could begin. I explained to him that BGC had $400,000 in cash and a line of credit for $800,000. The FDA wanted the patients treated two to three months apart. We were pretty much set for the next year. I left without budging him.

I called Dr. John Tisdale at the National Institutes of Health. He was willing to treat our patients for $50,000 each. We decided that KMC would do the first patient, and that, if needed, the rest would be treated at NIH. When Mr. Pickens heard my solution, he declared that BGC must find a commercialization partner before any patients would be treated.

I organized a meeting with our longtime friends, the Italian pharma giant Phi Stamin. Mr. Pickens attended and told Leroy Gertz, the CEO of Phi Stamin, that our product did not work and that they'd be foolish to invest. It was one of the craziest things I've ever seen, and I've seen crazy.

Leroy was undaunted. He believed in the product and he believed in BGC. He as well was confused by the behavior of the KMC executive, but they were more than ever convinced that they wanted to be the commercialization partner for our product. Weeks later, Phi Stamin made a proposal to KMC, which was immediately turned down. KMC then filed a lawsuit against BGC, claiming that we fell short of our obligations.

In March 2011, BGC sent a special courier to pick our medicine up and deliver it to Doctor John Tisdale at the National Institutes of Health (NIH). KMC turned the courier away. They would not return our drug.

Things dragged on, and finally, in June, after two days of negotiations with KMC, I picked up the phone and called Santino from my attorney Ken Sussmane's office. For the good of patients, I felt that we just couldn't afford to lose more time.

I spoke in Italian. "Son," I said as tears rolled, "I'm going to give the project back to KMC and they promised me that they'll fund it fully and run like hell to begin the clinical trials. I think it's the best thing for patients. VulturX 's product is shit, but they're gaining on us and we're losing precious time."

At a certain point, I lost control of my usually precise vocal prowess and cried into the shoulder of my teddy-bear-like attorney (in heart and body), Ken Sussmane.

Santino, on the other end of the world, waited until I spoke again.

"Son, I want your permission to do this."

There was an eternal silence as I waited for the verdict.

"Pà, you always do your best, and you told us that if we do our best, no matter what, it's the right thing to do." I remembered him telling me this when the first divorce papers arrived and I imagined that Santino was also feeling the weight of this moment. I wasn't really sure what the verdict was when he continued. "Pà, if you think it's the right thing to do, then it's right with me, too."

The vector production for ten patients alone had cost over $1,300,000. BGC handed everything over without compensation, maintaining a 50 percent interest in any future profit.

On June 17, 2011, I signed the settlement agreement, and Kragness Medical Center became the project's new owner. I looked at it from their point of view. It also made sense. They went from an upside of 4 to 6 percent royalties on a final product to 50 percent of whatever the project could become. The product was worth billions if placed in a publicly traded entity.

I knew that KMC had the resources to see Santino and all his brothers and sisters cured. It was in the best interest of our patients. After all, KMC, a *not-for-profit*, had an annual income of over three billion dollars. The CEO made $7,000,000 alone. KMC had billions in property and hundreds of millions in liquidity. They would easily be able to invest whatever was needed to bring our project home.

When Santino felt weak as a child, I would squeeze his hand in mine. We would close our eyes, and after 30 seconds his hand would tingle. I would release . . . *it was now KMC's turn to fly like a rondone*. I had no doubt that they would.

The flight took off from LAX. I would soon be home with my sons.

It had been eleven years since I met Pierre Shorf. It had been eleven years since he had published an article about curing five generations of Thalassemic mice in *Nature* Magazine. Eleven is a lucky number. *Soon Santino would be safe.* My investors would also be in the chips as they collectively still owned 50 percent of the greatest gene therapy project for Sickle Cell Disease and Thalassemia in the world.

There is nothing like playing soccer, or any sport for that matter, on the same field as your three sons. We sometimes played together twice a week. Four Girondis on the same or opposing team made for lots of kidding, especially when I, the new *Old Man*, scored a goal or dribbled past one of them.

I enjoyed my sons, and the legal separation was a piece of cake. I was with them whenever they chose and instead of it all costing tens of thousands, it cost a few thousand over years and years. I went to court maybe once annually, usually for something of minimal importance. Low stress.

I did a bunch of concerts with The Orphan Dream Band. More important, we continued to assist families who had children with rare diseases and perfected the technique. Within twenty-four hours, we were able to let them know of the clinical trials in their disease and a center of excellence in their geographical area. Finally, through our growing network of researchers, research centers, and doctors, we were usually able to connect them with a doctor and or researcher specialized in their affliction within a week. Nothing made us happier than assisting these folks.

In February 2012, Parker Branham wrote an article in the *New York Times.* The headline was "Kragness Medical Center Chief Is Accused of Taking Research." It said that the CEO of KMC, Dr. Ian R. Koke, was being sued by the Ferris Cancer Research Center, his employer of eleven years (1999–2010), for a billion dollars.

Dr. Ian R. Koke was hired by KMC in 2010.

Later on in February 2012, Dr. Koke made it to the front page again. "Dr. Ian R. Koke, Head of Kragness Medical Center, is Sued by Koenig University."

The Ferris Cancer Research Center/Koenig University complaint described Dr. Koke as an "unscrupulous, thieving doctor" who has caused an estimated $1 billion in damages. Also named as defendants were Karpa Science and Morgen Bio Corp.

Digging a bit deeper, I discovered that in 2007, Dr. Koke founded Karpa Science. According to the Ferris/Koenig lawsuit, Dr. Koke did this all without telling them, his full-time employer. Dr. Koke was an employee who was paid hundreds of thousands of dollars in salary per year. To establish Karpa Science in 2007, Dr. Koke transferred intellectual property in cancer treatments, which he personally invented, into Karpa Science. His contribution became Karpa Science company shares. *Dr. Koke invented this intellectual property, which turned into billions while he was the head of research at the Ferris Cancer institute.*

How Koke was able to do this without breaking the law is obvious. He invented all of the Karpa Science products in his garage with his own science kit in his spare time. Today, Karpa Science has a market cap in the BILLIONS. That's a big payback for part-time work.

Coincidentally in 2007, Karpa Science received $33 million in a raise run by Stair Seven LTD, the same company that owned VulturX Pharma, my main competitor and the same company that had tried to purchase BGC in 2010.

I began digging. Low and behold, our man Garth was quite busy. Aside from all of his other strenuous activities, Garth was a former partner of Stair Seven LTD and from 2009 to 2010 Chief Strategy Officer for Karpa Science.

On July 5, 2012, another relative article was published in *History Repeats* magazine, "Breaking Down CappasL's Billion-Dollar Wrongdoing."

In the largest settlement involving a pharmaceutical company ever, the US Justice Department announced in July 2012 that CappasL LLC would pay $3 billion in fines and plead guilty to marketing drugs for unapproved uses and failing to report drug safety information to the US Food and Drug Administration (FDA).

Nat Sacher, father of Garth Sacher, was the CEO of CappasL Pharma when much of the wrongdoing occurred between 1994 and 2000.

As the year progressed, we noticed our project slowing down. I called the head of research for all of KMC, Dr. Chauncey Manson. I inquired about progress and told him our concerns about Dr. Koke. Dr. Manson told me that things were progressing well and that there was a Chinese wall around Dr. Koke, who knew nothing about our project. After all, he stated, "KMC is involved in thousands of research programs going on at any given time."

In September 2012, the lawsuit between Koke, Ferris/Koenig, Karpa, and Morgen Bio was settled in a secret, forever sealed document for an unspecified sum.

Steal a car, go to jail; rob millions, resulting in lost lives, pay attorneys and go golfing.

I expected that Koke would quickly be ushered out of his spot. Kragness annually relies on over a half billion in donations from private individuals and over a billion in grants and payments from the federal and state governments. The board could not afford to have a cloud over their prestigious institute, which was founded over a century prior.

Koke remained and BGC sent a letter, signed by president Sam Salman, on November 19, 2012, to the Boards of Overseers and Managers of Kragness Medical Center:

> We are concerned that conflicts of interest between Covered Persons (per your website's Policy on Financial Conflicts of Interest and Conflict of Commitment document) with a Financial Interest may adversely affect the integrity of the commercialization and development opportunity for the Sickle Cell Disease, Thalassemia vector. Our concern is elevated by the possibility that a significant, embedded and long-term economic non-KMC relationship exists between at least three potential commercialization candidates and a Covered Person.

Specifically, Karpa Science, an entity in which it is well documented that Ian R. Koke MD, has a material economic interest, has received substantial investments from Stair Seven LTD, a leading biotech focused fund. Stair Seven LTD even has its co-founder, Mr. Nance Drewson, on the board of directors of Karpa Science. It is noted that Karpa Science's website describes Morgen Bio Corp Corporation as its major financial and developmental strategic partner. A Morgen Bio Corp executive is also on the board of Karpa Science.

We voiced our concerns about the conflicts of interest that lay in plain sight, and impressed upon them the urgency of the work they were doing. Dr. Chauncey Manson guaranteed that we had nothing to be concerned about. He promised to give us updates at monthly meetings. He also asked us to refrain from writing further to the KMC board.

Also in November 2012, I made it back to India. I had first been there in 2010, to meet with Advika Nutti and her team. Advika was the head of India Thal Foundation. India has the world's largest Thalassemia population, estimated at over 300,000.

Some patients and patient families traveled to visit me at the conference and at the hotel where I was staying.

Dr. Omar Achman, the Principal Investigator of our Clinical Trial at KMC, is a wonderful guy. He promised that the first treated patient would be my Christmas present. It was actually also a birthday present, which I wouldn't forget. KMC treated the first patient on November 23, 2012 in Los Angeles. It was actually November 24 in India, and my birthday.

The second patient was treated in February 2013.

Paulie had been out of prison for a few months. I was in Florida when I got a call from my brother Bobby. Not one to mince words, he told me that Paulie was gone. Like Mikey Fontana, Paulie got a hot dose and bled out at our sister Coleen's house.

The day after, I got a call from Peter Bellus. He had a book for me. I told him to send it to Florida. The book was from the US Department of Justice, Federal Bureau of Investigation. A decade prior I had asked my friend and attorney Joe Farrell to ask the government why they were hassling me. I assumed that it was for bailing out Martin Robin. I was wrong. The book began, "This interstate identification index response is the result of your record request for FBI/703536R8."

The FBI had investigated me for the murder of one of my best friends, Dirken Scott. They followed me around for two years, 2001 to 2003. All of the pages were filled with zebra stripes, so it was difficult to really make a lot of sense out of the novel. It was insane; Dirken committed suicide in Iowa. I had called the FBI to assist in following him and I was in Italy. It appears that someone had watched *The Godfather* and *Goodfellas* a few too many times. I can't say that I was shocked by the report, but it certainly saddened me. Dirken, Mikey, and Paulie, three of the closest people in my life, were all gone. I threw the book into my suitcase and have never really read it carefully.

ᚠ

In June 2013, the third patient was treated with our vector at KMC.

The first goal of a phase 1/2 clinical trial is, "Do no harm." There were no issues. Patients did wonderfully. The trial was going well.

Ironically, in 2013, VulturX abandoned the vector they paid $35,000,000 for in 2010.

Dr. Aurelio Maggio, in Palermo, was the personal doctor of two of the three patients treated.

I wanted Santino to be ready for the treatment. He needed to go through a series of tests to ensure that he would qualify for clinical trials. I made an appointment with Dr. Maggio and Santino and I drove down to the toe of Italy's boot, Villa San Giovanni in Calabria. From there we took a ferry to Messina, Sicily and drove on to Palermo.

I was satisfied. We were getting closer.

Our family has many friends in Palermo, and Santino and I ate out with them whenever he was not restricted by hospital exams. All of the tests were done at the Cervello Hospital where Dr. Maggio worked. Santino had three more tests/examinations to complete. The last would be done at the Policlinico Hospital of Palermo.

It was 10 a.m. Santino and I just returned to the hospital from breakfast. He turned to me. "Pà, alle du menegi," in his Arabic-like language this meant that at 2 p.m. he was leaving. I remembered the day he told me that he wouldn't finish school. I pleaded with him. This was crazy. He had only a few exams to complete. We had already been there for three days. He needed to be ready for his possible liberation!

I quietly sat, praying that he'd reconsider. We were in the hall waiting for him to be called for an MRI. Santino rose. I looked at my phone: 2 p.m.

Santino entered Dr. Maggio's office. I quietly followed. The doctor pleaded with him. To save time Dr. Maggio offered to have us accompanied to the expressway by an ambulance after the last exam. I was livid, afraid of exploding and actually physically harming my firstborn.

Santino signed the forms and we left. He drove. Not a word was spoken from Palermo to Messina. Santino maneuvered the car into the line to get on the ferry to return home.

I looked at him; he was twenty-three, handsome, and calm. "Son, do you know all that I've been through to get to this day?"

Santino looked kindly at me. "Pà, I never asked you to do what you do. This doesn't mean that I don't appreciate it."

I stared, not knowing what could possibly come next.

Santino continued with the same even-toned kindness. "Pà, you know what I say?"

I looked at him, the expression on my face begging him for clarification, explanation.

"You see that grocery store over there?"

I looked at the store in confusion.

"The sign says that they have arancini (Sicilian rice balls). I'm hungry, what do you say? Go get us a few."

And so I did and we never spoke about that day again. I'd figure something out when his turn to do the therapy came.

In 2013, Tarx Pharma was born around CAR T-cell Therapy for cancer. The founders were Radex Research Center and Kragness Medical Center. The core technology was invented by Pierre Shorf and his wife, Nancy Cuttings. They became scientific founders of Tarx Pharma.

In December 2013, I attended the North American Hematological Foundation in Nashville. The Shorf (BGC) SickleThalgen trial was a hit.

In the summer of 2014, *Rolling Stone* magazine sent Warren Braun, author of the book *Holdup*, a *New York Times* bestseller, to write my story, "The CEO Who Rocks." Warren spent ten days with me and my family. He interviewed everyone, including Lucrezia.

In the fall, *Rolling Stone* retracted a 2014 article, "Sexual Assault, Part of University Curriculum," a purported group sexual assault at the University of Townsend. The victim had invented it all. A few months later, Warren reported with great disappointment that *Rolling Stone* refused to publish my article. It was his opinion that they viewed the story a bit too controversial to publish right after "the sexual-assault-that-wasn't-a-sexual-assault scandal."

I had now been legally separated for more than ten years. The Italian system is very different from the American system, which seems hell-bent on turning spouses against each other so that the justice industry, with its many tentacles, can milk their family for every dime possible and then divide what's left (often nothing or debt) between two people who loathe each other.

Italian courts are far simpler. They see family assets as everyone's, including the children's. I had barely been to court, and my kids were happy. My wife felt that she should be able to get some of the marital property, but we were not in a communal property marriage. The marriage contract, which Lucrezia had signed twice, had been translated and attached to our marriage records in Italy. Lucrezia was a co-owner of property, which I had purchased in both of our names, but other than that, what was mine was mine and what was hers was hers.

I had been a wealthy guy before the marriage. Fighting Thalassemia had put a real dent in the resource column. Still, Santino was relatively well, and I was doing the best I could. The Italian health system, as far as our many experiences, is tops. Every twenty days, Santino walked into the hospital. They took care of him and he walked out. No insurance documents to fill out. No co-pay, no stress.

In December 2014, I was scheduled to leave the US for Italy. I knew that my wife (we were separated, not divorced, since 2003) was with her sister's family in Chicago. I called Lucrezia and asked if she wanted me to deposit her monthly alimony in her bank account in Italy, or if she preferred to receive it in Chicago so that she had money for gifts for her nieces.

The following evening, I waited for Lucrezia at a coffee shop on Archer Avenue in Oak Brook, Illinois. She walked in and stared at me. She was not an unattractive woman. I glanced and she sat down. I pulled twenty hundred-dollar bills out of my pocket and put them on the table.

"Are they real? I can expect anything from you," she said bitterly.

"Well, I don't want to stress you out. I'll take them back if you're that concerned."

I reached and she snatched the stack, stuffing it into her purse as if it was cocaine or heroin and not legal tender. She stared at me. I smiled. We had our issues, and I knew she didn't have a high regard for me, but it was satisfying, knowing that no matter what she said, no matter what lies her attorneys tried to tell, that I provided for her, and of course my children.

"Now I have something to show you," she said.

I was usually ready for most things. We were in the middle of a coffee shop. Was she going to flash me her tits, saying, "You don't get these anymore?"

While I was thinking, she rose and disappeared. In her place arrived an eight-foot-tall guy, dressed in black. What an idiot I had been.

"Mr. Girondi?" he asked.

I rose and headed for the door. "I'm not Girondi," I shouted.

He was in hot pursuit. "Yes, you are, I've seen pictures of you."

I got in my car and began pulling out of the parking lot.

He ran to where he was within 25 feet of my car.

"Sir, I'm sorry I have to do this. I know about your sick child, but I have kids too, and this is my job!" he screamed.

I pulled farther out.

"I'm going to say that I served you, even if you drive away! You may as well see when your court date is or they'll come and arrest you!"

He dropped the summons on the parking lot asphalt and walked away. I drove back and picked up the piece of paper, which would be responsible for ruining my life for the foreseeable future.

I left for home. It was Christmas, but I was aggravated at myself. Why did I insist on giving her the money in the US? What did I care about her convenience or her nieces? The answer is, "the Girondi Disease." Still, I had a marital agreement, which my wife had signed twice in front of attorneys. Our entire married life was in Italy. The separation was an Italian separation. Our children were in Italy. In Italy, our marital assets were already divided. How bad could it be?

On December 18, 2014, Garth Sacher, head of VulturX, and Henrich Vidal, head of Karpa Science, were chosen as CEOs of the Year by *Science Roadway*, a top Biotech publication. I'm not kidding. *The media cares little about how you got on top, but that you are on top.*

I was getting more than anxious. KMC had not treated a patient since June 2013.

Still trying to look out for our investors, by 2015, we, BGC, had almost made deals with two publicly traded companies. The idea was to fuse our 50 percent of eventual profit in the Sickle Cell Disease and Thalassemia gene therapy into a publicly traded company in exchange for shares. Our investors would then have liquidity if they chose to monetize their investment. Both companies' due diligence included confidential talks with KMC, which is why I suspect both deals failed.

I met with Chauncey Manson, the head of research of KMC, at the Pershing Square restaurant on Thursday, January 15, 2015. Unfortunately, he informed me that the clinical trial was blocked due to lack of funding. I was flabbergasted, given the fact that KMC had annual income of over $3 billion. KMC finished 2014 with over $240,000,000 in profit. That in itself is illogical. KMC is a NOT-FOR-PROFIT.

Chapter 27

A Struggle Against Overwhelming Odds

I contacted Edgar Diran, the attorney who represented Koenig University and the Ferris Cancer Research Center against Ian B. Koke, the CEO of KMC in 2012.

Diran agreed that clinical trials should move ahead, and we went in front of Judge Vience in the Federal Court of California, asking for replevin. Our claim was simple. KMC was no longer moving ahead with the project, so it should be returned to BGC, for the good of patients. According to Diran, it was a legally sound position. We didn't ask for damages.

The judge disagreed. There was no provision in the settlement agreement of 2011 for the return of the project for nonperformance. She did, however, suggest that BGC might search for alternative solutions for the product to be returned. Edgar Diran, attorney and friend, was not interested in a dragged-out litigation. BGC's attorney for years, Ken Sussmane, resumed the case in California Court. We filed a complaint against KMC for Breach of Contract.

The Orphan Dream Band's fourth CD, *Orphan's Cure*, was released in 2015. The whole five years of work on it may have been much wishful thinking. We were in a Grand Prix race. VulturX drove ahead with a junker, while our Ferrari was sitting in the garage without tires. There was no cure on the horizon that I could see.

In May, smelling gasoline, and not wanting to take any chances, I headed to Indiana, a one-party state, meaning that someone could record another person without consent for it to be admissible in court. Illinois was a two-party state.

I passed onto the Chicago Skyway and looked down onto some of the places I used to drive a truck and deliver to: Bethlehem Steel, Southworks, and US Steel. Unfortunately, most of the places looked like industrial ghost towns, as our corporate CEOs saw more profit in producing and buying from China. The corporations and a few families that own about everything in the US, blamed the unions. Any rational man now knows that it was corporate greed that did it. Executives didn't want to have decent employee wages and benefits cutting into their bottom line.

A whole new kind of executive arrived in the eighties. "I'll make your shareholders rich, just trust me." He fired or took away benefits from those employees he hadn't fired, and moved the production to China . . . real geniuses.

I paid the five bucks and got the receipt from the Skyway booth. It was time-stamped. I did the same on my return. I stopped at McDonald's, a thing I never do, to get a coffee I would never drink. The McDonald's franchise model made a few folks rich at the expense of millions, *poisoning people for generations*, some say. I just say it's sad.

I didn't have a lot of thoughts about what I would do, what I had to do. It was the right thing for my son, for patients. I looked for a quiet place to park and tape-recorded the researcher, my friend, Pierre Shorf.

From my call with Dr. Shorf, I understood that he was confident that our product was safer and overall superior to the VulturX product. He was desperate and frustrated that his project was blocked and not being funded by KMC. He was frightened by what he thought the VulturX and KMC executives at his own medical center could do to him.

It's May, 2015. Pierre believes in his vector, but is scared to death.

Things continued to get more crazy. It was like a script for a bad film, far too easy to figure out. On June 29, 2015, Morgen Bio Corp bought $1 billion of Tarx shares at twice the trading price. Morgen Bio Corp was one of the first investors in VulturX Pharma and licensing partners with Karpa Science and VulturX. At the same time, Morgen Bio Corp canceled $200,000,000 in funding for the CAR T-cell project at VulturX.

This may very well be the nut of the story. The pharmaceutical organized crime syndicate chose the KMC spinoff company, Tarx Pharma, to be the CAR T-cell company. In doing so, they made billions in profit.

In the same way, they picked VulturX to be the gene therapy company for Sickle Cell Disease and Thalassemia. To complete the maneuver, it was necessary to get Shorf's superior therapy out of the way.

Any way you spell it, Morgen Bio and the rest of the clan cleaned up in the scheme, at patients' expense.

I received tragic news on September 28, 2015, that Dr. Derek Persons, a gallant warrior of St. Jude and a personal friend, passed away. Dr. Brian Sorrentino, also of St Jude, asked that I make a trip and meet him to help evaluate their gene therapy vector. Of course, I made the trip.

Things often move strangely. *Rolling Stone* did not run my story. The *New York Times* did.

On October 16, 2015, I was on the front page of the business section of the *New York Times*: "Streetwise Father Takes on Kragness Medical Center to Save His Sick Son."

In 2016, Ken Sussmane sent out subpoenas to people at KMC and Garth Sacher, CEO of VulturX. VulturX immediately sent a motion to quash our request. KMC and VulturX attorneys then proceeded to convince Vience's Assistant, Magistrate Judge Bryant to grant KMC and VulturX 's wish for an Attorneys' Eyes Only (AEO) protective order.

This was an interesting situation. The corporations and their executives have their hands *so* deep into the cookie jar that they've actually convinced legislators to pass such a law. This protective order meant that my attorneys would never be able to show me our evidence. Only they could see it, and would be able to advise me based on what they saw. In the discovery, there were plenty of smoking guns. The problem was that I could not see any of them.

How would my attorneys who didn't know my business, ever know the intricate meaning of the evidence which was sealed away from the world, including from me, the plaintiff?!

We could not afford other legal help, so I became a paralegal to Ken Sussmane and eventually his partner. I read and investigated everything which was not sealed under protective order.

In Garth's motion to quash, there were two sentences that were of particular interest; the first said that Garth should not be called; *the subpoena represented an unjustifiable burden, particularly to the CEO of a publicly traded company.* The arrogance was baffling to me. The second was intriguing. It represented the first of many errors committed by their legal team; *VulturX's motivations for entering into a separate contract with KMC, is not an issue in this case.*

VulturX's attorneys were correct, VulturX was not a party to the Breach of Contract case; however, in their idiotic motion to quash, they told me that my product was given to VulturX in some backdoor deal. I was like a dog with a bone.

VulturX convinced Judge Bryant that we only subpoenaed Garth Sacher because AEO documents had been illegally shared with me. We were ordered to pay a fine of $88,000, the cost of the counterpart's legal fees for filing the motion for our violation of the AEO protective order.

This seemed unfair. We subpoenaed Garth Sacher because VulturX had met with KMC in 2010 and VulturX had told KMC executives that our product was superior and that they wanted to buy it. Truthfully, I had not seen one protected document.

I've done many things in my life. I'm a sinner. I won't likely get up and begin saying how sorry I am as I enjoyed many of them and find such acts mostly cowardly convenience. I confess to the Lord and each day try to improve. I try to follow the motto that "man's laws are optional and God's mandatory." But at this junction, with all the complications and thorny weeds in the garden, there is no way that I would not respect this corruptoration sponsored, man's Attorneys' Eyes Only law. Looking at those documents would endanger my patients. If Ken was looking at one of them on the computer, I didn't even want to be in the same room.

We withdrew the request to subpoena Garth Sacher and because BGC had shareholders who were residents of California, the case was moved to California Superior Court and assigned to Judge Gange in room 232.

Unfortunately, the AEO protective order followed us and remained a thorn. It was like fishing without hooks, at least for me. Ken had to tread carefully with what he showed and told me. He was allowed to give me advice but couldn't tell me why he advised me. The next infraction would get him disbarred.

Discovery saw the delivery of hundreds of thousands of pages. Most of them were sealed AEO. I scrutinized the ones that weren't like a gem dealer analyzing a diamond.

The Joe Feldman family saved the day by coming up with funding; an e-discovery firm took the documents from discovery and organized them into files. We were then able to search the files for names, like Sacher or Koke.

The story was coming together and no matter where I was, I spent hours each day reading. I also pestered every journalist I could.

In early December, I received a call from my friend, Vance Harris. In 2005, when his first child was diagnosed with a rare neurological disease, Vance contacted me through a friend on the trading floor. A few months later, their two-year-old son Redmond was diagnosed with the same disease. I did what I could and I became very close to the Harris family. The family lost their fourteen-year-old daughter Hannah in June 2016.

I arrived at the Harris home. Vance and his wife Kelly handed me a package. "We know that you will be heading home to do concerts. This is our Christmas gift to you. Please wear it and sing for our Hannah."

Inside the package was a beautiful black Versace La Greca Gabardine blazer. I was honored and humbled. I had done nothing special, just my duty.

On December 18, 2016, the day before my flight back to Italy, I was at a coffee shop, in Bridgeport, off 32nd and Halsted. I was in the company of an acquaintance and attorney, Terry Dicecca. She was Johnny Dicecca's first cousin. For decades, our families had been friends, and she was quite easy on the eyes.

When Terry went to the ladies' room, I scoped the joint out. There was a cute woman sitting in a booth about fifteen feet away. I approached her and we exchanged emails before Terry got back to the table. Now, that's efficiency.

Megan Euker and I began communicating. She was a thirty-two-year-old professor at the School of the Art Institute of Chicago. She immediately became a friend of all of our patients, and arrived at my house in Italy on January 2, 2017. She was intrigued by my court case and our mission for orphan diseases.

Megan, in Italy, became Margherita, as most of the Italians pronouced Megan making it sound like a German mouthwash.

Megan began working as my personal assistant, paralegal, and public relations person. She had soon amassed a list of over 250 journalists, and frequently sent out communications that explained BGC's side of the story. As a result, newspaper and online articles began emerging about the case.

There seemed to be nothing that Megan couldn't do. I told her the Versace jacket story and as a gift to the Harris family, she created a bronze statue of me wearing the gifted, mystical jacket. She then went on to create almost one hundred sculptures of various sizes and materials, continuing to depict me in the Versace blazer and trademark newsboy cap. She was able to sell some. Five alone went to a Los Angeles art dealer. The sculptures became a way to share the story of the jacket, and the larger story of my company, our legal battle, and orphan diseases.

We then came up with the idea to award one of the statues each year to a person who excelled in helping people with rare disease.

In concerts when I wore the gifted Versace, I knocked it out of the park.

In 2017, Ken Sussmane amended the complaint, this time including VulturX. *The plot thickens.*

The VulturX and KMC legal teams of course opposed. It was so strange to me that they collaborated as a team. This was insane. They were competitors. KMC controlled the Shorf vector and it was the only rival to the VulturX lemon vector.

Their opposition argument was that BGC would have never amended the complaint, and that the newspaper articles would have never been printed, unless my attorneys shared AEO information with me. I was now accused for the second time of divulging protected court documents to the press, and scheduled to go back in front of Judge Bryant, who had decreed the Attorneys' Eyes Only order.

Penal Code 166 PC is the California statute that defines the offense of contempt of court. A person commits this crime if he or she engages in any behavior that is disrespectful to the court process and carries a penalty of up to six months in jail.

The last time I was charged, it cost $88,000. Ken was as nervous as a person allergic to bee stings, sitting in a room full of honeycombs. I could end up in jail, and if Judge Bryant handed down a guilty verdict, this would likely convince Judge Gange to throw the case out of court and take steps to disbar my attorney.

Ken was working on contingency. He had mortgaged his house. Joe Feldman had borrowed money from his pension to finance our case.

The trial was set for 3 p.m. on June 27, 2017.

Mr. Respectful, me, I actually bought an $80 suit to go in front of the good judge.

Judge Bryant was an elderly, dark-skinned gent, with curly, salt-and-pepper hair.

The judge seemed irritated, not looking at Ken and me when he spoke. He began the proceedings by informing us that it was our obligation to convince him that we should not be fined, that our case should not be thrown out, and that I should not be imprisoned for breaching his protective order for the second time. His demeanor told me that he had already been convinced of my guilt by the hundreds of pages that KMC and VulturX attorneys had deposited in stating their breach of the Attorneys' Eyes Only court order.

Ken whispered, "Are you nervous?"

"Would it help?" I whispered back and smiled.

I was sworn in.

My mind was at peace. I had done my best and I would continue to do so.

I'm not sure that the lobbyists who got the AEO protective order on the books knew that it mostly shielded cowardly criminals and dishonest behavior . . . or, on second thought, I'm sure that they knew exactly what they were doing. Who do you think paid them?

Wayne Harlan, the Pitch and Balken attorney questioning me, was intense. By the time I had been on the stand for five minutes, I was calling him Wayne, WH, Wayney, and personally having a gay old time.

The judge seemed equally entertained and dozens of times pushed his glasses to his forehead and gazed at me. *WH* didn't understand the difference between Orphan Drug Designation and Orphan Drug Exclusivity as part of the 1983 Orphan Drug Act. I felt it was my duty to set him straight and began explaining how Wayney had it wrong. It was the only time that the good judge interrupted me. "Mr. Girondi, you don't need to educate opposing counsel on their misunderstandings of the material at hand."

"Yes sir," I replied.

In the summer of 2017, little had changed in the eight-hundred-year-old piazza. Santino, instead, was twenty-seven and had weathered almost twenty years of blood transfusions and iron chelation. I was certain that he should have been cured already. This was the toughest part for me to handle. Slowly but surely, I was convinced that the greed of a few men had dramatically shortened the life of my son.

As a man, should I have killed them, risking life in prison so that they couldn't repeat their behavior, stealing the lives of others? This question kept me awake at night and haunted the sunniest day. I knew where they worked, where they lived. It would be a piece of cake and I'd get away with it . . . at least in this world. *What's a Franciscan to do?*

My competitor VulturX's unsafe drug proceeded into clinical trials. Stair Seven LTD was still a major shareholder of VulturX and with billions at stake, KMC, Stair Seven LTD, and VulturX armed dozens of lawyers and Ivy League executives against a short and bald quixotic father.

Judge Bryant's sentence came out on October 16, 2017.

This is taken from the decision:

> *Girondi testified at length about his increasing concerns about potential conflict of interest between the CEO of KMC and his competitor VulturX. In support of his testimony, Girondi supplied letters to the Court that he or other executives of BGC wrote to the board of KMC dating back to 2012. The letters plainly state BGC's concerns regarding a conflict of interest. In addition, Girondi supplied news articles from 2012 that detail allegations against Ian R. Koke (CEO of KMC), claiming that he stole intellectual property from his former employer for his own business endeavors.*
>
> *Thus, the Court finds that BGC has met its burden of establishing an independent factual basis for its claims in the Amended California Complaint.*
>
> *The court finds the plain meaning of this sentence to be consistent with Girondi's testimony: that the CEO of KMC, Ian R. Koke has a company, Karpa Science, which raised money with the assistance from the owners of VulturX.*

The Court also notes that by failing to produce the full document and arguing that Koke was not a significant shareholder, KMC has made a misrepresentation to the Court in potential violation of its duty of candor to the Court.

We had dodged another bullet and would proceed, but nothing could have helped me prepare for the most surprising reading of my life, which was yet to come.

✒

Oddly enough, Garth Sacher, the handsome (if he had a choof of hair, he'd look exactly like a picture of the male sex organ) CEO of VulturX, did not want to appear in court and or speak with us, but he was fond of giving interviews on TED, *Wall Street Journal,* the *New York Times,* Bloomberg, and all sorts of other venues.

I chuckled when I read in one of the articles that he felt he was doing God's work. I'm not really sure who was handing out Garth's assignments. They didn't seem like things God would have ordered.

On November 27, 2017, Mr. Sacher gave an interview for a *New York Times* piece written by Kerry Green, titled, "A Virus Shortage Hits Gene Therapy."

Another error. What were his attorneys thinking? I guess they assumed that we didn't pay attention to the news or maybe that I, a high school dropout, couldn't read. Sacher's quotes were priceless. In our motions and eventual court appearances, time and time again, we were able to use his own words in our favor.

"Using VulturX 's original recipe in 2010, the manufacturing company said it was going to cost VulturX a million dollars to create enough viruses to treat one patient," Sacher told Green.

"We got no virus," Mr. Sacher said to the *New York Times* reporter.

"It was an Apollo 13 moment," he added. "We put everyone in a room and said, 'We have to figure this out. Everything at the company is now stopped. Nothing can be done without virus.'"

Wow, 2010, that was right before our project was sabotaged. What a coincidence. Garth meant to say that with no regard for patients, they put everyone in a room and mapped out the theft and destruction of BGC's life-saving therapy.

What an industrious fellow Garth Sacher was, a man of conscience and principle. He was a regular "Man for All Seasons" kind of guy, just doing God's work.

Garth Sacher was the hero of the planet. His name was everywhere. He was the toast of every medical convention and by giving out interviews, his hubris was forming around his neck like a noose.

Ken used the stimulus of these articles and the statements made by Sacher himself in the filing of the second amended complaint, court docket 123.

Each time Ken sent something to the court, his papers were followed by hundreds, if not thousands of pages of motions—motion to dismiss, motion to compel, motion to strike, and discovery motions written by the legions of KMC, VulturX, and Stair Seven LTD attorneys and paralegals, who were attempting to protect empire. This protection does not come cheap. The court case until then had to have cost our counterparts over $10,000,000.

This is why most cases never get to court and the ones that do settle more than 95 percent of the time. No single person and very few companies can afford justice. It was KMC, Stair Seven LTD, and VulturX strategy to outspend us. This strategy has another advantage. It wears the judge down and eventually he or she pushes hard for both sides to desist or settle.

It was the night of December 28, 2017. I was lying in my bed in Altamura. I couldn't afford a large heating bill and it was 11 Celsius or 51 degrees Fahrenheit in my room. The bed was finally more comfortable than the floor.

Ken called me. He was out of breath. The house was silent. "Judge Gange had ruled that the second amended complaint, could be seen by the world!"

Our complaint, which until then, I was not able to read because it was based on AEO documents, was now able to be read not only by me but by all.

I remained in bed and as the voice of my phone read the complaint, unexplainable tears rolled from my eyes.

I had listened to and read thousands of court document pages. I have been through so much in my wonderful life. Through all of the beautiful experiences (all meaning even the ones that most would say were not so good), I had been inoculated against being hurt, let down, etc.

The voice continued to read and for the first time, the worst of my suspicions were backed up with facts and documents and quotes. They confirmed what I had suspected but could not bring myself to believe, for years: the people I had trusted with my son's and our patients' lives had done a secret deal to destroy our project.

The unexplainable tears originated in the bottomless pond of hurt in my heart.

The following day, I read all fifty-four pages and the corroborating attachments to the second amendment complaint.

Unbeknownst to me, in May 2010, Stair Seven LTD, the owner of VulturX, contacted Pierre Shorf. They wanted to see synergies. This was a foul. BGC owned the product. Stair Seven LTD and VulturX were seeking to pilfer.

On June 22, 2010, Garth Sacher wrote an email to Rip Sarfel, the Chief Scientific Officer of VulturX, "Pat Girondi—need to shut him down . . . curious what he called about . . . my emails were clear want to get him to buy into a CDA to review Pierre's data. Be nice, suck up, etc . . . if you think (and I think) that Pierre has valuable data." A CDA is a confidential disclosure agreement.

After the *Nature* Article of September 2010, based on the E-beta patient treated by VulturX Pharma, we discovered that Pierre Shorf had written a letter to KMC executive Dill Pickens on September 16, 2010: "it's baffling that they (VulturX) would even continue with its vector, as admitted by Wright/Sarfel [Dr. Wright, Chief Medical Officer and Dr. Sarfel, Chief Scientific Officer of VulturX] at the meeting. Leukemia may develop. Their vector is still the same lemon and the paper was aimed at *Nature* to avoid key reviewers."

There was no doubt that VulturX Pharma's CEO had been behind the sabotage of the BGC product. There was no doubt that Sacher's scientific team believed that the BGC product was superior, and stated so in evidenced PowerPoints and emails.

In other words, there was no doubt that VulturX Pharma had delayed the treatment of hundreds of Sickle Cell Disease and Thalassemia patients, costing lives. Despite all of this, their stock was trading at $230 with a market cap of $13,000,000,0000.

Mr. Sacher told the *New York Times* about his Apollo 13 moment in 2010. To fix it, VulturX studied, gained from, and sabotaged our technology.

BGC's real problem began when I refused to sign a confidentiality agreement in October 2010. Most people with a lick of sense should not ever, ever sign confidentiality agreements.

Confidential agreements only protect the big guys. The court systems are so overloaded and expensive that if someone violates the agreement, it will take seven years and millions of dollars to get any justice, and by that time, what's the use? The hogs can afford the attorneys. They steal your technology and if, by the very rare chance, are caught red-handed, just burn you out in court. (Red-handed is a saying from the fifteenth century that refers to a murderer getting caught with the victim's blood on his hands.)

Confidential agreements allow the Goliaths to steal your ideas and technology. If you don't implicitly trust someone, don't share delicate information with them. The confidentiality agreements only give the little guy a false sense of hope so they can be legally raped, as it's not illegal until a judge and/or jury says it is so.

Court itself is a wild gamble. Judges and/or juries don't always get it right. The National Academy of Sciences reports that 4 percent of death row patients are innocent.

Me refusing to sign a CDA, handing my product to VulturX so that they could pillage, put Garth into desperation mode. By doing the smart thing and not playing their game, I left Garth no choice but to steal from and sabotage our life-saving product.

This was where the heartache for my patients really ratcheted up.

I, Ken, and Megan examined hundreds of thousands of pages. The evidence was overwhelming.

I saw how things were orchestrated. Ansel Droops, a hedge fund manager from Stoneclub (the Kennedy Family Fund), was the liaison between Sacher and Koke, to avoid the appearance of conflict of interest.

When I got suspicious, they labeled me crazy—an interesting strategy and easy to sell, the CEO who doesn't take a salary, invests his own assets, and does rock concerts.

Garth Sacher wrote to Elvin Krammel, Stair Seven partner, on October 30, 2010: "VulturX is in play at KMC and they're pulling vector from crazy pat."

We saw VulturX PowerPoints that admitted, "Getting BGC vector could increase target population by 50 percent and drive over $200M in current program value."

They also knew that the E-beta cure was a sham. It was written in plain daylight in another PowerPoint: "Getting BGC vector, [could] lead to a 3-5x improvement in copy expression vs VulturX vector and eliminates the most threatening competitor. Getting the BCG vector gives us a significantly increased probability of success in ß0ß0 [The sickest patients and Santino's type of Thalassemia]."

Of course, all of this was hidden from me in Attorneys' Eyes Only documents for years.

If BGC was such an insignificant, ineffective player and I was just a crazy guy, why did they need to get rid of us?

We were their most threatening competition. Greed commanded them to destroy my credibility and us.

These unfortunate men have a cancerous affliction that affects many corruptoration executives. Patient deaths are just a collateral effect of their disease, greed.

Chapter 28

Organized Crime Control over Not-for-Profits

Jane Nunn, KMC executive, wrote to Pierre Shorf on May 3, 2010, "Pierre, I don't quite see how Stair Seven/VulturX can make the best out of KMC/BGC technology w/o letting one sit on the shelf." So much for the Chinese Wall around Koke.

Nunn continued her letter, "Also, they know that we entered into a license with BGC, and they are coming to you, not to BGC, when they perfectly know that they should talk to BGC to get rights to the technology. I honestly do not see what they are seeking . . . besides competitive intelligence . . ."

Before BGC gave the product to KMC, in June 2011, and while Stair Seven LTD and Sacher knew that BGC owned the product, Stair Seven LTD, Garth Sacher, and VulturX executives began negotiating with KMC and drawing them into the "deadly agreement"—a term eventually used by Dr. Pierre Shorf.

BGC had every reason to believe that, by signing the June 17, 2011, agreement, the Investigational New Drug application would be submitted the following day and would be approved. In this scenario, KMC would be in patients by October 2011, as KMC (Dill Pickens) stated repeatedly during the negotiations to convince BGC to hand the project over to KMC.

Lots of crazy things went on behind the scenes as people tried to cover their tracks. KMC even erased board minutes to hide the intentional sabotage of our product.

"Efforts are underway to terminate the license with BGC, and once completed negotiate a license with VulturX Pharma."

This phrase was removed from minutes of a KMC Board Meeting in January 2011, attended by Ansel Droops, CEO Ian R. Koke, Chauncey Manson, KMC Chairmen Nester, and board member Timothy Treble.

Shorf was desperate. He understood that KMC didn't want to have anything further to do with BGC and Girondi. But there were patients, and this project was his life. Shorf approached board member Treble, attempting to prevent the project from being blocked.

Days later, Abdul Yenkin of VulturX wrote a congratulatory email to Garth Sacher with the subject line, "KMC-BGC license terminated!": "I can fill you in on the details later (at some point I may even write a screenplay for S. Spielberg . . .) But bottom line is that it ended better than we could have hoped."

Pierre Shorf and his wife Nancy Cuttings, one of the world's most renowned cell therapists, were now "technically and financially aligned with VulturX."

VulturX claimed to Shorf, that VulturX scientists would pick the best vector and or make a hybrid out of the two of them. Shorf was convinced that his product would be chosen. Only an idiot didn't realize that the VulturX vector was a lemon.

The idea of a hybrid was insane. VulturX was full press in an industry where greed reigns. They wouldn't afford the resources it would take to put quality and safety over ecomomics.

Before VulturX even signed the contract with KMC, on August 8, 2011, VulturX documents demonstrate that they had already decided that the VulturX vector would take the lead. It was written plainly in a PowerPoint presentation developed by VulturX: "VulturX's own vector development will take the lead due to earlier time to market opportunity."

Shorf's project, which he began in the 1980s, which had been mentioned as Nobel Prize–worthy, was over even before the collaboration agreement between KMC and VulturX was signed. VulturX only had plans to steal from it and destroy it.

The Shorf vector, the best choice for patients, would be shelved.

Discovery documents demonstrated other crazy facts.

On November 17, 2011, Stair Seven LTD secured another $78,000,000 for Karpa Science. KMC's board, should have been minimally cognizant of Stair Seven LTD's funding for their CEO's own company Karpa Science. Stair Seven LTD was a direct competitor of KMC's own gene therapy project for Sickle Cell Disease and Thalassemia, arguably the most important project of all of KMC's projects.

Finally, the Option Agreement was signed between KMC and VulturX on November 21, 2011. The indemnification was highly entertaining and unusual. I had to read it three times.

In paragraph 5.2 of the Option Agreement, KMC actually indemnifies VulturX for wrongdoing and gross negligence, only against BGC. As a result, the BGC court case cost KMC tens of millions in attorney fees. KMC was defending the same entity that directly damaged a KMC project and KMC patients. It was absurd behavior. KMC, a not-for-profit, was protecting VulturX with taxpayers' money.

In the same contract it was also stipulated that KMC could not seek any funding whatsoever for the SickleThalgen project until 2016.

So much for saying that KMC had all the funding needed for our project. In 2011, before KMC took over the Sickle Cell Disease and Thalassemia gene therapy product, it was already condemned to death.

You can't make this stuff up.

On January 27, 2012, Garth Sacher, CEO of VulturX, wrote an email to VulturX executives, Rip Sarfel, Vann Linge, Trip Cronin, and Abdul Yenkin, which stated: "First and foremost is getting Pierre to agree to give us samples of his vector so we can get it to AVC (Adolf Von Crooks) in Heidleberg, Germany. If he doesn't we need to go postal. We must get Pierre to see this the right way."

On June 9, 2012, Koke communicated to Garth to stay clear, as the appearance of conflict is too great, given their history with him and Stair Seven LTD. He suggested that Ansel Droops was the guy. Koke had already spoken to Droops about the situation.

On November 16, 2012, Sacher was asked by analyst Axel Dorn what was going on with the BGC vector.

Garth replied: "Part of our lock 'em up strategy. Please keep very tight . . . we did not disclose on purpose."

Pierre Shorf was livid, morally decapitated, and destroyed. He said, "VulturX has obtained a lot of information and future rights in exchange for next to nothing. Although they have already pillaged most of our know-how and strategic ideas, I would like to know whether the KMC/VulturX agreement can be rescinded. The recent realization by VulturX that our vector expresses better than theirs may provide a moment where they may pay attention."

Shorf also communicated to KMC executives, "VulturX benefitted from our expertise, getting our full Investigational New Drug application before submitting their own, sitting on our samples for months, pushing their vector ahead after having in effect neutralized our ability to seek new partners."

I contacted executives of Forbion Captial Partners, a Netherlands-based fund, to line up an eventual, possible collaboration. After receiving a request to speak, Forbion executives asked Garth about me. Garth replied, "Girondi off reservation. Do not respond."

❦

I read all of the damaging emails and analyzed all of the PowerPoints. We had been duped. I had let my patients down. I was thoroughly disappointed in myself.

Garth, on the other hand, had instructed analysts and fund executives to keep critical, disastrous information about the VulturX product from the public. During this time, he sold tens of millions of dollars in VulturX shares to vulnerable stock purchasers.

Ashamed, I began ripping things apart. I had to get to the bottom of this scandal that had robbed years of life from my son and all his brothers and sisters. More important, I had to save our patients from VulturX's less safe solution. I read that the VulturX, E-beta patient supposedly cured in 2007 transfused again in less than seven years. This was *quietly* published in *Human Gene Therapy*, January 22, 2016.

I couldn't get it out of my head. I had let them harm my patients and my son. I had let greed outsmart me.

We were in the middle of the court case. Joe Feldman was borrowing more money to finance the court case and Ken Sussmane had taken out a second mortgage on his home. Joe and Ken each had four high school and college-aged children. This all laid a foundation for many heated exchanges. Ken, though we loved each other with all our hearts, was quitting two to three times a week.

The weight we were carrying was grueling and mounted further, as dozens of KMC, Stair Seven LTD, and VulturX attorneys crammed the court dockets with more and more motions. Each court docket contained thousands of pages, and by 2018, there were over 500 dockets.

I settled into my role as a full-time attorney's assistant. Ken and I collaborated like affectionate brothers. Megan was meticulous about keeping things in order. She did the work of five paralegals and was, literally, a lifesaver.

One evening I received a text message from Vance Harris. "Pat, please also sing for Redmond." Their second child had left them, us.

The pain of these families battling these horrific diseases only made me resent the money changers more.

Later in 2018, ABC did a story on the Harris family struggle. The journalist went with a camera crew to their home. I watched the documentary and was moved when I saw the statue of the short little, hooked-nosed guy in a Versace behind Kelly Harris as she spoke.

I spent months in Los Angeles. When my friend Bobby Cotts was out of the country, he let me use his apartment on El Segundo Boulevard. A lot of my time was spent killing mice. I was happy that they now make mouse traps out of plastic. They were durable. One night I cleaned the trap ten times.

Nothing could distract me. I had 600,000 more pages of discovery to go through.

Jimmy Macchitelli was my attorney in Will County, where my wife had filed for divorce. Our judge was Rhonda Booth. From the beginning, things didn't go well for me. I would say that about any of the friends of mine who had gotten divorced in the US.

Divorces cost so much because they're worth it. I'm not sure.

Our marriage had been in Italy the whole of its existence. Our children lived in Italy. The majority of our property and possessions were in Italy. We were legally separated in Italy. I brought in an Italian divorce expert to speak to the judge, twice. The first time, he was not permitted to speak, because the interpreter was not accredited. The second time, he flew in from Italy to offer guidance and explain Italian law, the accredited interpreter did not speak fluent Italian. I am not kidding.

My wife first said that she never signed any marital agreements. When she was presented the agreements she said that she had signed blank pages.

"Absolutely blank?" Jimmy asked. "Not one line, no paragraphs, not one dot?"

"No," Lucrezia answered. "They were completely blank."

"Then how is it that your signature is written so straight, so perfectly straight right on the line?"

Lucrezia looked at her sister and burst into tears. "He told me he would beat me if I didn't sign them."

The judge scornfully looked at me. The contracts, signed in front of attorneys and witnesses thirty years ago, were not taken into consideration by the judge. If I didn't agree, after the divorce was final, I could appeal. Of course an appeal would take up to three years and cost maybe $50,000. In the meantime, I'd have to abide by any ruling. I couldn't afford my heating bill, let alone this.

Jimmy believes that the fix was in because the firm representing my wife was connected to the judge. I guess that we shouldn't blame the judge. She needed money to be reelected, and law firms can be very generous, or not.

KMC was having issues of their own. An article in the *New York Times* read, "Perez Chief Medical Officer of KMC failed to disclose millions of dollars in payments from drug and healthcare companies in recent years, omitting his financial ties from dozens of research articles in prestigious publications like *The US Medical Journal* and *Phenomenon Magazine*. Perez was also a Tarx Pharma consultant."

Another *New York Times* headline from September 9, 2018, reads: "KMC Cancer Center Orders Staff to 'Do a Better Job' of Disclosing Industry Ties."

A *New York Times* story from September 29, 2018, explained that KMC Executive Rafe Getz had to return $1.4 million after he was found to have personally profited from deals he made for KMC.

Getz was caught red-handed getting a kick-back for a KMC product licensed to a large pharmaceutical entity. In return, Getz got $1.4 million worth of shares of stock in the licensing company. In most places, this is called a bribe. Getz is still receiving his $1 million-plus salary at KMC today. Not bad cake for working at a not-for-profit.

In 2018, VulturX traded at a market cap of $13 billion. That same year, the company sold $1,100,000,000, one billion, one hundred million dollars worth of shares to unsuspecting investors at $185 and $165. Garth knew he had a bad product and was no one's fool. His take in 2018 for commandeering a company without even one product and a lemon in the pipeline . . . $24,000,000. Unlike Getz, Garth didn't have to return any of it.

In Chicago, I had dinner with a major analyst, who after hearing my insights about VulturX said, "I believe you Pat, but we've got all of our clients into the stock. If I went to my boss with this story I'd be fired." He looked at me seriously and added, "I got a mortgage and a family."

It was the sixteenth of October, 2018. My divorce was finally over. I was just glad to have it behind me. I harbor no ill-will toward my now ex-wife. We have three great children together, and she has some wonderful attributes, acting being one of them.

Santino, our oldest child, was an aspiring businessman. Cenzino qualified for state-sponsored years of architecture school in Portugal and Germany. Mariocarlo was attending Bari University, taking courses in finance. The Italian scholastic structure is a wonderful one. The poorest kids are entitled to a university education. Students like Cenzino who exceed are paid to study abroad. It's not a perfect system but it makes for a lot less stress and happier families.

On October 18, 2018, I was lying on my bed in Italy. My phone rang. With three sons, you always answer. There was no number on the phone screen. I answered.

"Pronto," I said.

"Watch *Michael Clayton*," the voice said, and then there was silence.

I'm not sure if it was a man or woman's voice, and I had no idea who Michael Clayton was or why I should be watching him. I googled Michael Clayton.

In the movie, Michael Clayton, an attorney who takes a stance against a corporation, is held down while a needle is inserted between his toes. The two men hold him steady while he dies of a phosphorus-induced heart failure.

I got the picture, but wasn't really sure if the person was friend or foe. The next day, I forbade my sons to sleep in the house.

On November 16, 2018, I received the tragic news that an incredible gene therapy researcher and a personal friend, Brian Sorrentino of Saint Jude, left us.

A four-page story ran in the *The New York Times* on December 31, 2018. The headline was *"Kragness Medical Center: A Year of Scandal."*

It was amazing to the world that the CEO remained in his $7,000,000 a year spot. Kragness is a "not-for-profit," living off the taxpayers—a not-for-profit that asks grandparents to donate, *even*, $10 for research after they've lost a grandchild. Haven't any of these kind donors calculated that at 260 work days/year, the CEO of KMC makes $27,000 every single day?

To some, the Kragness board seemed ineffective for patients, but the stock deals in which the institute was involved made many board members very effective for themselves. They were not getting rid of the goose that laid the golden egg.

By the beginning of 2019, the court case was within sight. The Joe Feldman family saved the day by coming up with still more funding for experts, court costs, and the continuation of the monthly fees paid to the e-discovery firm maintaining our evidence in a searchable, orderly manner on their company cloud.

As stated previously, ninety-five percent of these cases are settled out of court, the great majority because David ran out of resources before the finish line. This is the goal of the Goliaths. Connive, steal, and bully to get ahead, making enough graft to pay attorneys who keep you in the court system long enough to get you off the hook. The attorneys are only too happy to collect years in fees getting continuances, filing objections, and countersuing.

By now, there had been dozens of newspaper articles and blog posts written about our case. Over the years, I became friends with Dan O'Connor, a great guy and founder of TrialSite News. People like him helped me through some of the most dangerous passages. Publicity was cover for me, like wearing a bulletproof vest. The more articles written, and the more attention that our case received, the harder it would be for them to murder me . . . shoe-shining.

Our professional damage experts prepared reports. Ken, Kevin Murphy, our newly recruited lawyer, and I trudged back and forth to the courthouse. Ken and Kevin traveled with their office on wheels. Each wheeled suitcase weighed 50 pounds or more.

In April 2019, yet another scandal was unearthed in the *New York Times*. The headline read, "KMC Executives and Board Violated Conflict of Interest Rules." Still, no change from the management, no government investigation. Working under these conditions must present some trying situations. Many frustrated KMC workers commented to newspapers; one said that, "the nation had ceased to be free."

Garth and VulturX were also in the news. In one of the many lawsuits lodged against them, it was stated that each company board member made an absurdly irresponsible $750,000 a year. As the suits piled up, the VulturX legal team purposely hid the obvious from the unsuspecting public.

The VulturX share price headed south. The malevolent king and crew continued to pilfer the sinking ship, selling their holdings to unsuspecting investors as it sank.

Many patient lives were lost. My investors had been robbed. I had been outsmarted. This was also my responsibility. The guilt I felt was torturous and truly unexplainable in words.

In August, I sent this letter to my children.

Santino, Cenzino and Mariocarlo,

We've been pursuing the cure of Sickle Cell and Thalassemia for 27 years and it was within our grasp.

A week ago today, on August 12, 2019 we swatted the hornet's nest. Inside the nest were Karpa Science, VulturX, Morgen Bio Corp, Tarx, Stair Seven LTD, etc., a considerable axis of power in the modern Pharma world. This clan goes all the way back to the Xgerst (anti-depression drug which caused thousands of suicides in US children) scandal and CappasL Pharma when the US government levied a fine of 3 billion dollars in 2012; a small compensation for the thousands of families whose children committed suicide as a direct result of purposely hidden scientific data. The entities have different names but in fact are all the same. The corporate shield is impregnable and men who are responsible for more murders than Attila the Hun are golfing and the toast of the town.

I am not exaggerating. Look at the US opioid crisis. The culprits walk away with their billions and the victim's family with tears.

On August 12th, the appellate California judges ruled that over a billion dollars in damages is not speculative for BGC. The hornets have a decision to make. Had they known that we would survive so long, Papà would have been a victim of a hit and run, heart attack or the ever favorite, suicide; long ago.

There have been dozens of articles written about our case but they offer little cover when billions are at stake. The suspicious death of Mr. Epstein last week, protected by government guards, is yet another reminder that no one is untouchable.

I want you to know that I love you and I'd like to be remembered as a shoeshine boy, dishwasher, dockworker, truck driver, singer, uomo d'affari (business man) and most important as a father who did his best, who helped whoever he could whenever he could. I want *un brave uaggnòne* (nice guy) put on my stone and a picture of me in concert as my cemetery figure.

I want my last mass to be said in the Cathedral in Piazza Duomo where you all grew up and if possible Don Peppino from our parish and Don Vito from the cathedral to say the mass. I want the ex-bishop Don Mario and Santino to say a few words. Give Donato *ubrieich* (the town drunk) 500 Euro to head the guys carrying the flowers. Please put me in the wall at the Cemetery of Altamura and on the way to the cemetery in the procession, have Enzo, my beloved guitarist and Nanni Teot, my beloved trumpet player, perform some of my songs.

When you were little I obligated you to give toys to the gypsies outside of town for Christmas. I now again obligate you each Christmas to help those less fortunate than yourselves, whatever gesture you choose as the best way to honor my memory.

Tell Uncle Joe Feldman to organize a little get together in Bridgeport at the church of his choice. I love them all.

I am forbidding any tears of sadness at my passing. I was a lucky man and was given, in this life far, more than I deserved. Any tear must be a joyous one for the moments that we touched each other's lives and loved each other.

I want you to know that if I die of a heart attack, commit suicide and or become the victim of a mafia hit in Italy; it was not a heart attack, suicide or the Sacra Corona (name of the crime organization in Puglia). It was a group of greedy, little, coward gnats. I forgive them and ask that you do the same; for they are the true victims of their own avarice.

Whatever eternity is, I am ready and am hopeful of mercy and forgiveness for my many faults and sins.

I wrote in my mother tongue and I die a proud Catholic. If you have any trouble understanding let Cenzino translate as he is now prolific in English, Italian, Portuguese and soon enough German.

Papà

Chapter 29

The Final Round

In the spring of 2019, BGC hired Greenberg Traurig of Boston to come in and assist Ken and Kevin. Zack Kleinsasser, Gary Greenberg, and Mark Berthiaume were the new hired guns. They were great guys and an outstanding addition to the team.

We had looked into litigation financing, but Joe Feldman, my partner for as long as I could remember, didn't want us to pay the juice. The deal we almost consummated was $2 million now and $5 million (the first $5 million) paid out at the trial's end.

Joe was now writing checks for a hundred thousand a month on average, continuing to go in personal debt to finance the war.

His family's a whole book; his parents raised six children and have thirty-three grandchildren.

I'm not much on spectator sports, but I couldn't wait to see the Illinois High School Championship back in 2015. Joey Feldman's son Tommy was a star, along with three of his first cousins, Lee Barnes, Bobby Ernsting, and Michael Prasse. Their school, Benet Academy, gallantly lost three to two in overtime.

In June 2019, VulturX announced that they would raise the price of their therapy to $1,800,000 per patient. Prior to then, analysts assumed the price to be around $750,000.

By doing this, VulturX lost many of those who had supported them. Gene therapy is costly; we can compare it in certain ways to a bone marrow transplant which in the US costs around $300,000 to $700,000 (without issue with GVHD — Graft-versus-host disease). But $1,800,000 was more than anyone expected.

BGC planned to charge $700,000 for the first patients and to then move the price down as more patients were treated.

Finally on August 20, 2019, the tide began to change. It was BGC's third appearance in front of a judge on contempt charges. Judge Gange sanctioned VulturX $25,000 for wasting the court's time and making wild accusations against BGC.

Another huge error and one of the craziest things I've ever seen, was that the VulturX attorneys in an effort to smear BGC for using protected documents, displayed even more incriminating evidence in open court. During the proceedings our attorney, Kevin Murphy, made an objection to a comment made by VulturX attorney, Jacob Buttick.

"Sit down, Mr. Murphy," the judge said, "opposing counsel is doing a great job laying your story out for us."

VulturX attorney, Jacob Buttick dropped the binder from his pedestal and looked back at the dozen KMC and VulturX lawyers sitting behind him.

Judge Gange smiled, glanced at Buttick, and said, "please proceed."

By doing this, Jacob had done us a big favor. Any and all of the Attorneys' Eyes Only or confidential documents that he entered as exhibits that day were now available to the public, including the dozens of journalists following the case.

We weren't the only ones waking up to the reality of the drug companies. In September 2019, Professor Eugene McCarthy published a fifty-page document named: *A Call To Prosecute Drug Company Fraud as Organized Crime*. The article was broadcasted by countless newspapers, law schools, and legal organizations in part or in its entirety.

The document outlined the pharmaceutical industry's use of fraud and corruption to push their profits, consequentially harming and killing thousands. The solution according to McCarthy was to use the Racketeering Influenced and Corrupt Organizations (RICO) Act against corrupt executives in the pharmaceutical industry.

Professor McCarthy argued that as the government used RICO against the mafia, they should now use it against white-collar criminals, including executives, drug representatives, doctors, lawyers, and politicians who profit at the great cost of lives.

In January 2020 as the coronavirus took hold, VulturX won a partial approval to treat the least sick Thalassemia patients in Germany. As stated previously, a great majority of the Thalassemic patients in North America and Europe are not E-Beta or mildly afflicted patients; therefore, few could or would be treated with the approval.

From February 1, 2020 to July 1, 2020, Megan Euker's art exhibition about the trial, "The Cure," was held at the International Museum of Surgical Science, Chicago.

The exhibition placed the BGC legal case at the heart of an investigation into orphan diseases and the role the pharmaceutical industry has in controlling treatment research and patient access. Music and videos of Pat Girondi and the Orphan's Dream band, my group founded around orphan diseases, filled the space with blues, soul, and rock songs about the lives of people with rare diseases.

The exhibit included seventeen large graphics piecing the case together, along with music videos. It helped us gain traction, and the press began paying even more attention to the BGC Case.

VulturX had now made seven appeals. Each appeal costs anywhere from $200,000 to $5,000,000 in attorney fees to file and takes anywhere from four months to a year to be decided. On April 30, 2020 the appeals court decision was in.

The California Appeals Court ruled to uphold *all* of BGC's charges against VulturX Pharma and KMC. It was a good day.

Our trial was set for October 29, 2020.

In June 2020, an abstract by Doctor Aurelio Maggio, Pierre Shorf, and others was published at the European Hematology Society meeting demonstrating incredible results treating patients using mild myelosuppressive conditioning treatment for patients treated with our SickleThalgen vector.

The abstract demonstrated that after more than seven years, two out of three Italian patients have reduced transfusions of 48 and 38 percent. Italian Thalassemia patients represent the population with the most severe form of the disease. A 43 percent reduction in transfusions for Santino would knock his transfusions from 20 to 11 a year. It would be a miracle.

In other news, Tarx and KMC were awarded more than $1.1 billion in a final judgment on an intellectual property case. The inventor of the intellectual property at the heart of the case was our very own Pierre Shorf. Reading through the case documents, I discovered that KMC had received, in 2013 alone, $150,000,000 in payments from Tarx. Yet they didn't have a few million in funding for Dr. Shorf to proceed with his project.

With COVID raging, I left for Los Angeles from Italy in September, ensuring that I wouldn't get trapped outside the country before the trial. Court was virtual. We would use the offices of Greenberg Traurig in Boston for the trial. I left from Los Angeles to Boston on Monday, October 12.

I loved Boston, mostly because my ninety-one-year-old Aunt Vittoria lived there. I visited her a few times a week.

The offices of Greenberg Traurig were only a few miles away from where I slept. I walked back and forth each day, sometimes twice or even three times.

My attorneys and friends Ken and Kevin had their rolling suitcases to lug with them. They took cabs.

By now, Megan Euker had become an intrinsic part of the team. There are no words to express my gratitude and respect for her.

By the beginning of the trial, there were 1,177 dockets crammed with hundreds of thousands of pages. Megan, my partner Joe, Ken, and myself were all lodged in the same building that offered apartment suites. I woke up at 5 a.m. and did my exercises.

I had learned my routine from Mr. Arcieri ("u maest," dialect for *il maestro*), my buddies Rocco and Carmie Arcieri's dad. It's a kind of circuit, eight exercises times four. It took me anywhere from thirty five to fifty minutes, depending on who I was on the phone with while exercising.

I wasn't the least bit nervous the first day of the trial, but marveled that this part of my voyage was finally coming to an end. We walked into Greenberg Traurig all smiles.

It was October 29, the first day of our trial. Andy Martin, a great journalist, wrote an article published in *Bloomberg* with the headline, "Father Takes on Kragness Medical in a Billion Dollar Gene Therapy Deal."

I'll never understand how the board of a not-for-profit allowed their institute to indemnify a for-profit competitor company for wrongdoing. Estimating the amount of money that Kragness Medical Center spent defending themselves and VulturX had to be north of $30,000,000.

Now, in the ninth inning, KMC brought in a relief pitcher. The new Wyatt Earp was from a firm called Bush and Baker. I looked them up. They had also been counsel on the Theranos trial, in which the CEO was convicted for defrauding millions from investors. How fitting.

I was scheduled to be first. My job was the easiest of anyone's. Mine was not a technical presentation. All I had to do was tell the truth.

This may sound a bit elementary, but Ken had once complained to me, "In the law business, things have changed. All of the attorneys lie and the judge spends his time on the bench guessing who is lying the least. Clients shouldn't look for people who know the law. They should look for good actors."

It was a big day. If I failed, we likely failed; if I didn't slip up and was credible, we would likely succeed.

At 9 a.m., it was confirmed—I was in the hot seat first. The fellow running the virtual court informed the judge that there were more people watching this trial than any other online trial he had ever heard of.

I was arguably their most important witness. If I could be shaken, then maybe KMC and VulturX had a chance.

After my testimony, our attorneys were high-fiving. Mark Berthiaume, of Greenberg Traurig, made a swing with his imaginary bat. I had hit the ball out of the park.

Leroy Gertz, the ex-CEO of Phi Stamin, was next. He was an incredible plus for our team.

At the end of the day, I called my sons. Santino informed me that all three of them had watched me online. I had done my best and my sons had watched me. I felt as if I had fought an evil dragon in the colosseum, won, then unexpectedly discovered that my family had seen the victory.

My knees buckled, and I fell toward the ground. I had to grab the table to hold myself up, or I'd have fallen flat on my face.

Sam Salman began Friday, the next day. Like an elegant assassin, he killed it. Next were our damage experts, Stan Smith and Vlad Vitoc. They were incredible.

So, by the end of the two days, we proved that I was probably not completely insane. We also proved that BGC had a top team of doctors and researchers, but that corrupt executives blocked BGC from bringing our treatment to patients.

The weekend was tense for most. I went to see my Aunt Vittoria with Megan. At ninety-one, my aunt was still sharp as a tack. I loved being with her and miss her every day I'm not with her.

Sunday night, I received a call from Mark Berthiaume. The other side wanted to know what it would take to stop the trial. I told him that we'd tend to it in the a.m.

Monday morning, the attorneys raced to get a deal done.

I did as I did in June 2011. I called Santino and gave him an update, asking him if it was all right with him if we settled. It was almost ten years earlier that he gave me permission to hand the project over to KMC.

We settled. BGC was now again the owner of the vector, and after paying attorney fees of over $11 million, and all of BGC's debt and loans, we had enough to get the train back on the tracks. I could not wait to return to our goal of curing patients.

VutlurX's partial approval for their product in Germany (for the least sick) was a hollow victory. Their paid lobbyists failed to convince the various European nations that their product was worth $1,800,000 per patient.

Economically speaking, the Sacher family did a bit better than myself or our entire company. Knowing that he had a bad product which was demonstrated in countless pieces of evidence, Garth sold most or all of his shares in VulturX, pocketing over $100,000,000, in seven years as CEO. Most would regard this as insider trading. In the pharma industry it's just called normal.

On December 18, 2020, Garth Sacher was voted the worst CEO in biopharma. VulturX, which had been trading recently at over $230 with a market cap of over $13 billion was now trading at $18 with a market cap of $1.5 billion.

In August 2021, VulturX officially pulled their gene therapy product for the treatment of Sickle Cell Disease and Thalassemia out of Europe (they had only a partial approval, for the least sick patients in Germany). They had treated one patient.

"European players have not yet evolved their approach to gene therapy in a way that can recognize the innovation and the expected life-long benefit of these products," VulturX said in a press release. They would now seek approval only in the US.

VulturX's failure is a wake-up call for the industry. Deductible research expense and the price of medical therapies must be based on the cost of production and not on the profits made by pharma executives and pharma funds. At over a million dollars per patient for some drugs, few patients will ever be treated, anywhere.

In October 2021, instead of writing letters from a prison cell, Garth split VulturX into two companies and became the CEO of a newly founded cancer company. He had been voted the worst CEO in the pharmaceutical industry in 2020 but it appears that the "pillage and plunder" factor of greed, which has overtaken the world, has no bounds.

It's reminiscent of 2008. After thousands of Lehman Brothers employees lost their jobs and pensions, the CEO of the defunct company was rewarded with a golden parachute worth more than $30,000,000. The rest of his colleagues, all who helped create the subprime mortgage crisis of 2008, are today more powerful than ever, and worth billions.

In the beginning of 2022, Garth began referring to himself as the Chief Kairos Officer . . . you just can't make this stuff up.

Chapter 30

The Beginning of a New Love Story

BGC has changed its name to San Rocco Therapeutics. San Rocco is a patron saint of incurable disease. We are poised to continue where we left off more than a decade ago and hope to be back in clinical trials, treating patients soon.

Perez, the CMO caught up in the KMC scandal, died on March 21, 2021, in Spain. He was 62 years old.

Zia Maria from Modugno died on June 2, 2021. I was blessed. I visited her often in her last days.

Aunt Vittoria died October 21, 2021. In the last week of her life, my sons and I FaceTimed five times with her from Altamura. She was ninety-two years old. A fervent dying wish was that her father Santino's grandson and namesake would be cured.

On February 6, 2022, Ian R Koke resigned as the CEO of KMC. No one was really sure what to expect. Important work still needed to be completed before we would be back in patients.

On February 23, 2022, I received a call from an unlisted number. "Pat," the voice said, "I'm in a precarious situation here at KMC but I need to get you some data about the VulturX vector and the possibility of it creating leukemia in patients." The voice paused. "I will send the critical data to Santino's email. Please," he hesitated, "you must get the info to the FDA."

The line went dead.

By April 2022, VulturX shares were trading under $5. Laughably, the company warned investors of possible disaster. They should have done this when the stock was trading at $200. Of course if they had, the executives would not have been able to get out of their shares at such a high profit.

Steal a car, go to jail. Steal hundreds of millions, causing the deaths of patients, and go to dinner.

EXHIBITS USED IN COURT PROCEEDINGS

Exhibit 10

June 10, 2010

Email from Dill Pickens, Head of Industrial Affairs at KMC:

Pat,

I have been for some time now well aware of your dedication. That was part of the reason that I was so enthused, and now disappointed about Stair Seven. It was my short-lived dream that you would have their support. It's really too bad. We are lucky to have you on our team. It's Stair Seven's loss.

Dill

Exhibit 26

June 18, 2010

Email from Garth Sacher to Chief Scientific Officer, Rip Sarfel, and other VulturX executives:

Pat Girondi - need to shut him down . . . curious what he called about . . . my emails were clear want to get him to buy into a CDA [Confidential Disclosure Agreement] to review Shorf's data. Be nice, suck up, etc . . . if you think (and I think) that Shorf has valuable data.

Garth Sacher, Chief VX

Exhibit 37

October 30, 2010

Email from Garth Sacher to Stair Seven LTD and VulturX board and executives:

Great news, Ansel Droops can make things happen at KMC - I've had several chats with Ansel and we are now in play at KMC . . . they are pulling back their license and working on buying the vector from crazy Pat . . .

Garth Sacher Chief VX

Exhibit 43

November 2, 2010
VulturX PowerPoint Presentation
Demonstrated to Stair Seven LTD and VulturX executives:

Positives to getting the BGC Vector

Significant progress on vectorology vs. VX vector
leading to a 3-5x improvement in copy expression vs VX vector
Consolidation eliminates most threatening competitor
Significantly increased probability of success with sickest patients
More stable vector
Increases partnering potential
Better scale up possibility

November 16, 2010
VulturX PowerPoint Presentation
Demonstrated to Stair Seven LTD and VulturX executives:

Positives to getting the BGC Vector

Increase patient population by 50%
Will drive current market value by $100,000,000
Increasing probability will drive value up by $100,000,000

Exhibit 58

December 7, 2010
MINUTES FROM KMC BOARD MEETING OF DECEMBER 7, 2010

The minutes of the meeting of December 7, 2010 were approved with one correction. The following sentence was deleted: "Efforts are underway to terminate the license with Beta Gene Company, and once completed, negotiate a license with VulturX Pharma."

EXHIBIT 93

Sept 6, 2012

Email between Garth Sacher and VulturX Chief Scientific Officer Rip Sarfel and VulturX Executive Abdul Yenkin:

Fyi – Ian Koke just called me . . . had brief chat. We agreed it was best for him to stay clear as the appearance of conflict is too great given my past history w him and STAIR SEVEN. He agreed that Ansel Droops was the guy and he has already spoken to him about the situation . . . also they have apparently hired a new TT head named Rafe Getz that will start in a few weeks and is "great".

We'll see what Ansel says monday. I am taking earlier flight so i can meet him. Let me know any key messages.

Garth, Chief VX

Exhibit 113

March 8, 2013

Email communications between KMC Chauncey Manson, Head of Research and KMC Rafe Getz, Head of Industrial Affairs:

Chauncey Manson: Jenkins the guy interested in pushing ahead the Sickle Cell product just called again. I gave him the brush off.

Rafe Getz: Should have given him Girondi's phone number and home address. Would have got two birds with one stone.

Chauncey Manson: Yeah, would have buried them, I just dropped the shovel laughing.

LETTERS FROM ME

2017-12-20

To Franz Angst, once called, "the most feared journalist in Biotech."

His journal named CEO Garth Sacher of VulturX and CEO Henrich Vidal of Karpa as best CEOs of the year in 2014.

Dear Franz,

Karpa Science is founded on the theft of Koenig property. (Settled out of court). VulturX tried to buy the Shorf vector in 2010. Ronan Wright of Stair Seven LTD admitted Shorf's vector to be superior to the Redunt vector they had just spent (foolishly) 35 million on. BGC was the sponsor/owner of the superior vector.

We met with Stair Seven LTD, Rip Sarfel, Garth Sacher and Earl Lein in Cambridge, June 2010.

I told them the truth. They bought a hag which had created 'Clonal Dominance,' a precursor to cancer and that the E beta patient who has a fetal hemoglobin base of 40-80% higher than betas. My son and 85 percent of the patient base in Europe are beta patients. The subject of *Nature* article was not cured, but likely positively affected by myeloablation.

Many E beta's are completely relieved of symptoms by taking Hydroxyurea or other chemotherapeutic drugs, Busulfan . . . study by Tannoia among others.

Instead of dealing with the truth, KMC/Koke sabotaged my Clinical Trials which were commencing in late 2010, early 2011 at KMC-NIH (PI's Achman and Tisdale respectively) and gave my product to Redunt/Stair Seven LTD for free. Several major analysts valued the shit vector at 400 million in 2012–13. Free was a Great price to pay for our better vector.

Shorf, the ingenuous pawn/victim gave all of our data to VulturX in visits to Cambridge late 2010-early 2011, thinking VulturX would kill the Temple vector, his competition since early '90s for his own.

On November 27, 2017, in *New York Times* front page story about vector shortage, Garth admitted that in 2010, "it was an Apollo 13 moment, we had no product." Arrogance and selling shares for over $100 million could alter the perceptions of most. He was right: they had no product, so they stole from and shelved our superior product.

They then dumped their original product and caught up to where we were in 2010, in 2013, except we spent 10 million and they by then spent 500 million; great CEO, genius.

(I'm obtuse and nuts, that's the award I get. I guess I should have finished high school).

I had no idea of anything until 2012, when Koke (CEO of the not-for-profit, I hope I'm not being too obtuse) was sued by his past employer of 11 years for theft, described as an "unscrupulous doctor who absconded . . ." (Parker Branham article of February 12, the *New York Times*).

I only then began to get suspicious about the KMC sabotage that resulted in the return of my product to them . . .

I wrote to the board of KMC who promptly and emphatically ignored my warning of possible conflict.

I agonized as Shorf treated 3, very sick, older patients, from Italy, the worst Thalassemics with his vector using myelosuppression.

VulturX used myeloablation, apples and oranges.

There are very few E Thal experts in the US. Professor Galanello of Sardegna published why E betas are not betas and promptly died.

Anyway, Morgen Bio Corp buys a billion dollars of Tarx at 93 (it was trading at 46) and then cuts their Car T Cell deal with VulturX from 225 million to 25 million in June of 2015.

Shorf becomes founder of Tarx, a bitter Cupie doll indeed.

VulturX then becomes a Cancer company. Data is only as good as the flexibility of your researchers and the talent of the writers of the results.

I may be obtuse but the whole apparatus is corrupted, not broken but fixed by the bankers that invaded the camp.

Me communicating with you might be frowned upon by Judge Gange and or Bryant.

They had me on the hot seat for almost 3 hours explaining why I should not be fined/imprisoned for contempt of court.

I sent you Judge Bryant's ruling 177.

You see Franz, I'm just Santino's father and they stole 7 years from him and all SCD/Thal patient's. I don't have a crystal ball and can't guarantee that we'd have cured them but we would be in a better place and the Monopoly money would have gone into REAL RESEARCH, not fattening the wallets of investors and executives in the greatest pyramid scheme of our time.

These are only opinions. Every statement you should check.

My attorney would literally quit if he knew about this communication (Nah, he loves me too much).

This communication in no way should be taken as anything but information from Santino's father, an aging, obtuse, scared to death parent and proud patriot, I'm also a vet . . . just saying.

I can be much more specific. I am using no confidential material as Garthy informed us in a motion to quash about the 'secret agreement,' between he and Koke, I mean KMC and VulturX that basically blocked our vector, eliminating the company that was 3 years ahead of him with a better project in a 0 cost contract (I still have never seen).

Koke's attorney, Harlan's greatest move, was pumping 85 percent of all discovery in AEO protected order documents.

By the way, KMC is also a victim of these two Bozo's.

Try to get Ole VulturX to give you a copy of the sealed amended complaint.

For now the court has it protected, to shield corporate crimes, not competitive secrets . . .

You might understand why some call your CEO's picks of the year of 2014 also the picks of the greatest crimes of the 21st century thus far.

Steal, make hundreds of millions or even billions and then if you get caught, drag it out through the system and worst case, settle in a sealed agreement. Serves patients . . . right.

You must know that Stair Seven LTD raised 33 million in 2007 for the founding of Karpa Science and that Garth Sacher was the Business Development Officer for Karpa Science in 2009-10.

Noam Chomsky says that journalism is the search for truth . . . I'd like to believe so. Speak with your colleague Parker Branham, he might share notes.

Merry Christmas. I've given you your gifts. I hope you use them for the good of the whole industry, nation and world.

If you care to investigate, you'll discover that diseased, greedy executives are murdering innocent victims . . .

I guess that over 100,000,000 dollars in tainted stock has been sold by Garth. The AG would love that tidbit.

I had dinner in Chicago's Greek town recently with a major analyst, who said, "I believe you Pat, but we've got all of our clients into the stock. If I went to my boss with this story I'd be fired." He looked at me seriously and added, "I got a mortgage and a family."

my best,

patg the 'G's for got to do my duty, over attorney advice

Please understand that I am the father of 3, there are billions at stake and these Ivy League 'Commandos' are 'ends justifies the means.'

If I suddenly die of a heart attack, get hit by a car or choke on my baccala you'll know what happened.

This communication is my opinion and based on publicly available material. I have not seen AEO or have not used Confidential court protected information to base my opinions and statements.

I am the founder/shareholder of BGC, Santino's father and servant to my patients.

I will close before you lose your patience.

Any sarcasm is completely done with intent.

From: Patrick Girondi

Date: November 18, 2018 at 08:21 PM CST

To: Warren Braun (*New York Times* best-selling author and journalist sent by *Rolling Stone* to do a story on me, the CEO who rocks)

Subject: patg

Dear Warren,

I'm in LA combing through thousands of pages of documents, meeting with attorneys and writing letters to government officials. I now am closer to the truth, and as I feared, it was those who I suspected. They say things like, "we have to shut Girondi down," and "so it doesn't look like a conflict of interest we'll use a board member as the liaison." Of course they all have these things buried in court protected Attorneys' Eyes Only and Confidential, Court protected documents. I'm not sure that the protective orders were supposed to be used so that corporations could shield wrongdoing from the public, but that's the only thing it's done in this case.

They effectively destroyed a valid therapy for Sickle Cell Disease and Thalassemia. The patients . . .

I don't think that there's a person on the planet who will ever understand why I've done all this. Why I left a trading career and a life of dreams, why I traveled the world over and slept on floors and in cockroach infested hotels on Ardmore, why I left my wife and children in search of a dream.

I laugh inside remembering how I pestered *New York Times* reporter Parker Branham for years, trying to get him to shed a little light on a tragedy that I feared would only get worse.

Through this all I've learned who God is . . .

Today, the culprits have fortunes that reach several hundred million points. But what good are points when eventually there won't be enough to hide the decay, the rot which drives us to deceive one another and certainly ourselves; to grab for more power, more prestige and another zero to add at the end of our point tally.

In the end, I hope that at least one person understands that love necessitates drive and that God is the opposite of the impurity in our souls. The one person is my son Santino, who through his mighty spirit has taught me courage.

In time the guilty will be stripped of their prestige and their points and I will suffer along with them; as had I been a better man, I'd have prevented these people from hurting my loved ones and from destroying themselves.

Soon I'd have been up for parole.

patg

ϝ

From: Patrick Girondi
Data: 28 agosto 2019 02:55:43 GMT-5
To: Daniel O'Connor
Oggetto: patg

Dear Danny,

Thanks so much for your efforts for our patients.

I'm having my caffè in the place I have my caffè each day, Bar Della Antica Mura (old wall). In fact, it's walls have been stacked since the 1100's.

I read your new article about our case, for the first time and I'm actually crying. I don't know the right words in English.

We say in Italian, "mi commuovo," I think that the best translation is, "your words touch my heart."

As I look back, a voyage of 27 years I see myself as a fortuitous stumbling, bumbling fool saved only by the hands of dozens who helped me rise and my own sentimental persistence.

Santino began the passage with 2 brothers, Cenzino and Mariocarlo. After visits to patients in India, Morocco, and Saudi Arabia, Santino has been joined by thousands of brothers and sisters with Sickle Cell Disease and its cousin Thalassemia.

Each day I rise hoping to get them closer to salvation. Each night I close my eyes, asking for their patience and forgiveness.

There is a song by Nino D'angelo, Senza Giacca e Cravatta, that flows through the story of his rise in music, 'without a shirt and tie.'

His story in many ways is mine . . .

I showed up without a tie and jacket.

patg

2020-07-26 11:34 p.m.
From: Pat Girondi
To: Greenberg Traurig attorneys

Yes Guys,

I was actually there the night of the rock performance. John T has been a close friend of mine for decades.

He was Principal Investigator for BGC, 2005-13 . . . He could have left the NIH and moved to private industry a dozen times to make big bucks, but stays on his government salary where he believes he can help more folks.

When I was recently in Tanzania at the Muhimbili Hospital in Dar Es Salaam, I spoke to the medical community there about gene therapy and Dr. Lucio Luzzatto told them of my quest . . .

It is my dream that someday these poor people who have Santino's disease and Thalassemia's cousin Sickle Cell Disease will be cured.

In 2013 John called me to ask if I minded if he worked with VulturX. 60 Minutes patients were all treated with VulturX drug. Of course I told him that it was his obligation and my sincere wish that he collaborated with VulturX. I also said the same to my other friend in Italy, Franco Locatelli who also eventually treated patients for VulturX.

There are two major considerations. As you know, two out of three patients treated with the BGC vector have a 43% reduction in transfusions for over 9 years. Those patients did myelosuppression therapy. It would be a small miracle for patients to forgo the harsher myeloablative prep . . .

The other consideration is cost. As you know, VulturX's cost is $1.8M.

For me, I'm happy and have tears of joy in my eyes for these families. I don't care who cures them, as long as they are cured.

I'll be speaking to John and probably seeing him in late August, early September. As I told you, he's said in the past that he believes that the Temple (VulturX) vector or SickleThalgen could get the job done.

And as I said and repeat, I'm so happy for the patients and their families. Godspeed . . .

BGC and her investors saw this 60 Minutes document in our dreams when we met Shorf in 2000 . . . it has been our sincere goal for decades.

We will fight at your side for justice and pray that our mission will continue.

Who ends up in the Winner's Circle at the Derby is inconsequential. As Garth so eloquently said in the news article I sent. He believes that research is a dogfight. In a dogfight you have to kill all others to survive. He confuses getting rich with helping others.

We believe that research is a team game. Patients benefit most when we encourage and collaborate with competitors, not destroy them.

We want those patients treated.

pat girondi

ʄ

On Aug 17, 2020, at 9:41 p.m.

From: Patrick Girondi

To: Christie Walton:

Christie, I'll never forget the day John called. "Pat, I don't want to keep you, I know you're busy. I just want you to know that Lukas is fine. I'm gonna hand Beacon over to you. You go and cure our Santino."

His words compounded my resolve and destiny cemented the eternal bond at our family picnic.

You can be 1,000's of miles away from loved ones but it makes you no less part of them.

Please hug Lukas for Santino and I.

patg

ʄ

From: Patrick Girondi

Date: January 14, 2021 at 06:49:35 EST

To: Garth Sacher

Subject: patg

Dear Garth,

I hope you're well.

Our vector is safer and cheaper, meaning more accessible to patients.

Why don't you just abandon yours and jump on board like I suggested 10 years ago?

The $100,000,000 of investor/research money you stuffed in your pocket will only mean discomfort in the afterlife and some of the things you did to get the loot are illegal and worse, immoral.

My son Santino, would have been cured 3-5 years ago without your interference . . . Three-five more years of transfusions and iron overload on his organs. It rips my heart out and I lay awake at night wondering about what the right thing for a father to do is.

If someone did this to one of your children, what would you believe the right thing to do would be?

Decisions aren't always easy.

patg

LETTERS WRITTEN TO ME

On May 19, 2019, at 02:23, Stan Smith Ph.D. wrote:

Dear Pat,

I didn't listen to the music link you sent until tonight. Moving and beautiful!

As the father of a five-year-old boy whose life we are always fighting, for I admire and respect your drive and your passion.

Your quest is a gift to the world.

Count that I am on your team.

Always.

Best,

Stan Smith

From: John Aquino
Date: January 20, 2020 at 20:12:20 GMT+1
To: Patrick Girondi
Subject: Re: patg

Dear Pat,

You wrote me below, and I never answered, for which I am very sorry. I experienced some health problems, which required testing that, as of now, appear to have been false alarms. One big test on Feb. 3. But it was not forgivable for me not to respond.

Although we have never met personally, you are one of the best fathers I have ever communicated with and even heard of. When I think of the challenges you had and what you have accomplished--I don't have the words.

I hope you and your son were able to have an enjoyable holiday season and that his and your health remain well.

All the best,
John

From: Carl Segvich
Date: March 18, 2022 at 15:28
To: Patrick Girondi
Subject: praise

Dear Mr. Girondi,
I personally know the challenges which one faces when confronting a health issue.

Your battle to defeat Sickle Cell Disease and Thalassemia is an inspiration to Bridgeport, Canaryville and the world.

Carl Segvich, Republican Committeeman, 11th Ward Chicago

Character Index
(Alphabetical by First Name)

NAME IN BOOK	WHO/NOTES
Aarush Patelni	Father of patient
Abdul Yenkin	VulturX executive
Acme Armored Truck Heist	A famous heist
Adolf Von Crooks	German researcher affiliated with VulturX
Advika Nutti	Head of Thalassemia foundation in India
Agent Weatherspoon	FBI Agent
Al Smith	Larry Smith's dad
Alan Bino	Neighborhood guy
Alessandro Vali	Founder of Phi Stamin
Alfonso Prato	Patrick's cousin from Italy
Alice Girondi	Uncle Vince's wife
Alice Walton	Sister of John Walton
Andreas Schmitz	Friend of Patrick's from the military
Angela	Sister of Patrick's mother
Angela Iacono	President of Italian Thalassemia Federation
Anne	Sister of Patrick
Annunziata	Friend of Patrick
Ansel Droops	Liaison between Garth Sacher and Ian R. Koke
Antonia	Grandmother of Patrick
Archer	Name of street in Chicago
Art Nieman	First CEO of Beacon
Asman Temple	Created competing, but faulty gene therapy
Aunt Kay Brown	Babysitter of Patrick
Dr. Aurelio Maggio	Hematologist in Palermo
Axel Dorn	Stock analyst

Beacon	Second pharmaceutical company founded by Patrick
Benjamin Tisch	Trader in General Electric
Benet Academy	Joe Feldman's sons' high school
Berken Drick	Brokerage firm
Bernardo Cramarossa	Son of Italian crime boss, "One Arm Rico" Cramarossa
Beta Gene Company ("BGC")	Name of pharma company Patrick founded in 2003 in continuation of Beacon
Billy Fisch	Second-in-command to Stuart Wilmott at Birken Drick brokerage firm
Blake Ross	Patrick saved this trader's life
Blind Faith	Play written by Patrick; became runner-up in American Screenwriters Competition
Bloomberg	Important news publication that released a story about Patrick and BGC the day of the trial
Blue Ciacci	Neighborhood (Bridgeport) friend
Bobby Carmichael	Patrick's brother
Booby Suss	Trader in Houston Oil pit
Boston University	Dr. Perrine's affiliation; big US research university
Brad Wolf	Attorney for Beta Gene Company (BGC)
William Milton	Soybean trader
Brett Galen	Former CEO of VulturX
Brian Lantz	Thalassemia patient
Brinda	Patient (Aarush Paltelni's daughter)
Bruno	Broker in Houston Oil pit
Bruno Mauri	Executive at Phi Stamin
Buck Willis	Patrick's neighborhood friend
Burton Hartz	Boss at Chicago Corp, on exchange floor
Bush And Baker	Legal firm for KMC
Callom Stoke	Investment firm
CappasL Pharma	Company that was fined $3 billion for actions stemming from when Garth Sacher's father was the company's CEO

CAR T-cell Therapy	Cancer-fighting procedure
Carco Partners	Venture-capital firm in Cambridge; Nat Sacher's wife's father was a founder
Carl Mabry	CEO of biological material manufacturer
Carmichael	Last name of Patrick before taking his mother's last name
Carmine Ferri	Son of Zia Anna Ferri
Casey	Brother of Patrick
Champ	Kid from the neighborhood (Bridgeport)
Chauncey Manson	Head of research, Kragness Medical Center
Chenx Laboratories	Earl Lein, founder of Stair Seven LTD, had previous executive role here
Chicago News	Chicago newspaper
Chicago Post	Chicago newspaper
Christie Walton	Wife of John Walton/mother of Lukas Walton
Chris Wiech	Son of Norb Wiech
Christopher Ballas	BGC scientist
Cinzia (Dr.)	Doctor of Santino
Clara	Sister of Patrick
Clay Canon	Board of Trade former president
Coleen	Sister of Patrick
Colonel Armstrong	Base commander who rushedly approved Patrick's hardship discharge
Community Hospital in Bethesda	Where Lucrezia did IVF
Congressman Patowskus	Chicago Congressman
Cory Vann	Teledyne trader
Craig Butler	Trader in Houston Oil pit
Crete Hogg	Teledyne trader
Dan	Owner's son, Club el Bianco
Daniel O'Connor	Editor of TrialSite News
Darren Stokes	Judge
Dennis O'Rourke	Friend responsible for Patrick taking a job on the trading floor
Dent Firm	Trading firm

Derek Holmes	Friend of Patrick's and son of Big Mamma
Derek Persons	Doctor at St. Jude Children's Research Hospital
Dicecca	DiCecca family from Bridgeport, friends of Patrick's
Diego Rato	Son of Serge Rato
Dill Pickens	Head of Industrial Affairs Dept. at Kragness Medical Center
Dirken Scott	Friend of Patrick and manager of Bridgeport Securities Group (Patrick's trading company)
Dominick	Boss of the Italian crime organization in Bridgeport
Donald Brath	Chicago Journalist
Donald Winski	Chicago ward committeeman of Polish descent living in Florida
Dr. Ferdinand Torre	Santino's doctor
Dr. Ronan Wright	Stair Seven LTD medical advisor
Dr. Tirelli	New York hematologist
Drew Norte	Former CEO of VulturX
Duke Rymt	Attorney for Beacon
Earl Black	Phone clerk
Earl Lein	Founder of Stair Seven LTD
Ed's Street	A Chicago bar
Eddy Shinnick	Owner of Shinnick's Bar Bridgeport
Edgar Diran	The attorney who represented Koenig University in their suit against Ian R. Koke and first represented BGC against KMC
Egidio Cramarossa ("Il Nero")	Brother of crime boss "One Arm Rico" Cramarossa
Elaine Sussmane	Wife of Patrick's attorney, Ken Sussmane
Emmett	Neighborhood friend of Patrick's
Emmy Brown	Aunt Kay's daughter
Enrico	Owner of Club El Bianco
Enrico ("One Arm Rico") Cramarossa	Mob boss
Eric Sarr	Patrick's supervisor when working for Morgan Church in the Teledyne pit

Ernest Givings	Teledyne trader
Falo Twist	Notre Dame professor/inventor
Fanny Tifo	Canadian doctor
Ethan Hansel	Trade checker/phone clerk
Father Edward	Priest at Saint Joseph's Seminary
Father Pasquale Faro	Priest who got Patrick into Saint Joseph's Seminary
Feeralx	Medicine
Ferris Cancer Research Center	Where Ian R. Koke worked and was accused of intellectual property theft; one of the top US research centers
Forbion Capital Partners	Netherlands-based funding firm
Fortissa	Trading company in Switzerland
Francis	Brother of Patrick
Franco Locatelli	President of Italy's Higher Health Counsel
Franz Angst	Reporter
Gant Hert	CEO of pharmaceutical company and analyst
Garby	Attorney for Martin Robin
Garth Sacher	CEO VulturX
Gary Greenberg	Attorney at Greenberg Traurig
Gary Mason	Bridgeport Securities Group broker in the soybean pit
George Murphy	Irish hitman and friend of Patrick's father
Giovanna Ferri	Zia Anna Ferri's daughter
Girondi	Last name of Patrick
Greenberg Traurig	Legal firm used by BGC
Greg	Patrick's brother
Guido Lucarelli	Italian transplant doctor
Gustus Antybulos	Greek doctor
Hannah Harris	Child of Kelly and Vance Harris
Harvard University	Ivy League university
Harvey Wan	Patrick's boss at Chicago Board of Options Exchange from Taiwan
Heather Stucker	Candidate for Clerk of Cook County
Henrich Vidal	CEO of Karpa Science

Herman Maily	Executive at Phi Stamin
Hiney Ciacci	Friend from Bridgeport
History Repeats Magazine	Important crime journal
Holdup	Name of book by Warren Braun
Human Gene Therapy	Magazine
Hopkins	Undercover FBI agent on the floor
Ian R. Koke	CEO of Kragness Medical Center
IBM	Stock
India Thal Foundation	Thalassemic foundation India
International Museum of Surgical Science, Chicago	Megan Euker exhibited graphics and information about the court case here
International Thalassemia Alliance	World Health Organization, Thalassemia foundation headquartered in Cypress
Irwin Rothstein	Door-to-door merchant
Italian Thalassemia Federation	Thalassemia foundation
Jackie Burke	Friend of Patrick's and commander of police station in Bridgeport
Jacob Buttick	Attorney for VulturX
Jake Nolan	Trader
Jane Smith	Larry Smith's daughter
Jane Nunn	Industrial affairs department, KMC
Jarrett Rose	Owner of trading firm, SOC
Jasmine Carmichael	Bobby Carmichael's daughter
Jefferson Harding	Undercover FBI agent
Jessica Holmes	Wife of Derek Holmes
Jim Bob Hailey	Friend from Bridgeport
Jim Remenick	Attorney friend of Patrick's and Susan Perrine
Jimmy	Patrick's brother
Jimmy Macchitelli	Friend of Patrick's and divorce attorney
Joe Feldman Jr.	Patrick's best friend and business partner
Joe Horvat	Croatian boss who worked at the docks with Patrick
John Aquino	Reporter for *Bloomberg*
Dr. John Gray	Doctor, St. Jude Children's Research Hospital

John Tisdale	Hematologist and friend of Patrick's
John Walton	Son of Sam Walton
Johnny Griff	Worker at Great Lakes Supply
Johnny Rossi	Aunt Angela's husband
Jonas Hoffman	Stock analyst with Callom Stoke
Josh Balkus	Criminal attorney for Patrick
Joshua Bandik	Administrative head of BGC
Judge Bryant	Magistrate judge for federal case
Judge Gange	Judge for trial against KMC and VulturX
Judge Vience	Judge in federal case filed by BGC against KMC and VulturX
Justice Ford	Doctor/professor, could take a cell off an embryo and label its HLA antigens
Karpa Science	Pharmaceutical company founded by Ian R. Koke
Katy	Sister of Patrick
Kaylen Holmes	Son of Derek Holmes
Kelly Harris	Wife of Vance Harris; lost two children to a rare disease
Ken Sussmane	Patrick's attorney
Kevin Brown	Aunt Kay's kid
Kevin Murphy	Patrick's attorney
Knuckles Ciacci	Friend from the neighborhood/Bridgeport
Koenig University	US Ivy League University
Kragness Medical Center LA	Medical center
L'Olmo	Patrick's Italy wedding recpetion was here; this is the hotel owned by Don Enrico
Lance Rolf (Rofanowski)	New York wheeler-dealer
Laro	Swiss trader who created a loss in Fortissa Company and substantial economic loss to Patrick
Larry Smith	Patrick's friend
Lenonardo Franco	Unsuccessful buyer of BPT trading; later imprisoned for embezzlement
Leonard Dent	Founder of Dent Trading Firm

Leone	Family with the outfit in Bridgeport
Leroy Gertz	CEO of Phi Stamin
Linda Wiech	Wife of Norb Wiech
Lippi	Enrico's doctor in Florence
Lonny Katz	Trader at Chicago Board of Options Exchange
Lorry Irving	Trader in Houston Oil pit
Louis Fellini	Neighborhood guy
Lucio Luzzatto	Hematologist and mentor to Patrick
Ludwig Bigi	Owner of Swiss trading firm Fortissa
Lukas Walton	Son of John Walton
Maria	Sister of Patrick's mother
Maria Trian	Patient's mother
Marie	Patrick Girondi's sister
Mariocarlo	Patrick's son
Mark	Patrick's brother
Markum	Sergeant in basic training
Mark Berthiaume	Attorney at Greenberg Traurig
Marlin International Trading	Faux name of FBI agents' undercover company
Marshall Holmes	Derek Holmes Son
Marshall Polcari	Italian police captain
Martin Robin	Patrick's friend
Martin Tenniswood	Doctor/researcher
Matty	The Old Man, father of Patrick
Maynard Racic	Cook County Clerk
Megan Euker	Close friend of Patrick's, assistant to the lawsuit and his company; artist
Mercurio Ferri	Zia Anna Ferri's Son
Mike Nolan	Trader; Jake Nolan's Brother
Mikey Fontana	Patrick's brother
Milly	Mother of Rita, a Canadian Thalassemic patient
Mithu Sen	Formerly worked for Phi Stamen
Morgan Church	Patrick's boss in the Teledyne pit
Morgen Bio Corp	Pharmaceutical company
Morris Greenberger (Morry Green)	Owner Silver Transmission Shop

Nance Drewson	Cofounder of Stair Seven
Nancy Cuttings	Researcher/Pierre Shorf's wife
Nat Sacher	Garth Sacher's father
Nathaniel and Nathaniel	Pharma company
Nathaniel Poppel	Guy who hired Patrick at Great Lakes Supply
National Role Corp	Options unit with huge losses in 1987 crash, in great part created by Harvey Wan, Patrick's old boss
Nature	Magazine where Dr. Shorf published about curing Thalassemic mice
Nelly Gester	Researcher for Beacon
Nica Cappellini	Doctor in Milan
Nicky Tarson	Trader
Nicola Melo (Nicky)	Cousin of Patrick, Aunt Vittoria's son who was killed in Tucson
Nius Pharmaceuticals	Earl Lein had previous executive role here
Norb Wiech	Founder of BGC
Novak Brothers	Auto repair shop
O'Halloran	Broker for Dent Trading firm
Oakland Children's Hospital	Santino treated here
Olive	Dale; Tom; Rochelle; Terry neighbors of Patrick
Omar Achman	Doctor at KMC (Kragness Medical Center)
Ontario Children's Hospital	Hospital in Canada
Oscar Novak	Novak Brothers car shop
Oscar Rays	Transplant doctor at KMC (Kragness Medical Center)
Otello Mirizza	Patrick's friend in Italy
Packy Schultz	Phone clerk at Chicago Corp on the trading floor
Parker Branham	Journalist for the *New York Times*
Patricia Giardina	Doctor at Cornell
Dr. Patrick Tian	Doctor friend of Patrick's
Paulie Carmichael	Brother of Patrick
Penny Candy	Ran the biggest book for the outfit at the Board of Trade

Percy University	US university
Perez	Doctor forced to resign from KMC (Kragness Medical Center)
Perry Sand	Professor from LA
Peter Bellus	Patrick's friend and employee at Bridgeport Securities Group
Pharma Today	Weekly magazine
Phenomenon Magazine	Scientific journal
Phi Stamin	Italian pharmaceutical company
Philly Melo	Cousin of Patrick, Aunt Vittoria's son
Pierre Shorf	Scientist and inventor of Patrick's company's product
Pierson Reins	Researcher at Notre Dame
Pistol Ciacci	Friend from the neighborhood (Bridgeport)
Pitch and Balken	Legal firm for KMC
Provenzano	Employee of Rezac Pharma
Rachele Ferri	Zia Anna Ferri's daughter
Radex Research Center	A research center
Rafe Getz	Head Of Industrial Affairs Kragness Medical Center/KMC
Raimondo Culatto	Accountant friend of Patrick's and father of a Thalassemic patient
Randall Farms	Broker and Floor Governer in Houston Oil pit
Raymond	One of the brothers who owned Novak's Auto Repair
Reardon	Undercover FBI agent
Redmond Harris	Daughter of Kelly and Vance Harris
Redunt	The prior name of VulturX
Research Center Of Philadelphia (RCOP)	Where BGC manufacturing took place
Rezac Pharmaceuticals	Pharma company
Rhonda Booth	Divorce judge
Ricky Stanic	Patrick's shoeshine friend
Rino Fini (Penny Candy)	Ran the biggest book for the outfit at the Board of Trade

Rino Vullo	Doctor, Ferrarra, Thalassemia Specialist
Rip Sarfel	CSO of VulturX Pharma
Rob Kelly	Neighborhood friend of Patrick
Robert Meyer	Patrick's stepfather
Rodolfo Marche	Thalassemic patient
Roger Nimitz	Trader in the soybean pit
Rolexgen	Earl Lein helped lead the sale of this company
Ronald Troy	Assistant to John Walton
Ronnie Moreno	Political figure in Chicago
Rooks	Public relations guy for Dominick and the Chicago outfit
Rosalba	Annunziata's sister
Rossi Calo	Neighborhood guy
Rudy Cepak	Alderman of far South Side Chicago ward
Ruggero Ciacci	Friend from the neighborhood in Bridgeport
RWG	German trading company
Ryan Banks	Bully who worked in Northwestern Hospital kitchen with Patrick
Sam Salman	President of Patrick's company
Sam Walton	Creator of Walmart
Sammy Bino	Neighborhood guy
Samuele Prete	Director of Italian Telethon
Santino	Patrick's firstborn son
Sara	Patrick's stepmother
Sara	Mother of Patrick
Sarge	The family dog who attacked on Patrick's father's command
Science Roadway	A top biotech publication
Sean McCrory	Neighborhood guy
Sebastiano Morici	Swiss trader and friend of Patrick's
Sergio Rato	President of Thalassemia International Foundation
SickleThalgen	Trademarked name for BGC vector
Sid Feldman	Joe Feldman's grandfather
Silvia	Girl who comes to the house from time to time

Sipich	Pharmacy
Skippy Stein	Owner of Security Options Corp, firm where Patrick cleared his trades
Slim Traino	One of Dominick's guys who went to prison for murder
Sonny Handelsman	Trader who Patrick had altercations with
Stair Seven LTD	Funding firm
Stanlo Pharmaceuticals	Firm where Earl Lein was former Chief Business Officer
Stan Smith	Expert witness for BGC
Steve Tyler	Trader and friend of Patrick's
Stoneclub	Funding firm
Stuart Martin	Undercover FBI agent
Stuart Wilmott	Berken Drick (brokerage firm)
Susan Perrine	Doctor at Boston University
Sweetboy Leone	One of Dominick's captains
Tam	Larry Smith's Mom
Tarx Pharma	Pharma company
Thalassemia Anemia International	Thalassemia Foundation
The *New York Times*	Patrick was on the front page of this news publication for the story of his court case in 2015
The Turk	Broker in Houston Oil pit
The *Wall Street Journal*	Newspaper
Tisravno	Pharmaceutical company
Todd Mann	Merill Lynch Broker
Tony Burke	Friend of Patrick's who stabbed a guy and was sent to the military around the same time as Patrick
Travis Dunn	Assistant to John Walton
TrialSite News	Clinical trial publication (online)
Trip Cronin	VulturX executive
Uncle Rory Brown	Aunt Kay's husband

Vance Harris	Friend of Patrick's with two children with rare diseases
Vann Linge	VulturX researcher
Vince Berke	Politician
Vincenzo Girondi	Patrick's second son
Vincenzo/Uncle Vince	Brother of Patrick's mother
Vittoria Melo	Sister of Patrick's mother
Vlad Vitoc	Expert witness for BGC
VulturX Pharma	Patrick's competitor
Walter Hayhurst	Texas pharmacist
Wanda Smith	Daughter of Larry Smith
Warren Braun	Author of *Holdup*
Wayne Harlan	Kragness Medical Center (KMC) attorney
Wilem Masters	CEO of Callom Stoke
Will County	County of Patrick's divorce
William Milton	Founder of Milton Trading and soybean pit trader
Willy Banto	Ed's Street owner soybean trader
Xavier Earp	Journalist, *Pharma Today*
Xgerst	Medication for depression
Zack Kleinsasser	Attorney at Greenberg Traurig
Zia Anna Ferri	Patrick's adopted Bridgeport mother
Zia Maria Prato	Patrick's aunt in Italy